Biblical Quotations

FOR ALL OCCASIONS

J. STEPHEN LANG

Biblical
Quotations

FOR ALL OCCASIONS

From the World's Greatest Source,
Over 2,000 Timeless Quotes
to Enrich Your Message

PRIMA PUBLISHING

Contents

PREFACE • XI

PART ONE: FAMILIAR PHRASES
FROM THE BIBLE • 1

PART TWO: QUOTATIONS
FOR ALL OCCASIONS • 5

PART THREE: QUOTATIONS, ALPHABETICAL BY TOPIC • 31

Preface

ETERNALLY INTERESTING — AND QUOTABLE

THE BIBLE IS an old, old, *old* book, but it is eternally up to date, for there is no topic of interest to contemporary man that the Bible does not address. Consider a sample of the topics included here—Abuse, Adultery, Aging, Alcohol and Other Substance Abuse, Ambition, Angels, Anger, Anxiety, Arrogance—and that's just the letter "A." Under these and other headings are quotations that are profound, dramatic, colorful, and occasionally even witty. Some of them are so familiar that you may find yourself saying, "I never knew that was from the Bible!" But the book you are holding also includes many lesser-known quotations, some neglected gems that deserve to be better known and appreciated.

The Bible is the Book for all seasons—and for all occasions as well. For this reason we have included not only chapters arranged by topic but also a section for special occasions—personal red-letter days such as birthdays, weddings, graduation, new jobs, retirement, housewarming, and so on—and also major holidays such as Independence Day, Thanksgiving, Christmas, Easter, and others.

We intended this to be a book for all readers—a resource for speakers and writers, for pastors, for those who read the Bible for their devotions, and even for people who are just plain curious about what the amazing Book has to say on a particular topic. We believe that the topical arrangement, with the topics in alphabetical order, will make this book supremely "user friendly." At the end of each topical chapter, the reader is referred to other related topics. At the book's end is an index to aid in finding the correct topical chapter.

In each chapter of the book, the quotations are placed in a Genesis-to-Revelation sequence—that is, they are in the order in which they would occur in the Bible. Thus, under the section on Children, verses from Deuteronomy precede those from the Psalms, which precede those from Proverbs.

A NOTE ON THE USE
OF THE KING JAMES VERSION

Most everyone agrees that the King James Version of the Bible, published way back in 1611, was, and probably always will be, the most poetic English translation ever. There are many superb contemporary translations, but none has grasped the reading public's consciousness as the King James Version has. Why so? Were the King James translators more "poetic" in their talents, or was the English language in those days just more *quotable*? Remember that this was the age of Shakespeare as well as a hundred other phenomenally gifted authors. The English language was having its golden age when this most loved of all Bibles had its birth. So it is no wonder that when English-speaking people think of phrases from the Bible, the phrases are those of the King James.

But this version was born almost four hundred years ago. Languages change, as individual words change in meaning or fall out of use altogether. Even patterns of thought change. In short, no matter how impressive a translation is, it becomes, alas, dated. The King James Version has endured more than most. In some ways it may endure forever.

This book of quotations uses the King James Version—but with a slight (but very significant) difference. When necessary to communicate the meaning, I have paraphrased, substituting a more understandable word or phrase. In many cases this was unnecessary: Some of the quotes needed no changes at all. But many did, and in the process I consulted a number of modern translations as well as commentaries on the Bible. The aim was this: to retain, as much as possible, the beauty and poetry of the King James Version and, when the wording of the King James Version is unclear, to paraphrase but in no way change the meaning. *In no sense do the quotations in this book distort or alter the meaning of the original Hebrew and Greek books of the Bible.*

Readers will notice immediately that pronouns have been changed to their contemporary equivalents—that is, *thou* and *thine* have been replaced with *you* and *yours*. Verbs have also been modernized—for example, *he walketh* changed to *he walks*. While some people like the "quaint" quality of the older words, most people prefer the more modern wording. In a few quotations—such as the Lord's Prayer—I have retained the King James Version's wording completely since these verses are so familiar.

We hope that this system gives the reader the best of all possible worlds: the majesty and memorable quality of the King James Version but without any words or phrases that might cause confusion. No contemporary version of the Bible seemed to achieve this to our satisfaction, but we hope that the book you are holding has the best collection of Bible quotations—poetic, readable, and based on a great tradition but fully understandable.

PART ONE

Familiar Phrases
from the Bible

Eye for an eye

Life shall go for life, eye for eye, tooth for tooth, hand for hand, foot for foot. DEUTERONOMY 19:21

Go the extra mile

Whosoever shall compel you to go a mile, go with him two. MATTHEW 5:41

Turn the other cheek

I say unto you, that you resist not evil: but whosoever shall smite you on thy right cheek, turn to him the other also. MATTHEW 5:39

Wolf in sheep's clothing

Beware of false prophets, who come to you in sheep's clothing, but inwardly they are ravening wolves. MATTHEW 7:15

Salt of the earth

You are the salt of the earth. MATTHEW 5:13

Drop in the bucket

Behold, the nations are as a drop of a bucket. ISAIAH 40:15

Fat of the land

I will give you the good of the land of Egypt, and you shall eat the fat of the land. GENESIS 45:18

My brother's keeper

The LORD said unto Cain, "Where is Abel thy brother?" And he said, "I know not: Am I my brother's keeper?" GENESIS 4:9

Spare the rod and spoil the child

He that spareth his rod hateth his son. PROVERBS 13:24

Giving up the ghost

Man dies, and wastes away: yes, man gives up the ghost, and where is he? JOB 14:10

The skin of my teeth

I am escaped with the skin of my teeth. JOB 19:20

Woe is me!

Then said I, Woe is me! for I am undone.   ISAIAH 6:5

Pride goes before a fall

Pride goeth before destruction, and a haughty spirit before a fall.

PROVERBS 16:18

Eat, drink, and be merry

A man hath no better thing under the sun, than to eat, and to drink, and to be merry.   ECCLESIASTES 8:15

And also:

Take thine ease, eat, drink, and be merry.   LUKE 12:19

A lamb to the slaughter

He is brought as a lamb to the slaughter.   ISAIAH 53:7

Can a leopard change his spots?

Can the Ethiopian change his skin, or the leopard his spots?

JEREMIAH 13:23

Holier than thou

Come not near to me, for I am holier than thou.   ISAIAH 65:5

PART TWO

Quotations for All Occasions

ANNIVERSARIES

If you think about it, we ought to celebrate anniversaries more than we do weddings, for weddings are only beginnings, while anniversaries commemorate something that has endured. Love is a beautiful thing when observed in two newlyweds, but even more impressive is the mellowing (but also strengthening) of love as the years pass by.

The LORD has done great things for us, and so we are glad.

PSALM 126:3

Let your fountain be blessed, and rejoice with the wife of your youth.

PROVERBS 5:18

Whoever finds a wife finds a good thing, and obtains favor from the LORD.

PROVERBS 18:22

House and riches are the inheritance of fathers, and a prudent wife is from the LORD.

PROVERBS 19:14

Love bears all things, believes all things, hopes all things, endures all things.

1 CORINTHIANS 13:7

I pray that God would grant you, according to the riches of his glory, strength and might through his Spirit in the inner man, and that Christ may dwell in your hearts by faith, as you are being rooted and grounded in love. I pray you may be able to comprehend with all saints what is the breadth and length and depth and height, and to know the love of Christ, which surpasses knowledge, so that you might be filled with all the fullness of God.

EPHESIANS 3:14–19

Wives, submit yourselves to your own husbands, as it is fitting in the Lord. Husbands, love your wives, and be not harsh with them.

COLOSSIANS 3:18–19

If we love one another, God dwells in us, and his love is perfected in us.

I JOHN 4:12

Marriage is honorable in all, and the bed undefiled.

HEBREWS 13:4

BIRTH OR ADOPTION

Children are a tremendous responsibility, which the Bible takes very seriously. But the Bible also shares in the basic human delight in the birth of a child. Parents may need reminding of their moral duties toward their children, but they probably need no reminder of the pleasure of looking into a newborn's face.

These words, which I command you this day, shall be in your heart. And you shall teach them diligently to your children, and shall talk of them when you sit in your house, and when you walk by the way, and when you lie down, and when you rise up. And you shall bind them for a sign upon your hand, and they shall be as emblems before your eyes. And you shall write them upon the posts of your house and on your gates.

DEUTERONOMY 6:6–9

As for me and my house, we will serve the LORD. JOSHUA 24:15

Children are a heritage from the LORD, and the fruit of the womb is his reward. As arrows are in the hand of a mighty man, so are children of one's youth. Happy is the man that has his quiver full of them.

PSALM 127:3–4

Children's children are the crown of old men, and the glory of children are their fathers. PROVERBS 17:6

Train up a child in the way he should go, and when he is old, he will not depart from it. PROVERBS 22:6

All your children shall be taught by the LORD, and great shall be the peace of your children. ISAIAH 54:13

Jesus called a little child to him, and set him in the midst of them, and said, "Truly I say to you, unless you are converted, and become like little children, you shall not enter the kingdom of heaven. Whoever shall humble himself as this little child, the same is greatest in the kingdom of heaven. And whoever shall receive one such little child in my name receives me." MATTHEW 18:2–5

They brought young children to Jesus so that he should touch them, and his disciples scolded those that brought them. But when Jesus saw it, he was much displeased, and said to them, "Permit the little children to come to me, and forbid them not, for of such is the kingdom of God. Truly I say to you, whoever shall not receive the kingdom of God as a little child, he shall not enter it." And he took them up in his arms, put his hands upon them, and blessed them. MARK 10:13–16

Fathers, provoke not your children to wrath, but bring them up in the nurture and instruction of the Lord. EPHESIANS 6:4

BIRTHDAYS

Birthdays are viewed with eager anticipation when we're young, less so as we age. To a child, it represents one wonderful year closer to being "grown up," but the grown-ups are not so sure that aging is a good thing. In fact, the birthdays seem to come around a lot faster and with a lot less anticipation. Even so, looking at things from the Bible's point of view, life itself is a good thing, and living one more year is worth celebrating, especially if we are not only aging but maturing as well. Birthdays are a fine time to recall that God watches over each person.

A Bible trivia tidbit: The only times that birthday celebrations are mentioned are in Genesis 40:20, which refers to the birthday feast of Egypt's pharaoh, and in Matthew 14:6, which mentions the birthday of Herod.

The joy of the LORD is your strength. NEHEMIAH 8:10

You will show me the path of life. In your presence is fullness of joy; at your right hand are pleasures for evermore.   PSALM 16:11

One thing have I desired of the LORD, and that will I seek after: that I may dwell in the house of the LORD all the days of my life, to behold the beauty of the LORD, and to inquire in his temple.   PSALM 27:4

Delight yourself in the LORD, and he shall give you the desires of your heart.
                    PSALM 37:4

The LORD knows the days of the upright, and their inheritance shall be forever.   PSALM 37:18

Whom have I in heaven but you? And there is none upon earth that I desire beside you. My flesh and my heart fail, but God is the strength of my heart, and my portion forever.   PSALM 73:25–26

A day in your courts is better than a thousand.   PSALM 84:10

LORD, you have been our dwelling place in all generations. Before the mountains were brought forth, or ever you had formed the earth and the world, even from everlasting to everlasting, you are God. You turn man to destruction, and say, "Return, you children of men." For a thousand years in your sight are but as yesterday when it is past, and as a watch in the night. You carry them away as with a flood; they are as a sleep; in the morning they are like grass that grows up. In the morning it flourishes, and grows up; in the evening it is cut down and withers.

The days of our years are seventy, and if by reason of strength they be eighty years, yet their span is trouble and sorrow. For it is soon cut off, and we fly away. Who knows the power of your anger? Even according to your fear, so is your wrath. So teach us to number our days, that we may apply our hearts to wisdom.   PSALM 90:1–6, 10–12

This is the day the LORD has made; we will rejoice and be glad in it.
                    PSALM 118:24

Your hands have made me and fashioned me; give me understanding, so that I may learn your commandments.   PSALM 119:73

The LORD will perfect what concerns me; your mercy, O LORD, endures forever. Forsake not the works of your own hands.   PSALM 138:8

O LORD, you have searched me and known me. You know my sitting down and my rising up; you understand my thoughts from afar. You encompass my path and my lying down, and you know all my ways. There is not a word on my tongue, but, lo, O LORD, you know it altogether. You press upon me behind and before, and lay your hand on me. Such knowledge is too wonderful for me; it is so high I cannot attain it.

Where can I go from your Spirit? Where can I flee from your presence? If I ascend up to heaven, you are there; if I make my bed in the grave, behold, you are there. If I take the wings of the morning, and dwell in the uttermost parts of the sea, even there shall your hand lead me, and your right hand shall hold me. If I say, "Surely the darkness shall cover me, and the light around me turn to night." The darkness and light to you are both alike.

You created my inmost parts; you knit me together in my mother's womb. I will praise you, for I am fearfully and wonderfully made. Marvelous are your works, and my soul knows this well. My body was not hid from you when I was made in secret, made in the depths of the earth. Your eyes beheld my substance while it was still incomplete, and in your book all my members were written.

How precious are your thoughts to me, O God! How great is the sum of them! If I should count them, they are more in number than the sand. When I awake, I am still with you.

Search me, O God, and know my heart; try me, and know my thoughts. See if there is any wicked way in me, and lead me in the way everlasting.

                                                          PSALM 139

Even to your old age I am he, and even to gray hairs will I carry you; I have made you, and I will bear you; I will carry you, and will deliver you.

                                                        ISAIAH 46:4

Thus says the LORD who created you and formed you, "Fear not, for I have redeemed you; I have called you by name; you are mine. When you pass through the waters, I will be with you; and through the rivers, they shall not overflow you; when you walk through the fire, you shall not be burned; neither shall the flame kindle upon you. For I am the LORD, your God.

ISAIAH 43:1–3

O LORD, you are our father; we are the clay, and you our potter, and we all are the work of your hand.   ISAIAH 64:8

"I know the thoughts that I think about you," says the LORD, "thoughts of peace, and not of evil, to give you a future with hope. Then shall you call upon me, and you shall go and pray to me, and I will hearken to you. And you shall seek me, and find me, when you shall search for me with all your heart."   JEREMIAH 29:11–13

I have come that they might have life, and that they might have it more abundantly.   JOHN 10:10

Eye has not seen, nor ear heard, neither have entered into the heart of man the things God has prepared for those who love him.

I CORINTHIANS 2:9

CHRISTMAS

Forget for a moment the tree, the gifts, the food, the parties, and the decorations and focus on the Nativity scene—the one in the Bible, that is. The Bible passages concerning the birth of Jesus Christ remind us that there was only one Christmas—all the rest are merely anniversaries.

For unto us a child is born, unto us a son is given; and the government shall be upon his shoulder; and his name shall be called Wonderful, Counselor, the Mighty God, the Everlasting Father, the Prince of Peace.

ISAIAH 9:6

Now the birth of Jesus Christ took place in this way: when his mother Mary was betrothed to Joseph, before they came together, she was found to be with child by the Holy Spirit. Then Joseph her husband, being a just man, and not willing to make her a public example, was minded to put her away secretly. But while he thought on these things, behold, the angel of the Lord appeared to him in a dream, saying, "Joseph, you son of David, fear not to take to you Mary your wife, for what is conceived in her is from the Holy Spirit. And she shall bring forth a son, and you shall call his name JESUS, for he shall save his people from their sins." Now all this was done, so that it might be fulfilled what was spoken of the Lord by the prophet, saying, "Behold, a virgin shall be with child, and shall bring forth a son, and they shall call his name 'Immanuel,' which means 'God with us.' "

Then Joseph being raised from sleep did as the angel of the LORD had told him, and took to him his wife. And he knew her not till she had brought forth her firstborn son, and he called his name JESUS.

Now when Jesus was born in Bethlehem of Judea in the days of Herod the king, behold, there came wise men from the east to Jerusalem, saying, "Where is he who is born King of the Jews? For we have seen his star in the east, and have come to worship him." When Herod the king had heard these things, he was troubled, and all Jerusalem with him. And when he had gathered all the chief priests and scribes of the people together, he demanded of them where Christ should be born. And they said to him, "In Bethlehem of Judea, for thus it is written by the prophet, 'And you Bethlehem, in the land of Judah, are not the least among the princes of Judah, for out of you shall come a Governor who shall rule my people Israel.'" Then Herod, when he had secretly called the wise men, inquired of them diligently what time the star appeared. And he sent them to Bethlehem, and said, "Go and search diligently for the young child, and when you have found him, bring me word again, so that I may come and worship him also." When they had heard the king, they departed, and, lo, the star, which they saw in the east, went before them, till it came and stood over where the young child was. When they saw the star, they rejoiced with great joy. And when they went into the house, they saw the young child with Mary his mother, and fell down, and worshipped him. And when they had opened their treasures, they presented to him gifts—

gold, frankincense, and myrrh. And being warned by God in a dream that they should not return to Herod, they departed into their own country by another way.   MATTHEW 1:18–2:12

It came to pass in those days that there went out a decree from Caesar Augustus, that all the world should be taxed. . . . And all went to be taxed, everyone to his own city. And Joseph went up from Galilee, out of the city of Nazareth, into Judea, to the city of David, which is called Bethlehem (because he was of the house and lineage of David) to be taxed with Mary his espoused wife, who was great with child. And so it was that while they were there, the days were accomplished that she should be delivered. And she brought forth her firstborn son, and wrapped him in swaddling clothes, and laid him in a manger, because there was no room for them in the inn.

And there were in the same country shepherds abiding in the field, keeping watch over their flocks by night. And, lo, the angel of the Lord came upon them, and the glory of the Lord shone round about them, and they were very afraid. And the angel said to them, "Fear not, for, behold, I bring you good tidings of great joy, which shall be to all people. For to you is born this day in the city of David a Savior, who is Christ the Lord. And this shall be a sign to you: You shall find the babe wrapped in swaddling clothes, lying in a manger." And suddenly there was with the angel a multitude of the heavenly host praising God and saying, "Glory to God in the highest, and on earth peace, good will toward men." And it came to pass, when the angels were gone away from them into heaven, the shepherds said one to another, "Let us now go to Bethlehem, and see this thing which has come to pass, which the Lord has made known to us." And they came with haste, and found Mary, and Joseph, and the babe lying in a manger. . . . And the shepherds returned, glorifying and praising God for all the things that they had heard and seen.   LUKE 2:1–20

EASTER

It surprises many people that the Bible says very little about Christmas (the birth of Jesus, that is) but a great deal about Easter, Jesus' resurrection from the dead. In fact, this was the key belief of the earliest Christians: Jesus had been crucified on a Friday but was miraculously raised to life the following Sunday. Hard to accept? No doubt it was hard for them also. But a lot of skeptics must have become believers, for the faith in the risen Jesus spread like a wildfire.

As it began to dawn toward the first day of the week, there came Mary Magdalene and the other Mary to see the tomb. And, behold, there was a great earthquake, for the angel of the Lord descended from heaven, and came and rolled back the stone from the entrance, and sat upon it. His face was like lightning, and his clothing white as snow. And for fear of him the keepers did shake, and became as dead men. And the angel answered and said to the women, "Fear not, for I know that you seek Jesus, who was crucified. He is not here, for he is risen, as he said. Come, see the place where the Lord lay. And go quickly, and tell his disciples that he is risen from the dead, and, behold, he goes before you into Galilee; there shall you see him; lo, I have told you."

And they departed quickly from the tomb with fear and great joy, and ran to bring his disciples word. And as they went to tell his disciples, behold, Jesus met them, saying, "Greetings." And they came and held him by the feet, and worshipped him. Then said Jesus to them, "Be not afraid; go tell my brethren that they go into Galilee, and there shall they see me. . . ."

Then the eleven disciples went away into Galilee, to a mountain where Jesus had appointed them. And when they saw him, they worshipped him, but some doubted. And Jesus came and spoke to them, saying, "All power is given to me in heaven and in earth. Go you therefore, and teach all nations, baptizing them in the name of the Father, and of the Son, and of the Holy Spirit; teaching them to observe all things whatever I have commanded you. And, lo, I am with you always, even to the end of the world."

MATTHEW 28:1–10, 16–19

At evening on the first day of the week, when the doors were shut where the disciples were assembled for fear of the Jews, Jesus came and stood in the midst, and said to them, "Peace be with you." And when he had so said, he showed to them his hands and his side. Then were the disciples glad, when they saw the Lord. Then said Jesus to them again, "Peace be with you. As my Father has sent me, even so send I you." And when he had said this, he breathed upon them, and said to them, "Receive the Holy Spirit. If you forgive anyone's sins, they are forgiven. And if you do not forgive their sins, they are not forgiven."

But one of the twelve, Thomas, called Didymus, was not with them when Jesus came. The other disciples said to him, "We have seen the Lord." But he said to them, "Unless I shall see in his hands the nail prints, and put my finger into the nail prints and thrust my hand into his side, I will not believe." And after eight days his disciples were inside the house, and Thomas with them. Then came Jesus, the doors being shut, and stood in the midst, and said, "Peace be with you." Then said he to Thomas, "Reach here your finger, and behold my hands, and reach here your hand, and thrust it into my side, and be not faithless, but believing." And Thomas answered and said to him, "My Lord and my God." Jesus said to him, "Thomas, because you have seen me, you have believed. Blessed are they that have not seen, and yet believe."

JOHN 20:19–29

God has both raised up the Lord, and will also raise up us by his own power.

1 CORINTHIANS 6:14

He who raised up the Lord Jesus shall raise up us also.

2 CORINTHIANS 4:14

FATHER'S DAY

The "sensitive man" is supposed to be a recent invention, but everyone who ever had a caring father knows that there have always been kind, compassionate, and loving men. In fact, nothing seems to bring out men's sensitive side as much as their own children. The Bible has a high view of fatherhood, setting the highest standard of all, God the Father—loving, merciful, and patient but also firm, demanding in the area of morality, and someone to revere and respect as well as love.

As a father pities his children, so the LORD pities those who fear him.

PSALM 103:13

A wise son makes a glad father. PROVERBS 15:20

Children's children are the crown of old men, and the glory of children are their fathers.   PROVERBS 17:6

The just man walks in his integrity; his children are blessed after him.

PROVERBS 20:7

The father of the righteous shall greatly rejoice, and he who begets a wise child shall have joy of him.   PROVERBS 23:24

Honor your father and mother, which is the first commandment with promise.   EPHESIANS 6:2

GRADUATION

Graduations are exciting—but also stress producing—because the future looks both bright and uncertain. While the graduate is rightly celebrating the completion of one education, it is that other education—the one in the "school of hard knocks"—that is intimidating. The Bible is not lacking in either wisdom or comfort for the new graduate.

Delight yourself in the LORD, and he shall give you the desires of your heart.

PSALM 37:4

How shall a young man cleanse his way? By taking heed according to your word.   PSALM 119:9

What is a man profited, if he shall gain the whole world, and lose his own soul? Or what shall a man give in exchange for his soul?

MATTHEW 16:26

Whatever things are true, whatever things are honest, whatever things are just, whatever things are pure, whatever things are lovely, whatever things are admirable—if anything is excellent or praiseworthy—think on these things.   PHILIPPIANS 4:8

You are the salt of the earth, but if the salt has lost its savor, how can it be salty again? It is no longer good for anything, but to be cast out, and to be trampled underfoot.

You are the light of the world. A city that is set on a hill cannot be hid. Neither do men light a candle and put it under a bushel, but on a candlestick, and it gives light to all that are in the house. Let your light so shine before men that they may see your good works and glorify your Father who is in heaven.   MATTHEW 5:13–16

Seek first the kingdom of God, and his righteousness, and all these things shall be added to you.   MATTHEW 6:33

Are not two sparrows sold for a penny? And not one of them shall fall on the ground without your Father knowing. Even the very hairs of your head are all numbered. Fear you not therefore, you are of more value than many sparrows.   MATTHEW 10:29–31

He that finds his life shall lose it, and he who loses his life for my sake shall find it.   MATTHEW 10:39

He that loves his life shall lose it, and he who hates his life in this world shall keep it to life eternal.   JOHN 12:25

Be not conformed to this world, but be transformed by the renewing of your mind.   ROMANS 12:2

Where is the wise? Where is the scribe? Where is the disputer of this world? Has not God made foolish the wisdom of this world?

I CORINTHIANS 1:20

If any man be in Christ, he is a new creature; old things have passed away— behold, all things have become new. And all things are from God, who has reconciled us to himself through Jesus Christ.

2 CORINTHIANS 5:17–18

He that glories, let him glory in the Lord. For not he who commends himself is approved, but him whom the Lord commends.

2 CORINTHIANS 10:17–18

You are a chosen generation, a royal priesthood, a holy nation, a distinctive people, so you should show forth the praises of him who has called you out of darkness into his marvelous light. In time past you were not a people, but now are the people of God.   I PETER 2:9–10

Love not the world, neither the things that are in the world. If any man love the world, the love of the Father is not in him. For all that is in the world, the lust of the flesh, and the lust of the eyes, and the pride of life, is not of the Father, but is of the world. And the world passes away, and the lust thereof, but he who does the will of God abides forever.

I JOHN 2:15–17

HOUSEWARMING

An old proverb tells us that to be happy at home is the greatest thing of all. Well, perhaps it isn't the greatest, but it surely ranks high. Whether the household is one person or a dozen, it is at its best (according to the Bible) when dedicated to the Lord.

As for me and my house, we will serve the LORD.   JOSHUA 24:15

Except the LORD build the house, they that build it labor in vain.

PSALM 127:1

The curse of the LORD is on the house of the wicked, but he blesses the habitation of the just.   PROVERBS 3:33

The house of the righteous shall stand firm.   PROVERBS 12:7

In the house of the righteous is much treasure.   PROVERBS 15:6

Through wisdom is a house built, and by understanding it is established.

PROVERBS 24:3

Every house is built by some man; but he who built all things is God.

HEBREWS 3:4

Be not forgetful to entertain strangers, for thereby some have entertained angels unawares.   HEBREWS 13:2

Show hospitality one to another without grudging.   1 PETER 4:9

INDEPENDENCE DAY AND OTHER PATRIOTIC HOLIDAYS

Patriotism has not, thankfully, gone out of style. For all our griping, most of us are pleased to live in this country, certain that the good outweighs the bad. The Bible encourages us to be good citizens while reminding us that God is in control of all nations and that nations and empires have perished when they lost their moral vision.

Proclaim liberty throughout all the land to all the inhabitants thereof.
                                                    LEVITICUS 25:10

[These are the words inscribed on the Liberty Bell in Philadelphia.]

If my people, which are called by my name, shall humble themselves and pray and seek my face and turn from their wicked ways, then will I hear from heaven, and will forgive their sin, and heal their land.
                                                    2 CHRONICLES 7:14

The LORD brings the counsel of the nations to nothing; he frustrates the plans of the peoples. The counsel of the LORD stands forever, the thoughts of his heart to all generations. Blessed is the nation whose God is the LORD, and the people he has chosen for his inheritance. The LORD looks from heaven; he beholds all the sons of men. From the place of his habitation he looks upon all the inhabitants of the earth. He fashions their hearts alike; he observes all their deeds. There is no king saved by the multitude of an army; a mighty man is not delivered by great strength.   PSALM 33:10–16

Be still, and know that I am God; I will be exalted among the nations, I will be exalted in the earth. The LORD Almighty is with us; the God of Jacob is our refuge.   PSALM 46:10–11

God reigns over the nations; God sits upon the throne of his holiness.

PSALM 47:8

God be merciful to us, and bless us, and cause his face to shine upon us, that your way may be known upon earth, your saving health among all nations. Let the people praise you, O God; let all the people praise you. O let the nations be glad and sing for joy; for you shall judge the people righteously, and govern the nations upon earth. Let the people praise you, O God; let all the people praise you.   PSALM 67:1–5

Arise, O God, judge the earth; for all the nations belong to you.

PSALM 82:8

Ascribe to the LORD, O you families of the earth, ascribe to the LORD glory and strength.   PSALM 96:7

Happy is that people whose God is the LORD.   PSALM 144:15

Righteousness exalts a nation, but sin is a reproach to any people.

PROVERBS 14:34

Where there is no vision, the people perish.   PROVERBS 29:18

Behold, the nations are as a drop in the bucket, and are regarded as small dust on the scales. Behold, he takes up the isles as a very little thing. . . . All nations before him are as nothing, and they are counted to him less than nothing, mere emptiness.

It is he who sits upon the circle of the earth, and the inhabitants of it are like grasshoppers; he stretches out the heavens like a curtain and spreads them out as a tent to dwell in; he brings the rulers to nothing; he makes the judges of the earth to be emptiness.   ISAIAH 40:15–17, 21–23

You shall know the truth, and the truth shall make you free.

JOHN 8:32

I urge therefore, that supplications, prayers, intercessions, and thanksgiving be made for all men; for rulers, and for all that are in authority; that we may lead a quiet and peaceable life in all godliness and honesty.

I TIMOTHY 2:1–2

MOTHER'S DAY

Abraham Lincoln, reared in poverty, claimed, "No man is poor who has a godly mother." (Lincoln, in fact, was twice blessed. After his beloved mother's death, he was very close to his stepmother.) The Bible shares this high view of motherhood, especially in the famous passage from Proverbs 31. Note the quotation below from John's Gospel: Jesus, in agony on the cross, thought highly enough of his mother to commend her to the keeping of one of his followers.

A gracious woman retains honor.   PROVERBS 11:16

Every wise woman builds her house, but the foolish plucks it down with her hands.   PROVERBS 14:1

Strength and honor are her clothing, and she shall rejoice in time to come. She opens her mouth with wisdom, and on her tongue is the law of kindness. She looks well to the ways of her household, and eats not the bread of idleness. Her children rise up and call her blessed; her husband also, and he praises her. Many daughters have done virtuously, but you excel them all. Favor is deceitful, and beauty is vain, but a woman that fears the LORD, she shall be praised. Give her of the fruit of her hands, and let her own works praise her in the gates.   PROVERBS 31:25–31

Now there stood by the cross of Jesus his mother. . . . When Jesus therefore saw his mother, and the disciple whom he loved standing by, he said unto his mother, "Woman, behold your son!" Then said he to the disciple, "Behold your mother!" And from that hour that disciple took her unto his own home.   JOHN 19:25–27

NEW JOB/PROMOTION

A new job or a promotion is always exciting but also a bit intimidating. What if I'm not up to the standards of this new position? What if I fail? What if the new post is too stressful? What if I had just stayed in my old position? What if . . . ? Well, amidst all the agonizing there is still pleasure, especially for the worker who acts to the best of his or her ability and who leaves the outcome to God, whom the Bible presents as the one Master who ultimately rewards our labors.

He that tills his land shall be satisfied with bread, but he who chases worthless pursuits is void of understanding.   PROVERBS 12:11

The hand of the diligent shall rule, but the lazy will be forced into slave labor.   PROVERBS 12:24

The slothful man does not roast what he took in hunting, but the diligent man gains precious wealth.   PROVERBS 12:27

In all labor there is profit, but mere talk leads only to poverty.   PROVERBS 14:23

The thoughts of the diligent lead only to prosperity, but those of the hasty lead only to want.   PROVERBS 21:5

See you a man diligent in his business? He shall stand before kings.   PROVERBS 22:29

He that tills his land shall have food in abundance, but he who follows fleeting fantasies shall have poverty.   PROVERBS 28:19

The sleep of a laboring man is sweet, whether he eat little or much, but the abundance of the rich will not allow him to sleep.

ECCLESIASTES 5:12

Behold what I have seen: it is good and fitting for one to eat and to drink, and to enjoy the good of all his labor that he does under the sun all the days of his life, which God gives him, for this is his lot; this is the gift of God.

ECCLESIASTES 5:18–19

Whatever your hand finds to do, do it with your might.

ECCLESIASTES 9:10

Be not slothful in business; be fervent in spirit, serving the Lord.

ROMANS 12:11

Whether you eat, or drink, or whatever you do, do all to the glory of God.

I CORINTHIANS 10:31

My beloved brethren, be steadfast, unmovable, always abounding in the work of the Lord, since you know that your labor is not in vain in the Lord.

I CORINTHIANS 15:58

Serve with good will, as doing it for the Lord, not for men.

EPHESIANS 6:6–7

Study to lead a quiet life, and to do your own business, and to work with your own hands, as we commanded you, so that you may walk honestly toward outsiders, and that you may have lack of nothing.

I THESSALONIANS 4:11–12

RETIREMENT

As much as people claim to dislike working, we must admit that work does give our lives a certain amount of structure and predictability. With retirement, that is all taken away, which may be why some retirees have difficulty adjusting. But for many, retirement is pure pleasure, a freedom to do things at leisure, to try new things, and maybe even to reflect on our spiritual condition and, if needed, to improve it.

The LORD is good; his mercy is everlasting, and his truth endures to all generations.   PSALM 100:5

Better is a handful with quietness, than both the hands full with toil and a chasing after the wind.   ECCLESIASTES 4:6

Let us not be weary in doing right, for in due season we shall reap, if we faint not. As we have therefore opportunity, let us do good to all men, especially to them who are of the household of faith.

GALATIANS 6:9–10

Being confident of this very thing, that he who has begun a good work in you will perform it until the day of Jesus Christ.   PHILIPPIANS 1:6

Walk in wisdom toward outsiders, making the most of opportunities. Let your speech be always with grace, seasoned with salt, so that you may know how you ought to answer every man.   COLOSSIANS 4:5–6

I have fought a good fight, I have finished my course, I have kept the faith.

2 TIMOTHY 4:7

THANKSGIVING

A bit of historical trivia: In the midst of the Civil War, Abraham Lincoln proclaimed the last Thursday in November as a national day of thanksgiving to God, stating that the gifts of God should be "solemnly, reverently, and gratefully acknowledged." It is easy to forget, in the thick of feasting and fellowship and football, that the holiday originally had this deeply spiritual purpose. In fact, it is the only national holiday rooted in the simple desire to show gratitude to God.

We your people and sheep of your pasture will give you thanks forever; we will show forth your praise to all generations.   PSALM 79:13

It is a good thing to give thanks unto the LORD, and to sing praises unto your name, O most High.   PSALM 92:1

Make a joyful noise to the LORD, all you lands. Serve the LORD with gladness; come before his presence with singing. Know you that the LORD he is God; it is he who has made us, and not we ourselves. We are his people, and the sheep of his pasture. Enter into his gates with thanksgiving, and into his courts with praise. Be thankful to him, and bless his name. For the LORD is good; his mercy is everlasting, and his truth endures to all generations.
                                                    PSALM 100:1–5

Bless the LORD, O my soul, and all that is within me, bless his holy name. Bless the LORD, O my soul, and forget not all his benefits.
                                                    PSALM 103:1–2

Bless the LORD, O my soul. O LORD my God, you are very great; you are clothed with honor and majesty. You cause the grass to grow for the cattle, and plants for the service of man, that he may bring forth food out of the earth.   PSALM 104:1, 14

Praise the LORD. O give thanks to the LORD; for he is good, for his mercy endures forever.   PSALM 106:1

Thanks be to God, who gives us the victory through our Lord Jesus Christ.
                                                    1 CORINTHIANS 15:57

Thanks be to God for his unspeakable gift.   2 CORINTHIANS 9:15

Give thanks to the Father, who has made us fit to be partakers of the inheritance of the saints in light.   COLOSSIANS 1:12

Be anxious for nothing, but in every thing by prayer and supplication with thanksgiving let your requests be made known to God. And the peace of God, which surpasses all understanding, shall keep your hearts and minds through Christ Jesus.   PHILIPPIANS 4:6–7

Rejoice evermore. Pray without ceasing. In everything give thanks, for this is the will of God in Christ Jesus concerning you.

I THESSALONIANS 5:16–18

Everything created by God is good, and nothing to be refused if it be received with thanksgiving, for it is made holy by the word of God and prayer.

I TIMOTHY 4:4–5

WEDDINGS

Someone is always predicting the demise of marriage, yet it endures, and so do weddings. There is something about a ceremony uniting two people for life that tugs on the heartstrings. The Bible takes a rosy but realistic view of marriage: It is for life; it is not heaven on earth; it is at its best when the two people are willing to think less of their own egos and more of the worth of the spouse. This is something to celebrate.

Let your fountain be blessed, and rejoice in the wife of your youth. Let her be as the loving deer, the pleasant doe; let her breasts satisfy you at all times, and be you intoxicated always with her love.   PROVERBS 5:17–19

Whoever finds a wife finds a good thing, and obtains favor from the LORD.

PROVERBS 18:22

Live joyfully with the wife whom you love all the days of this meaningless life under the sun.   ECCLESIASTES 9:9

My beloved spoke, and said to me, "Rise up, my love, my fair one, and come away. For, lo, the winter is past, the rain is over and gone. The flowers appear on the earth; the time of the singing of birds is come, and the voice of the turtle-dove is heard in our land. The fig tree puts forth her green figs, and the vines with the tender grape give a pleasant fragrance. Arise, my love, my fair one, and come away."   SONG OF SOLOMON 2:10–13

My beloved is mine, and I am his.   SONG OF SOLOMON 2:16

Set me as a seal upon your heart, as a seal upon your arm. For love is strong as death. . . . Its flashes are like flashes of fire, a raging flame. Many waters cannot quench love, neither can the floods drown it. If a man would give all the wealth of his house for love, it would utterly be scorned.

SONG OF SOLOMON 8:6–7

From the beginning of creation God made them male and female. For this cause shall a man leave his father and mother and unite with his wife, and the two shall be one flesh; so they are no longer two, but one flesh. What therefore God has joined together, let not man put asunder.

MARK 10:7–9

I pray that God would grant you, according to the riches of his glory, strength and might through his Spirit in the inner man, and that Christ may dwell in your hearts by faith, as you are being rooted and grounded in love. I pray you may be able to comprehend with all saints what is the breadth and length and depth and height, and to know the love of Christ, which surpasses knowledge, so that you might be filled with all the fullness of God.

EPHESIANS 3:14–19

Submit to one another out of reverence for Christ.

Wives, submit yourselves to your own husbands, as to the Lord. For the husband is the head of the wife, just as Christ is the head of the church, and he is the Savior of the body. Just as the church is subject to Christ, so let the wives be to their own husbands in everything.

Husbands, love your wives, just as Christ loved the church and gave himself for it, that he might sanctify and cleanse it with the washing of water by the word, so that he might present it to himself a glorious church, not having blemish or wrinkle or any such thing, but that it should be holy and without fault. So ought men to love their wives as their own bodies. He that loves his wife loves himself. For no man ever yet hated his own body, but rather he nourishes and cherishes it, just as the Lord loves the church; for we are members of his body, of his flesh, and of his bones. For this cause shall a man leave his father and mother, and shall be joined to his wife, and the two shall be one flesh. This is a great mystery, but I speak concerning Christ and the church. Nevertheless let everyone of you in particular so love his wife just as himself, and the wife see that she reverence her husband.

EPHESIANS 5:21–33

Whatever you do in word or deed, do all in the name of the Lord Jesus, giving thanks to God and the Father through him. Wives, submit yourselves to your own husbands, as it is fitting in the Lord. Husbands, love your wives, and be not harsh with them. COLOSSIANS 3:18–19

The Lord make you to increase and abound in love one toward another.

I THESSALONIANS 3:12

Marriage is honorable in all, and the bed undefiled.

HEBREWS 13:4

AND FOR ALL OCCASIONS . . .

Thanks to Pete Seeger's folk song "Turn, Turn, Turn," Ecclesiastes 3:1–8 is probably one of the most quoted passages from the Bible. Seeger took the Bible's words and added a few of his own, and the song became a hit for the pop group The Byrds in 1965. Even people who have never heard of the Old Testament book of Ecclesiastes have heard the familiar text that begins, "To everything there is a season . . ."

To every thing there is a season, and a time to every purpose under the heaven: a time to be born, and a time to die; a time to plant, and a time to pluck up that which is planted; a time to kill, and a time to heal; a time to break down, and a time to build up; a time to weep, and a time to laugh; a time to mourn, and a time to dance; a time to cast away stones, and a time to gather stones together; a time to embrace, and a time to refrain from embracing; a time to get, and a time to lose; a time to keep, and a time to cast away; a time to rend, and a time to sew; a time to keep silence, and a time to speak; a time to love, and a time to hate; a time of war, and a time of peace.

PART THREE

Quotations

Alphabetical by Topic

ABUSE

The word abuse *is used so often today that we begin to wonder whether everyone* is abused. *It's true that all human beings suffer, but genuine abuse involves willfully persecuting another human being. This can be physical or verbal, and the Bible strongly condemns all of it. The key teaching of the Bible is that the abused person can take comfort in knowing that God is the great Comforter of the abused. This leaves no place for retaliation, for God alone will judge and pay back the abuser. The worst thing an abused person can do is to add his or her own bitterness to the heavy burden of abuse.*

You shall not mistreat a stranger, nor oppress him, for you were strangers in the land of Egypt. You shall not afflict any widow, or fatherless child. If you afflict them in any way, and they cry at all to me, I will surely hear their cry.

EXODUS 22:21–24

O LORD my God, in you do I put my trust. Save me from all those who persecute me, and deliver me. PSALM 7:1

The LORD will be a refuge for the oppressed, a refuge in times of trouble.

PSALM 9:9

The poor commits himself to you; you are the helper of the fatherless.

PSALM 10:14

This poor man cried, and the LORD heard him, and saved him out of all his troubles. PSALM 34:6

The LORD is near to those that are of a broken heart; and he saves those who are of contrite spirit. PSALM 34:18

In God have I put my trust; I will not be afraid what man can do to me.

PSALM 56:11

Incline my heart to your commandments, and not to covetousness. Turn away my eyes from beholding worthless things.   PSALM 119:36-37

Do not say, "I will recompense evil," but wait on the LORD, and he shall save you.   PROVERBS 20:22

You will keep him in perfect peace, whose mind is stayed on you, because he trusts in you.   ISAIAH 26:3

He that walks righteously, and speaks uprightly, who despises the gain of oppressions, who keeps his hands from taking of bribes, who stops his ears against hearing of bloodshed, and shuts his eyes from seeing evil—he shall dwell on high; his place of defense shall be the rocky fortress. Bread shall be given him; his waters shall not fail.   ISAIAH 33:15-16

Execute justice in the morning, and deliver him that is robbed out of the hand of the oppressor, lest my fury break out like fire, and burn that none can quench it, because of the evil of your doings.   JEREMIAH 21:12

They hate him that rebukes in the gate, and they abhor him that speaks up-rightly. Therefore, since you tread upon the poor, and you take from him his grain: you have built houses of stone, but you shall not dwell in them; you have planted pleasant vineyards, but you shall not drink wine of them. For I know your manifold transgressions, and your mighty sins: they afflict the just, they take a bribe, and they turn aside the poor in the gate from their right. Therefore the prudent shall keep silence in that time; for it is an evil time. Seek good, and not evil, that you may live, and so the LORD, the God Almighty, shall be with you, as you have spoken. Hate the evil, and love the good.   AMOS 5:10-15

Woe to those who devise iniquity, and work evil upon their beds! When the morning is light, they practice it, because it is in the power of their hand. And they covet fields, and take them by violence, and houses, and take them away. So they oppress a man and his house, even a man and his heritage.

Therefore thus says the LORD, "Behold, against this family do I devise an evil, from which you shall not remove your necks, neither shall you go haughtily, for this time is evil." MICAH 2:1–3

Blessed are the merciful, for they shall obtain mercy. MATTHEW 5:7

[Jesus:] "I say to you, resist not evil, but whoever shall strike you on your right cheek, turn to him the other also. And if any man will sue you at the law, and take away your coat, let him have your cloak also. And whoever shall compel you to go a mile, go with him two. Give to him that asks you, and do not turn away from him that would borrow of you. You have heard that it has been said, 'You shall love your neighbor, and hate your enemy.' But I say to you, love your enemies, bless those who curse you, do good to those who hate you, and pray for them which spitefully use you and persecute you, that you may be the children of your Father who is in heaven, for he makes his sun to rise on the evil and on the good, and sends rain on the just and on the unjust. For if you love them which love you, what reward have you?" MATTHEW 5:39–46

If you forgive men their trespasses, your heavenly Father will also forgive you. But if you forgive not men their trespasses, neither will your Father forgive your trespasses. MATTHEW 6:14–15

[Jesus, reading from the Book of Isaiah:] "The Spirit of the Lord is upon me, because he has anointed me to preach the gospel to the poor. He has sent me to heal the brokenhearted, to preach deliverance to the captives, and recovering of sight to the blind, to set at liberty those who are bruised, to preach the acceptable year of the Lord." And he closed the book, and he gave it again to the minister, and sat down. And the eyes of all those who were in the synagogue were fastened on him. And he began to say to them, "This day is this scripture fulfilled in your ears." LUKE 4:18–21

Bless them which persecute you; bless, and curse not. Recompense no man evil for evil. Dearly beloved, avenge not yourselves, but rather give place to wrath, for it is written, "Vengeance is mine; I will repay," said the Lord. Therefore if your enemy hungers, feed him; if he thirsts, give him drink, for in so doing you shall heap coals of fire on his head. Be not overcome by evil, but overcome evil with good. ROMANS 12:14, 17, 19, 20–21

Let all bitterness and wrath and anger and brawling and evil speaking be put away from you, with all malice. And be kind to one another, tenderhearted, forgiving one another, even as God for Christ's sake has forgiven you.

EPHESIANS 4:31–32

Bear with one another, and forgive one another, if any man have a quarrel against any; even as Christ forgave you, so also do you.

COLOSSIANS 3:13

See also Anger, Enemies, Forgiveness, Mercy, Revenge.

ADULTERY

If adultery is so common, then it must be okay, right? Hardly. The Bible presents us with a high view of marriage, the most intimate human relation that two people can enter into. Whatever threatens that intimate bond is wrong in the eyes of God and a cruelty to one's spouse. The people of biblical times were not bombarded by seductive media images of the joys of adultery, but the temptation was there nonetheless. It is amazing how contemporary the Bible sounds in its description of the fleeting joys of hidden encounters. But one message comes through clearly: Fidelity to one's spouse is the standard. Why else would God have set this high standard in one of his Ten Commandments in Exodus 20?

You shall not commit adultery. EXODUS 20:14

The eye of the adulterer waits for the twilight, saying, "No eye shall see me," and conceals his face. . . . They know not the light. For the morning is to them like the shadow of death. . . . Drought and heat consume the snow waters, so does the grave those which have sinned. JOB 24:15–19

The Adulterers' Bible

As any writer knows, good proofreaders are a critical part of publishing. Perhaps the printers who produced the English Bible in 1631 needed a better proofreader. A thousand copies of the Bible were printed with a key word missing from one of the Ten Commandments: not. *This misprinted Bible had the verse "Thou shalt commit adultery." The printers were fined 3,000 pounds.*

The lips of a strange woman drip like a honeycomb, and her speech is smoother than oil. But her end is bitter as wormwood, sharp as a two-edged sword.   PROVERBS 5:3–4

Why will you, my son, be ravished with a strange woman, and embrace the bosom of a stranger? For the ways of man are before the eyes of the LORD, and he ponders all his goings. His own iniquities shall take the wicked himself, and he shall be held with the cords of his sins. He shall die without instruction, and in the greatness of his folly he shall go astray.
                                                PROVERBS 5:20–23

By means of a whorish woman a man is reduced to a piece of bread, and the adulteress will prey upon his precious life. Can a man take fire in his bosom, and his clothes not be burned? Can one walk upon hot coals, and his feet not be burned? So he who goes in to his neighbor's wife; whoever touches her shall not be innocent. Men do not despise a thief, if he steal to satisfy his soul when he is hungry. But if he is found, he must restore sevenfold; he shall give all the substance of his house. But whoever commits adultery with a woman lacks understanding. He that does it destroys his own soul.   PROVERBS 6:26–32

[Jesus:] You have heard that it was said by them of old time, "You shall not commit adultery." But I say to you, whoever looks on a woman to lust after her has committed adultery with her already in his heart.

MATTHEW 5:27–28

Out of the heart proceed evil thoughts, murders, adulteries, fornications, thefts, false witness, blasphemies. These are the things which defile a man.

MATTHEW 15:19–20

The scribes and Pharisees brought to him a woman taken in adultery, and when they had set her in the midst, they said to him, "Master, this woman was taken in adultery, in the very act. Now Moses in the law commanded us, that such should be stoned, but what say you?" This they said to test him, that they might have grounds to accuse him.

But Jesus stooped down, and with his finger wrote on the ground, as though he heard them not. So when they continued asking him, he lifted up himself, and said to them, "He that is without sin among you, let him first cast a stone at her." And again he stooped down, and wrote on the ground. And they which heard it, being convicted by their own conscience, went out one by one, beginning at the eldest, even to the last, and Jesus was left alone, with the woman standing in the midst.

When Jesus had lifted up himself, and saw none but the woman, he said to her, "Woman, where are your accusers? Has no man condemned you?" She said, "No man, Lord." And Jesus said to her, "Neither do I condemn you. Go, and sin no more."

JOHN 8:3–11

Know you not that the unrighteous shall not inherit the kingdom of God? Be not deceived; neither fornicators, nor idolaters, nor adulterers, nor homosexuals, nor abusers of themselves with mankind, nor thieves, nor covetous, nor drunkards, nor slanderers, nor swindlers shall inherit the kingdom of God.

I CORINTHIANS 6:9–10

Flee fornication. Every sin that a man does is outside the body, but he who commits fornication sins against his own body.

I CORINTHIANS 6:18

Fornication, and all uncleanness, or covetousness, let it not be even hinted at among you, as becomes saints.   EPHESIANS 5:3

Marriage is honorable in all, and the bed undefiled, but whoremongers and adulterers God will judge.   HEBREWS 13:4

See also Marriage, Sexuality, Temptation.

AGING

Our society is beginning to recover some of its respect for senior citizens, and rightly so. But the media, with the attractive images of youthful beauty, still dominate our thinking, leading us to believe that preservation of the body is the chief goal in life. This is obvious in the number of seniors obsessed with diet and fitness, with covering up gray and struggling to keep away flab and wrinkles. But the Bible has a different view of gray and wrinkles: They are—or should be—badges of maturity, the "battle scars" indicating maturity and wisdom after enduring life's hardships. It may sound hopelessly old-fashioned, but "respect your elders" is sound biblical advice.

You shall rise up in the presence of the gray head, and honor the face of the old man, and fear your God.   LEVITICUS 19:32

With the ancient is wisdom, and in length of days there is understanding.
                                                    JOB 12:12

When I am old and grayheaded, O God, forsake me not.
                                                    PSALM 71:18

LORD, you have been our dwelling place in all generations. Before the mountains were brought forth, or ever you had formed the earth and the world, even from everlasting to everlasting, you are God. You turn man to destruction, and say, "Return, you children of men." For a thousand years in your sight are but as yesterday when it is past, and as a watch in the night. You carry them away as with a flood; they are as a sleep; in the morning they are

> *"Nobody ever outgrows Scripture; the Book widens and deepens with our years."*
>
> —C. H. SPURGEON, THE MOST FAMOUS PREACHER IN VICTORIAN ENGLAND

like grass that grows up. In the morning it flourishes, and grows up; in the evening it is cut down and withers.

The days of our years are seventy, and if by reason of strength they be eighty years, yet their span is trouble and sorrow. For it is soon cut off, and we fly away. Who knows the power of your anger? Even according to your fear, so is your wrath. So teach us to number our days, that we may apply our hearts to wisdom.   PSALM 90:1–6, 10–12

The righteous shall flourish like the palm tree; he shall grow like a cedar in Lebanon. Those that are planted in the house of the LORD shall flourish in the courts of our God. They shall still bring forth fruit in old age; they shall be fresh and flourishing.   PSALM 92:12–14

Blessed is the man that fears the LORD, that delights greatly in his commandments. His children shall be mighty upon earth; the generation of the upright shall be blessed.   PSALM 112:1–2

The gray head is a crown of glory, if it be found in the way of righteousness.   PROVERBS 16:31

Children's children are the crown of old men, and the glory of children are their fathers.   PROVERBS 17:6

The glory of young men is their strength, and the beauty of old men is the gray head.   PROVERBS 20:29

Even to your old age I am he, and even to gray hairs will I sustain you; I have made you and I will carry you.   ISAIAH 46:4

"It shall come to pass in the last days," said God, "I will pour out of my Spirit upon all flesh, and your sons and your daughters shall prophesy, and your young men shall see visions, and your old men shall dream dreams. And on my servants and on my handmaidens I will pour out in those days of my Spirit, and they shall prophesy." ACTS 2:17–18

Be confident of this very thing, that he who has begun a good work in you will perform it until the day of Jesus Christ. PHILIPPIANS 1:6

Rebuke not an old man, but appeal to him as a father. Treat the younger men as brothers, the elder women as mothers, the younger as sisters, with all purity. I TIMOTHY 5:1–2

Speak the things which agree with sound doctrine. Teach that the aged men be sober, sensible, self-controlled, sound in faith, in charity, in patience. Teach the aged women likewise, that they behave as becomes holiness, not false accusers, not addicted to wine, but teachers of good things.

TITUS 2:1–3

See also Hope, Personal Growth.

ALCOHOL AND OTHER SUBSTANCE ABUSE

No, the Bible does not actually condemn alcohol. But it does take a harsh view of those who let alcohol or any other substance wreak havoc with their lives and the lives of others. Some people accuse the Bible of being anti-pleasure, but it is more accurate to say that it is pro-health and pro-moderation. It is also clear, especially in the New Testament, that the fleeting pleasures of drinking are small compared with the greater, more enduring, life-affirming joy of fellowship with God.

Wine is a mocker, strong drink is raging, and whoever is deceived thereby is not wise. PROVERBS 20:1

He that loves pleasure shall be a poor man; he who loves wine and oil shall not be rich. PROVERBS 21:17

Be not among wine guzzlers, nor among gluttonous eaters of food. For the drunkard and the glutton shall come to poverty, and laziness shall clothe a man with rags.   PROVERBS 23:20–21

Who has woe? Who has sorrow? Who has strife? Who has complaints? Who has wounds without cause? Who has redness of eyes? They that tarry long at the wine, they that go to seek mixed wine. Look not upon the wine when it is red, when it sparkles in the cup, when it goes down smoothly. At the last it bites like a serpent, and stings like an adder. Your eyes shall behold strange women, and your heart shall utter perverse things. Yes, you shall be like one who lies down in the midst of the sea, or as he who lies upon the top of a mast. "They have struck me," you shall say, "and I was not sick. They have beaten me, and I felt it not. When shall I awake? I will seek it yet again."
PROVERBS 23:29–35

Give strong drink to him that is ready to perish, and wine to those that are of heavy hearts. Let him drink, and forget his poverty, and remember his misery no more.   PROVERBS 31:6–7

Woe to those who rise up early in the morning, that they may follow strong drink, that continue until night, till wine inflames them! . . . they regard not the work of the LORD, neither consider the operation of his hands.
ISAIAH 5:11–12

Whoredom and wine and new wine take away the heart.   HOSEA 4:11

Take heed to yourselves, lest at any time your hearts be occupied with dissipation, and drunkenness, and worries of this life, or that day may come upon you unawares.   LUKE 21:34

Let us walk honestly, as in the day, not in orgies and drunkenness, not in debauchery and immorality, not in strife and envying.   ROMANS 13:13

Be not drunk with wine, wherein is excess, but be filled with the Spirit.
EPHESIANS 5:18

They that sleep sleep in the night, and they that are drunk are drunk in the night. But let us, who are of the day, be sober.   I THESSALONIANS 5:7

> *"I have spent a lot of time searching through the Bible for loopholes."*
>
> —HARD-DRINKING FILM COMIC W. C. FIELDS

In the past you spent enough time doing as the pagans do, walking in debauchery, lusts, excess of wine, orgies, carousing, and abominable idolatries. They think it strange that you no longer join with them to the same excess of dissipation, so they speak evil of you. They shall give account to him who is ready to judge the living and the dead.   I PETER 4:3–5

See also Bad Company, The Body, Sickness, Temptation.

AMBITION

Is ambition a bad thing? If it involves making oneself and one's career into one's own private god, then, yes, it is possible to worship and serve ambition rather than serving the true God. If ambition means attempting to do great things for God and mankind, then, no, it is not bad at all. But the Bible takes a realistic view of human aspiration, especially in the Old Testament books of Psalms, Proverbs, and Ecclesiastes, which compare the brevity of human achievements with the eternal God. The message is reiterated in the New Testament: Possessions and fame pass away, and we are left facing the more important questions of our relation with God and our fellow man.

Trust in the LORD, and do good, so shall you dwell in the land, and truly you shall be fed.   PSALM 37:3

Wise men die, likewise the fool and the senseless perish, and leave their wealth to others. Their inward thought is that their houses shall continue forever, and their dwelling places to all generations; they call their lands after their own names. Nevertheless man, despite his honors, abides not; he is like the beasts that perish. Such is the fate of the foolish, and of their followers who approve their sayings. Like sheep they are laid in the grave; death shall feed on them; and the upright shall have dominion over them in the morning; and their beauty shall decay in the grave, far from their dwelling. But God will redeem my soul from the power of the grave; for he shall receive me.

Be not afraid when one is made rich, when the glory of his house is increased, for when he dies he shall carry nothing with him; his glory shall not descend with him. Though while he lived he was counted as blessed—and men will praise you when you prosper—he shall go to the generation of his fathers; they shall never see light. Man that is held in honor and lacking in understanding is like the beasts that perish.   PSALM 49:10–20

He that is greedy of gain troubles his own house.   PROVERBS 15:27

Better it is to be of humble spirit with the lowly than to divide the spoil with the proud.   PROVERBS 16:19

There are many devices in a man's heart; nevertheless the purpose of the LORD, that shall stand.   PROVERBS 19:21

Better is a handful with quietness, than both the hands full with toil and a chasing after the wind.   ECCLESIASTES 4:6

In many dreams and many words there is also meaninglessness.
                                                    ECCLESIASTES 5:7

The race is not to the swift, nor the battle to the strong, nor bread to the wise, nor riches to men of understanding, nor favor to men of skill; but time and chance happen to them all.   ECCLESIASTES 9:11

Woe to those who add house to house, that lay field to field, till there are no places left, that they may live alone in the midst of the earth! In mine ears said the LORD Almighty, "Surely the many houses shall be desolate, even great and fair, without inhabitants."   ISAIAH 5:8–9

"Let him that glories glory in this, that he understands and knows me, that I am the LORD which exercise lovingkindness, judgment, and righteousness, in the earth, for in these things I delight," says the LORD.

JEREMIAH 9:24

The devil took him up into an exceedingly high mountain, and showed him all the kingdoms of the world, and the glory of them, and said to him, "All these things will I give you, if you will fall down and worship me." Then said Jesus to him, "Get you hence, Satan, for it is written, 'You shall worship the Lord your God, and him only shall you serve.'"

MATTHEW 4:8–10

What is a man profited, if he shall gain the whole world, and lose his own soul? Or what shall a man give in exchange for his soul?

MATTHEW 16:26

Whoever will be great among you, let him be your servant.

MATTHEW 20:26

Whoever shall exalt himself shall be abased, and he who shall humble himself shall be exalted.   MATTHEW 23:12

Woe to you who are rich, for you have already received your consolation. Woe to you who are full, for you shall hunger. Woe to you that laugh now, for you shall mourn and weep.   LUKE 6:24–25

Jesus spoke a parable to them, saying, "The ground of a certain rich man brought forth plentifully. And he thought within himself, saying, 'What shall I do, because I have no room to store my fruits?' And he said, 'This will I do: I will pull down my barns, and build larger, and there will I store all my fruits and my goods. And I will say to my soul, Soul, you have much goods laid up for many years; take your ease, eat, drink, and be merry.' But God said to him, 'You fool, this night your soul shall be required of you. Then whose shall those things be, which you have provided?' So is he who lays up treasure for himself, and is not rich toward God."   LUKE 12:16–21

The great (and highly ambitious) Napoleon wasn't exactly religious, but he did make this statement: "The Bible is no mere book, but a Living Creature, with a power that conquers all that oppose it." It has certainly outlasted Napoleon and his empire.

Behold, some that are last shall be first, and some that are first shall be last.

LUKE 13:30

That which is highly esteemed among men is abomination in the sight of God.

LUKE 16:15

Jesus said to them, "The kings of the pagans exercise lordship over them, and they that exercise authority upon them are called benefactors. But you shall not be so, but he who is greatest among you, let him be as the younger, and he who is chief, as he who does serve. For which is greater, he who sits at the table, or he who serves? Is it not he who sits at food? But I am among you as he who serves." LUKE 22:25–27

How can you believe, you who accept honor from one another but seek not the honor that comes from God only? JOHN 5:44

I am come that they might have life, and that they might have it more abundantly. JOHN 10:10

Let nothing be done through ambition or vain conceit, but in humility let each esteem others better than themselves. PHILIPPIANS 2:3

Set your affection on things above, not on things on the earth.

COLOSSIANS 3:2

Study to lead a quiet life, and to do your own business, and to work with your own hands, as we commanded you, so that you may walk honestly toward outsiders, and that you may have lack of nothing.

I THESSALONIANS 4:11–12

If you have bitter envying and strife in your hearts, do not boast of it, and do not deny the truth. This so-called wisdom descends not from heaven, but is earthly, sensual, devilish. For where envying and strife are, there is disorder and every evil work. But the wisdom that is from above is first pure, then peaceable, gentle, and easy to be entreated, full of mercy and good fruits, without partiality, and without hypocrisy.   JAMES 3:14–17

All that is in the world, the cravings of the sinful nature, and the lust of the eyes, and the pride of life, is not of the Father, but is of the world.

I JOHN 2:16

See also Self-Esteem, Success.

ANGELS

Angels have become a "hot topic" in recent years, as seen in so many books, calendars, motion pictures, and so on. Curiously, the angels that the Bible presents us with are not the cute, chubby infants seen in old paintings. Rather, they are majestic, awe-inspiring messengers of God. The people in the Bible who encountered angels were often frightened at first, for those heavenly beings are anything but cute and adorable. On the other hand, because they are powerful and watchful, we can take comfort in knowing that such beings guide and protect us. A curious thing: On several occasions people encountered angels without being aware of it at first. The "angel in disguise" phenomenon raises an obvious question: Have I encountered one of God's angels in my own life?

The angel of the LORD encamps round about those who fear him, and delivers them. O taste and see that the LORD is good; blessed is the man that trusts in him.   PSALM 34:7–8

He shall give his angels charge over you, to keep you in all your ways. They shall bear you up in their hands, lest you dash your foot against a stone.

PSALM 91:9–12

The Son of man shall send forth his angels, and they shall gather out of his kingdom all things that offend, and those who do evil, and shall cast them into a furnace of fire. There shall be wailing and gnashing of teeth. Then shall the righteous shine forth as the sun in the kingdom of their Father.

MATTHEW 13:41–43

Take heed that you despise not one of these little ones; for I say to you, that in heaven their angels do always behold the face of my Father who is in heaven.   MATTHEW 18:10

Then shall appear the sign of the Son of man in heaven, and then shall all the tribes of the earth mourn. And they shall see the Son of man coming in the clouds of heaven with power and great glory. And he shall send his angels with a great sound of a trumpet, and they shall gather together his elect from the four winds, from one end of heaven to the other.

MATTHEW 24:30–31

Of that day and hour knows no man, no, not the angels of heaven, but my Father only.   MATTHEW 24:36

Whoever shall confess me before men, him shall the Son of man also confess before the angels of God. But he who denies me before men shall be denied before the angels of God.   LUKE 12:8–9

There is joy in the presence of the angels of God over one sinner who repents.

LUKE 15:10

The high priest rose up, and all they that were with him who were of the sect of the Sadducees, and they were filled with indignation. They laid their hands on the apostles, and put them in the common prison. But the angel of the Lord by night opened the prison doors, and brought them forth, and said, "Go, stand and speak in the temple to the people all the words of this life."

ACTS 5:17–20

We think of "cherubs" as cute, chubby infant angels with wings. But cherubs in the Bible are awesome creatures, angels that symbolize divine power and energy. Gold figures of two of these, with their great wings outstretched, were on top of Israel's ark of the covenant—just as depicted in the hit movie Raiders of the Lost Ark.

The angel of the Lord came upon him, and a light shone in the prison, and he touched Peter on the side, and raised him up, saying, "Arise up quickly." And his chains fell off from his hands. And the angel said to him, "Tie up your belt and put on your sandals." And so he did. And the angel said to him, "Put your garment around you, and follow me." And he went out, and followed him, and knew not that it was real what was done by the angel, but he thought he was seeing a vision. When they were past the first and the second guard station, they came to the iron gate that leads to the city, and it opened for them of its own accord. They went out, and passed on through a street, and suddenly the angel departed from him. And when Peter was come to himself, he said, "Now I know for certain that the Lord has sent his angel, and has delivered me out of the hand of Herod, and from all that the Jews expected to occur."   ACTS 12:7–11

Such are false apostles, deceitful workers, transforming themselves into the apostles of Christ. Satan himself is transformed into an angel of light. Therefore it is no great thing if his servants also be transformed as the ministers of righteousness. Their end shall be according to their works.

2 CORINTHIANS 11:14

The Lord himself shall descend from heaven with a shout, with the voice of the archangel and with the trumpet of God, and the dead in Christ shall rise first. Then we who are alive and remain shall be caught up together with them in the clouds to meet the Lord in the air, and so shall we ever be with the Lord. So comfort one another with these words.

I THESSALONIANS 4:16–18

Are they not all ministering spirits, sent forth to minister for them who shall be heirs of salvation? HEBREWS 1:14

You are come to Mount Zion, to the city of the living God, the heavenly Jerusalem, and to an innumerable company of angels.

HEBREWS 12:22

Be not forgetful to entertain strangers, for thereby some have entertained angels unawares. HEBREWS 13:2

God spared not the angels that sinned, but cast them down to hell, and delivered them into chains of darkness, to be reserved for judgment.

2 PETER 2:4

The angels which kept not their first estate, but left their own habitation, he has reserved in everlasting chains under darkness to the judgment of the great day. JUDE 6

See also The Devil.

ANGER

The level of violence in our society suggests that a lot of people are angry and that they aren't dealing with it very constructively. While there is sometimes a place in life for righteous anger (see John 2:14–16 below, depicting an angry Jesus), the Bible takes a realistic view of human anger, seeing it as arising from a selfish sense of wounded honor. More often than not, it is purely destructive, hurting not only the angry person but others as well. The Book of Proverbs in particular has much to say about the foolishness of the hothead.

Wrath kills the foolish man, and envy slays the simpleminded one.

JOB 5:2

A fool's anger is quickly known, but a prudent man ignores insults.

PROVERBS 12:16

He that is easily angered deals foolishly, and a man of wicked devices is hated.

PROVERBS 14:17

A soft answer turns away wrath, but grievous words stir up anger.

PROVERBS 15:1

A wrathful man stirs up strife, but he who is slow to anger calms strife.

PROVERBS 15:18

He that is slow to anger is better than the mighty, and he who rules his spirit than he who takes a city.

PROVERBS 16:32

The beginning of strife is as when water breaks out of a dam.

PROVERBS 17:14

The discretion of a man defers his anger, and it is his glory to ignore a transgression.

PROVERBS 19:11

A man of great wrath shall suffer punishment, for if you deliver him, yet you must do it again.

PROVERBS 19:19

Make no friendship with an angry man, and with a furious man you shall not go, lest you learn his ways, and get a snare to your soul.

PROVERBS 22:24–25

Scornful men bring a city into a snare, but wise men turn away anger.

PROVERBS 29:8

An angry man stirs up strife, and a furious man abounds in transgression.

PROVERBS 29:22

Be not hasty in your spirit to be angry, for anger rests in the bosom of fools.

ECCLESIASTES 7:9

Whoever is angry with his brother without a cause shall be in danger of the judgment, and whoever shall say to his brother, "You fool" shall be in danger of hell fire. MATTHEW 5:22

Jesus found in the temple those that sold oxen and sheep and doves, and the money-changers were sitting there. And when he had made a whip out of small cords, he drove them all out of the temple, along with the sheep and the oxen, and he poured out the changers' money, and overturned the tables. And he said to those who sold doves, "Take these things away; do not make my Father's house a house of merchandise." JOHN 2:14–16

Dearly beloved, avenge not yourselves, but rather give place to wrath, for it is written, "Vengeance is mine; I will repay," says the Lord. Therefore if your enemy hungers, feed him; if he thirsts, give him drink, for in so doing you shall heap coals of fire on his head. Be not overcome of evil, but overcome evil with good. ROMANS 12:19–21

Be angry, and sin not; let not the sun go down upon your wrath.

EPHESIANS 4:26

Let all bitterness and wrath and anger and brawling and evil speaking be put away from you, with all malice. And be kind to one another, tenderhearted, forgiving one another, even as God for Christ's sake has forgiven you.

EPHESIANS 4:31–32

Now you also put off all these; anger, wrath, malice, blasphemy, filthy communication out of your mouth. Lie not to one another, seeing that you have put off the old man with his deeds, and have put on the new man, which is renewed in knowledge after the image of him that created him.

COLOSSIANS 3:8–10

I will therefore that men pray every where, lifting up holy hands, without wrath and doubting. I TIMOTHY 2:8

My beloved brethren, let every man be swift to hear, slow to speak, slow to anger; for the wrath of man works not the righteousness of God.

JAMES 1:19–20

See also Hate, Meekness/Gentleness, Pride, Self-Control/Self-Denial.

ANXIETY

One thing that rich and poor and everyone in between have in common is anxiety. Despite therapy, self-help books, drugs, alcohol, and positive-thinking seminars, anxiety still prevails. Why? Because we don't like uncertainty—because humans want to know what lies ahead and to be prepared for it. Regrettably, this hankering to plan ahead only makes us anxious, sapping the joy of the present moment. While the Bible urges people to take thought for the future (at least in the sense of preparing ourselves for eternity), it also urges us to "loosen up," to recognize that our control of events is limited and that only God is truly in control of all things.

Yea, though I walk through the valley of the shadow of death, I will fear no evil, for you are with me; your rod and your staff they comfort me. You prepare a table before me in the presence of my enemies: you anoint my head with oil; my cup runs over. Surely goodness and mercy shall follow me all the days of my life, and I will dwell in the house of the LORD forever.

PSALM 23:4

I sought the LORD, and he heard me, and delivered me from all my fears.

PSALM 34:3

Rest in the LORD, and wait patiently for him. PSALM 37:7

Do not call a conspiracy all that this people calls conspiracy; do not fear what it fears, nor be in dread. But the LORD Almighty, him you shall regard as holy, him alone shall you fear and dread. ISAIAH 8:12–13

It shall come to pass in the day that the LORD shall give you rest from your sorrow and from your fear and from the hard bondage in which you were made to serve. ISAIAH 14:3

Take no thought for your life, what you shall eat, or what you shall drink; nor yet for your body, what you shall put on. Is not life more than food, and the body than clothing? Behold the birds of the air, for they sow not, neither do they reap, nor gather into barns, yet your heavenly Father feeds them. Are you not much better than they? Which of you by worrying can add a single hour to his life span? MATTHEW 6:25–27

Be anxious for nothing, but in everything by prayer and supplication with thanksgiving let your requests be made known to God. And the peace of God, which passes all understanding, will keep your hearts and minds in Christ Jesus. PHILIPPIANS 4:6

There is no fear in love; but perfect love casts out fear; because fear has to do with punishment. He that fears is not made perfect in love.

I JOHN 4:18

See also **Worry.**

ARROGANCE

The attitude of arrogance has always repelled some people and attracted others. We look at the arrogant person and ask, "Who does he think he is? God?" In fact, the answer may be, "Yes, he does." But that very attitude draws others, who see the arrogant person as independent, aggressive, a climber, and one who lives by his or her own rules. But most of us know that the arrogant always end up hurting others, and in the eternal sense they have spent their lives worshiping the wrong God: themselves. The Bible opposes any kind of idolatry, including one's own ego. It presents us with an alternative: the true God who is in control of the universe. He alone deserves worship. He also lifts from us the burden of always having to guard our own fragile egos.

Talk no more so exceeding proudly; let not arrogance come out of your mouth, for the LORD is a God of knowledge, and by him actions are weighed.   I SAMUEL 2:3

The afflicted people you will save, but your eyes are upon the haughty, that you may bring them down.   2 SAMUEL 22:28

There is no fear of God before his eyes, for he flatters himself in his own eyes.   PSALM 36:1–2

Him that has a high look and a proud heart I will not endure.
                                                          PSALM 101:5

The fear of the LORD is to hate evil; pride, and arrogance, and the evil way, and the perverse mouth, do I hate.   PROVERBS 8:13

Pride goes before destruction, and a haughty spirit before a fall.
                                                       PROVERBS 16:18

The lofty looks of man shall be humbled, and the haughtiness of men shall be bowed down, and the LORD alone shall be exalted in that day.
                                                          ISAIAH 2:11

Behold, the LORD, the LORD Almighty, shall lop the bough with terror, and the high ones of stature shall be cut down, and the haughty shall be humbled.   ISAIAH 10:33

I will punish the world for their evil, and the wicked for their iniquity, and I will cause the arrogance of the proud to cease, and will lay low the haughtiness of the terrible.   ISAIAH 13:11

"Behold, I am against you, O you most proud," says the LORD God Almighty, "for your day is come, the time that I will visit you."
                                                       JEREMIAH 50:31

Your heart is lifted up, and you have said, "I am a God, I sit in the seat of God" . . . yet you are a man, and not God.   EZEKIEL 28:2

England's King Henry VIII (famous for having six wives) did a famous flip-flop. He executed William Tyndale for translating the Bible into English. Years later, Henry ordered that every English church have a copy of the Bible in English. Before Tyndale was burned at the stake, he had prayed, "Lord, open the king of England's eyes!" Obviously, his prayer was answered.

There are some who are last who shall be first, and there are some first who shall be last.   LUKE 13:30

Listen, now, you who say, "Today or tomorrow we will go into such a city, and continue there a year, and buy and sell, and make money." And yet you do not know what will happen tomorrow. For what is your life? It is like a vapor, that appears for a little time, and then vanishes away. Rather, you ought to say, "If the Lord wills, we shall live, and do this or that."

                                                                JAMES 4:13—15

See also Conceit, Pride.

BACKSLIDING

Making promises is a human trait. So is breaking them. While we are all full of good intentions, promising ourselves and others that we will do better in the future, we inevitably fail, falling back into our familiar patterns. While this can make us appreciate God (who makes promises and never breaks them), it can make us angry and frustrated with ourselves and others. In fact, God himself is angry when people turn to him when they need him and then (like a bad habit) turn away again. Happily, the Bible tells us that God shows his mercy again and again and is always willing to forgive the repentant sinner.

Take heed to yourself, and keep your soul diligently, lest you forget the things which your eyes have seen, and lest they depart from your heart all the days of your life.   DEUTERONOMY 4:9

If you forsake the LORD and serve strange gods, then he will turn and do you hurt and consume you.   JOSHUA 24:20

The children of Israel remembered not the LORD their God, who had delivered them out of the hands of all their enemies on every side.

JUDGES 8:34

If you seek him, he will be found of you; but if you forsake him, he will cast you off forever.   I CHRONICLES 28:9

If my people, which are called by my name, shall humble themselves, and pray, and seek my face, and turn from their wicked ways; then will I hear from heaven, and will forgive their sin, and will heal their land.

2 CHRONICLES 7:14

My steps have held to your paths; my feet have not slipped.

PSALM 17:5

As a dog returns to his vomit, so a fool returns to his folly.

PROVERBS 26:11

The ox knows his owner, and the donkey knows his master's crib, but Israel does not know, my people do not understand.   ISAIAH 1:3

"Return, backsliding Israel," says the LORD, "and I will not cause my anger to fall upon you; for I am merciful, and I will not keep anger forever."

JEREMIAH 3:12

"As I live," says the LORD God, "I have no pleasure in the death of the wicked; but I desire that the wicked turn from his way and live. Turn, turn you from your evil ways; for why will you die, O house of Israel?"

EZEKIEL 33:11

"Even from the days of your fathers you are gone away from mine laws, and have not kept them. Return to me, and I will return to you," says the LORD Almighty.   MALACHI 3:7

If any man obey not our word by this letter, note that man, and have no company with him, that he may be ashamed. Yet count him not as an enemy, but admonish him as a brother.   2 THESSALONIANS 3:14–15

Brethren, if any of you err from the truth, and someone converts him, let him know that he who converts the sinner from the error of his ways shall save a soul from death, and shall hide a multitude of sins.

JAMES 5:19–20

See also God's Mercy.

BAD COMPANY

Peer pressure can be a positive thing as well as a negative one. But anyone who has children (or who has ever been a child, which includes all of us) knows that it is so much easier to follow the group that does bad than the group that does good. In fact, caving in to negative peer pressure is a form of laziness, taking the path of least resistance. It is always harder—and also more courageous—to swim upstream, to fly in the face of peer pressure, to stand one's ground morally. The Bible speaks many times of a faithful "remnant," those people who have resisted the temptations of bad companions and have remained faithful to God. And for those who have not resisted, the Bible offers a clear call to change, to follow God's way instead of the crowd's way.

You shall not follow a crowd to do evil. EXODUS 23:2

Blessed is the man that walks not in the counsel of the ungodly, nor stands in the way of sinners, nor sits in the seat of the scornful. But his delight is in the law of the LORD, and in his law does he meditate day and night. And he shall be like a tree planted by the rivers of water, that brings forth his fruit in his season. His leaf shall not wither, and whatever he does shall prosper.

The ungodly are not so, but are like the chaff which the wind drives away. Therefore the ungodly shall not stand in the judgment, nor sinners in the congregation of the righteous. For the Lord knows the way of the righteous, but the way of the ungodly shall perish. PSALM I

I had rather be a doorkeeper in the house of my God, than to dwell in the tents of wickedness. PSALM 84:10

Discretion shall preserve you, understanding shall keep you, to deliver you from the way of the evil man, from the man that speaks perverse things.

PROVERBS 2:11—12

The righteous is more excellent than his neighbor, but the way of the wicked seduces them. PROVERBS 12:26

He that walks with wise men shall be wise, but a companion of fools shall be destroyed.   PROVERBS 13:20

He that handles a matter wisely shall find good, and whoever trusts in the LORD, happy is he.   PROVERBS 16:20

Whoever keeps the law is a wise son, but he who is a companion of gluttons shames his father.   PROVERBS 28:7

Do not call a conspiracy all that this people calls conspiracy; do not fear what it fears, nor be in dread. But the LORD Almighty, him you shall regard as holy, him alone shall you fear and dread.   ISAIAH 8:12–13

Be not conformed to this world, but be transformed by the renewing of your mind, that you may prove what is the good and acceptable and perfect will of God.   ROMANS 12:2

Be not deceived: bad companions corrupt good morals.

1 CORINTHIANS 15:33

In the past you already spent enough time doing as the pagans do, walking in debauchery, lusts, excess of wine, orgies, carousing, and abominable idolatries. They think it strange that you no longer join with them to the same excess of dissipation, so they speak evil of you. They shall give account to him that is ready to judge the living and the dead.   1 PETER 4:3–5

See also Fellowship with Other Believers, Friends, Trendiness, Witnessing/Evangelism.

BAPTISM

Baptism in the New Testament is rich with meaning. It symbolizes the washing away of one's past sins, the "burial" of one's former life and the beginning of a new spiritual life. The first generation of Christians saw it as absolutely essential, for it was a way of indicating—both to the public and to the person being baptized—that something new and dramatic had occurred.

Jesus himself set the pattern when his kinsman, the great wilderness prophet known as John the Baptist, baptized him in the Jordan River. This marked the beginning of Jesus' public ministry as teacher, miracle worker, and Savior.

[John the Baptist:] "I indeed baptize you with water for repentance, but he who comes after me is mightier than I, whose shoes I am not worthy to carry. He shall baptize you with the Holy Spirit and with fire."

MATTHEW 3:11

Then came Jesus from Galilee to John, to be baptized by him. But John forbade him, saying, "I have need to be baptized of you, and come you to me?" And Jesus answering said to him, "Let it to be so now, for thus it becomes us to fulfill all righteousness." And Jesus, when he was baptized, went up straightaway out of the water, and, lo, the heavens were opened to him, and he saw the Spirit of God descending like a dove, and lighting upon him. And, lo, a voice from heaven, said, "This is my beloved Son, in whom I am well pleased."   MATTHEW 3:13–17

Go you therefore, and teach all nations, baptizing them in the name of the Father, and of the Son, and of the Holy Spirit.   MATTHEW 28:19

John did baptize in the wilderness, and preach the baptism of repentance for the remission of sins. And there went out to him all the land of Judea, and they of Jerusalem, and were all baptized of him in the Jordan River, confessing their sins.   MARK 1:4–5

He that believes and is baptized shall be saved; but he who believes not shall be damned.   MARK 16:16

Peter said to them, "Repent, and be baptized everyone of you in the name of Jesus Christ for the forgiveness of sins, and you shall receive the gift of the Holy Spirit."   ACTS 2:38

We are buried with him by baptism into death: that as Christ was raised up from the dead by the glory of the Father, even so we also should walk in newness of life.   ROMANS 6:4

As many of you as have been baptized into Christ have put on Christ.

GALATIANS 3:27

There is one body and one Spirit, even as you are called in one hope of your calling: one Lord, one faith, one baptism.   EPHESIANS 4:4–5

When you were buried with him in baptism, you also were raised with him through the faith of the power of God, who has raised him from the dead.

COLOSSIANS 2:12

BAPTISM OF THE SPIRIT/GIFTS OF THE SPIRIT

Baptism in water is a practice going back to Jesus himself. But the New Testament presents us with another sort of baptism, one in which God's people are given life-changing spiritual power, the power of the Holy Spirit. This amazing empowerment was predicted in the Old Testament, and in the New it was seen in the many miracles and other signs of the Spirit's working. Jesus himself had predicted that his followers would do amazing works. For many generations people neglected this important teaching, but in recent years there has been a renewed interest in the baptism of the Spirit and the gifts that the Spirit bestows on God's people. There is ample evidence around the world that the Spirit is still working through people of faith, and the gifts of the Spirit were definitely not limited to the age of the first Christians.

I will pour water upon him that is thirsty, and floods upon the dry ground. I will pour my Spirit upon your children, and my blessing upon your offspring.   ISAIAH 44:3

It shall come to pass afterward, that I will pour out my Spirit upon all flesh, and your sons and your daughters shall prophesy, your old men shall dream dreams, your young men shall see visions. And also upon the servants and upon the handmaids in those days will I pour out my Spirit.

JOEL 2:28–29

[John the Baptist:] "I indeed baptize you with water to repentance, but he who comes after me is mightier than I, whose shoes I am not worthy, to carry; he shall baptize you with the Holy Spirit and with fire."

MATTHEW 3:11

Jesus answered, "Truly, truly, I say to you, except a man be born of water and of the Spirit, he cannot enter into the kingdom of God."

JOHN 3:5

When the day of Pentecost had come, they [the apostles] were all together in one place. And suddenly there came a sound from heaven like the rushing of a mighty wind, and it filled all the house where they were sitting. And there appeared to them tongues of fire that separated and sat upon each of them. And they were all filled with the Holy Spirit, and began to speak with other tongues, as the Spirit gave them ability. ACTS 2:1–4

Then Peter said to them, "Repent, and be baptized everyone of you in the name of Jesus Christ for the forgiveness of sins, and you shall receive the gift of the Holy Spirit. For the promise is to you, and to your children, and to all that are far away, even as many as the Lord our God shall call." And with many other words did he testify and exhort, saying, "Save yourselves from this corrupt generation." Then they that gladly received his word were baptized, and the same day there were added to them about three thousand souls. ACTS 2:38–41

As I [the apostle Paul] began to speak, the Holy Spirit fell on them, as on us at the beginning. Then I remembered the word of the Lord, how he had said, "John indeed baptized with water, but you shall be baptized with the Holy Spirit." ACTS 11:15–16

As we have many members in one body, and all members have not the same function, so we, being many, are one body in Christ, and all are members of one another. We have gifts differing according to the grace that is given to us: prophecy, in proportion to faith; ministry, in ministering; the teacher, in teaching; the exhorter, in exhortation; the giver, in generosity; the leader, in diligence; the compassionate, in cheerfulness. ROMANS 12:4–8

By one Spirit are we all baptized into one body, whether we be Jews or Gentiles, whether we be slave or free, and have been all made to drink into one Spirit.   I CORINTHIANS 12:13

Now there are diversities of gifts, but the same Spirit. And there are differences of services, but the same Lord. And there are diversities of activities, but it is the same God who works all in all. But the manifestation of the Spirit is given to every man to profit all.

For to one is given by the Spirit the word of wisdom; to another the word of knowledge by the same Spirit; to another faith by the same Spirit; to another the gifts of healing by the same Spirit; to another the working of miracles; to another prophecy; to another discerning of spirits; to another various kinds of tongues; to another the interpretation of tongues. But in all these work that one and the selfsame Spirit, allotting to every man individually as he chooses.

For as the body is one, and has many members, and all the members of that one body, being many, are one body: so also is Christ. For by one Spirit are we all baptized into one body, whether we be Jews or Gentiles, whether we be slave or free, and have been all made to drink into one Spirit. For the body is not one member, but many. If the foot shall say, "Because I am not the hand, I am not of the body," is it therefore not part of the body? And if the ear shall say, "Because I am not the eye, I am not of the body," is it therefore not of the body? If the whole body were an eye, where would the hearing be? If the whole body were hearing, where would the sense of smell be? But now has God set the members every one of them in the body, as it has pleased him. And if they were all one member, where would the body be? But now they are many members, yet only one body. And the eye cannot say to the hand, "I have no need of you," nor can the head say to the feet, "I have no need of you." No, those members of the body which seem to be weaker are necessary.

Now you are the body of Christ, and individually members of it. And God has appointed some in the church, first apostles, second prophets, third teachers, after that miracles, then gifts of healings, forms of assistance, leadership, diversities of tongues. Are all apostles? Are all prophets? Are all teachers? Are all workers of miracles? Have all the gifts of healing? Do all speak with tongues? Do all interpret? But desire earnestly the best gifts.

I CORINTHIANS 12:4–23, 27–31

Not by works of righteousness which we have done, but according to his mercy he saved us, by the washing of regeneration, and renewing of the Holy Spirit.

TITUS 3:5

God also bore them witness, both with signs and wonders, and with various miracles, and gifts of the Holy Spirit, according to his own will.

HEBREWS 2:4

See also The Holy Spirit.

BEAUTY

The Bible shows a deep appreciation of the attractions of the human body. If you don't believe this, check out any verse from the Song of Solomon. Yet the Bible takes a more balanced view of outward beauty—that is, it reminds us again and again that it is possible to be pretty on the outside and horrible on the inside. Needless to say, inner beauty is better and more enduring to boot.

The Bible also has a lot to say about the beauties of creation. Nature as God created it is a beautiful thing and deserves our praise—so long as we remember to save our deepest praise for the Creator himself.

God saw every thing that he had made, and, behold, it was good.

GENESIS 1:31

Give unto the LORD the glory due unto his name; bring an offering, and come before him; worship the LORD in the beauty of holiness.

I CHRONICLES 16:29

Stand still, and consider the wondrous works of God.

JOB 37:14

The Heavens declare the glory of God, and the firmament shows his handiwork.

PSALM 19:1

Beautiful Bibles

William Tyndale produced his English translation of the New Testament in 1524. It was the first English Bible produced on a printing press. It was also the first English Bible to include a word that we now use everyday: beautiful. *It was still a fairly new word at the time, and some people were amazed that Tyndale would use such a "novel" word in the Bible.*

One thing have I desired of the LORD and that will I seek after: that I may dwell in the house of the LORD all the days of my life, to behold the beauty of the LORD, and to inquire in his temple.   PSALM 27:4

Let the beauty of the LORD our God be upon us.   PSALM 90:17

Honor and majesty are before him; strength and beauty are in his sanctuary.   PSALM 96:6

The LORD takes pleasure in his people; he will beautify the meek with salvation.   PSALM 149:4

As a jewel of gold in a swine's snout, so is a beautiful woman who is without discretion.   PROVERBS 11:22

The glory of young men is their strength, and the beauty of old men is the grey head.   PROVERBS 20:29

Through wisdom is a house built, and by understanding it is established; and by knowledge shall the chambers be filled with all pleasant riches.   PROVERBS 24:3–4

Favor is deceitful, and beauty is vain; but a woman that fears the LORD, she shall be praised. PROVERBS 31:30

He has made every thing beautiful in his time. ECCLESIASTES 3:11

Woe to you, scribes and Pharisees, hypocrites! For you are like whitewashed tombs, which appear beautiful outwardly, but within are full of dead men's bones, and of all kinds of filth. Even so, you outwardly appear righteous to men, but within you are full of hypocrisy and dishonor. MATTHEW 23:27

Consider the lilies, how they grow; they toil not, they spin not, and yet I say to you that Solomon in all his glory was not arrayed like one of these. LUKE 12:27

Though our outward man perish, yet the inward man is renowned day by day. 2 CORINTHIANS 4:16

Whatever things are true, whatever things are honest, whatever things are just, whatever things are pure, whatever things are lovely, whatever things are admirable—if anything is excellent or praiseworthy—think on these things. PHILIPPIANS 4:8

Unto the pure all things are pure. TITUS 1:15

Let it not be that outward adorning of arranging the hair, or of wearing of gold, or of putting on clothing. But let it be that the hidden man of the heart, in that which is not corruptible, the ornament of a gentle and quiet spirit, which is precious in the sight of God. I PETER 3:3–4

All that is in the world, the cravings of the sinful nature, and the lust of the eyes, and the pride of life, is not of the Father, but is of the world. And the world passes away, and the lust thereof, but he who does the will of God abides forever. I JOHN 2:16–17

See also The Body, Nature and the Earth, Self-Esteem.

THE BIBLE

We talk about the Bible as being "inspired," but what exactly does that mean? Great authors like Shakespeare and Dickens were also "inspired," weren't they? Well, in a sense, every great writer or artist uses talent and gifts given to him or her by God. But tradition tells us that the Bible is special in this sense: God guided the authors in some special way so that they set down in words the eternal truths he wished to communicate. They were not writing textbooks on science (so we should forget all the useless arguments over the "six days of creation" in the Book of Genesis). Rather, they were communicating everything necessary about living rightly in fellowship with God and our fellow man. Can anyone prove that God guided these authors? No. It is a matter of faith. But millions of people across the centuries have accepted that the Bible truly does communicate the will of God. The message of the Bible itself is this: Trust these words because they are from the God who can be trusted. It is for this reason that people of faith have always yearned to study the Bible closely and (more important than merely studying) to apply it to life.

This book of the law shall not depart out of your mouth; but you shall meditate upon it day and night, that you may observe to do according to all that is written therein, for then you shall make your way prosperous, and then you shall have good success.   JOSHUA 1:8

The LORD gave the word: great was the company of those that published it.

PSALM 68:11

Your word is a lamp to my feet, and a light to my path.

PSALM 119:105

The commandment is a lamp, and the law is light, and reproofs of instruction are the way of life.   PROVERBS 6:23

The Comforter, which is the Holy Spirit, whom the Father will send in my name, he shall teach you all things, and bring all things to your remembrance, whatever I have said to you.   JOHN 14:26

> *Some statistics (in case you're interested):*
>
> *The Bible has 66 books:*
> *39 in the Old Testament,*
> *27 in the New Testament.*
>
> *There are 1,189 chapters in the Bible:*
> *929 in the Old Testament,*
> *260 in the New Testament.*
>
> *There are 31,173 verses in the Bible:*
> *23,214 in the Old Testament,*
> *7,959 in the New Testament.*
>
> *The most common word in English Bibles is (surprise!) and.*
>
> *The shortest verse in the Bible is two words: "Jesus wept" (John 11:35).*

I am not ashamed of the gospel of Christ, for it is the power of God to salvation to every one that believes; to the Jew first, and also to the Gentile.

ROMANS 1:16

Faith comes by hearing, and hearing by the word of God.

ROMANS 10:17

Whatever things were written in the past were written for our learning, that we through patience and comfort of the scriptures might have hope.

ROMANS 15:4

Take the helmet of salvation, and the sword of the Spirit, which is the word of God.

EPHESIANS 6:17

From childhood you have known the holy scriptures, which are able to make you wise to salvation through faith which is in Christ Jesus. All scripture is given by inspiration of God, and is profitable for doctrine, for reproof, for correction, for instruction in righteousness, so that the man of God may be perfect, thoroughly furnished to all good works.

2 TIMOTHY 3:15–17

The word of God is living, and powerful, and sharper than any two-edged sword, piercing even to the dividing apart of soul and spirit, and of the joints and marrow; it is a discerner of the thoughts and intents of the heart. There is no creature that is not manifest in his sight, but all things are laid bare and opened to the eyes of him with whom we must render account.

HEBREWS 4:12–13

No prophecy of the scripture is of any private interpretation. For the prophecy came not in old time by the will of man, but holy men of God spoke as they were moved by the Holy Spirit.　2 PETER 1:20–21

Our beloved brother Paul, according to the wisdom given to him, has written to you in his epistles. . . . In them are some things hard to understand, which those who are unlearned and unstable twist, as they do also the other scriptures, to their own destruction.　2 PETER 3:15–16

BLESSING

Blessing and cursing are opposites, and we definitely hear more cursing today than blessing. Every individual and group seems to see itself as "victimized," eager to point a blaming finger at someone else. But the Bible has a lot to say about blessing, not only about God blessing people of goodwill but also about people blessing one another. In other words, the Bible "accentuates the positive," urging us to focus more on the good things God does for us and the good things we can and should do for one another. It also urges people to pursue the moral, God-centered life that will lead to blessing not only in this life but also in the hereafter.

The LORD bless you, and keep you; the LORD make his face shine upon you, and be gracious to you; the LORD lift up his countenance upon you, and give you peace.   NUMBERS 6:24–26

Behold, I set before you this day a blessing and a curse—a blessing, if you obey the commandments of the LORD your God, which I command you this day, and a curse, if you will not obey the commandments of the LORD your God, but turn aside out of the way which I command you this day, to go after other gods, which you have not known.

DEUTERONOMY 11:26–28

The LORD has blessed his people.   2 CHRONICLES 31:10

The LORD our God be with us, as he was with our fathers: let him not leave us, nor forsake us.   1 KINGS 8:57

God be merciful to us, and bless us, and cause his face to shine upon us.

PSALM 67:1

Bless the LORD, O my soul, and all that is within me, bless his holy name. Bless the LORD, O my soul, and forget not all his benefits.

PSALM 103:1–2

Blessed are they whose iniquities are forgiven, and whose sins are covered.

ROMANS 4:7

Bless them which persecute you: bless, and curse not.

ROMANS 12:14

Eye has not seen, nor ear heard, neither have entered into the heart of man, the things which God has prepared for those who love him.

1 CORINTHIANS 2:9

Blessed is the man that endures temptation, for when he is tested, he shall receive the crown of life, which the Lord has promised to those who love him.

JAMES 1:12

Be you all of one mind, having compassion for one another; love as brethren, be considerate, be courteous, not rendering evil for evil, or insult for insult, but, on the contrary, blessing; knowing that you are called for this, that you should inherit a blessing.   I PETER 3:8–9

Blessed is he who reads, and they that hear the words of this prophecy, and keep those things which are written within it, for the time is at hand.

                                                                    REVELATION 1:3

I heard a voice from heaven saying to me, "Write, 'Blessed are the dead which die in the Lord from henceforth.' Yes," said the Spirit, "that they may rest from their labors, and their works follow them."

                                                                    REVELATION 14:13

Behold, I come quickly: blessed is he who keeps the sayings of the prophecy of this book.   REVELATION 22:7

Blessed are they that do his commandments, that they may have right to the tree of life, and may enter in through the gates into the city [the New Jerusalem, heaven].   REVELATION 22:14

See also Fellowship with God, God's Love.

THE BODY

A visitor from an earlier century might well wonder if the god we worship today is the human body. While we don't actually bow down and worship human-shaped statues, we do devote time, money, and energy to pursuing the idealized image of the human body. So, strictly speaking, we live in an idolatrous society, forgetting the true God and focusing on the flesh. Of course, it isn't wrong to take care of one's body, maintaining good health, and taking reasonable pride in one's appearance. But moderation is hard to find, and so our culture errs on the side of obsession. How could it be otherwise since the video age is saturated with images of youth and beauty? It is easy to forget the invisible God and give our attention to what we can actually see.

But the Bible whispers, "What about the eternal things?" The flesh passes away despite our anxious efforts to stave off aging and decline. Not only does bodily obsession take our minds off the hereafter, but it also makes us neglect our inner selves. No wonder the Bible gives so much attention to that invisible part of us, the soul, the part that never ages, the part that can endure forever if God is the priority.

In brief: The Bible is not anti-body, it is pro-eternity.

In the sweat of your face shall you eat bread, till you return to the ground; for out of it were you taken, for dust you are, and to dust shall you return.

GENESIS 3:19

The LORD said to Samuel, "Look not on his appearance, or on the height of his stature, because I have refused him, for the LORD sees not as man sees. For man looks on the outward appearance, but the LORD looks on the heart."

I SAMUEL 16:7

As a jewel of gold in a swine's snout, so is a fair woman who is without discretion.

PROVERBS 11:22

All go to one place; all are of the dust, and all turn to dust again.

ECCLESIASTES 3:20

If your right eye offend you, pluck it out, and cast it away from you, for it is better for you that one of your members should perish, and not that your whole body should be cast into hell.

MATTHEW 5:29

Watch and pray, that you enter not into temptation. The spirit indeed is willing, but the flesh is weak.

MATTHEW 26:41

Jesus said to his disciples, "Therefore I say to you, take no thought for your life, what you shall eat; neither for the body, what you shall put on. Life is more than food, and the body is more than clothing. Consider the ravens, for they neither sow nor reap, they have neither storehouse nor barn, and God feeds them. How much more are you better than the birds? And which

of you with taking thought can add to his stature one foot? If you then are
not able to do that thing which is least, why take you thought for the rest?"

LUKE 12:22–26

Judge not according to the appearance, but make a right judgment.

JOHN 7:24

Let not sin reign in your mortal body, that you should obey its lusts. Neither
yield you your members as instruments of unrighteousness to sin, but yield
yourselves to God, as those that are alive from the dead, and yield your
members as instruments of righteousness to God. For sin shall not have dominion over you, for you are not under the law, but under grace.

ROMANS 6:12–14

There is therefore now no condemnation to them which are in Christ Jesus,
who walk not after the sinful nature, but after the Spirit.   ROMANS 8:1

I beseech you therefore, brethren, by the mercies of God, that you present
your bodies a living sacrifice, holy, acceptable to God, which is your reasonable worship. And be not conformed to this world, but be transformed by
the renewing of your mind, that you may prove what is the good and acceptable and perfect will of God.   ROMANS 12:1–2

Put on the Lord Jesus Christ, and make no provision for the sinful nature, to
gratify its lusts.   ROMANS 13:14

Know you not that the unrighteous shall not inherit the kingdom of God?
Be not deceived: neither fornicators, nor idolaters, nor adulterers, nor homosexuals, nor abusers of themselves with mankind, nor thieves, nor covetous, nor drunkards, nor slanderers, nor swindlers shall inherit the
kingdom of God. And such were some of you. But you are washed, you are
sanctified, you are justified in the name of the Lord Jesus, and by the Spirit
of our God.

All things are permissible for me, but all things are not beneficial: all
things are permissible for me, but I will not be brought under the power of
any. Food for the belly, and the belly for foods, but God shall destroy both it

and them. Now the body is not for fornication, but for the Lord, and the Lord for the body. And God has both raised up the Lord, and will also raise up us by his own power.   I CORINTHIANS 6:9–14

What? Know you not that your body is the temple of the Holy Spirit which is in you, which you have from God, and you are not your own? For you are bought with a price. Therefore glorify God in your body, and in your spirit, which are God's.   I CORINTHIANS 6:19–20

Though our outward man perish, yet the inward man is renewed day by day.
                    2 CORINTHIANS 4:16

We know that if this earthly tent we live in is destroyed, we have a building from God, a house not made with hands, eternal in the heavens. For in this tent we groan, earnestly desiring to be clothed with our dwelling from heaven. . . . For we who are in this tent do groan, being burdened, for we wish not to be unclothed but to be further clothed, so that mortality might be swallowed up by life. Now he who has made us for this very thing is God, who also has given to us the guarantee of the Spirit. Therefore we are always confident, knowing that, while we are at home in the body, we are absent from the Lord. (For we walk by faith, not by sight.)
                    2 CORINTHIANS 5:1–7

Having therefore these promises, dearly beloved, let us cleanse ourselves from all filthiness of the flesh and spirit, perfecting holiness in the fear of God.   2 CORINTHIANS 7:1

Do you look at things after the outward appearance? If any man have confidence that he is Christ's, let him consider this: that as he is Christ's, so we also are Christ's.   2 CORINTHIANS 10:7

Walk in the Spirit, and you shall not fulfill the lust of the sinful nature. For the sinful nature lusts against the Spirit, and the Spirit against the sinful nature, and these are contrary to one another, so that you cannot do the things that you wish. But if you are led by the Spirit, you are not under the law.
                    GALATIANS 5:16–18

> ### The Lump in Your Throat
> *The human body's Adam's apple takes it name from Genesis 3, which tells of Adam, the first man, eating the fruit that God had forbidden him to eat. According to an old legend, a piece of the forbidden fruit became stuck in Adam's throat. So the bulge in the average male throat is called the Adam's apple.*

Brethren, you have been called to liberty; only do not use your liberty as an opportunity for the sinful nature, but by love serve one another. Now the works of the sinful nature are manifest, which are these: fornication, uncleanness, debauchery. . . . They that are Christ's have crucified the sinful nature with its affections and lusts.   GALATIANS 5:13, 19, 24

I have told you often, and now tell you with tears, that there are many who are the enemies of the cross of Christ. Their destiny is destruction, their God is their belly, and their glory is in their shame. Their mind is on earthly things.   PHILIPPIANS 3:18–19

This is the will of God, your sanctification, that you should abstain from fornication; that each one of you should know how to control his own body in holiness and honor, not in the lust of immorality, like the pagans who do not know God; that no man go beyond and exploit his brother in any way; because the Lord is the avenger in all these things, just as we also have forewarned you and testified. For God has not called us to uncleanness, but to holiness.   I THESSALONIANS 4:3–7

Bodily exercise profits some, but godliness is profitable to all things, having promise of the life that now is, and of the life which is to come.

I TIMOTHY 4:8

If a man will purge himself from these, he shall be a vessel of honor, sanctified, and right for the master's use, and prepared for every good work. Flee also youthful lusts, but follow righteousness, faith, charity, peace with those who call on the Lord out of a pure heart.   2 TIMOTHY 2:21–22

The grace of God that brings salvation has appeared to all men, teaching us that, denying ungodliness and worldly lusts, we should live soberly, righteously, and godly, in this present world; looking for that blessed hope, and the glorious appearing of the great God and our Savior Jesus Christ.

TITUS 2:11–13

Every man is tempted, when he is drawn away by his own lust and enticed. Then when lust has conceived, it brings forth sin; and sin, when it is finished, brings forth death.   JAMES 1:14–15

Let it not be that outward adorning of arranging the hair, or of wearing of gold, or of putting on clothing. But let it be the hidden man of the heart, in that which is not corruptible, the ornament of a gentle and quiet spirit, which is precious in the sight of God.   I PETER 3:3–4

All that is in the world, the cravings of the sinful nature, and the lust of the eyes, and the pride of life, is not of the Father, but is of the world. And the world passes away, and the lust thereof, but he who does the will of God abides forever.   I JOHN 2:16–17

See also Alcohol and Other Substance Abuse, Food, Pride, Self–Esteem, Sexuality, Temptation.

BRIBERY/CORRUPTION

Power and influence are so desirable that people have always been willing to buy and sell them. This was true in biblical days, and it is no less true today, when any newscast reminds us that politicians and other leaders are not above bribery and other forms of corruption. While this state of affairs can make us cynical about our leaders, it also reminds us that God alone is the one judge and ruler who shows no partiality and accepts no bribes.

You shall take no gift, for the gift blinds the wise and perverts the words of the righteous.   EXODUS 23:8

The LORD your God is God of gods, and LORD of lords, a great God, a mighty, and a terrible, who shows no partiality, nor accepts bribes.

DEUTERONOMY 10:17

You shall not show partiality, nor take a bribe: for a bribe blinds the eyes of the wise and perverts the words of the righteous.

DEUTERONOMY 16:19

Let the fear of the LORD be upon you; take heed and do it: for there is no iniquity with the LORD our God, nor respect of persons, nor taking of bribes.

2 CHRONICLES 19:7

The congregation of hypocrites shall be desolate, and fire shall consume the dwelling places of bribery.   JOB 15:34

Gather not my soul with sinners, nor my life with bloody men, in whose hands is mischief, and their right hand is full of bribes.   PSALM 26:9

He that is greedy for gain troubles his own house; but he that hates bribes shall live.   PROVERBS 15:27

A wicked man takes a bribe secretly to pervert the ways of justice.

PROVERBS 17:23

The king by justice establishes the land, but he that receives bribes overthrows it.   PROVERBS 29:4

Surely oppression makes a wise man mad, and a bribe destroys the heart.

ECCLESIASTES 7:7

The good man is perished out of the earth: and there is none upright among men: they all lie in wait for blood; they hunt every man his brother with a net. That they may do evil with both hands earnestly, the ruler and the judge asks for bribes.   MICAH 7:2–3

See also God As Judge, God's Fairness.

CHEERFULNESS

We all like to be around cheerful people, but they're becoming rare, aren't they? So many people cultivate a cynical attitude, and everyone seems to carry a grievance of some kind. While the cheerful person attracts us, we get a little suspicious also. We wonder, "With everyone else so cynical and anxious, what makes this person different?" The Bible is, naturally, pro-cheerfulness and anti-cynicism. But cheerfulness is more than just a pose, more than just making a choice to be sunny spirited. Real cheerfulness is rooted in being free from anxiety, knowing that God is in control no matter what happens.

A merry heart makes a cheerful countenance, but by sorrow of the heart the spirit is broken.   PROVERBS 15:13

All the days of the afflicted are evil, but he who is of a merry heart has a continual feast.   PROVERBS 15:15

A merry heart does good like a medicine.   PROVERBS 17:22

Go your way, eat your bread with joy, and drink your wine with a merry heart.   ECCLESIASTES 9:7

Rejoice, O young man, in your youth, and let your heart cheer you in the days of your youth. Walk in the ways of your heart, and whatever your eyes see, but know that for all these things God will bring you into judgment.
ECCLESIASTES 11:9

These things I have spoken to you, that in me you might have peace. In the world you shall have tribulation, but be of good cheer; I have overcome the world.   JOHN 16:33

> *Evangelist Billy Graham is quoted as saying, "I'm an optimist. I've read the last page of the Bible."*

God loves a cheerful giver.   2 CORINTHIANS 9:7

Is any among you afflicted? Let him pray. Is any merry? Let him sing psalms.
                                               JAMES 5:13

See also Joy.

CHILDREN

On some days children can seem like a burden and a cross. On others they seem like life's greatest blessing. Of course, children probably see their parents in the same ways. While the Bible sees children as a blessing from God, there is no sentimental view of child rearing in the Bible. It is seen as a serious task, one in which parents may have to play the role of "bad guy" and apply discipline with firmness. In the short term, this seems painful for both parent and children. In the long term, it is for the best. This is probably the one issue on which the Bible differs most radically from our present society. In fact, people of faith have come under fire, accused of abuse because they are considered too strict with their children. But no one ever said that the Bible's standards would be popular with the world at large.

These words, which I command you this day, shall be in your heart. And you shall teach them diligently to your children, and shall talk of them when you sit in your house, and when you walk by the way, and when you lie down, and when you rise up. And you shall bind them for a sign upon your hand, and they shall be as emblems between your eyes. And you shall write them upon the posts of your house, and on your gates.

                                               DEUTERONOMY 6:6–9

Gather the people together, men, women, and children, and the stranger that is within your gates, that they may hear, and that they may learn, and fear the LORD your God, and observe to do all the words of this law.

DEUTERONOMY 31:12

Children are a heritage from the LORD, and the fruit of the womb is his reward. As arrows are in the hand of a mighty man, so are children of one's youth. Happy is the man that has his quiver full of them.

PSALM 127:3–4

My son, forget not my law, but let your heart keep my commandments; for length of days and long life and peace shall they add to you.

PROVERBS 3:1–2

Hear, you children, the instruction of a father, and attend to know understanding. For I give you good doctrine. Forsake you not my law. For I was my father's son, tender and only beloved in the sight of my mother. He taught me also, and said to me, "Let your heart retain my words: keep my commandments, and live. Get wisdom, get understanding, forget it not; neither decline from the words of my mouth. Forsake her not, and she shall preserve you: love her, and she shall keep you. Wisdom is the principal thing; therefore get wisdom, and with all your getting get understanding."

PROVERBS 4:1–7

My son, keep your father's commandment, and forsake not the law of your mother. PROVERBS 6:20

A wise son makes a glad father, but a foolish son is the grief of his mother.

PROVERBS 10:1

A wise son hears his father's instruction, but a scorner hears not rebuke.

PROVERBS 13:1

He that spares his rod hates his son, but he who loves him chastens him quickly. PROVERBS 13:24

A fool despises his father's instruction, but he who regards reproof is prudent.   PROVERBS 15:5

Children's children are the crown of old men, and the glory of children are their fathers.   PROVERBS 17:6

Chasten your son while there is hope, and do not set your heart on his destruction.   PROVERBS 19:18

Even a child is known by his doings, whether his work be pure, and whether it be right.   PROVERBS 20:11

Train up a child in the way he should go, and when he is old he will not depart from it.   PROVERBS 22:6

Foolishness is bound in the heart of a child; but the rod of correction shall drive it far from him.   PROVERBS 22:15

Withhold not correction from the child, for if you beat him with the rod, he shall not die.   PROVERBS 23:13

Hearken to your father who begot you, and despise not your mother when she is old.   PROVERBS 23:22

The father of the righteous shall greatly rejoice, and he who begets a wise child shall have joy of him. Your father and your mother shall be glad, and she who bore you shall rejoice.   PROVERBS 23:24–26

Whoever keeps the law is a wise son, but he who is a companion of wild-living men shames his father.   PROVERBS 28:7

The rod and reproof give wisdom, but a child left to himself brings his mother to shame.   PROVERBS 29:15

All your children shall be taught by the LORD, and great shall be the peace of your children.   ISAIAH 54:13

Jesus called a little child to him, and set him in the midst of them, and said, "Truly I say to you, except you be converted, and become like little children, you shall not enter into the kingdom of heaven. Whoever therefore shall humble himself like this little child, the same is greatest in the kingdom of heaven. And whoever shall receive one such little child in my name receives me."

MATTHEW 18:2–5

Out of the mouths of children and infants you have ordained praise.

MATTHEW 21:16

They brought young children to him, that he should touch them, and his disciples rebuked those that brought them. But when Jesus saw it, he was much displeased, and said to them, "Let the little children come to me, and forbid them not, for of such is the kingdom of God. Truly I say to you, whoever shall not receive the kingdom of God as a little child, he shall not enter it."

MARK 10:14–15

Children, obey your parents in the Lord, for this is right. Honor your father and mother; which is the first commandment with promise; that it may be well with you, and you may live long on the earth.

EPHESIANS 6:1–4

See also **Marriage, Parents.**

CHOICES

Choices *is a magic word today, for everyone likes to be able to choose. We see life as a giant cafeteria where we have unlimited options in careers, place of residence, spouse, and so on. We even apply the "cafeteria mentality" to morals, and so people assume that the ability to choose is more important than the choice itself. It is as if the best thing is not being* right *or* moral *but rather being* free to choose. *The Bible does affirm that human beings have free will, able to choose the good—but also able to choose the bad. The fact that we can do so is good: It means that we are not robots but are living, moral beings who can please God and enrich our own lives by doing the right thing. It is not our freedom to choose that pleases God but rather the fact that we use that freedom to do what is right, even when that means self-denial, thinking more of others than our own selfish desires.*

I set before you this day a blessing and a curse—a blessing, if you obey the commandments of the LORD your God, which I command you this day; and a curse, if you will not obey the commandments of the LORD your God.

DEUTERONOMY 11:26–28

Choose life, that both you and your offspring may live.

DEUTERONOMY 30:19

Choose you this day whom you will serve . . . as for me and my house, we will serve the LORD. JOSHUA 24:15

Elijah came to all the people, and said, "How long will you waver between two opinions? If the LORD be God, follow him, but if Baal, then follow him." I KINGS 18:21

[NOTE: *Baal was a fertility god, and the people of Israel were constantly tempted to worship him instead of God. Baal worship often involved ritual orgies and violence.*]

Refuse the evil, and choose the good. ISAIAH 7:15

Seek good, and not evil, that you may live, and so the LORD, the God Almighty, shall be with you. AMOS 5:14

Whoever hears these sayings of mine, and does them, will be like a wise man who built his house upon a rock. And the rain descended, and the floods came, and the winds blew and beat upon that house, yet it fell not, for it was founded upon a rock. And everyone that hears these sayings of mine, and

Bibliomancy *is the name given to the practice of opening the Bible and reading a passage at random. Some people do this when they're looking for guidance in life. We don't recommend this. After all, a person considering suicide might open to the passage that says, "Judas went away and hanged himself."*

does them not, shall be like a foolish man who built his house upon the sand. And the rain descended, and the floods came, and the winds blew and beat upon that house, and it fell, and great was the fall of it.

MATTHEW 7:24–27

He that believes and is baptized shall be saved; but he who believes not shall be damned. MARK 16:16

Jesus said to him, "No man who puts his hand to the plow then looks back is fit for the kingdom of God." LUKE 9:62

No servant can serve two masters, for either he will hate the one and love the other; or else he will hold to the one and despise the other. You cannot serve God and money. LUKE 16:13

A double-minded man is unstable in all his ways. JAMES 1:8

Draw near to God, and he will draw near to you. Cleanse your hands, you sinners, and purify your hearts, you double-minded. JAMES 4:8

I know your works, that you are neither cold nor hot: I wish you were cold or hot. So then because you are lukewarm, and neither cold nor hot, I will spew you out of my mouth. REVELATION 3:16

CITIZENSHIP

How easy it is to get cynical about citizenship! While we still fly the flag on national holidays, low voter turnout shows that old-style patriotism is becoming rarer. Bombarded with news about corruption in high places, we naturally assume that we are citizens living under corrupt leaders. But this is nothing new. History is one long tale of corrupt leadership, interrupted by the occasional righteous leader. The Bible, with its painfully realistic view of human life, makes it clear that we should not put our ultimate faith in human leaders, even the best ones. Our ultimate allegiance is to God alone, and our ultimate citizenship is in heaven. On the other hand, the Bible urges us to be good and moral citizens here. In a sense, people of faith have "dual citizenship," looking forward to their ultimate destination hereafter but also living moral, God-centered lives wherever they happen to be.

A Bible tidbit: The well-known phrase "the powers that be" is from Romans 13:1, found below.

Happy is that people whose God is the LORD.   PSALM 144:15

Where there is no vision, the people perish.   PROVERBS 29:18

Then went the Pharisees, and plotted how they might entrap Jesus in his talk. And they sent out to him their disciples, along with the Herodians, saying, "Master, we know that you are sincere, and teach the way of God in truth, showing no deference to, for you do not regard men with partiality. Tell us therefore what you think of this: Is it lawful to give taxes to Caesar or not?" But Jesus perceived their wickedness, and said, "Why do you test me, you hypocrites? Show me the tribute money." And they brought to him a penny. And he said to them, "Whose image and title are on this?" They said to him, "Caesar's." Then said he to them, "Render therefore to Caesar the things that are Caesar's, and to God the things that are God's."

MATTHEW 22:15–21

Pilate entered into the judgment hall again, and called Jesus, and said to him, "Are you the King of the Jews?" Jesus answered him, "Do you say this thing of yourself, or did others tell it you of me?" Pilate answered, "Am I a Jew? Your own nation and the chief priests have delivered you to me. What have you done?" Jesus answered, "My kingdom is not of this world. If my kingdom were of this world, then would my servants fight, that I should not be delivered to the Jews, but now is my kingdom not from here." Pilate therefore said to him, "Are you a king then?" Jesus answered, "You say that I am a king. To this end was I born, and for this cause came I into the world, that I should bear witness to the truth. Every one that is of the truth hears my voice."

JOHN 18:33–37

Then went the captain with the officers, and brought them [the apostles] without violence, for they feared the people, lest they should have been stoned. And when they had brought them, they set them before the council, and the high priest asked them, saying, "Did not we strictly command you that you should not teach in this name? And, behold, you have filled Jerusalem with your doctrine, and intend to bring this man's blood upon us." Then Peter and the other apostles answered and said, "We ought to obey God rather than men."

ACTS 5:26–29

Let every soul be subject to the higher powers. For there is no authority except from God: the powers that be are ordained of God. Whoever therefore resists the power is resisting what God has instituted, and they that resist shall receive damnation. For rulers are not a terror to good conduct but to evil. Will you then not be afraid of the power? Do that which is good, and you shall have praise from the same, for he is the minister of God to you for good. But if you do that which is evil, be afraid; for he bears not the sword in vain, for he is the minister of God, a revenger to execute wrath upon him that does evil. Therefore you must be subject, not only because of wrath, but also for conscience's sake. For this cause pay you taxes also, for they are God's servants, attending continually upon this very thing. Render therefore to all their dues: taxes to whom taxes are due, revenue to whom revenue is due, respect to whom respect is due, honor to whom honor is due.

ROMANS 13:1–7

You are no longer strangers and foreigners, but fellow citizens with the saints, and of the household of God, and are built upon the foundation of the apostles and prophets, Jesus Christ himself being the chief cornerstone.

EPHESIANS 2:19–20

> "*I always say that the studious perusal of the Sacred Volume will make better citizens, better fathers, and better husbands.*"
>
> —THOMAS JEFFERSON, THIRD U.S. PRESIDENT

Our citizenship is in heaven; from whence also we look for the Savior, the Lord Jesus Christ, who shall change our vile body, that it may be fashioned like his glorious body, according to the working whereby he is able even to subdue all things to himself.　　　　PHILIPPIANS 3:20–21

I urge therefore, that supplications, prayers, intercessions, and thanksgiving be made for all men; for rulers, and for all that are in authority; that we may lead a quiet and peaceable life in all godliness and honesty. For this is good and acceptable in the sight of God our Savior, who will have all men to be saved, and to come to the knowledge of the truth.

I TIMOTHY 2:1–4

Remind them to be subject to rulers and authorities, to obey magistrates, to be ready to every good work.　　　　TITUS 3:1

Submit yourselves to every ordinance of man for the Lord's sake: whether it be to the king, as supreme; or to governors, as to those who are sent by him for the punishment of evildoers, and for the praise of those who do well. For this is the will of God, that by doing right you may silence the ignorance of foolish men. As servants of God, live as free men, but do not use your freedom as a pretext for evil. Honor everyone. Love the brethren. Fear God. Honor the king.　　　　I PETER 2:13–17

They confessed that they were strangers and aliens on the earth, for those who speak in this way make it clear that they are seeking a homeland. . . . Now they desire a better country, that is, a heavenly one: therefore God is not ashamed to be called their God, for he has prepared for them a city. For here have we no continuing city, but we seek one to come.

HEBREWS 11:13–14, 16; 13:14

See also Politics and Government.

COMFORT IN TIMES OF TROUBLE

Abraham Lincoln claimed that reading the Bible was "the best cure for the blues." Many readers through the centuries have agreed with him. This is because the Bible, page after page, presents us with a loving, compassionate God who is always willing to aid those who turn to him. There is no problem, physical or mental, that is too small or too trivial to bring to God. This is the greatest comfort of all: The Ruler of the universe, the Almighty, lends his ear to us.

The eyes of the LORD run to and fro throughout the whole earth, to show himself strong on behalf of those whose hearts are committed to him.

2 CHRONICLES 16:9

Behold, God will not cast away a blameless man, neither will he help the evildoers.

JOB 8:20

The LORD also will be a refuge for the oppressed, a refuge in times of trouble.

PSALM 9:9

The LORD is my rock, and my fortres, and my deliverer; my God, my strength, in whom I will trust; my shield, and the horn of my salvation, and my high tower.

PSALM 18:2

The LORD is my shepherd; I shall not want. He makes me to lie down in green pastures: he leads me beside the still waters. He restores my soul: he leads me in the paths of righteousness for his name's sake. Yes, though I walk through the valley of the shadow of death, I will fear no evil, for you are with me; your rod and your staff they comfort me.

PSALM 23:1–4

His anger endures but a moment; in his favor is life. Weeping may endure for a night, but joy comes in the morning. PSALM 30:5

I will be glad and rejoice in your mercy, for you have considered my trouble. You have known my soul in adversities. PSALM 31:7

I sought the LORD, and he heard me, and delivered me from all my fears.

PSALM 34:4

The salvation of the righteous is of the LORD: he is their strength in the time of trouble. And the LORD shall help them, and deliver them: he shall deliver them from the wicked, and save them, because they trust in him.

PSALM 37:39–40

God is our refuge and strength, a very present help in trouble. Therefore will not we fear, though the earth be removed, and though the mountains be carried into the midst of the sea. PSALM 46:1–2

Call upon me in the day of trouble: I will deliver you, and you shall glorify me. PSALM 50:15

Cast your burden upon the LORD, and he shall sustain you. He shall never suffer the righteous to be moved. PSALM 55:22

You, who have shown me great and bitter troubles, shall quicken me again, and shall bring me up again from the depths of the earth.

PSALM 71:20

Whom have I in heaven but you? And there is none upon earth that I desire beside you. My flesh and my heart fail, but God is the strength of my heart, and my portion forever. But it is good for me to draw near to God: I have put my trust in the LORD God, that I may declare all your works.

PSALM 73:25–26, 28

He shall give his angels charge over you, to keep you in all your ways.

PSALM 91:11

Like a father pities his children, so the LORD pities those who fear him.

PSALM 103:13

O that my ways were directed to keep your statutes!   PSALM 119:50

They that sow in tears shall reap in joy.   PSALM 126:5

He heals the broken in heart, and binds up their wounds.   PSALM 147:3

The fear of man brings a snare, but whoever puts his trust in the LORD shall be safe.   PROVERBS 29:25

Fear you not; for I am with you: be not dismayed; for I am your God. I will strengthen you; yes, I will help you; yes, I will uphold you with the right hand of my righteousness.   ISAIAH 41:10

When you pass through the waters, I will be with you, and through the rivers, they shall not overflow you. When you walk through the fire, you shall not be burned; neither shall the flame kindle upon you.

ISAIAH 43:2

Sing, O heavens, and be joyful, O earth, and break forth into singing, O mountains, for the LORD has comforted his people, and will have mercy upon his afflicted.   ISAIAH 49:13

"I know the thoughts that I think toward you," says the LORD, "thoughts of peace, and not of evil, to give you an expected end. Then shall you call upon me, and you shall go and pray to me, and I will hearken to you. And you shall seek me, and find me, when you shall search for me with all your heart."   JEREMIAH 29:11–13

The LORD will not cast off forever, but though he cause grief, yet will he have compassion according to the multitude of his mercies. For he does not afflict willingly nor grieve the children of men.

LAMENTATIONS 3:31–33

Blessed are they that mourn, for they shall be comforted. Blessed are they which are persecuted for righteousness' sake, for theirs is the kingdom of heaven. Blessed are you when men shall slander you, and persecute you, and shall say all manner of evil against you falsely for my sake. Rejoice, and be exceedingly glad, for great is your reward in heaven, for so persecuted they the prophets who were before you.   MATTHEW 5:4, 10–12

Are not two sparrows sold for a penny? And one of them shall not fall on the ground without your Father. But the very hairs of your head are all numbered. Fear you not therefore; you are of more value than many sparrows.
MATTHEW 10:29–31

Come to me, all you that labor and are heavy laden, and I will give you rest. Take my yoke upon you, and learn from me; for I am meek and lowly in heart, and you shall find rest to your souls. For my yoke is easy, and my burden is light.   MATTHEW 11:28–30

Lo, I am with you always, even to the end of the world.
MATTHEW 28:20

Jesus took with him Peter and James and John, and began to be greatly distressed and agitated. And he said to them, "My soul is exceeding sorrowful, even to death. Remain here, and keep awake." And he went forward a little, and fell on the ground, and prayed that, if it were possible, the hour might pass from him. And he said, "Abba, father, all things are possible to you; take away this cup from me: nevertheless not what I will, but what you will."
MARK 14:33–36

Peace I leave with you, my peace I give to you: not as the world gives, give I to you. Let not your heart be troubled, neither let it be afraid.
JOHN 14:27

These things I have spoken to you, that in me you might have peace. In the world you shall have tribulation, but be of good cheer; I have overcome the world.   JOHN 16:33

We know that all things work together for good to those who love God, to them who are the called according to his purpose. Who shall separate us from the love of Christ? Shall tribulation, or distress, or persecution, or famine, or nakedness, or peril, or sword?   ROMANS 8:28, 35

Blessed be God, even the Father of our Lord Jesus Christ, the Father of mercies, and the God of all comfort. He comforts us in all our tribulation, that we may be able to comfort those who are in any trouble, by the comfort with which we ourselves are comforted by God. For as the sufferings of Christ abound in us, so our consolation also abounds through Christ. And if we are afflicted, it is for your consolation and salvation, which is effectual in the enduring of the same sufferings which we also suffer. And if we are comforted, it is for your consolation and salvation. And our hope of you is steadfast, knowing, that as you are partakers of the sufferings, so shall you be also partakers of the consolation.   2 CORINTHIANS 1:3–7

We are troubled on every side, yet not distressed. We are perplexed, but not in despair; for which cause we faint not; For though our outward man perish, yet the inward man is renewed day by day. For our light affliction, which is but for a moment, works for us a far more exceeding and eternal weight of glory.   2 CORINTHIANS 4:8, 16–17

To keep me from being too exalted through the abundance of the revelations, there was given to me a thorn in the flesh, the messenger of Satan to torment me, lest I should be exalted above measure. For this thing I appealed to the Lord three times, that it might depart from me. And he said to me, "My grace is sufficient for you, for my strength is made perfect in weakness." Most gladly therefore will I glory in my infirmities, that the power of Christ may rest upon me. Therefore I take pleasure in infirmities, in insults, in hardships, in persecutions, in calamities for Christ's sake, for when I am weak, then am I strong.   2 CORINTHIANS 12:7–10

Since the children are partakers of flesh and blood, he also himself likewise took part in the same; that through death he might destroy him that had the power of death, that is, the devil; . . . For we have not a high priest who

> *"To the influence of this Book we are indebted for all the progress made in true civilization."*
>
> —ULYSSES S. GRANT, AMERICAN GENERAL AND EIGHTEENTH U.S. PRESIDENT

cannot be touched with the feeling of our infirmities; but was in all points tempted as we are, yet without sin. HEBREWS 2:14, 4:15

Blessed is the man that endures temptation, for when he is tested, he shall receive the crown of life, which the Lord has promised to those who love him. JAMES 1:12

Beloved, think it not strange concerning the fiery trial which is to test you, as though some strange thing happened to you. But rejoice, inasmuch as you are sharers of Christ's sufferings; that, when his glory shall be revealed, you may be glad also with exceeding joy. If you are reviled for the name of Christ, you are blessed, for the Spirit of glory and of God rests upon you. I PETER 4:12–14

I saw a new heaven and a new earth, for the first heaven and the first earth were passed away, and there was no more sea. And I John saw the holy city, New Jerusalem, coming down from God out of heaven, prepared as a bride adorned for her husband. And I heard a great voice out of heaven saying, "Behold, the dwelling place of God is with men, and he will dwell with them, and they shall be his people, and God himself shall be with them, and be their God. And God shall wipe away all tears from their eyes, and there shall be no more death, neither sorrow, nor crying, neither shall there be any more pain, for the former things are passed away." And he who sat upon the throne said, "Behold, I make all things new." REVELATION 21:1–5

See also Patience, Peace, Perseverance, Sickness, Trusting God, Worldly Cares, Worry.

CONCEIT

Most people hate conceit in others—but not necessarily in themselves. It is so easy to focus on our looks, our possessions, our achievements, our future, and so on. In the process we forget that it could all be taken away in a moment. We also forget that God alone is in control of all things. What is the best antidote for conceit? A realistic look at God and at ourselves.

He catches the wise in their own craftiness, and the schemes of the cunning are swept away. JOB 5:13

There is no fear of God before his eyes, for he flatters himself in his own eyes. PSALM 36:1–2

The way of a fool is right in his own eyes. PROVERBS 12:15

The rich man's wealth is his strong city, and like a high wall in his own conceit. PROVERBS 18:11

See you a man wise in his own conceit? There is more hope for a fool than for him. PROVERBS 26:12

He that trusts in his own heart is a fool. PROVERBS 28:26

Behold, some that are last shall be first, and some that are first shall be last. LUKE 13:30

Professing themselves to be wise, they became fools. ROMANS 1:22

Be of the same mind one toward another. Be not high-minded, but be willing to condescend to men of low estate. Be not wise in your own conceits. ROMANS 12:16

Let him that thinks he stands firm take heed lest he fall. I CORINTHIANS 10:12

See also Arrogance, Pride, Self-Deception.

CONFESSION

The old proverb "Confession is good for the soul" is not in the Bible, but it does reflect the Bible's view. Admitting that we have done wrong is the first step in healing a broken relationship with God and with others. But today we tend to take a limited view of confession, as if saying "I'm sorry" is sufficient. It isn't. The Bible won't allow us to "talk the talk" unless we "walk the walk." Saying the words is only the first step. The second step involves making amends when possible and (of course) a determination not to repeat our wrongs. Happily, God takes pleasure in our admitting our sins and even more pleasure when we turn from the wrong and do right.

Psalm 51, below, is considered the great "confession hymn" of the Bible. It is attributed to King David, who had been confronted with his adultery with another man's wife.

When a man or woman shall commit any sin that men commit, to do a trespass against the LORD, and that person is guilty, then they shall confess their sin which they have done; and he shall pay restitution for his wrong.

NUMBERS 5:6–7

Blessed is he whose transgression is forgiven, whose sin is covered. Blessed is the man to whom the LORD imputes no iniquity, and in whose spirit there is no deceit. When I kept silent, my body wasted through my groaning all the day long. For day and night your hand was heavy upon me. My strength dried up as in the drought of summer. Then I acknowledged my sin to you, and my iniquity I did not hide. I said, "I will confess my transgressions to the LORD," and you forgave the guilt of my sin. For this shall everyone that is godly pray to you in a time when you may be found. Surely in the floods of great waters they shall not come near him. PSALM 32:1–6

LORD, be merciful to me: heal my soul; for I have sinned against you.

PSALM 41:4

Have mercy upon me, O God, according to your lovingkindness; according to the multitude of your tender mercies, blot out my transgressions. Wash me thoroughly from my iniquity, and cleanse me from my sin. For I acknowledge my transgressions, and my sin is ever before me. Against you, you only, have I sinned, and done this evil in your sight: that you might be justified when you speak, and be blameless when you pass judgment. Behold, I was formed in iniquity, and in sin did my mother conceive me. Behold, you desire truth in the inward being, and in the hidden part you shall make me to know wisdom.

Purge me with hyssop, and I shall be clean. Wash me, and I shall be whiter than snow. Make me to hear joy and gladness; let the bones which you have broken rejoice. Hide your face from my sins, and blot out all my iniquities. Create in me a clean heart, O God, and renew a right spirit within me.

PSALM 51:1-10

He that covers his sins shall not prosper, but whoever confesses and forsakes them shall have mercy. PROVERBS 28:13

I will sprinkle clean water upon you, and you shall be clean. From all your filthiness, and from all your idols, will I cleanse you. A new heart also will I give you, and a new spirit will I put within you. And I will take away the stony heart out of your flesh, and I will give you a heart of flesh. And I will put my Spirit within you, and cause you to walk in my statutes, and you shall keep my judgments, and do them. And you shall dwell in the land that I gave to your fathers, and you shall be my people, and I will be your God.

EZEKIEL 36:25-28

I say to you, that every idle word that men shall speak, they shall give account of in the day of judgment. MATTHEW 12:36

It is written, "As I live, said the Lord, every knee shall bow to me, and every tongue shall confess to God." So then every one of us shall give account of himself to God. ROMANS 14:11-12

You, being dead in your sins and the uncircumcision of your flesh, has he made alive together with him, having forgiven you all trespasses; blotting out the handwriting of the record that was against us, which was contrary to us, and took it out of the way, nailing it to his cross.

COLOSSIANS 2:13-14

Confess your faults one to another, and pray one for another, that you may be healed. The prayer of a righteous man is powerful and effective.

JAMES 5:16

If we confess our sins, he is faithful and just to forgive us our sins, and to cleanse us from all unrighteousness.   I JOHN 1:9

See also Guilt, Repentance, Sin and Redemption.

CONFLICT

Every writer knows that every good story must have conflict. Well, by that standard, human life is a very good story. But life has enough conflict without anyone deliberately adding more. For this reason the Bible takes a harsh view of people who deliberately create and sustain strife. While the Bible pronounces blessing on peacemakers, it continually warns against quarrels, not just quarrels between neighbors but between groups and nations as well. Those who love God and their fellow man will want to sow peace, not discord. No wonder the Bible's last book, Revelation, pictures heaven as a place where all conflict has been banished forever.

Hatred stirs up quarrels, but love covers all sins.   PROVERBS 10:12

Only by pride come quarrels, but with the well-advised is wisdom.

PROVERBS 13:10

A soft answer turns away wrath, but grievous words stir up anger.

PROVERBS 15:1

A wrathful man stirs up strife, but he who is slow to anger calms strife.

PROVERBS 15:18

A perverse man sows strife, and a whisperer separates chief friends.

PROVERBS 16:28

He who loves transgression loves strife, and he who builds his gate high invites destruction. PROVERBS 17:19

It is an honor for a man to cease from strife, but every fool is quick to quarrel. PROVERBS 20:3

Cast out the scoffer and strife shall go out; yes, strife and abuse shall cease. PROVERBS 22:10

He that is of a proud heart stirs up strife, but he who puts his trust in the LORD shall be made prosperous. PROVERBS 28:25

An angry man stirs up strife, and a furious man abounds in transgression. PROVERBS 29:22

Blessed are the peacemakers, for they shall be called the children of God. MATTHEW 5:9

These things I have spoken unto you, that in me you might have peace. In the world you shall have tribulation, but be of good cheer; I have overcome the world. JOHN 16:33

You are still carnal, for since there is among you envying and strife and divisions, are you not carnal, and walk as mere men? I CORINTHIANS 3:3

Dare any of you, having a grievance against another, go to court before unbelievers, and not before the saints? Do you not know that the saints shall judge the world? And if the world shall be judged by you, are you not competent to judge the smallest cases? Know you not that we shall judge angels? How much more things that pertain to this life? I CORINTHIANS 6:1–3

Continue in the things which you have learned and have been assured of, knowing of whom you have learned them; but avoid profane chatter, for it will only lead to more ungodliness. 2 TIMOTHY 2:14, 16

Avoid foolish and senseless controversies, knowing that they breed quarrels. And the servant of the Lord must not be quarrelsome, but must be gentle to all men, an apt teacher, patient, gently instructing his opponents. God may perhaps grant that they may repent and come to the acknowledging of the truth.   2 TIMOTHY 2:23–25

Where do these conflicts and disputes among you arise from? Do they not come from your cravings that war within you? You crave, and have not, so you kill. You desire to have, and cannot obtain, so you fight and war. You have not because you ask not. You ask, and receive not, because you ask wrongly, that you may spend it upon your pleasures. You adulterers and adulteresses, know you not that the friendship of the world is enmity with God? Whoever therefore will be a friend of the world is the enemy of God.
                                                    JAMES 4:1–4

See also Fellowship with Other Believers, Hate, Peace.

CONTENTMENT

We hear a great deal about happiness *but not much about* contentment. *The word* contentment *is probably not popular today because it suggests enjoying life "as is," whereas most people are focused on change, improving, or buying that new product that will (so they think) make life better. While the Bible does encourage people to be constantly improving, it also encourages us to enjoy the present, to accept life "as is" and find pleasure in it. Even though the ultimate contentment is to be found in the afterlife, God also urges us to enjoy life now. Instead of frantically seeking after whatever is "new and improved," we can actually savor the present. This view would quickly put advertisers and marketers out of business, but it is the Bible's view.*

A sound heart is the life of the body, but envy the rottenness of the bones.
                                                    PROVERBS 14:30

All the days of the afflicted are evil, but he who is of a merry heart has a continual feast.   PROVERBS 15:15

Better is a little with righteousness than great revenues gained dishonestly.

PROVERBS 16:8

Better is a dry morsel, and quietness with it, than a banquet in a house full of troubles.

PROVERBS 17:1

A merry heart does good like a medicine, but a broken spirit dries up the bones.

PROVERBS 17:22

Let not your heart envy sinners, but be in the fear of the LORD all the day long.

PROVERBS 23:17

Give me neither poverty nor riches; feed me with only as much food as I need.

PROVERBS 30:8

There is nothing better for a man, than that he should eat and drink, and that he should make his soul enjoy good in his labor. This also, I saw, was from the hand of God.

ECCLESIASTES 2:24

The sleep of a laboring man is sweet, whether he eats little or much, but the abundance of the rich will not allow him to sleep.

ECCLESIASTES 5:12

Better is what the eye sees than the wandering of desire: this is futile, a chasing after the wind.

ECCLESIASTES 6:9

I have learned, in whatever state I am, to be content. I know what it is to have little, and I know what it is to have plenty. Everywhere and in all things I have learned to endure both fullness and hunger, both to have plenty and to be in need. I can do all things through Christ who strengthens me.

PHILIPPIANS 4:11–13

Godliness with contentment is great gain. For we brought nothing into this world, and it is certain we can carry nothing out. And having food and clothing, let us be content.

I TIMOTHY 6:6–8

The word Hallelujah *(or* Alleluia) *is often used in Christian worship and prayer. The only book of the Bible to use it is Revelation (19:1, 3–4, 6). But the original Hebrew word* Hallelujah *occurs many times in Psalms. It is translated as "praise the Lord"— which is exactly what it means.*

Let your lives be free from covetousness, and be content with such things as you have, for he has said, "I will never leave you, nor forsake you."

HEBREWS 13:5

See also Ambition, Envy, Peace, Worldly Cares, Worry.

COURAGE

We associate courage with the death-defying deeds in action movies—the lone hero or a small band taking on a larger, hostile force. But for most people courage is a much quieter matter, the daily matter of making the right moral choices when it is easier to do the wrong thing. Courage is found when the heart says "No" to temptation or peer pressure. There is courage in saying "No" to our own selfish desires.

But courage is more than the right moral choices. It is the quality we need when life simply seems overwhelming, when it seems like us against a cruel world. For this the Bible offers us a God who is in control, who can see us through the worst disaster even when our own hearts have given up. True courage does not always involve pulling ourselves up by our own bootstraps but may involve recognizing what our limits are and turning to God as the one Helper who will never fail.

You shall not be partial in judgment, but you shall hear the small as well as the great. You shall not be afraid of the face of man, for the judgment is God's. DEUTERONOMY 1:17

Yes, though I walk through the valley of the shadow of death, I will fear no evil, for you are with me; your rod and your staff they comfort me.

PSALM 23:4

The LORD is my light and my salvation; whom shall I fear? The LORD is the strength of my life; of whom shall I be afraid? PSALM 27:1

Wait on the LORD: be of good courage, and he shall strengthen your heart.

PSALM 27:14

I sought the LORD, and he heard me, and delivered me from all my fears.

PSALM 34:4

In God I will praise his word, in God I have put my trust; I will not fear what man can do to me. PSALM 56:4

In the day when I called, you answered me, and strengthened me with strength in my soul. PSALM 138:3

The wicked flee when no man pursues, but the righteous are bold as a lion.

PROVERBS 28:1

They that wait upon the LORD shall renew their strength; they shall mount up with wings as eagles; they shall run, and not be weary, and they shall walk, and not faint. ISAIAH 40:31

These things I have spoken to you, that in me you might have peace. In the world you shall have tribulation, but be of good cheer; I have overcome the world. JOHN 16:33

> *"The true hero of the Bible is God. All the other men in it are his aides and foot soldiers."*
>
> —THOMAS "STONEWALL" JACKSON, CONFEDERATE GENERAL

When they saw the boldness of Peter and John, and perceived that they were unschooled and ordinary men, they marveled, and they took note of them, that they had been with Jesus. ACTS 4:13

When they had prayed, the place was shaken where they were assembled together, and they were all filled with the Holy Spirit, and they spoke the word of God with boldness. ACTS 4:31

If God be for us, who can be against us? ROMANS 8:31

In Christ we have boldness and access with confidence by the faith of him. EPHESIANS 3:12

Let us therefore come boldly unto the throne of grace, that we may obtain mercy, and find grace to help in time of need. HEBREWS 4:16

The Lord is my helper, and I will not fear what man shall do to me. HEBREWS 13:6

See also Fear, God's Guidance.

CRITICISM

This is one area of life in which we are extremely generous: We are more than happy to give criticism but never to receive it. While we may feel close enough to someone to respect and heed helpful advice, most often we see criticism for what it is: verbal cruelty. We take joy in putting someone else in the wrong, in seeming more clever than another, in wounding someone without leaving cuts or bruises. Isn't it possible that more harm is done in the world by a spiteful tongue than by weapons of war?

Sadly, even the most moral people are not free from criticism. In fact, as Jesus himself predicted, good people often suffer the worst forms of abuse. But the Bible warns us not to fight fire with fire nor harsh words with harsh words. We can—as Jesus did himself—endure the harshness of people's words, knowing that the approval of God is more important than whatever humans can do or say to us.

Whoever secretly slanders his neighbor, him will I cut off: him that has a high look and a proud heart will not I endure.   PSALM 101:5

There is one who speaks like the piercings of a sword, but the tongue of the wise is health.   PROVERBS 12:18

A perverse man sows strife, and a whisperer separates chief friends.

PROVERBS 16:28

The words of a talebearer are like delicious morsels; they go down into the innermost parts of the body.   PROVERBS 18:8

He that goes about as a talebearer reveals secrets: therefore associate not with him that flatters with his lips.   PROVERBS 20:19

The north wind produces rain, and a backbiting tongue produces angry looks.   PROVERBS 25:23

Fear not the harsh words of men, neither be afraid of their insults. For the moth shall eat them up like a garment, and the worm shall eat them like wool. But my righteousness shall be forever, and my salvation from generation to generation.   ISAIAH 51:7–8

Blessed are you when men shall slander you, and persecute you, and shall say all manner of evil against you falsely, for my sake. Rejoice, and be exceedingly glad, for great is your reward in heaven, for so persecuted they the prophets who came before you.   MATTHEW 5:11–12

How can you say to your brother, "Let me pull out the speck out of your eye," and, behold, a plank is in your own eye? You hypocrite, first take out the plank from your own eye, and then shall you see clearly to take out the speck from your brother's eye.   MATTHEW 7:3–5

O generation of vipers, how can you, being evil, speak good things? For out of the abundance of the heart the mouth speaks. A good man out of the good treasure of the heart brings forth good things, and an evil man out of the evil treasure brings forth evil things. But I say to you, that every idle word that men shall speak, they shall give account of in the day of judgment. For by your words you shall be justified, and by your words you shall be condemned.   MATTHEW 12:33–37

Judge not, and you shall not be judged. Condemn not, and you shall not be condemned. Forgive, and you shall be forgiven.   LUKE 6:37

Let all bitterness and wrath and anger and brawling and evil speaking be put away from you, along with all malice. And be kind one to another, tenderhearted, forgiving one another, even as God for Christ's sake has forgiven you.   EPHESIANS 4:31–32

If any man among you seem to be religious, and bridles not his tongue, but deceives his own heart, this man's religion is worthless.   JAMES 1:26

We put bits in horses' mouths so that they may obey us, and we direct their whole body. Behold also ships, which though they be so large, and are driven by fierce winds, yet are they guided by a small rudder, wherever the pilot chooses. Even so, the tongue is a little member, yet it boasts great things. Behold, a great forest is set aflame by a little fire! And the tongue is a fire, a world of iniquity: so is the tongue among our members, so that it defiles the whole body, and sets on fire the course of nature, and it is set on fire by hell. For every kind of beasts and birds and serpents and things in the sea is tamed, and has been tamed by mankind, but the tongue can no man tame. It is an unruly evil, full of deadly poison. With it we bless God, even the Father, and with it we curse men, who are made in the image of God. Out of the same mouth proceed blessing and cursing. My brethren, these things ought not to be.   JAMES 3:3–10

Speak not evil one of another, brethren. . . . There is one lawgiver, who is able to save and to destroy. Who are you that judge another?

JAMES 4:11−12

Lay aside all malice, and all deceit, and hypocrisy, and envies, and all evil speaking.   I PETER 2:1

Be ready always to give an answer to every man that asks you a reason of the hope that is in you with gentleness and respect.   I PETER 3:15

They [the unbelievers] think it strange that you no longer join with them to the same excess of dissipation, so they speak evil of you. They shall give account to him that is ready to judge the living and the dead.

I PETER 4:4−5

If you are insulted for the name of Christ, you are blessed, for the Spirit of glory and of God rests upon you.   I PETER 4:14

See also **Anger, Envy, Hate, Judging Others, Self-Righteousness, The Tongue.**

DEATH

Belief in some kind of afterlife is pretty much universal, but you might not guess that from the media. Video and advertising focus on the here-and-now, so in place of the traditional belief in an afterlife is the belief in extending one's youth and physical health as long as possible. The problem: Even at its healthiest, the body still dies. No one has figured out a way around that yet. In the meantime, most people prefer not to think about death. Or, if they think about it, they may latch on to the popular belief in reincarnation—in other words, death, followed by another life, with no stopping place in sight. But the Bible affirms something most of us know deep down: Each person dies once, and after this comes the judgment of God. This view is less popular in our scientific age, but the many verified accounts of "near-death experiences" support what people have long believed—there is heaven and (gulp!) hell after the earthly body dies.

Death is real, and man is mortal—the Bible makes no bones about that. But at the end, the Book of Revelation affirms a strong belief in a joyous afterlife with no death or any hurtful thing. Just as Jesus was raised from the dead into a new form of life, so all of God's faithful people will live with him forever.

In the sweat of your face shall you eat bread, till you return to the ground; for out of it were you taken, for dust you are, and to dust shall you return.

GENESIS 3:19

Yes, though I walk through the valley of the shadow of death, I will fear no evil, for you are with me; your rod and your staff they comfort me.

PSALM 23:4

God will redeem my soul from the power of the grave, for he shall receive me.

PSALM 49:15

You shall guide me with your counsel, and afterward receive me to glory.

PSALM 73:24

Teach us to number our days, that we may apply our hearts to wisdom.

PSALM 90:12

Precious in the sight of the LORD is the death of his saints.

PSALM 116:15

He will swallow up death in victory, and the LORD God will wipe away tears from off all faces, and the disgrace of his people shall he take away from off the earth, for the LORD has spoken it.　　　　ISAIAH 25:8

"Have I any pleasure at all that the wicked should die?" says the LORD God, "and not that he should turn from his ways, and live?"

EZEKIEL 18:23

Many of those who sleep in the dust of the earth shall awake, some to everlasting life, and some to shame and everlasting contempt. And they that are wise shall shine as the brightness of the heavens, and they that turn many to righteousness shall shine as the stars forever and ever.

DANIEL 12:2–3

Blessed are they that mourn, for they shall be comforted.

MATTHEW 5:4

In the resurrection they neither marry, nor are given in marriage, but are like the angels of God in heaven.　　　　MATTHEW 22:30

He is not a God of the dead, but of the living: for to him all are alive.

LUKE 20:38

That which is born of the flesh is flesh, and that which is born of the Spirit is spirit.　　　　JOHN 3:6

He that believes in the Son has everlasting life, and he who believes not the Son shall not see life; but the wrath of God abides on him.　　　　JOHN 3:36

Truly, truly, I say to you, he who hears my word, and believes in him that sent me, has everlasting life, and shall not come into condemnation; but is passed from death to life. JOHN 5:24

I am the resurrection and the life: he who believes in me, though he were dead, yet shall he live. JOHN 11:25

When Jesus saw her weeping, and the Jews also weeping who came with her, he groaned in his spirit, and was troubled, and said, "Where have you laid him?" They said to him, "Lord, come and see." Jesus wept. Then said the Jews, "See how he loved him!" JOHN 11:33–36

Who shall separate us from the love of Christ? Shall tribulation, or distress, or persecution, or famine, or nakedness, or peril, or sword? No, in all these things we are more than conquerors through him that loved us. For I am persuaded, that neither death, nor life, nor angels, nor demons, nor powers, nor things present, nor things to come, nor height, nor depth, nor anything else in all creation will be able to separate us from the love of God. ROMANS 8:35, 37–38

None of us lives to himself, and no man dies to himself. ROMANS 14:7

Since by man came death, by man came also the resurrection of the dead. For as in Adam all die, even so in Christ shall all be made alive. I CORINTHIANS 15:21–22

Behold, I show you a mystery: We shall not all sleep, but we shall all be changed. In a moment, in the twinkling of an eye, at the last trumpet. The trumpet shall sound, and the dead shall be raised incorruptible, and we shall be changed. For this corruptible must put on incorruption, and this mortal must put on immortality. So when this corruptible has put on incorruption, and this mortal has put on immortality, then shall be brought to pass the saying that is written, "Death is swallowed up in victory. O death, where is your sting? O grave, where is your victory?" I CORINTHIANS 15:51–55

> *"The devil can cite Scripture for his purpose."*
>
> —WILLIAM SHAKESPEARE, *The Merchant of Venice*

We know that if this earthly tent we live in is destroyed, we have a building from God, a house not made with hands, eternal in the heavens. For in this tent we groan, earnestly desiring to be clothed with our dwelling from heaven. . . . For we who are in this tent do groan, being burdened, for we wish not to be unclothed but to be further clothed, so that mortality might be swallowed up by life. Now he who has made us for this very thing is God, who also has given to us the guarantee of the Spirit. Therefore we are always confident, knowing that, while we are at home in the body, we are absent from the Lord. (For we walk by faith, not by sight.)

2 CORINTHIANS 5:1–7

For me, to live is Christ, and to die is gain. But if I live in the body, that means fruitful labor for me. Yet what I shall choose? I know not. For I am hard pressed between the two, having a desire to depart and to be with Christ, which is far better.   PHILIPPIANS 1:21–23

Since the children are partakers of flesh and blood, Christ himself likewise took part in the same, so that through death he might destroy him that had the power of death, that is, the devil, and deliver them who through fear of death were all their lifetime subject to bondage.   HEBREWS 2:14–15

I heard a voice from heaven saying to me, "Write, 'Blessed are the dead which die in the Lord from now on.' Yes," said the Spirit, "that they may rest from their labors, and their works do follow them."

REVELATION 14:13

I saw a great white throne, and him that sat on it. From his face the earth and the heaven fled away, and there was found no place for them. And I saw the dead, small and great, stand before God, and the books were opened, and another book was opened, which is the Book of Life, and the dead were judged out of those things which were written in the books, according to their deeds. And the sea gave up the dead which were in it, and death and hell delivered up the dead which were in them, and they were judged every man according to their deeds. And death and hell were cast into the lake of fire. This is the second death. And whoever was not found written in the Book of Life was cast into the lake of fire.　REVELATION 20:11–15

I John saw the holy city, New Jerusalem, coming down from God out of heaven, prepared as a bride adorned for her husband. And I heard a great voice out of heaven saying, "Behold, the dwelling place of God is with men, and he will dwell with them, and they shall be his people, and God himself shall be with them and be their God. And God shall wipe away all tears from their eyes, and there shall be no more death, neither sorrow, nor crying, neither shall there be any more pain, for the former things are passed away."　REVELATION 21:2–4

See also Eternal Life, Heaven, Hell, Hope, Jesus' Second Coming.

DECEIT

People often assume that "sin" in the Bible always refers to something sexual. In fact, while the Bible does condemn sexual immorality, it says a lot more about honesty—or, rather, the absence of honesty, which seems to be part of the human condition. It is one of the curiosities of human life that we all know instinctively that honesty is absolutely essential, yet we constantly deceive each other. God, the Bible tells us, is not fooled by our deceit, no matter how successful we are in fooling others—or fooling ourselves.

The LORD will abhor the bloody and deceitful man.　PSALM 5:6

He that works deceit shall not dwell within my house: he who tells lies shall not tarry in my sight.　PSALM 101:7

Deliver my soul, O LORD, from lying lips, and from a deceitful tongue.

PSALM 120:2

The lip of truth shall be established forever, but a lying tongue is but for a moment.

PROVERBS 12:19

Lying lips are abomination to the LORD, but they that deal honestly are his delight.

PROVERBS 12:22

A wicked doer pays heed to false lips, and a liar gives ear to a mischievous tongue.

PROVERBS 17:4

Food gained by deceit is sweet to a man; but afterwards his mouth shall be filled with gravel.

PROVERBS 20:17

You are of your father the devil, and the desires of your father you will do. He was a murderer from the beginning, and does not stand in the truth, because there is no truth in him. When he speaks a lie, he speaks according to his nature, for he is a liar, and the father of lies.

JOHN 8:44

A double-minded man is unstable in all his ways.

JAMES 1:8

See also Lying.

DEPRESSION

You won't find the word depression *in most translations of the Bible, but the idea is certainly there. The feeling that life is bad and unlikely to get any better is as old as humanity, and the Bible presents us with many people— including saints—who felt abandoned by man and by God. But God never truly abandons his people. In the midst of the deepest depression, people of faith have found their one consolation in this: God is in charge, and regardless of what afflicts us in this life, our ultimate destiny is in God's hands. It is easy to lose sight of this when all seems hopeless, yet this truth bears constantly repeating: Events do not control God, and events do not separate us from God.*

The needy shall not always be forgotten: the expectation of the poor shall not perish forever.   PSALM 9:18

Turn to me, and have mercy upon me; for I am desolate and afflicted.
                                                               PSALM 25:16, 21

O love the LORD, all you his saints, for the LORD preserves the faithful, and plentifully pays back the proud. Be of good courage, and he shall strengthen your heart, all you that hope in the LORD.   PSALM 31:23–24

The LORD redeems the soul of his servants, and none of those who trust in him shall be desolate.   PSALM 34:22

I am poor and needy; yet the LORD thinks upon me: you are my help and my deliverer.   PSALM 40:17

Why are you cast down, O my soul? And why are you disquieted within me? Hope in God, for I shall yet praise him, who is the health of my countenance, and my God.   PSALM 42:11

My heart is in anguish within me, and the terrors of death are fallen upon me. Fearfulness and trembling are come upon me, and horror has overwhelmed me. And I said, "Oh, that I had wings like a dove, for then would I fly away, and be at rest!"   PSALM 55:4–6

You are my hope, O LORD God: you are my trust since my youth. By you have I been sustained since my birth; you are he who took me out of my mother's womb. My praise shall be continually of you.
                                                               PSALM 71:5–6

The LORD God is a sun and shield: the LORD will give grace and glory: no good thing will he withhold from those who walk uprightly. O LORD Almighty, blessed is the man that trusts in you.   PSALM 84:11–12

Out of the depths have I cried to you, O LORD. LORD, hear my voice; let your ears be attentive to the voice of my supplications. If you, LORD, should mark iniquities, O LORD, who shall stand? But there is forgiveness with you, so that you may be feared. I wait for the LORD, my soul does wait, and in his word do I hope. My soul waits for the LORD more than they that watch for the morning. PSALM 130:1–6

I looked on my right hand, and there was no man that would know me; I had no refuge; no man cared for my soul. I cried to you, O LORD; I said, "You are my refuge and my portion in the land of the living." Attend to my cry; for I am brought very low; deliver me from my persecutors; for they are stronger than I. PSALM 142:4–6

A merry heart does good like a medicine, but a broken spirit dries up the bones. PROVERBS 17:22

The spirit of a man will endure sickness, but who can bear a wounded spirit? PROVERBS 18:14

Blessed is the man that trusts in the LORD, and whose hope the LORD is. JEREMIAH 17:7

"I know the thoughts that I think about you," says the LORD, "thoughts of peace, and not of evil, to give you a future with hope. Then shall you call upon me, and you shall go and pray to me, and I will hearken to you. And you shall seek me, and find me, when you shall search for me with all your heart." JEREMIAH 29:11–13

My soul is far removed from peace, and I have forgotten happiness. And I said, "Gone are my glory and my expectation from the LORD." Remembering my affliction and my misery, the wormwood and the gall. My soul has them still in remembrance, and is bowed down within me. This I recall to my mind, therefore have I hope.

It is due to the LORD's mercies that we are not consumed, because his compassions fail not. They are new every morning: great is your faithfulness. The LORD is my portion, said my soul, therefore will I hope in him. The LORD is good to those who wait for him, to the soul that seeks him. It is good that a man should both hope and quietly wait for the salvation of the LORD. LAMENTATIONS 3:17–26

Blessed are they that mourn: for they shall be comforted.

MATTHEW 5:4

You shall be sorrowful, but your sorrow shall be turned into joy.

JOHN 16:20

If in this life only we have hope in Christ, we are of all men most miserable.

I CORINTHIANS 15:19

We are troubled on every side, yet not distressed; we are perplexed, but not in despair; persecuted, but not forsaken; cast down, but not destroyed; always bearing about in the body the dying of the Lord Jesus, that the life also of Jesus might be made manifest in our body.

2 CORINTHIANS 4:8–10

There is one body, and one Spirit, even as you are called in one hope of your calling. EPHESIANS 4:4

The love of money is the root of all evil. Some who have coveted after it have strayed from the faith and pierced themselves through with many sorrows.

I TIMOTHY 6:10

Faith is the substance of things hoped for, the evidence of things not seen.

HEBREWS 11:1

Blessed be the God and Father of our Lord Jesus Christ, who according to his abundant mercy has given us a new birth into a living hope by the resurrection of Jesus Christ from the dead, to an imperishable inheritance, one undefiled, which never fades away, reserved in heaven for you. You are protected by the power of God through faith for a salvation ready to be revealed in the last time. In this you greatly rejoice, though now for a time you are in heaviness through various trials. I PETER 1:3–6

> *Abraham Lincoln claimed that reading the Bible was "the best cure for the blues." Lincoln also claimed that "this great Book is the best gift God has given to man. But for it, we could not know right from wrong."*

Prepare your minds for action, be self-controlled, and set your hope on the grace that is to be brought to you when Jesus Christ is revealed.

I PETER 1:13

Cast all your care upon him; for he cares for you.　　　I PETER 5:7

See also Eternal Life, Faith, Heaven, Hope, Loneliness, Trusting God.

THE DEVIL

Does that evil being with horns and a pitchfork really exist? Well, in the first place, the Bible says nothing whatever about Satan's appearance. The Book of Revelation refers to him as the "Dragon," and since he is evil, artists have naturally made him look ugly. But the Bible is more concerned with his activity than his looks. He is real, and he opposes God and people of faith. He is the Adversary, and though he can vex people and temporarily thwart God, he and his followers face a final defeat at the end of the world.

Remember the old line "The devil made me do it"? It isn't accurate. The devil is a tempter, but we ourselves are responsible for our own moral failings. When we give in to our selfish impulses, we are, in a sense, following the Adversary instead of following God. Powerful as the devil is, he is no match for God. Jesus made it clear that Satan's kingdom was already in the process of being torn down.

If I cast out devils by the Spirit of God, then the kingdom of God has come to you. MATTHEW 12:28

The Lord appointed seventy others also, and sent them two by two ahead of him into every city and place that he himself would go. . . . The Seventy returned again with joy, saying, "Lord, even the devils are subject to us through your name." And he said to them, "I beheld Satan fall like lightning from heaven. Behold, I give to you power to tread on serpents and scorpions, and over all the power of the enemy, and nothing shall by any means hurt you. Nevertheless, do not rejoice that the spirits are subject to you, but rather rejoice because your names are written in heaven." LUKE 10:1, 17–20

Jesus said to them, "If God were your Father, you would love me: for I proceeded forth and came from God; neither came I of myself, but he sent me. Why do you not understand what I say? Because ye cannot hear my word. You are of your father, the devil, and the desires of him you will do. He was a murderer from the beginning, and held not to the truth, because there is no truth in him. When he speaks a lie, he speaks his own language; for he is a liar, and the father of lies." JOHN 8:42–44

Now is the time for the judgment of this world; now shall the prince of this world [Satan] be cast out. JOHN 12:31

God anointed Jesus of Nazareth with the Holy Spirit and with power. He went about doing good, and healing all that were oppressed by the devil, for God was with him. ACTS 10:37–38

Open their eyes, and turn them from darkness to light, and from the power of Satan to God, that they may receive forgiveness of sins, and inheritance among those who are sanctified by faith that is in me. ACTS 26:18

The God of peace shall bruise Satan under your feet shortly.

ROMANS 16:20

Satan himself is disguised as an angel of light. Therefore it is no great thing if his ministers also be disguised as the ministers of righteousness. Their end shall be according to their deeds.   2 CORINTHIANS 11:14–15

Be angry, and sin not: let not the sun go down upon your wrath, neither give place to the devil.   EPHESIANS 4:26–27

Put on the whole armor of God, that you may be able to stand against the wiles of the devil. For we struggle not against flesh and blood, but against principalities, against powers, against the rulers of the darkness of this world, against spiritual wickedness in high places. Therefore take up the whole armor of God, that you may be able to withstand on the evil day, and having done all, to stand firm. Stand therefore, having your waist belted with truth, and having on the breastplate of righteousness, and your feet shod with the preparation of the gospel of peace. Above all, take up the shield of faith, with which you shall be able to quench all the fiery arrows of the wicked. And take the helmet of salvation, and the sword of the Spirit, which is the word of God.   EPHESIANS 6:11–17

The Spirit speaks clearly that in the last times some shall depart from the faith, giving heed to deceitful spirits and doctrines of devils, through the hypocrisy of liars whose consciences are seared with a hot iron.

1 TIMOTHY 4:1–2

Since the children are partakers of flesh and blood, he [Jesus] also himself likewise took part in the same, that through death he might destroy him that had the power of death, that is, the devil.   HEBREWS 2:14

This so-called wisdom descends not from heaven, but is earthly, sensual, devilish. For where envying and strife are, there is disorder and every evil work. But the wisdom that is from above is first pure, then peaceable, gentle, and easy to be entreated, full of mercy and good fruits, without partiality, and without hypocrisy.   JAMES 3:15–16

Submit yourselves to God. Resist the devil, and he will flee from you. Draw near to God, and he will draw near to you. Cleanse your hands, you sinners, and purify your hearts, you double-minded.   JAMES 4:7–8

In Act II of William Shakespeare's Hamlet, *the title character states that "the Devil hath power to assume a pleasing shape." This perfectly echoes Paul's words in 2 Corinthians 11:14: "Satan himself is disguised as an angel of light."*

Be disciplined, be vigilant, because your adversary the devil, like a roaring lion, walks about, seeking whom he may devour. Resist him, steadfast in the faith, knowing that your brethren in all the world are undergoing the same afflictions. 1 PETER 5:8–9

He that commits sin is of the devil; for the devil sins from the beginning. For this purpose the Son of God was revealed, that he might destroy the works of the devil. Whoever is born of God does not commit sin, for God's seed remains in him, and he cannot sin, because he is born of God. In this the children of God are revealed, as are the children of the devil. Whoever does not righteousness is not of God, neither he who loves not his brother.

1 JOHN 3:8–10

The devil that deceived them was cast into the lake of fire and brimstone, where the beast and the false prophet are, and shall be tormented day and night forever and ever. REVELATION 20:10

There was war in heaven: Michael and his angels fought against the dragon, and the dragon and his angels fought, but did not prevail, neither was their place found any more in heaven. And the great dragon was cast out, that old serpent, called the Devil, and Satan, who deceives the whole world: he was cast out into the earth, and his angels were cast out with him.

REVELATION 12:7–9

See also Angels, Hell, Spiritual Power, Temptation.

DISCIPLINE AND CORRECTION

The health clubs and jogging trails are filled with people eager to discipline their bodies, submitting to diet and fitness regimens based on the philosophy "No pain, no gain." Funny that so many people deny themselves in order to achieve the perfect body, yet how many are willing to discipline themselves to become better on the inside?

Of course, life itself has a way of "correcting" us, throwing enough trouble at us to puncture our oversized egos and make us aware of our own limitations. No one enjoys this, and, regrettably, too often we respond to adversity by becoming bitter and cynical. Why isn't life easy and carefree? Why can't it be all "ups" without any "downs"? A more sensible question would be, Why don't we realize that the philosophy of "No pain, no gain" applies to our inner selves as well as our bodies? It's sad, but true: We usually don't grow and mature unless we deal with hardship.

You shall also consider in your heart, that, as a man chastens his son, so the LORD your God chastens you. Therefore you shall keep the commandments of the LORD your God, to walk in his ways, and to fear him.

DEUTERONOMY 8:5–6

Behold, happy is the man whom God corrects: therefore despise not the chastening of the Almighty, for he makes sore, and binds up; he wounds, and his hands make whole. JOB 5:17–18

When he has tested me, I shall come forth as gold. JOB 23:10

He that chastises the heathen, shall he not correct? He that teaches man knowledge, shall he not know? The LORD knows the thoughts of man, that they are futile. Blessed is the man whom you chasten, O LORD, and teach him out of your law. PSALM 94:10–12

The fear of the LORD is the beginning of knowledge, but fools despise wisdom and instruction. PROVERBS 1:7

Whom the LORD loves he corrects, even as a father corrects the son in whom he delights. PROVERBS 3:12

The commandment is a lamp, and the law is light, and reproofs of instruction are the way of life. PROVERBS 6:23

Reprove not a scorner, lest he hate you; rebuke a wise man, and he will love you. PROVERBS 9:8

Whoever loves instruction loves knowledge, but he who hates reproof is stupid. PROVERBS 12:1

A fool despises his father's instruction, but he who regards reproof is prudent. PROVERBS 15:5

He that refuses instruction despises his own soul, but he who hears reproof gets understanding. PROVERBS 15:32

A reproof enters more into a wise man than a hundred stripes into a fool. PROVERBS 17:10

As an earring of gold, and an ornament of fine gold, so is a wise man's reproof to an obedient ear. PROVERBS 25:12

Open rebuke is better than secret love. Faithful are the wounds of a friend; but the kisses of an enemy are deceitful. PROVERBS 27:5–6

It is better to hear the rebuke of the wise than for a man to hear the song of fools. ECCLESIASTES 7:5

When we are judged, we are chastened of the Lord, that we should not be condemned with the world. I CORINTHIANS 11:32

Our light affliction, which is but for a moment, works for us a far more exceeding and eternal weight of glory; while we look not at the things which are seen, but at the things which are not seen, for the things which are seen are temporal; but the things which are not seen are eternal.

2 CORINTHIANS 4:17–18

Rebuke publicly those who sin, so that others also may take warning.

1 TIMOTHY 5:20

All scripture is given by inspiration of God, and is profitable for doctrine, for reproof, for correction, for instruction in righteousness: that the man of God may be perfect, thoroughly furnished to all good works. 2 TIMOTHY 3:16–17

Exhort one another daily, while it is still today, lest any of you be hardened through the deceitfulness of sin.

HEBREWS 3:13

You have forgotten the exhortation which speaks to you as to children. My son, despise not the chastening of the Lord, nor faint when you are rebuked by him, for whom the Lord loves he chastens, and scourges every son whom he receives. If you endure chastening, God deals with you as with sons; for what son is he whom the father chastens not? . . . We have had fathers of our flesh who corrected us, and we gave them reverence: shall we not much rather be in subjection to the Father of spirits, and live? For they truly for a few days chastened us after their own pleasure; but he for our profit, that we might be partakers of his holiness.

Now no chastening for the present seems to be joyous, but grievous. Nevertheless, afterward it yields the peaceable fruit of righteousness to them which are trained by it. HEBREWS 12:5–12

As many as I love, I rebuke and chasten: be zealous therefore, and repent.

REVELATION 3:19

See also Fellowship with God, Patience, Perseverance, Personal Growth.

DUTY

"You owe it to yourself" is a good line to help sell a product or service. But most of us become so concerned about what we owe ourselves that we cast aside the thought of what we owe to others—or to God. In fact, the Bible says nothing whatever about what we "owe to ourselves," since it assumes (correctly) that we will look after our own interests without having to be told to. Rather, the Bible reminds us again and again that we owe love and kindness to our fellow man and love and reverence to God. Selfish as we are by nature, we have to be told—sometimes very loudly—that the world is a horrible place when each person is guided only by his or her own selfish desires.

Fear God, and keep his commandments, for this is the whole duty of man.
ECCLESIASTES 12:13

He has showed you, O man, what is good. And what does the LORD require of you, but to do justly, and to love mercy, and to walk humbly with your God?
MICAH 6:8

Jesus said to them, "Render therefore to Caesar the things which are Caesar's, and to God the things which be God's."   LUKE 20:25

Owe no man any thing, but to love one another, for he who loves another has fulfilled the law.   ROMANS 13:8

We ought to obey God rather than men.   ACTS 5:29

DUTY TO THE POOR

People accuse the Bible of being an "otherworldly" book, but they might be surprised how often it speaks of such earthly matters as the poor and our duty to help them. The Old Testament law shows amazing compassion for the poorest members of society, and that compassion is evident in the New Testament as well. Living in a society where government welfare programs are in place, it is easy for us to neglect the poor since we readily assume that we "gave at the IRS." But welfare isn't a cure-all, and many truly poor people do not benefit from government programs. There is no substitute, in God's eyes, for our genuine and active compassion for the destitute people of the world.

If there is among you a poor man of one of your brethren within any of your gates in your land which the LORD your God gives you, you shall not harden your heart, nor shut your hand from your poor brother.

For the poor shall never cease out of the land: therefore I command you, saying, you shall open your hand wide to your brother, to your poor, and to your needy, in your land. DEUTERONOMY 15:7, 11

Blessed is he who considers the poor: the LORD will deliver him in time of trouble. The LORD will preserve him, and keep him alive, and he shall be blessed upon the earth, and you will not deliver him to the will of his enemies. The LORD will strengthen him upon his sickbed and restore him.

PSALM 41:1–3

He that has pity on the poor lends to the LORD. PROVERBS 19:17

Whoever shuts his ears to the cry of the poor, he himself shall cry out but shall not be heard. PROVERBS 21:13

The righteous considers the cause of the poor, but the wicked closes his eyes to them. PROVERBS 28:27

If you do away with the yoke of oppression, the pointing of the finger, and malicious speaking, and if you work to feed the hungry and satisfy the needs of the afflicted, then your light shall rise in the darkness, and your night will be like the noonday. ISAIAH 58:9–10

Oppress not the widow, nor the fatherless, the stranger, nor the poor, and let none of you imagine evil against his brother in your heart.

ZECHARIAH 7:10

Jesus said to him, "If you will be perfect, go and sell what you have, and give to the poor, and you shall have treasure in heaven, and come and follow me."

MATTHEW 19:21

Sell what you have, and give to the poor; provide yourselves purses which grow not old, a treasure in the heavens that fails not, where no thief approaches, neither moth corrupts. For where your treasure is, there will your heart be also. LUKE 12:33–34

When you make a dinner or a supper, call not your friends, nor your brethren, neither your kinsmen, nor your rich neighbors; lest they also invite you again, and a recompense be made you. But when you make a feast, call the poor, the maimed, the lame, the blind. And you shall be blessed; for they cannot recompense you, for you shall be recompensed at the resurrection of the just. LUKE 14:12–14

Though I bestow all my goods to feed the poor, and though I give my body to be burned, and have not charity, it profits me nothing.

I CORINTHIANS 13:3

Every man according as he decides in his heart, so let him give; not grudgingly, or from necessity, for God loves a cheerful giver.

2 CORINTHIANS 9:7

Pure religion and undefiled before God and the Father is this, to visit the fatherless and widows in their affliction, and to keep himself unspotted from the world. JAMES 1:27

My brethren, with your acts of favoritism do you truly have faith in our Lord Jesus Christ, the Lord of glory? For if there comes to your assembly a man with a gold ring, in fine apparel, and there comes in also a poor man in dirty clothing, and you show favoritism to him that wears the fine clothing, and say to him, "Sit here in a good place," and say to the poor, "Stand you there, or sit here under my footstool"—are you not then showing partiality, and are become judges of evil thoughts? Hearken, my beloved brethren: has not God chosen the poor of this world to be rich in faith, and heirs of the kingdom which he has promised to those who love him? JAMES 2:1–5

You have despised the poor. Is it not the rich men who oppress you, and drag you before the judgment seats? JAMES 2:6

Whoever has this world's goods, and sees his brother in need, and has no pity on him, how dwells the love of God in him? My little children, let us not love merely in word, neither in speech, but in deed and in truth.

I JOHN 3:17–18

See also Generosity, God's Compassion for the Poor, Kindness, Money.

ENEMIES

One of the supreme ironies of life is that the best people are often the most hated. While it makes sense that wicked people would have enemies, it offends our sense of righteousness that good people are often despised. It offends God as well, and the Bible has much to say about God's anger toward those who persecute the righteous. Happily, no matter how many enemies we may have, the great Friend and Defender is God, who is more than a match for any human foe. And because God is on the side of his faithful ones, there is no place for revenge in their lives. In fact, the Bible turns the world's standards upside down: Instead of wishing harm to our enemies, we are to show them kindness.

If you see your enemy's ox or donkey going astray, you shall lead it back to him. If thou see the donkey of one who hates you fallen down under his load, do not leave it there, but help him with it.   EXODUS 23:4–5

In famine he shall redeem you from death, and in war from the power of the sword.   JOB 5:20

You prepare a table before me in the presence of mine enemies.

PSALM 23:5

In the time of trouble he shall hide me in his pavilion; in the secret of his dwelling place shall he hide me; he shall set me up upon a rock. And now shall my head be lifted up above my enemies round about me: therefore will I offer in his dwelling place sacrifices of joy; I will sing, yes, I will sing praises to the LORD.   PSALM 27:5–6

The LORD shall help them, and deliver them: he shall deliver them from the wicked, and save them, because they trust in him.   PSALM 37:40

Through God we shall do valiantly, for he it is that shall tread down our enemies.　　　　　　　　　　　　　　　　　　　　　PSALM 60:12

They that hate me without a cause are more than the hairs of my head: they that would destroy me, being my enemies wrongfully, are mighty.

PSALM 69:4

You that love the LORD, hate evil: he preserves the souls of his saints; he delivers them out of the hand of the wicked.　　　　　PSALM 97:10

The LORD is on my side; I will not fear. What can man do to me? The LORD takes my part with those who help me; therefore shall I see my desire upon those who hate me. It is better to trust in the LORD than to put confidence in man. It is better to trust in the LORD than to put confidence in princes.

PSALM 118:6–9

When a man's ways please the LORD, he makes even his enemies to be at peace with him.　　　　　　　　　　　　　　　　　　　PROVERBS 16:7

Rejoice not when your enemy falls, and let not your heart be glad when he stumbles, lest the LORD see it, and it displease him, and he turn away his wrath from him.　　　　　　　　　　　　　　　PROVERBS 24:17–18

The fear of man brings a snare, but whoever puts his trust in the LORD shall be safe.　　　　　　　　　　　　　　　　　　　　　PROVERBS 29:25

Do not call a conspiracy all that this people calls conspiracy; do not fear what it fears, nor be in dread. But the LORD Almighty, him you shall regard as holy, him alone shall you fear and dread.　　　　　ISAIAH 8:12–13

Behold, all they that were incensed against you shall be ashamed and confounded: they shall be as nothing, and they that strive with you shall perish.

ISAIAH 41:11

I will deliver you in that day, says the LORD, and you shall not be given into the hand of the men of whom you are afraid.　　　JEREMIAH 39:17

Rejoice not against me, O my enemy: when I fall, I shall arise; when I sit in darkness, the LORD shall be a light to me.   MICAH 7:8

You have heard that it has been said, "You shall love your neighbor, and hate your enemy." But I say to you, love your enemies, bless those who curse you, do good to those who hate you, and pray for them that spitefully use you, and persecute you; that you may be the children of your Father who is in heaven, for he makes his sun to rise on the evil and on the good, and sends rain on the just and on the unjust. For if you love them who love you, what reward have you? Do not even the tax collectors the same? And if you salute your brethren only, what do you more than others? Do not even the tax collectors do so? Be you therefore perfect, even as your Father who is in heaven is perfect.   MATTHEW 5:43–48

Shall not God avenge his own elect, who cry day and night to him, though he bear long with them? I tell you that he will avenge them speedily. Nevertheless, when the Son of man comes, shall he find faith on the earth?   LUKE 18:7–8

These things I have spoken to you, that in me you might have peace. In the world you shall have tribulation, but be of good cheer; I have overcome the world.   JOHN 16:33

If God be for us, who can be against us?   ROMANS 8:31

Bless them which persecute you: bless, and curse not. If your enemy hungers, feed him; if he thirsts, give him drink, for in so doing you shall heap coals of fire on his head.   ROMANS 12:14, 20

We wrestle not against flesh and blood, but against principalities, against powers, against the rulers of the darkness of this world, against spiritual wickedness in high places.   EPHESIANS 6:12

See also Forgiveness, Mercy, Revenge.

ENVY

Admiring someone's looks or personality or possessions is no sin. But want-ing to have them for ourselves is, especially when we allow ourselves to feel resentment. This is rooted in our offended sense of justice: "He doesn't deserve that new car, but I certainly do." or "Why should she get that promotion when I was the one who deserved it?" While sometimes we do see an actual injustice, more often than not envy grows out of plain old self-ishness. We want something that someone else has, and we would willingly take it away if we could. The Bible drives home the point that this has no place in life. It can lead to bitterness, frustration, and anger against God.

For a moral person, one of the most painful sensations is seeing the wicked prosper. It is tempting in this situation to envy the wicked person and to wonder why God allows some good people to live in poverty and some wicked people to gather wealth. The Bible assures us that justice will come, if not in this life, then in the next.

You shall not covet your neighbor's house, you shall not covet your neigh-bor's wife, nor his manservant, nor his maidservant, nor his ox, nor his don-key, nor anything that is your neighbor's.   EXODUS 20:17

Wrath kills the foolish man, and envy slays the simpleminded one.

JOB 5:2

Rest in the LORD, and wait patiently for him. Fret not yourself because of him who prospers in his way, because of the man who brings wicked devices to pass. Cease from anger, and forsake wrath: fret not yourself in any way to do evil. For evildoers shall be cut off, but those that wait upon the LORD, they shall inherit the earth.   PSALM 37:7–9

Envy not the oppressor, and choose none of his ways. For the perverse is abomination to the LORD, but his secret is with the righteous.

PROVERBS 3:31–32

A sound heart is the life of the flesh, but envy is the rottenness of the bones.

PROVERBS 14:30

Let not your heart envy sinners, but be in the fear of the LORD all the day long. For surely there is an end, and your expectation shall not be cut off.

PROVERBS 23:17–18

Be not envious against evil men, neither desire to be with them. For their heart studies destruction, and their lips talk of mischief.

PROVERBS 24:1–2

Wrath is cruel, and anger is outrageous; but who is able to stand before envy?

PROVERBS 27:4

I considered that all toil and all skill in work arise from a man's envy of his neighbor. This is also meaningless, a chasing after the wind.

ECCLESIASTES 4:4

Let us walk honestly, as in the day; not in orgies and drunkenness, not in sexual immorality and debauchery, not in strife and envying. But put on the Lord Jesus Christ, and make no provision for the sinful nature, to fulfill its lusts.

ROMANS 13:13–14

You are still carnal, for since there is among you envying and quarreling, are you not carnal, and walking like mere men?

I CORINTHIANS 3:3

Charity endures long, and is kind; charity envies not; charity boasts not; is not puffed up, does not behave itself wrongly, seeks not its own, is not easily provoked, thinks no evil.

I CORINTHIANS 13:4–5

Now the works of the sinful nature are obvious, which are these: adultery, fornication, impurity, debauchery, idolatry, witchcraft, hatred, discord, jealousy, wrath, strife, seditions, heresies, envyings, murders, drunkenness, carousing, and the like. I warn you, as I have also told you in the past, that those who do such things shall not inherit the kingdom of God. But the fruit of the Spirit is love, joy, peace, longsuffering, gentleness, goodness, faith, meekness, self-control—against such there is no law. And they that are Christ's have crucified the sinful nature with its passions and lusts. If we live in the Spirit, let us also walk in the Spirit. Let us not be conceited, competing with one another, envying one another.

GALATIANS 5:19–26

We ourselves also were sometimes foolish, disobedient, deceived, serving various lusts and pleasures, living in malice and envy, hateful, and hating one another. But after that the kindness and love of God our Savior toward man appeared, not by works of righteousness which we have done, but according to his mercy he saved us, by the washing of regeneration, and renewing of the Holy Spirit.

TITUS 3:3−5

Where do these conflicts and disputes among you arise from? Do they not come from your cravings that war within you? You crave, and have not, so you kill. You desire to have, and cannot obtain, so you fight and war. You have not because you ask not. You ask, and receive not, because you ask wrongly, that you may spend it upon your pleasures. You adulterers and adulteresses, know you not that the friendship of the world is enmity with God? Whoever therefore will be a friend of the world is the enemy of God.

JAMES 4:1−4

Lay aside all malice, and all deceit, and hypocrisies, and envies, and all evil speaking.

I PETER 2:1

See also Contentment, Hate.

EQUALITY/FAIRNESS

If equal means "equally precious in the sight of God," then, yes, all people are equal. But if equal means "exactly alike," then obviously we are not all alike since each of us has differing abilities and handicaps. It is hard to find the "level playing field" in life, and the courts are full of people bringing their lawsuits and charging someone else with "unfairness." The Bible has a lot to say about human judges and the necessity to show as much fairness as possible. But, ultimately, the only Judge who can finally judge with complete fairness is God himself. In the meantime, we can only strive for fairness in our human relations, knowing that just as we may sometimes be unfair to others, we ourselves must sometimes bear the injustice of others. But with God the only thing that matters is our hearts—not our looks, our family, or our achievements, but only our hearts.

I charged your judges at that time, saying, hear the causes between your brethren, and judge righteously between every man and his brother, and the stranger that is with him. You shall not show partiality toward persons in judgment; but you shall hear the small as well as the great; you shall not be afraid of the face of man; for the judgment is God's.

DEUTERONOMY 1:16–17

There is no iniquity with the LORD our God, nor favoritism toward persons, nor taking of gifts.   2 CHRONICLES 19:7

He comes to judge the earth; with righteousness shall he judge the world, and the people with equality.   PSALM 98:9

The rich and poor meet together: the LORD is the maker of them all.

PROVERBS 22:2

All are of the dust, and all turn to dust again.   ECCLESIASTES 3:20

There shall come forth a shoot from the stump of Jesse, and a branch shall grow out of his roots. And the Spirit of the LORD shall rest upon him, the Spirit of wisdom and understanding, the Spirit of counsel and might, the Spirit of knowledge and of the fear of the LORD. He shall not judge by what his eyes see, nor decide by what his ears hear; but with righteousness shall he judge the poor, and decide with equity for the meek of the earth.

ISAIAH 11:1–4

[NOTE: *The early Christians believed that this Old Testament prophecy was fulfilled in the life of Jesus.*]

Let justice flow down like waters, and righteousness as a mighty stream.

AMOS 5:24

He makes his sun to rise on the evil and on the good, and sends rain on the just and on the unjust.   MATTHEW 5:45

Judge not according to the appearance, but judge righteous judgment.

JOHN 7:24

I perceive that God shows no favoritism. But in every nation he who fears him, and works righteousness, is accepted by him.   ACTS 10:34–35

God has made of one blood all nations of men to dwell on all the face of the earth.   ACTS 17:26

There is neither Jew nor Greek, there is neither slave nor free, there is neither male nor female, for you are all one in Christ Jesus.

GALATIANS 3:28

There is neither Greek nor Jew, circumcision nor uncircumcision, barbarian, Scythian, slave nor free, but Christ is all, and in all.

COLOSSIANS 3:11

He that does wrong shall receive for the wrong which he has done, and there is no partiality.   COLOSSIANS 3:25

If you fulfill the royal law according to the scripture, you shall love your neighbor as yourself, you do well, but if you show favoritism, you commit sin.

JAMES 2:9

The Father, who without favoritism judges according to every man's work.

I PETER 1:17

ETERNAL LIFE

The key teaching of the New Testament is this: The crucified, dead, and buried Jesus was raised to life again by God. Not everyone can accept this grand miracle, but it was joyfully accepted and preached by the early Christians, who based their gospel on their life-changing belief that all believers would someday be as Jesus himself was—raised to glorious life and reigning forever in heaven with God. Appropriately, the Bible ends with the Book of Revelation's stirring picture of God's people gathered together in the heavenly city.

The eternal God is your refuge, and underneath are the everlasting arms.

DEUTERONOMY 33:27

I know that my redeemer lives, and that he shall stand at the latter day upon the earth. JOB 19:25

You will not leave my soul in hell; neither will you suffer your Holy One to see corruption. You will show me the path of life; in your presence is fullness of joy; at your right hand there are pleasures forevermore.

PSALM 16:10—11

Thy dead men shall live, together with my dead body shall they arise. Awake and sing, you that dwell in dust, for your dew is as the dew of herbs, and the earth shall cast out the dead. ISAIAH 26:19

Many of those who sleep in the dust of the earth shall awake, some to everlasting life, and some to shame and everlasting contempt. And they that are wise shall shine as the brightness of the heavens, and they that turn many to righteousness as the stars forever and ever. DANIEL 12:2—3

The kingdom of heaven is like a treasure hid in a field. When a man found it, he hid it again, and in joy went and sold all that he had, and bought that field. Again, the kingdom of heaven is like a merchant man, seeking goodly pearls; when he had found one pearl of great price, he went and sold all that he had, and bought it. MATTHEW 13:44—46

Now that the dead are raised, even Moses showed at the bush, when he calls the Lord the God of Abraham, and the God of Isaac, and the God of Jacob. For he is not a God of the dead, but of the living, for all live to him.

LUKE 20:37—38

That which is born of the flesh is flesh, and that which is born of the Spirit is spirit. . . . He that believes in the Son has everlasting life, and he who believes not the Son shall not see life; but the wrath of God abides on him.

JOHN 3:6, 36

God so loved the world that he gave his only begotten Son, that whoever believes in him should not perish, but have everlasting life. For God sent not his Son into the world to condemn the world, but that the world through him might be saved.

JOHN 3:16–17

This is the will of the Father who sent me, that of all which he has given me I should lose nothing, but should raise it up again at the last day. And this is the will of him that sent me, that everyone who sees the Son, and believes in him, may have everlasting life, and I will raise him up at the last day.

JOHN 6:39–40

Truly, truly, I say to you, if a man keep my sayings, he shall never see death.

JOHN 8:51

Jesus said to her, "I am the resurrection, and the life: he who believes in me, though he were dead, yet shall he live. And whoever lives and believes in me shall never die."

JOHN 11:25–26

He that loves his life shall lose it, and he who hates his life in this world shall keep it to life eternal.

JOHN 12:25

In my Father's house are many mansions: if it were not so, I would have told you. I go to prepare a place for you. And if I go and prepare a place for you, I will come again, and receive you to myself, so that where I am, there you may be also.

JOHN 14:2–3

The wages of sin is death; but the gift of God is eternal life through Jesus Christ our Lord.

ROMANS 6:23

If the Spirit of him that raised up Jesus from the dead dwells in you, he who raised up Christ from the dead shall also give life to your mortal bodies by his Spirit that dwells in you.   ROMANS 8:11

If in this life only we have hope in Christ, we are of all men most miserable. But now is Christ risen from the dead, and become the firstfruits of those who slept. For since by man came death, by man came also the resurrection of the dead. For as in Adam all die, even so in Christ shall all be made alive.

I CORINTHIANS 15:19–22

So also is the resurrection of the dead. It is sown in corruption; it is raised in incorruption. It is sown in dishonor; it is raised in glory. It is sown in weakness; it is raised in power. It is sown a natural body; it is raised a spiritual body. There is a natural body, and there is a spiritual body. And so it is written, "The first man Adam was made a living soul"; the last Adam was made a life-giving spirit. But it is not the spiritual that is first, but the physical, and afterward that which is spiritual. The first man is from the earth, earthy: the second man is the Lord from heaven. As is the earthy, such are they also that are earthy; and as is the heavenly, such are they also that are heavenly. Just as we have borne the image of the earthy, we shall also bear the image of the heavenly. Now this I say, brethren, that flesh and blood cannot inherit the kingdom of God; neither does corruption inherit incorruption.   I CORINTHIANS 15:42–50

Behold, I show you a mystery; we shall not all sleep, but we shall all be changed, in a moment, in the twinkling of an eye, at the last trumpet. For the trumpet shall sound, and the dead shall be raised incorruptible, and we shall be changed. For this corruptible must put on incorruption, and this mortal must put on immortality. So when this corruptible shall have put on incorruption, and this mortal shall have put on immortality, then shall be brought to pass the saying that is written, "Death is swallowed up in victory."   I CORINTHIANS 15:51–54

Though our outward man perishes, yet the inward man is renewed day by day. For our light affliction, which is but for a moment, prepares us for a far more exceeding and eternal weight of glory, because we look not at the things which are seen, but at the things which are not seen; for the things which are seen are temporary, but the things which are not seen are eternal. We know that if our earthly house, this tent, were dissolved, we have a building from God, a house not made with hands, eternal in the heavens. For in this we groan, earnestly desiring to be clothed upon with our house which is from heaven. . . . Therefore we are always confident, knowing that, while we are at home in the body, we are absent from the Lord.

2 CORINTHIANS 4:16–5:2, 6

He that sows to his sinful nature shall of the sinful nature reap corruption; but he who sows to the Spirit shall reap from the Spirit life everlasting.

GALATIANS 6:8

Concerning this salvation the prophets who prophesied of the grace that should come to you carefully searched and inquired, inquiring about what manner of time the Spirit of Christ which was in them indicated when it testified in advance the sufferings of Christ, and the glory that should follow.

I PETER 1:10–11

After you have suffered a little while, the God of all grace, who has called us to his eternal glory by Christ Jesus, will himself make you perfect, establish, strengthen, settle you.

I PETER 5:10–11

Love not the world, neither the things that are in the world. If any man love the world, the love of the Father is not in him. For all that is in the world, the cravings of the sinful nature, and the lust of the eyes, and the pride of life, is not of the Father, but is of the world. And the world passes away, and all its lusts, but he who does the will of God abides forever.

I JOHN 2:15–17

Beloved, now are we the sons of God, and it does not yet appear what we shall be, but we know that, when he shall appear, we shall be like him; for we shall see him as he is.

I JOHN 3:2

God has given to us eternal life, and this life is in his Son. He that has the Son has life, and he who has not the Son of God has not life. These things have I written to you that believe in the name of the Son of God, that you may know that you have eternal life, and that you may believe in the name of the Son of God.   I JOHN 5:11–14

I beheld a great multitude, which no man could count, from all nations and tribes and peoples and languages. They stood before the throne, and before the Lamb, clothed with white robes, with palm branches in their hands, and they cried with a loud voice, saying, "Salvation to our God who sits upon the throne, and to the Lamb." And all the angels stood round about the throne, and about the elders and the four beasts, and fell before the throne on their faces, and worshipped God, saying, "Amen: blessing, and glory, and wisdom, and thanksgiving, and honor, and power, and might, be to our God forever and ever. Amen." And one of the elders answered, saying to me, "Who are these that are arrayed in white robes? And whence came they?" And I said to him, "Sir, you know." And he said to me, "These are the ones who came out of great tribulation, and have washed their robes, and made them white in the blood of the Lamb. Therefore are they before the throne of God, and serve him day and night in his temple, and he who sits on the throne shall dwell among them. They shall hunger no more, neither thirst any more; neither shall the sun light on them, nor any heat. For the Lamb which is in the midst of the throne shall feed them, and shall lead them to living fountains of waters, and God shall wipe away all tears from their eyes."

REVELATION 7:9–17

I heard a great voice out of heaven saying, "Behold, the dwelling place of God is with men, and he will dwell with them, and they shall be his people, and God himself shall be with them, and be their God. And God shall wipe away all tears from their eyes, and there shall be no more death, neither sorrow, nor crying, neither shall there be any more pain, for the former things are passed away." And he who sat upon the throne said, "Behold, I make all things new. And he said to me: write, for these words are true and faithful."

REVELATION 21:3–5

See also Heaven, Hell, Jesus' Second Coming, Worldly Cares.

EVIL

Man, according to the Bible, was originally created in God's image, but it wasn't long before evil entered the picture, and we have been dealing with it ever since. Evil is universal, not limited to any particular individual, nation, group, or party. The Bible affirms that evil is never "out there" somewhere but rather that it is wherever man is. Even the best people are, at times, capable of doing bad things. So widespread is evil that mankind is in need of a divine Savior to restore a right relationship with God. Even better, the Bible promises that the world will finally, at the end, see the ultimate triumph of God over evil.

God saw that the wickedness of man was great in the earth, and that every inclination of the thoughts of his heart was continually evil. And the LORD was sorry that he had made man on the earth, and it grieved him to his heart. And the LORD said, "I will destroy man whom I have created from the face of the earth; both man, and beast, and the creeping thing, and the birds of the air; for I am sorry that I have made them." But Noah found grace in the eyes of the LORD.   GENESIS 6:5–8

The fear of the LORD, that is wisdom, and to depart from evil is understanding.
                                                              JOB 28:28

The wicked walk about freely when the vilest men are exalted.
                                                              PSALM 12:8

They are all gone astray, they are all together become filthy; there is no one that does good, no, not one.
                                                              PSALM 14:3

The face of the LORD is against those who do evil, to cut off the remembrance of them from the earth.
                                                              PSALM 34:16

Evil shall slay the wicked, and they that hate the righteous shall be desolate.
                                                              PSALM 34:21

I have seen the wicked in great power, and spreading himself like a green bay tree.   PSALM 37:35

You that love the LORD, hate evil. He preserves the souls of his saints; he delivers them out of the hand of the wicked.   PSALM 97:10

Let not an evil speaker be established in the earth; evil shall hunt the violent man to overthrow him.   PSALM 140:11

Incline not my heart to any evil thing, to practice wicked works with men that work iniquity.   PSALM 141:4

Their feet run to do evil, and make haste to shed blood.
                                                                                PROVERBS 1:16

The eyes of the LORD are in every place, beholding the evil and the good.
                                                                                PROVERBS 15:3

Be not envious of evil men, neither desire to be with them.
                                                                                PROVERBS 24:1

The heart of the sons of men is full of evil, and madness is in their heart while they live, and after that they go to the dead.
                                                                                ECCLESIASTES 9:3

All we like sheep have gone astray; we have turned every one to his own way.
                                                                                ISAIAH 53:6

There is no peace, says the LORD, for the wicked.   ISAIAH 48:22

The heart is deceitful above all things, and desperately wicked: who can understand it?   JEREMIAH 17:9

You have plowed wickedness, you have reaped iniquity; you have eaten the fruit of lies.   HOSEA 10:13

Seek good, and not evil, that you may live; and so the LORD, God Almighty, shall be with you, as you have spoken. Hate the evil, and love the good, and establish justice in the gate. AMOS 5:14–15

Woe to those who devise iniquity, and work evil upon their beds! When the morning is light, they practice it, because it is in the power of their hand.

MICAH 2:1

Every good tree brings forth good fruit; but a corrupt tree brings forth evil fruit. A good tree cannot bring forth evil fruit, neither can a corrupt tree bring forth good fruit. MATTHEW 7:17–18

O generation of vipers, how can you, being evil, speak good things? For out of the abundance of the heart the mouth speaks. MATTHEW 12:34

From within, out of the heart of men, proceed evil thoughts, adulteries, fornications, murders, thefts, covetousness, wickedness, deceit, debauchery, an evil eye, blasphemy, pride, foolishness. All these evil things come from within, and defile the man. MARK 7:21–23

A good man out of the good treasure of his heart brings forth that which is good, and an evil man out of the evil treasure of his heart brings forth that which is evil, for from the abundance of the heart his mouth speaks.

LUKE 6:45

This is the condemnation, that light is come into the world, and men loved darkness rather than light, because their deeds were evil. For everyone that does evil hates the light, neither comes to the light, lest his deeds should be reproved. JOHN 3:19–20

All have sinned, and come short of the glory of God. ROMANS 3:23

Be not overcome by evil, but overcome evil with good. ROMANS 12:21

Our Lord Jesus Christ gave himself for our sins, that he might deliver us from this present evil world, according to the will of God and our Father.

GALATIANS 1:3–4

We struggle not against flesh and blood, but against principalities, against powers, against the rulers of the darkness of this world, against spiritual wickedness in high places.   EPHESIANS 6:12

Abstain from all appearance of evil.   1 THESSALONIANS 5:22

The tongue can no man tame; it is an unruly evil, full of deadly poison.

JAMES 3:8

Beloved, follow not that which is evil, but that which is good. He that does good is of God, but he who does evil has not seen God.   1 JOHN 3:11

See also Sin and Redemption.

FAITH

Like love, *the word* faith *is so vague that it has lost virtually all its meaning. But the word, as the Bible uses it, is rich with meaning. The key idea is* holding to something with conviction and confidence. *What we are told to hold to is, of course, God, who is completely trustworthy and steadfast. By extension, by holding to something—or Someone, rather—who is so reliable, we become more reliable ourselves. In fact, faith means that in a world where nothing and no one seems 100 percent reliable, the only reliable One is God. So we put faith not in an idea or a set of beliefs, nor in a vague "faith in faith," but in a Person.*

Trust in the LORD with all your heart, and lean not on your own understanding.

PROVERBS 3:5

Truly I say to you, if you have faith like a grain of mustard seed, you shall say to this mountain, "Move from here to another place," and it shall move, and nothing shall be impossible for you.　　MATTHEW 17:20

Truly, truly, I say to you, he who believes in me, the works that I do he shall do also, and greater works than these shall he do; because I go to my Father. And whatever you shall ask in my name, that will I do, that the Father may be glorified in the Son. If you shall ask anything in my name, I will do it.

JOHN 14:12–14

Being justified by faith, we have peace with God through our Lord Jesus Christ, through whom also we have access to this grace in which we stand. And we rejoice in hope of the glory of God. And not only that, but we glory in sufferings also, knowing that suffering produces patience.

ROMANS 5:1–3

Welcome those who are weak in the faith, but not for the purpose of disputing.

ROMANS 14:1

Now abide faith, hope, charity, these three.

I CORINTHIANS 13:13

We walk by faith, not by sight. 2 CORINTHIANS 5:7

I am crucified with Christ: nevertheless I live; yet not I, but Christ lives in me. And the life which I now live in the flesh I live by the faith of the Son of God, who loved me, and gave himself for me. GALATIANS 2:20

You are all the children of God by faith in Christ Jesus. For as many of you as have been baptized into Christ have put on Christ.

GALATIANS 3:26–27

By grace are you saved through faith, and that not of yourselves: it is the gift of God—not of works, lest any man should boast. For we are his workman-ship, created in Christ Jesus for good works, which God has before ordained that we should walk in. EPHESIANS 2:8–10

Take up the shield of faith, with which you shall be able to quench all the fiery arrows of the wicked. And take the helmet of salvation, and the sword of the Spirit, which is the word of God. EPHESIANS 6:16–17

That Christ may dwell in your hearts by faith; that you, being rooted and grounded in love, may be able to comprehend with all saints what is the breadth, and length, and depth, and height, and to know the love of Christ, which surpasses knowledge, that you might be filled with all the fullness of God. EPHESIANS 3:17–19

Fight the good fight of faith, lay hold of eternal life.

I TIMOTHY 6:12

Faith is the substance of things hoped for, the evidence of things not seen. For by it our ancestors obtained approval. Through faith we understand that the worlds were formed by the word of God, so that things which are seen were not made of things which are visible. By faith Abel offered to God a more excellent sacrifice than Cain, by which he obtained evidence that he was righteous, God giving approval to his gifts. . . . Without faith it is impossible to please him, for he who comes to God must believe that he is, and that he rewards those who diligently seek him. By faith Noah, being warned of God of events not seen as yet, moved with fear, built an ark for the saving of his household; by this he condemned the world and became heir of the righteousness which is by faith. By faith Abraham obeyed when he was called to go out into a place which he should after-ward receive as an inheritance, and he set out, not knowing where he went. By faith he sojourned in the land of promise, as in a strange country, for he looked for a city which has foundations, whose builder and maker is God.

These all died in faith, not having received the promises, but having seen them far off, and were persuaded of them, and embraced them, and con-fessed that they were strangers and pilgrims on the earth. For they that say such things declare plainly that they seek a homeland. And truly, if they had been mindful of that country they had left behind, they might have had op-portunity to return. But they desire a better country, that is, a heavenly one. Therefore God is not ashamed to be called their God, for he has prepared for them a city.

HEBREWS 11:1–10, 13–16

What shall I more say? For the time would fail me to tell of Gideon, and of Barak, and of Samson, and of Jephthah; of David also, and Samuel, and of the prophets: who through faith subdued kingdoms, made righteousness, obtained promises, stopped the mouths of lions, quenched the violence of fire, escaped the edge of the sword, out of weakness were made strong, waxed valiant in fight, turned to flight the armies of the aliens. Women

> *"The greatest source of material for motion pictures is the Bible, and almost any chapter would serve as a basic idea for a motion picture."*
>
> —MOVIE DIRECTOR CECIL B. DEMILLE, FAMOUS FOR *The Ten Commandments*

received their dead raised to life again, and others were tortured, not accepting deliverance, that they might obtain a better resurrection. And others had trial of cruel mockings and floggings, even slavery and imprisonment. They were stoned, they were sawn asunder, were tempted, were destitute, afflicted, tormented—of them the world was not worthy. They wandered in deserts, and in mountains, and in dens and caves of the earth. And these all, having been commended for their faith, received not what was promised, since God had provided something better for us, so that they should not be made perfect apart from us.

Therefore, seeing we are surrounded by so great a cloud of witnesses, let us lay aside every weight, and the sin which does so easily beset us, and let us run with perseverance the race that is set before us, looking to Jesus, the author and finisher of our faith, who for the joy that was set before him endured the cross, disregarding its shame, and is set down at the right hand of the throne of God.   HEBREWS 11:32–12:2

My brethren, count it all joy when you fall into various temptations, knowing that the testing of your faith produces patience. But let patience have its full effect, so that you may be mature and complete, lacking nothing.   JAMES 1:2–4

What good is it, my brethren, when a man says he has faith but has no works? Can faith save him? If a brother or sister be naked and lacking daily food, and one of you says to them, "Depart in peace, be warmed and filled," and yet you give them not those things which are needful to the body, what is the good of that? Even so faith by itself, if it has no works, is dead. Yes, a man may say, "You have faith and I have works." Show me your faith without your works, and I will show you my faith by my works. You believe that there is one God; you do well: the devils also believe, and tremble. But will you know, O vain man, that faith without works is dead?   JAMES 2:14–20

Whatever is born of God overcomes the world, and this is the victory that overcomes the world, our faith.   I JOHN 5:4

See also God's Guidance, Hope, Trusting God.

FALSE TEACHINGS/HERESY

A browse through any bookstore reminds us that we are living in an age that is very spiritual—in a general way. But when we refer to someone as "religious" or "spiritual," just what do we mean? The words are now so vague that they are almost empty of meaning.

The Bible has a lot to say about "religious people"—and much of it is not good. It is possible to be very religious and yet to be far from God. Put another way, believing something strongly is not what pleases God. Believing in the true God and his teachings are what matter. Yes, this runs counter to our contemporary sense of tolerance, our desire not to offend anyone. But the Bible is pretty plain: Some beliefs are true, some are not. And it does matter what we believe, for we serve God with our minds. Words matter. Ideas matter. They matter because we base our lives on those words and ideas.

Whoever shall break one of these least commandments, and shall teach men to do so, he shall be called the least in the kingdom of heaven; but whoever shall do and teach them, the same shall be called great in the kingdom of heaven.   MATTHEW 5:19

Beware of false prophets, who come to you in sheep's clothing, but inwardly they are ravenous wolves. You shall know them by their fruits. Do men gather grapes from thorns, or figs from thistles? Even so, every good tree brings forth good fruit, but a corrupt tree brings forth bad fruit. A good tree cannot bring forth evil fruit, neither can a corrupt tree bring forth good fruit. Every tree that brings not forth good fruit is chopped down and cast into the fire. Therefore by their fruits you shall know them.   MATTHEW 7:15–20

Not everyone that says to me, "Lord, Lord," shall enter into the kingdom of heaven; but he who does the will of my Father who is in heaven.

MATTHEW 7:21

Jesus said to him, "You shall love the Lord your God with all your heart, and with all your soul, and with all your mind."   MATTHEW 22:37

Many false prophets shall rise, and shall deceive many. For there shall arise false Christs, and false prophets, and they shall show great signs and wonders, so much so that, if it were possible, they shall deceive the very elect.   MATTHEW 24:11, 24

Woe to you, when all men shall speak well of you, for so did their fathers to the false prophets.   LUKE 6:26

Jesus answered them, and said, "My doctrine is not mine, but his that sent me."   JOHN 7:16

Now I urge you, brethren, watch those who cause divisions and offenses contrary to the doctrine which you have learned, and avoid them.

ROMANS 16:17

Other foundation can no man lay than that which is laid, Jesus Christ.

I CORINTHIANS 3:11

When you come together in the church, I hear that there are divisions among you, and I partly believe it. For there must be heresies among you, so that they who are approved may be clearly seen among you.

I CORINTHIANS 11:18–19

Such are false apostles, deceitful workers, disguising themselves as the apostles of Christ. And no wonder, for Satan himself is disguised as an angel of light. Therefore it is no surprise if his ministers also be disguised as the ministers of righteousness. Their end shall be according to their works.

2 CORINTHIANS 11:13–15

As you have received Christ Jesus the Lord, so walk in him. . . . Beware lest any man spoil you through philosophy and empty deceit, according to the tradition of men, after the principles of the world, and not after Christ.

COLOSSIANS 2:6, 8

Since you are dead with Christ to the principles of the world, why, as though living in the world, are you subject to regulations—"Touch not, taste not, handle not"? All such regulations will perish with use and are merely human commandments and teachings. These things have indeed an appearance of wisdom in promoting self-imposed worship, false humility, and severe treatment of the body, but are of no value in controlling self-indulgence.

COLOSSIANS 2:20–23

The Spirit speaks clearly that in the last times some shall depart from the faith, giving heed to deceitful spirits and doctrines of devils, through the hypocrisy of liars whose consciences are seared with a hot iron. They will forbid people to marry, and command them to abstain from certain foods, which God has created to be received with thanksgiving by them which believe and know the truth.

I TIMOTHY 4:1–4

If any man teach otherwise and does not agree with the sound teachings of our Lord Jesus Christ, and to the doctrine which is according to godliness, he is conceited, knowing nothing, but craves controversy and quarrels over words. From these come envy, strife, slander, evil suspicions, perverse disputes of men of corrupt minds, lacking the truth, supposing that godliness is a means of gain. From such people withdraw yourself.

I TIMOTHY 6:3—5

Evil men and seducers shall grow worse and worse, deceiving, and being deceived.

2 TIMOTHY 3:13

The time will come when they will not endure sound doctrine; but, having itching ears, they will gather for themselves teachers to suit their own desires, and they shall turn away their ears from the truth, and shall be turned to myths.

2 TIMOTHY 4:3—4

Be not carried about with various and strange teachings. For it is a good thing that the heart be established with grace; not with regulations about foods, which are of no benefit.

HEBREWS 13:9

There shall be false teachers among you, who secretly shall bring in destructive heresies, even denying the Lord that bought them, and bring upon themselves swift destruction. And many shall follow their shameful ways; by reason of them the way of truth shall be evil spoken of. And through their greed shall they exploit you with deceptive words. Their judgment, pronounced on them long ago, hangs over them, and their damnation slumbers not. For God spared not the angels that sinned, but cast them down to hell, and delivered them into chains of darkness, to be reserved for judgment; and he spared not the old world, but saved Noah, a preacher of righteousness, bringing the flood upon the world of the ungodly.

2 PETER 2:1—5

These, like brute beasts, made to be taken and destroyed, speak evil of the things they do not understand. They shall utterly perish in their own corruption, and shall receive the reward of unrighteousness, as they that count it pleasure to carouse in broad daylight. They are blots and blemishes, reveling in their immoral pleasures while they feast with you. They have eyes full of adultery, and they cannot cease from sin. They entice unstable souls. They have hearts trained in greed. Accursed children! They have forsaken the right way, and are gone astray. . . . They are wells without water, clouds blown along by a storm, for whom deepest darkness is reserved forever. When they speak empty and boastful words, they entice through the

> *The common phrase "wolf in sheep's clothing" is from Matthew 7:15. Jesus was describing false prophets as those who appear good and innocent on the outside but who are "ravenous wolves" on the inside.*

immoral lusts of the sinful nature those who have just escaped from those who live in error. While they promise them liberty, they themselves are the slaves of corruption. For a man is a slave to whatever has mastered him.

2 PETER 2:12–19

Beloved, believe not every spirit, but test the spirits whether they are from God, because many false prophets have gone out into the world. Here is how you know the Spirit of God: every spirit that confesses that Jesus Christ is come in the flesh is of God. And every spirit that confesses not that Jesus Christ is come in the flesh is not of God. This is that spirit of antichrist, of which you have heard that it is coming, and even now already is in the world. You are of God, little children, and have overcome them: because greater is he who is in you, than he who is in the world. They are of the world: therefore what they say is from the world, and the world hears them. We are of God; he who knows God hears us; he who is not of God hears not us. From this we know the spirit of truth and the spirit of error.   1 JOHN 4:1–6

See also Wisdom and Discernment.

FEAR

The Bible tells us many times to "fear God." That doesn't set well with many people since we prefer to think of God as "approachable" and "user friendly." But let's face it: The Creator and Ruler of the universe must be pretty awesome. So fear—knowing that he rules, knowing that he can reward and punish us—is a sensible response. The flip side of this is that God is approachable, a loving Father who cares so much for us that he can take away our fears of whatever it is that plagues us. In other words, if we fear (and love) God, we need fear nothing else. It seems like a good deal, all in all.

The Bible shows how people of faith were often persecuted, even suffering martyrdom. Yet it is amazing how bold some of them were. How so? Because they truly believed that God was greater than any foe they might face, even if that foe caused their death.

Yes, though I walk through the valley of the shadow of death, I will fear no evil, for you are with me; your rod and your staff they comfort me. You prepare a table before me in the presence of mine enemies: you anoint my head with oil; my cup runs over. PSALM 23:4–5

The LORD is my light and my salvation; whom shall I fear? The LORD is the strength of my life; of whom shall I be afraid? When the wicked, even my enemies and my foes, came upon me to devour me, they stumbled and fell. Though an army should encamp against me, my heart shall not fear: though war should rise against me, in this will I be confident. PSALM 27:1–3

Fret not yourself because of evildoers, neither be envious of the workers of iniquity. PSALM 37:1

God is our refuge and strength, a very present help in trouble. Therefore will we not fear, though the earth be moved, and though the mountains be toppled into the depths of the sea; though the waters rage and foam, and though the mountains tremble at its tumult.

There is a river whose streams make glad the city of God, the holy habitation of the Most High. God is in the midst of her; she shall not be overthrown; God shall help her at the break of day. PSALM 46:1–5

He shall cover you with his feathers, and under his wings shall you trust. His truth shall be your shield and protection. You shall not be afraid for the terror by night, nor for the arrow that flies by day, nor for the sickness that stalks in the darkness, nor for the destruction that wastes at noonday.

PSALM 91:4–6

As the heaven is high above the earth, so great is his mercy toward them that fear him. Like a father pities his children, so the LORD pities them that fear him.   PSALM 103:11, 13

The LORD is on my side; I will not fear; what can man do unto me?
                                                                    PSALM 118:6

Keep sound wisdom and discretion: they shall be life to your soul, an ornament to grace your neck. Then shall you walk in your way safely, and your foot shall not stumble. When you lie down, you shall not be afraid; yes, you shall lie down, and your sleep shall be sweet.   PROVERBS 3:21–24

The fear of man brings a snare, but whoever puts his trust in the LORD shall be safe.   PROVERBS 29:25

Do not call a conspiracy all that this people calls conspiracy; do not fear what it fears, nor be in dread. But the LORD Almighty, him you shall regard as holy, him alone shall you fear and dread.   ISAIAH 8:12–13

I the LORD your God will hold your right hand, saying to you, "Fear not; I will help you."   ISAIAH 41:13

Thus says the LORD that created you, O Jacob, and he who formed you, O Israel, Fear not, for I have redeemed you, I have called you by your name; you are mine. When you pass through the waters, I will be with you, and through the rivers, they shall not overflow you. When you walk through the fire, you shall not be burned, neither shall the flame consume you. For I am the LORD your God, the Holy One of Israel, your Savior.   ISAIAH 43:1–3

The redeemed of the LORD shall return, and come with singing to Zion, and everlasting joy shall be upon their head. They shall obtain gladness and joy, and sorrow and mourning shall flee away. I, even I, am he who comforts you. Who are you, that you should be afraid of a man that shall die, and of the son of man who shall be made as grass?   ISAIAH 51:11–12

Do you fear bugs? Coverdale's English translation of the Bible, published in 1535, has this for Psalm 91:5: "Thou shalt not need to be afraid for any bugs by night." The King James Version puts it this way: "You will not fear the terror of night." Some book collectors refer to Coverdale's Bible as the "Bug Bible."

Fear not them which kill the body, but are not able to kill the soul; but rather fear him which is able to destroy both soul and body in hell.

MATTHEW 10:28

Fear not, little flock; for it is your Father's good pleasure to give you the kingdom.   LUKE 12:32

Peace I leave with you, my peace I give to you: not as the world gives, give I to you. Let not your heart be troubled, neither let it be afraid.

JOHN 14:27

You have not received the spirit of slavery to fall again into fear, but you have received the Spirit of adoption. When we cry, "Abba, Father," the Spirit itself bears witness with our spirit, that we are the children of God. And if children, then heirs, heirs of God and joint heirs with Christ—if we suffer with him so that we may be also glorified with him.   ROMANS 8:15–17

In all these things we are more than conquerors through him that loved us. For I am persuaded, that neither death, nor life, nor angels, nor principalities, nor powers, nor things present, nor things to come, nor height, nor depth, nor any other creature, shall be able to separate us from the love of God, which is in Christ Jesus our Lord.   ROMANS 8:37–39

We have boldness and access with confidence by the faith of him.

EPHESIANS 3:12

God has not given us the spirit of fear, but of power, and of love, and of a sound mind.

2 TIMOTHY 1:6–7

There is no fear in love, but perfect love casts out fear; because fear has to do with punishment. He that fears is not made perfect in love.

1 JOHN 4:18

Fear none of those things which you shall suffer. Behold, the devil shall cast some of you into prison, that you may be tried, and you shall have tribulation ten days: be faithful unto death, and I will give you a crown of life.

REVELATION 2:10

See also Contentment, Hope, Worry.

FELLOWSHIP WITH GOD

We talk a lot about "relationships," so the older word fellowship *seems a bit quaint. But it is also a richer word than* relationship *because fellowship involves deep sharing, intimacy, a common purpose, and (of course) a joy in one another's company. The Bible presents us with the Almighty God, Creator and Ruler of all things, magnificent, and awesome—and yet this same Almighty One desires fellowship with what he has created. Difficult as it is to grasp, each individual human being is called to fellowship with the One who made us all.*

I will walk among you, and will be your God, and you shall be my people.

LEVITICUS 26:12

The name of the city from that day shall be, "The LORD Is There."

EZEKIEL 48:35

Behold, a virgin shall be with child, and shall bring forth a son, and they shall call his name "Immanuel," which being interpreted is, "God with us."

MATTHEW 1:23

Where two or three are gathered together in my name, there am I in the midst of them. MATTHEW 18:20

Jesus answered and said to him, "If a man loves me, he will keep my words, and my Father will love him, and we will come to him, and make our abode with him." JOHN 14:23

Abide in me, and I in you. As the branch cannot bear fruit by itself, except it abide in the vine, no more can you, except you abide in me. I am the vine, you are the branches; he who abides in me, and I in him, the same brings forth much fruit, for without me you can do nothing. If you abide in me, and my words abide in you, you shall ask what you will, and it shall be done to you. JOHN 15:4–5, 7

As you, Father, are in me, and I in you, may they also be in us, so that the world may believe that you have sent me. And the glory which you gave me I have given them, so that they may be one, even as we are one. I in them, and you in me, that they may be made completely one, so that the world may know that you have sent me, and have loved them as you have loved me. Father, I desire that they also, whom you have given to me, be with me where I am, to behold my glory, which you have given me, for you loved me before the foundation of the world. O righteous Father, the world has not known you, but I have known you, and have known these that you have sent me. And I have declared to them your name, and will declare it, so that the love with which you have loved me may be in them, and I in them.

JOHN 17:21–26

If Christ is in you, the body is dead because of sin; but the Spirit is life because of righteousness. And if children, then heirs; heirs of God and joint heirs with Christ, if we suffer with him so that we may be also glorified with him. ROMANS 8:10, 17

We declare to you what we have seen and heard so that you also may have fellowship with us, and truly our fellowship is with the Father, and with his Son Jesus Christ. This then is the message which we have heard from him,

---

Does God Have Fingers?

God, according to the Bible, is an invisible spirit. But the Bible speaks—figuratively—of God's body parts. One example: Exodus 31:18 states that the Ten Commandments were given to Moses on stone tablets, "written with the finger of God." So the mysterious "fiery finger" in the movie The Ten Commandments *is not as farfetched as it appears.*

---

and declare to you, that God is light, and in him is no darkness at all. If we say that we have fellowship with him, and walk in darkness, we lie, and do not the truth. But if we walk in the light, as he is in the light, we have fellowship with one another, and the blood of Jesus Christ his Son cleanses us from all sin. 1 JOHN 1:3, 5–7

He that keeps his [Christ's] commandments dwells in him, and he in him. And hereby we know that he abides in us, by the Spirit which he has given us. 1 JOHN 3:24

Whoever transgresses, and continues not in the doctrine of Christ, has not God. He that continues in the doctrine of Christ, he has both the Father and the Son. 2 JOHN 9

Behold, I stand at the door, and knock; if any man hears my voice and opens the door, I will come in to him, and will dine with him, and he with me. REVELATION 3:20

See also Eternal Life, Heaven, Loneliness, Prayer.

FELLOWSHIP WITH OTHER BELIEVERS

The word church *immediately makes us think of a building, but that isn't what the word means in the Bible, for in those days fellowships of believers met in homes, not in special "church" buildings. The "church" in the New Testament meant "assembly" or "gathering" of the faithful, wherever they might be. This fellowship was too vital, too dynamic to be tied to any building, for it was a* living *fellowship, not a building of stone or brick.*

The New Testament church had its problems, and these are not glossed over in the New Testament. We may feel—should feel—a kinship with all other believers, but the fact is that, as human beings, we do not always get along. The New Testament is blunt in depicting the conflicts of the early believers. They had their problems, but they also had the promise that they could all look forward to having a fuller, more complete fellowship in heaven.

There shall be one fold, and one shepherd. JOHN 10:16

They continued steadfastly in the apostles' teaching and fellowship, and in breaking of bread, and in prayers. And awe came upon every soul, and many wonders and signs were done by the apostles. And all that believed were together, and had all things common. They sold their possessions and goods, and divided the proceeds among all, according to each man's need. And they, continuing daily in the temple, and breaking bread from house to house, did eat their food with gladness and singleness of heart, praising God, and having the good will of all the people. And the Lord added to the church daily those who were saved. ACTS 2:42—47

The multitude of those who believed were of one heart and one soul, and no one claimed private ownership of his own possessions, but they had all things in common. And with great power the apostles witnessed to the resurrection of the Lord Jesus, and great grace was upon them all. There was not any needy among them, for as many as were possessors of lands or houses sold them and brought the proceeds of the things that were sold, and laid them down at the apostles' feet, and it was distributed to every man according as he had need. ACTS 4:32—35

As we have many members in one body, and all members have not the same function, so we, being many, are one body in Christ, and all are members of one another. We have gifts differing according to the grace that is given to us: prophecy, in proportion to faith; ministry, in ministering; the teacher, in teaching; the exhorter, in exhortation; the giver, in generosity; the leader, in diligence; the compassionate, in cheerfulness.   ROMANS 12:4–8

Let love be genuine. Abhor what is evil; hold fast to what is good. Be kindly affectioned to one another with brotherly love. Honor one another above yourselves. Rejoice with those who rejoice, and weep with those who weep. Be of the same mind one toward another. Do not be haughty, but be willing to associate with men of low estate. Be not wise in your own conceit.

ROMANS 12:9–10, 15–16

Why do you judge your brother? Or why do you look down on your brother? For we shall all stand before the judgment seat of Christ. So let us not judge one another any more, but rather resolve that no man put a stumblingblock or a hindrance in his brother's way.   ROMANS 14:10, 13

Now I appeal to you, brethren, in the name of our Lord Jesus Christ, that you all agree together, and that there be no divisions among you; but that you are perfectly united together in the same mind and in the same purpose.

1 CORINTHIANS 1:10

The cup of blessing which we bless, is it not the communion of the blood of Christ? The bread which we break, is it not the communion of the body of Christ? For we being many are one bread, and one body, for we are all partakers of that one bread.   1 CORINTHIANS 10:16–17

When you come together in the church, I hear that there are divisions among you, and I partly believe it. For there must be also heresies among you so that those who are genuine may be clearly seen among you.

1 CORINTHIANS 11:18–19

Brethren, if a man is caught in a sin, you who are spiritual should restore him in the spirit of meekness. But take care, lest you also be tempted. Bear

The New Testament is a Christian book, but the word Christian *appears only three times. Its first appearance is in the Book of Acts: "The disciples were called Christians first at Antioch" (Acts 11:26).*

you one another's burdens, and so fulfill the law of Christ. For if a man think himself to be something, when he is nothing, he deceives himself.

GALATIANS 6:1–3

As we have opportunity, let us do good to all men, especially to them who are of the household of faith.   GALATIANS 6:10

You are no longer strangers and foreigners, but fellow citizens with the saints, and of the household of God.   EPHESIANS 2:19

Christ is before all things, and in him all things hold together. And he is the head of the body, the church; he is the beginning, the firstborn from the dead, so that in all things he might have first place.

COLOSSIANS 1:17–18

Do not forsake the assembling of yourselves together, as the manner of some is, but encourage one another.   HEBREWS 10:25

What good is it, my brethren, when a man says he has faith but has no works? Can faith save him? If a brother or sister be naked and lacking daily food, and one of you says to them, "Depart in peace, be warmed and filled," and yet you give them not those things which are needful to the body, what is the good of that? Even so faith by itself, if it has no works, is dead. Yes, a man may say, "You have faith and I have works." Show me your faith without your works, and I will show you my faith by my works. You believe that there is one God; you do well: the devils also believe, and tremble. But will you know, O vain man, that faith without works is dead?

JAMES 2:14–20

Love the brotherhood. Fear God. I PETER 2:17

That which we have seen and heard we declare to you so that you also may have fellowship with us; and truly our fellowship is with the Father, and with his Son Jesus Christ. I JOHN 1:3

If we walk in the light, as he is in the light, we have fellowship with one another, and the blood of Jesus Christ his Son cleanses us from all sin.

I JOHN 1:7

He that says he is in the light, and hates his brother, is in darkness even now. He that loves his brother dwells in the light, and there is no occasion of stumbling in him. But he who hates his brother is in darkness, and walks in darkness, and knows not where he goes, because that darkness has blinded his eyes. I JOHN 2:9–11

We know that we have passed from death to life, because we love the brethren. He that loves not his brother abides in death. I JOHN 3:14

See also Bad Company, Fellowship with God, Friends, Loneliness, Temptation.

FLATTERY

Two basic things about human nature: 1. No one believes that he or she is susceptible to flattery. 2. Most people are. The Bible's main beef against flattery is that it is dishonest, being the use of praise when it isn't due. This can sometimes be harmless, yet it can do great harm, especially when someone with authority is praised for acts that should be condemned. People of faith have this commandment from the Bible: Seek to please God, not to please people with flattery.

Everyone speaks falsely with his neighbor: with flattering lips they speak from a double heart. The LORD shall cut off all flattering lips, and the tongue that speaks proud things.   PSALM 12:2–3

The poor is hated even by his own neighbor, but the rich has many friends.
                                                               PROVERBS 14:20

He that goes about as a talebearer reveals secrets: therefore associate not with him that flatters with his lips.   PROVERBS 20:19

He that says to the wicked, "You are righteous," him shall the people curse; nations shall abhor him.   PROVERBS 24:24

A lying tongue hates those that are afflicted by it, and a flattering mouth works ruin.   PROVERBS 26:28

A man that flatters his neighbor spreads a net for his feet.
                                                               PROVERBS 29:5

Woe to you, when all men shall speak well of you, for so did their fathers to the false prophets.   LUKE 6:26

Among the chief rulers many believed in him [Jesus]; but because of the Pharisees they did not confess him, lest they should be put out of the synagogue. For they loved the praise of men more than the praise of God.
                                                               JOHN 12:42–43

Do I now persuade men, or God? Or do I seek to please men? For if I pleased men, I should not be the servant of Christ.   GALATIANS 1:10

We speak not to please men, but to please God, who tests our hearts.
                                                     1 THESSALONIANS 2:4

FOOD

The Old Testament contains the well-known laws of kosher, but the New Testament has a whole new perspective on food: Everything is permissible, as long as we live for the glory of God. Yet our culture today is obsessed with food, not from religious motivations but out of the neurotic fear of harming the body and shortening one's life span. While the Bible tells us to take care of our earthly bodies, it condemns fanaticism over food. Just as we are not to make an idol of our own bodies, we are not to make a life-dominating religion out of what we eat and drink.

Go your way, eat your bread with joy, and drink your wine with a merry heart.   ECCLESIASTES 9:7

[Jesus:] "Do you not understand that whatever enters into a man from outside cannot defile him; because it enters not into his heart, but into the belly, and then out of his body?" (Thus he declared all foods clean.) And he said, "It is what comes out of the man that defiles the man. For from within, out of the heart of men, proceed evil thoughts, adulteries, fornications, murders, . . . pride, foolishness. All these evil things come from within and defile the man."   MARK 7:18–20

I know, and am persuaded by the Lord Jesus, that there is nothing unclean in itself; but to him that believes any thing to be unclean, to him it is unclean. For the kingdom of God is not food and drink, but righteousness and peace, and joy in the Holy Spirit.   ROMANS 14:14, 17

Whether you eat or drink, or whatever you do, do all to the glory of God.
                                                      I CORINTHIANS 10:30–31

Let no man judge you in food, or in drink, or in observing of a holy day, new moon festivals, or sabbaths. These are only a shadow of things to come, but the substance belongs to Christ. Let no man disqualify you, insisting on self-abasement and worshipping angels, dwelling on things which he has not seen, vainly puffed up by his unspiritual mind, and not connected to the

Our familiar phrase "Eat, drink, and be merry" is from the Bible:
"A man hath no better thing under the sun, than to eat, and to drink, and to be merry" (Ecclesiastes 8:15).
And also:
"Take thine ease, eat, drink, and be merry" (Luke 12:19).

Head, from which all the body grows with the growth that is from God. Since with Christ you died to the principles of the world, why, as though living in the world, do you submit to regulations—"Touch not, taste not, handle not"? All these refer to things that perish with use. They are the commandments and teachings of men. These things have an appearance of wisdom in their self-imposed worship, false humility, and severe treatment of the body, but are of no value in controlling physical passions.

COLOSSIANS 2:16–23

The Spirit speaks clearly that in the last times some shall depart from the faith, giving heed to deceitful spirits and teachings of devils, through the hypocrisy of liars whose consciences are seared with a hot iron. They will forbid people to marry, and command them to abstain from foods, which God has created to be received with thanksgiving by them which believe and know the truth. For every creature of God is good, and nothing to be refused, if it is received with thanksgiving, for it is sanctified by the word of God and prayer.

I TIMOTHY 4:1–5

To the pure all things are pure; but to those who are defiled and unbelieving, nothing is pure; but even their mind and conscience is defiled.

TITUS 1:15

Every good gift and every perfect gift is from above, and comes down from the Father of lights.

JAMES 1:17

See also The Body, Worldly Cares, Worry.

FORGIVENESS

Forgiveness is a divine thing, and also a human thing, for animals cannot forgive their enemies. Humans can, and the Bible repeatedly tells us to do so, just as it tells us again and again of God's forgiveness of us. It presents forgiveness as a kind of "trickle down" process: God forgives our failings, so we in turn forgive others. In a sense, every time we forgive someone, we reflect the image of God in us.

This is not easy. It is especially difficult for the innocent person who has been severely wronged to forgive the perpetrator. Yet the Bible gives us examples—most notably Jesus himself—of innocent people who showed mercy to their enemies.

The discretion of a man defers his anger, and it is his glory to overlook a transgression. PROVERBS 19:11

Do not say, "I will recompense evil," but wait on the LORD, and he shall save you. PROVERBS 20:22

Blessed are the merciful, for they shall obtain mercy. MATTHEW 5:7

I say to you, resist not evil, but whoever shall strike you on your right cheek, turn to him the other also. And if any man sue you at the law, and take away your coat, let him have your cloak also. And whoever shall compel you to go a mile, go with him two. Give to him that asks you, and turn not away from him that would borrow from you.

You have heard that it has been said, "You shall love your neighbor, and hate your enemy." But I say to you, love your enemies, bless those who curse you, do good to those who hate you, and pray for those who spitefully use you and persecute you; that you may be the children of your Father who is in heaven. For he makes his sun to rise on the evil and on the good, and sends rain on the just and on the unjust. For if you love those who love you, what reward have you? MATTHEW 5:39–46

If you forgive men their trespasses, your heavenly Father will also forgive you. But if you forgive not men their trespasses, neither will your Father forgive your trespasses. MATTHEW 6:14–15

Then came Peter to him, and said, "Lord, if my brother sins against me, how many times should I forgive him? As many as seven times?" Jesus said to him, "I say to you, not seven times, but seventy times seven."

MATTHEW 18:21–22

When you stand praying, forgive, if you have anything against anyone, so that your Father who is in heaven may forgive you your trespasses.

MARK 11:25–26

Love your enemies, and do good; and lend, hoping for nothing in return. And your reward shall be great, and you shall be the children of the Highest, for he is kind to the ungrateful and to the evil. Be therefore merciful, as your Father also is merciful.

LUKE 6:35–36

Be on your guard: If your brother sins against you, rebuke him, and if he repents, forgive him. And if he sins against you seven times in a day, and seven times in a day turns again to you, saying, "I repent," you shall forgive him.

LUKE 17:3–4

Then said Jesus [on the cross], "Father, forgive them, for they know not what they do."

LUKE 23:34

Bless those who persecute you: bless, and curse not.

ROMANS 12:14

Repay no man evil for evil. Dearly beloved, avenge not yourselves, but rather leave room for the wrath of God, for it is written, "'Vengeance is mine; I will repay,' says the Lord." Therefore if your enemy hungers, feed him; if he thirsts, give him drink, for in so doing you shall heap coals of fire on his head. Be not overcome by evil, but overcome evil with good.

ROMANS 12:19–21

Bear with one another, and forgive one another, if any man has a quarrel against another; just as Christ forgave you, so also you must forgive.

COLOSSIANS 3:13

Let all bitterness and wrath and anger and brawling and evil speaking be put away from you, along with all malice. And be kind one to another, tenderhearted, forgiving one another, even as God for Christ's sake has forgiven you.   EPHESIANS 4:31–32

Be united in spirit, having compassion for one another; love as brethren, be tenderhearted, be courteous, not repaying evil for evil, or abuse for abuse, but, on the contrary, blessing, knowing that you are called so that you should inherit a blessing.   1 PETER 3:8–9

See also Anger, Enemies, Mercy, Revenge.

FREEDOM

We think of freedom as having no strings, no boundaries—in other words, do whatever you like. The Bible saw freedom in a more concrete way: to be set free from slavery. So many people in biblical days were slaves—some temporarily, some permanently. Being free meant "no longer a slave," not "free to lead a wild and selfish life."

Of course, there are different types of slavery. One can be not only a slave to a cruel human master but also a slave to peer pressure, to one's possessions, and even to one's own passions and desires. The promise to God's people is that we need not be a slave to such things. In fact, a key message of the New Testament is that we can be set free from the one thing that enslaves all human beings: sin. So freedom can mean "free to do the right thing, free to please God."

Proclaim liberty throughout all the land to all the inhabitants thereof.
                                             LEVITICUS 25:10
[This verse is inscribed on the Liberty Bell in Philadelphia.]

I called upon the LORD in distress; the Lord answered me, and set me free.

PSALM 118:5

[Jesus:] "Come to me, all you that labor and are heavy laden, and I will give you rest. Take my yoke upon you, and learn from me; for I am gentle and lowly in heart, and you shall find rest for your souls. For my yoke is easy, and my burden is light." MATTHEW 11:28–30

The Spirit of the Lord is upon me, because he has anointed me to preach the gospel to the poor; he has sent me to heal the brokenhearted, to preach deliverance to the captives, and recovering of sight to the blind, to set at liberty those who are oppressed. LUKE 4:18

You shall know the truth, and the truth shall make you free. JOHN 8:32

If the Son shall make you free, you shall be free indeed. JOHN 8:36

We are justified freely by his grace through the redemption that came through in Christ Jesus. ROMANS 3:24

We are buried with him by baptism into death, so that just as Christ was raised from the dead by the glory of the Father, so we too should walk in newness of life. For if we have been united with him in a death like his, we shall be also united with him in a resurrection like his. We know that our old man is crucified with him, so that the body of sin might be destroyed, and afterward we should not serve sin. For he who is dead is freed from sin. Now if we be dead with Christ, we believe that we shall also live with him.

ROMANS 6:4–8

Being made free from sin, you became the servants of righteousness. But now being made free from sin and made servants of God, you have your fruit of holiness, and the end is everlasting life. ROMANS 6:18, 22

I delight in the law of God in my inward man, but I see another law in my members, warring against the law of my mind, and bringing me into captivity to the law of sin which is in my members. O wretched man that I am! Who

shall deliver me from the body of this death? I thank God through Jesus
Christ our Lord.   ROMANS 7:22–25

The creation waits in eager expectation for the revealing of the sons of God.
For the creation was subject to futility, not of its own will, but by the will of
him who subjected it, in that the creation itself shall be set free from the
bondage to corruption into the glorious liberty of the children of God.

ROMANS 8:19–21

Though I be free from all men, yet have I made myself servant to all so that I
might gain more.   I CORINTHIANS 9:19

Where the Spirit of the Lord is, there is liberty.   2 CORINTHIANS 3:17

Stand fast in the liberty in which Christ has made us free, and be not entan-
gled again with the yoke of bondage.   GALATIANS 5:1

Brethren, you have been called to liberty; only use not liberty to indulge the
sinful nature; rather, with love serve one another. For all the law is fulfilled
in one word, "You shall love your neighbor as yourself."

GALATIANS 5:13–14

As you have therefore received Christ Jesus the Lord, so walk in him.

COLOSSIANS 2:6

Since you are dead with Christ to the principles of the world, why, as though
living in the world, are you subject to regulations—"Touch not, taste not,
handle not"? All such regulations will perish with use and are merely human
commandments and teachings. These things have indeed an appearance of
wisdom in promoting self-imposed worship, false humility, and severe treatment of the body, but are of no value in controlling self-indulgence.

COLOSSIANS 2:20–23

Whoever looks into the perfect law of liberty, and persevere in it, being not
a hearer who forgets but a doer who acts, this man shall be blessed in what
he does.   JAMES 1:25

> "It is impossible mentally or socially to enslave a Bible-reading people."
>
> —AMERICAN JOURNALIST HORACE GREELEY
> (FAMOUS FOR SUPPOSEDLY COINING THE PHRASE "GO WEST, YOUNG MAN.")

So speak and act as they that shall be judged by the law of liberty.

JAMES 2:12

This is the will of God, that by doing right you may silence the ignorance of foolish men. As free men, do not use your liberty as a cover for wickedness, but live as the servants of God. Honor all men. Love the brotherhood. Fear God. Honor the king.   1 PETER 2:15–17

When they [false teachers] speak empty and boastful words, they entice through the immoral lusts of the sinful nature those who have just escaped from those who live in error. While they promise them liberty, they themselves are the slaves of corruption. For a man is a slave to whatever has mastered him.   2 PETER 2:19

See also Contentment, Sin and Redemption, Temptation, Worldly Cares, Worry.

FRIENDS

The great English author Samuel Johnson was opinionated and cranky at times, yet he had many loyal friends, and he valued them all highly. He wrote, "A man should keep his friendships in constant repair." Johnson, an aging widower, treasured the company of people who were more than just pleasant companions but were also "friends in need." The Bible also places a high value on such people, just as it criticizes "fair-weather friends."

Two of the most famous friendships in history are beautifully recorded in the Bible—that between the warriors David and Jonathan and that between Ruth and her mother-in-law, Naomi.

The soul of Jonathan was united with the soul of David, and Jonathan loved him as his own soul. . . . Then Jonathan and David made a covenant, because he loved him as his own soul. And Jonathan took off his own robe and gave it to David, along with his garments, even his sword and his bow.

I SAMUEL 18:1–4

She [Naomi] said, "Behold, your sister-in-law has gone back to her people, and to her gods: return you after your sister-in-law." And Ruth said, "Entreat me not to leave you, or to return from following after you; for wherever you go, I will go, and where you lodge, I will lodge. Your people shall be my people, and your God my God. Where you die, I will die, and there will I be buried. The LORD deal with me severely if anything but death separates you and me." RUTH 1:15–17

A hypocrite with his mouth destroys his neighbor, but through knowledge shall the just be delivered. PROVERBS 11:9

The poor is hated even by his own neighbor, but the rich has many friends.

PROVERBS 14:20

A perverse man sows strife, and a gossip separates close friends.

PROVERBS 16:28

He that forgives a transgression promotes love, but he who repeats a matter separates true friends. PROVERBS 17:9

A friend loves at all times, and a brother is born for adversity.

PROVERBS 17:17

A man that has friends must show himself friendly, and there is a friend that sticks closer than a brother. PROVERBS 18:24

Most men will proclaim their own goodness, but a faithful man who can find?   PROVERBS 20:6

Make no friendship with an angry man, and with a furious man you shall not go, lest you learn his ways, and set a snare for your soul.

PROVERBS 22:24–25

Withdraw your foot from your neighbor's house, lest he grow weary of you and so hate you.   PROVERBS 25:17

As a mad man who shoots firebrands, arrows, and death, so is the man who deceives his neighbor and says, "I am only joking."

PROVERBS 26:18–19

Faithful are the wounds of a friend; but the kisses of an enemy are deceitful.

PROVERBS 27:6

Two are better than one; because they have a good reward for their labor. For if they fall, the one will lift up his fellow, but woe to him that is alone when he falls; for he has not another to help him up. Again, if two lie together, then they have heat, but how can one be warm alone? And though one may overpower another, yet two shall withstand him; and a threefold cord is not easily broken.   ECCLESIASTES 4:9–12

This is my commandment, that you love one another, as I have loved you. Greater love has no man than this, that a man lay down his life for his friends. You are my friends if you do whatever I command you. Henceforth I call you not servants, for the servant knows not what his Lord does. But I have called you friends; for all things that I have heard from my Father I have made known to you.   JOHN 15:12–15

Regarding brotherly love, you need not that I write to you, for you yourselves are taught by God to love one another. And indeed you do it toward all the brethren which are in all Macedonia, but we appeal to you, brethren, that you increase more and more.   I THESSALONIANS 4:9–10

Let us consider how to provoke one another to love and good works, not forsaking the assembling of ourselves together, as the habit of some is, but encouraging one another, and so much the more, as you see the day approaching.   HEBREWS 10:24–25

What good is it, my brethren, when a man says he has faith but has no works? Can faith save him? If a brother or sister be naked and lacking daily food, and one of you says to them, "Depart in peace, be warmed and filled," and yet you give them not those things which are needful to the body, what is the good of that? Even so faith by itself, if it has no works, is dead. Yes, a man may say, "You have faith and I have works." Show me your faith without your works, and I will show you my faith by my works. You believe that there is one God; you do well: the devils also believe, and tremble. But will you know, O vain man, that faith without works is dead?

                                                                  JAMES 2:14–20

Grumble not against one another, brethren, lest you be condemned. Behold, the Judge stands before the door.   JAMES 5:9

Brethren, if any of you errs from the truth, and someone bring him back, know this: that he who converts the sinner from the error of his way shall save a soul from death, and shall hide a multitude of sins.

                                                                  JAMES 5:19–20

Be all of one mind, having compassion for one another; love as brethren, be tenderhearted, be courteous: not rendering evil for evil, or abuse for abuse, but, on the contrary, blessing; knowing that you are called so that you should inherit a blessing.   I PETER 3:8–9

This is how we know the love of God, because he laid down his life for us, and we ought to lay down our lives for the brethren.   I JOHN 3:16

See also Bad Company, Fellowship with God, Fellowship with Other Believers, Loneliness, Trendiness.

FRUSTRATION

Living in the "instant" age, we have a low tolerance for anything that takes too much time. Naturally we become easily frustrated. The Bible takes the eternal view of things, so it values patience very highly. It also emphasizes the importance of turning over all our cares and worries to God, who is bigger than them all. If we are frustrated because we are "out of control" of our lives, we can find comfort with the God who is in control of all things.

Evildoers aim to confound the plans of the afflicted, because the LORD is his refuge. PSALM 14:6

In my distress I called upon the LORD, and cried to my God; he heard my voice out of his temple, and my cry came before him, even into his ears. PSALM 18:6

Fret not yourself because of evildoers, neither be envious of those who do wrong. For they shall soon be cut down like the grass, and wither as the green plants. PSALM 37:1–2

A little that a righteous man has is better than the riches of many wicked. PSALM 37:16

Be still, and know that I am God. PSALM 46:10

Trouble and anguish have taken hold on me, yet your commandments are my delights. PSALM 119:143

Hope deferred makes the heart sick, but when the desire comes, it is a tree of life. PROVERBS 13:12

I have seen all the works that are done under the sun, and, behold, all is futility, a chasing after the wind. Then I looked on all the works that my hands had made, and on the labor that I had labored to do, and, behold, all was futility, a chasing after the wind, and there was no profit under the sun.

Therefore I hated life, because the work that is made under the sun is grievous to me, for all is futility, a chasing after the wind.

ECCLESIASTES 1:14, 2:11, 17

What does man gain from all his labor, from all his anxious striving and toiling under the sun? For all his days are sorrowful, and his work brings grief; yes, his heart takes not rest in the night. This is also futility.

ECCLESIASTES 2:22–23

In quietness and in confidence shall be your strength. ISAIAH 30:15

They that wait upon the LORD shall renew their strength; they shall mount up with wings as eagles; they shall run, and not be weary, and they shall walk, and not faint. ISAIAH 40:31

Blessed is the man that trusts in the LORD, and whose hope the LORD is.

JEREMIAH 17:7

Take no thought for your life, what you shall eat, or what you shall drink, nor worry about your body, what you shall put on. Is not the life more than food, and the body than clothing? Behold the birds of the air, for they sow not, neither do they reap, nor gather into barns, yet your heavenly Father feeds them. Are you not much better than they? Which of you by worrying can add one single hour to his life span? MATTHEW 6:25–27

If God be for us, who can be against us? He that spared not his own Son, but delivered him up for us all, how shall he not with him also freely give us all things? ROMANS 8:31–32

I will destroy the wisdom of the wise, and will bring to nothing the understanding of the prudent. I CORINTHIANS 1:19

Let all bitterness and wrath and anger and brawling and evil speaking be put away from you, along with all malice. And be kind one to another, tenderhearted, forgiving one another, even as God for Christ's sake has forgiven you. EPHESIANS 4:31–32

Be anxious for nothing, but in everything by prayer and supplication with thanksgiving let your requests be made known to God. And the peace of God, which passes all understanding, will keep your hearts and minds in Christ Jesus. Finally, brethren, whatever things are true, whatever things are honest, whatever things are just, whatever things are pure, whatever things are lovely, whatever things are of good report; if there is any virtue, and if there are any praise, think on these things.   PHILIPPIANS 4:6–8

Humble yourselves under the mighty hand of God so that he may exalt you in due time, casting all your care upon him, for he cares for you.

I PETER 5:6–7

See also Anxiety, Contentment, Worry.

GENEROSITY

Stinginess was the vice of Ebenezer Scrooge in A Christmas Carol, *and it is a sin that the Bible heartily condemns. To be able to help others and not to do so is a cruelty. To have enough money to fritter it away on luxuries and amusements may be perfectly legal, but it is not moral. To live as God intended us, we must give, and we must give generously. As Winston Churchill put it, "We make a living by what we get, but we make a life by what we give."*

The Bible has some harsh words for people who toot their own horns, who give to charity so they will receive praise and publicity. In the Bible's view, the best way—perhaps the only right way—to be generous is to do it as anonymously as possible. The motivation for helping someone else is that it is right, not that it will gain us a reputation.

You shall not harden your heart nor shut your hand from your poor brother, but you shall open your hand wide to him, and shall surely lend him sufficient for his need, in what he wants. . . . You shall surely give him, and your heart shall not be grieved when you give to him, because for this thing the LORD your God shall bless you in all your works, and in all that you put your hand to. DEUTERONOMY 15:7–10

Blessed is he who considers the poor; the LORD will deliver him in time of trouble. The LORD will preserve him, and keep him alive, and he shall be blessed upon the earth, and you will not deliver him to the will of his enemies. The LORD will strengthen him upon the bed of sickness. PSALM 41:1–3

Honor the LORD with your substance, and with the firstfruits of all your produce. PROVERBS 3:9

There is one who gives freely, and yet increases; and there is another who withholds what is due, yet it leads to poverty.   PROVERBS 11:24

The generous soul shall be enriched, and he that gives water shall be watered himself.   PROVERBS 11:25

He that despises his neighbor sins, but he who has mercy on the poor, happy is he.   PROVERBS 14:21

Whoever mocks the poor reproaches his Maker.   PROVERBS 17:5

He that has pity upon the poor lends to the LORD, and what he has given will he pay him again.   PROVERBS 19:17

He that has a bountiful eye shall be blessed, for he gives of his bread to the poor.   PROVERBS 22:9

He that gives to the poor shall not lack, but he who hides his eyes from them shall have many a curse.   PROVERBS 28:27

Cast your bread upon the waters, for you shall find it after many days. Give a portion to seven, and even to eight; for you know not what disaster shall be upon the land.   ECCLESIASTES 11:1–2

If you work on behalf of the hungry and satisfy the afflicted, then shall your light rise in the darkness, and your night shall be as the noonday.

ISAIAH 58:10

Bring all the tithes into the storehouse, that there may be food in my house; and test me in this, says the LORD Almighty, if I will not open you the windows of heaven, and pour you out such a blessing that there shall not be room enough to receive it.   MALACHI 3:10

Take heed that you do not your charity before men, to be seen by them: otherwise you have no reward from your Father who is in heaven. Therefore when you do your alms, do not sound a trumpet before you, as the hypocrites do in the synagogues and in the streets, that they may receive glory from men. Truly I say to you, they have their reward. But when you do alms, let not your left hand know what your right hand does, that your alms may be in secret, and your Father who sees in secret himself shall reward you openly.   MATTHEW 6:1–4

Love your enemies, and do good; and lend, hoping for nothing in return. And your reward shall be great, and you shall be the children of the Highest, for he is kind to the ungrateful and to the evil. Be therefore merciful, as your Father also is merciful. Judge not, and you shall not be judged: condemn not, and you shall not be condemned, forgive, and you shall be forgiven.
                                                        LUKE 6:35–37

Give, and it shall be given to you; a good measure, pressed down, shaken together, and running over, shall men give into your lap. For the measure that you give shall be the measure you get back.   LUKE 6:38

When you make a dinner or a supper, call not your friends, nor your brethren, neither your kinsmen, nor your rich neighbors; lest they also invite you in return, and a recompense be made you. But when you make a feast, call the poor, the maimed, the lame, the blind. And you shall be blessed; for they cannot recompense you, for you shall be recompensed at the resurrection of the just.   LUKE 14:12–14

Jesus looked up and saw the rich men casting their gifts into the treasury. And he saw also a certain poor widow casting in there two small coins. And he said, "Truly, I say to you that this poor widow has cast in more than they all."   LUKE 21:1–3

You know the grace of our Lord Jesus Christ, that, though he was rich, yet for your sakes he became poor, that you through his poverty might be rich.
                                                    2 CORINTHIANS 8:9

He who sows sparingly shall reap also sparingly, and he who sows bountifully shall reap also bountifully. Every man should give what his heart has decided—not grudgingly, or from necessity, for God loves a cheerful giver. 2 CORINTHIANS 9:6–7

As we have opportunity, let us do good to all men, especially to them who are of the household of faith. GALATIANS 6:10

If any provide not for his own, and specially for those of his own house, he has denied the faith, and is worse than an unbeliever. 1 TIMOTHY 5:8

Command those who are rich in this world that they be not arrogant, nor trust in uncertain riches, but in the living God, who gives us richly all things to enjoy. Command that they do good, that they be rich in good works, ready to distribute, willing to share, laying up in store for themselves a good foundation against the time to come, that they may lay hold of eternal life. 1 TIMOTHY 6:17–19

God is not unrighteous to forget your work and labor of love, which you have showed toward his name, in that you have ministered to the saints, and still do so. HEBREWS 6:10

Whoever has this world's goods, and sees his brother in need, and has no pity on him, how dwells the love of God in him? My little children, let us not love merely in word, neither in speech, but in deed and in truth. 1 JOHN 3:17–18

See also Duty to the Poor, Kindness, Money.

GOD AS CREATOR

Critics have been grousing about the creation story in Genesis for centuries, casting doubts on whether it is "literally true" that God created everything in six days. They are missing the point of Genesis: God created everything. Even more so, he pronounced that the created order was "good." It did not evolve out of nothing, with no purpose behind it. It was made—and it exists—because God wanted it to be. In other words, nature exists with meaning and purpose.

There is no trace of "Mother Earth" religion in the Bible. God takes pleasure in his creation, and so should we, but we should admire and care for the created world, not worship it.

In the beginning God created the heaven and the earth. And the earth was without form, and void, and darkness was upon the face of the deep. And the Spirit of God moved upon the face of the waters. And God said, "Let there be light," and there was light. And God saw the light, that it was good, and God divided the light from the darkness. And God called the light Day, and the darkness he called Night. And the evening and the morning were the first day.   GENESIS 1:1–5

God said, "Let us make man in our image, after our likeness, and let them have dominion over the fish of the sea, and over the birds of the air, and over the cattle, and over all the earth, and over every creeping thing that creeps upon the earth." So God created man in his own image; in the image of God created he him; male and female created he them. And God blessed them, and God said to them, "Be fruitful, and multiply, and replenish the earth, and subdue it, and have dominion over the fish of the sea, and over the birds of the air, and over every living thing that moves upon the earth."

And God saw every thing that he had made, and, behold, it was very good. And the evening and the morning were the sixth day.

GENESIS 1:26–28, 31

On the seventh day God ceased from his work which he had made, and he rested on the seventh day from all his work which he had made. And God blessed the seventh day and sanctified it, because on it he had rested from all his work which God created and made.   GENESIS 2:2–3

The pillars of the earth are the LORD's, and he has set the world upon them.

I SAMUEL 2:8

All the gods of the people are idols, but the LORD made the heavens.

I CHRONICLES 16:26

When I consider your heavens, the work of your fingers, the moon and the stars that you have set in their courses, what is man, that you are mindful of him? And the son of man, that you seek him out?   PSALM 8:3–4

The heavens declare the glory of God, and the firmament shows his handiwork.   PSALM 19:1

The earth is the LORD'S, and all that is in it, the world, and they that dwell therein. For he has founded it upon the seas, and established it upon the floods.   PSALM 24:1–2

Every beast of the forest is mine, and the cattle upon a thousand hills. I know all the birds of the mountains, and the wild beasts of the field are mine.   PSALM 50:10–11

Before the mountains were brought forth, or ever you had formed the earth and the world, even from everlasting to everlasting, you are God.

PSALM 90:2

Know you that the LORD he is God; it is he who has made us, and not we ourselves; we are his people, and the sheep of his pasture.

PSALM 100:3

Remember now your Creator in the days of your youth.

ECCLESIASTES 12:1

Have you not known? Have you not heard, that the everlasting God, the LORD, the Creator of the ends of the earth, faints not, neither is weary? There is no searching of his understanding.   ISAIAH 40:28

Ah LORD God! behold, you have made the heaven and the earth by your great power and outstretched arm, and there is nothing too hard for you.

JEREMIAH 32:17

God who made the world and all things in it, the One who is Lord of heaven and earth, dwells not in temples made with hands, nor is he worshipped

The King and I *and Genesis*

You may have seen the popular musical The King and I. *In the play, the King of Siam complains to Anna, the English schoolteacher, that English books are inconsistent. The books of science say that the universe took millions of years to form. But the Bible claims that creation took only six days. Which is correct? asks the King. Why do English books contradict each other?*

Anna explains, politely and firmly, that there is no contradiction. The men who wrote the Bible were not scientists, she says. They were men of faith who explained creation in a simple and poetic way, communicating the belief that God made everything in the world and made it for a purpose. The scientists have not been able to disprove this.

with men's hands, as though he needed anything, since he gives to all life, and breath, and all things. He has made from one blood all nations of men to dwell on all the face of the earth, and has determined the times before appointed, and the bounds of their habitation, so that they should seek the Lord, and perhaps they might grope after him and find him, though he is not far from each one of us. For in him we live, and move, and have our being.   ACTS 17:24–28

I saw a new heaven and a new earth: for the first heaven and the first earth were passed away; and there was no more sea. And I John saw the holy city, new Jerusalem, coming down from God out of heaven.

                    REVELATION 21:1–2

See also Nature and the Earth.

GOD AS JUDGE

We have a right to demand justice in human courtrooms, but we needn't be surprised when we don't get it. Even the best of human judges are, well, human, and the sad truth is that there is no full and ultimate justice in this world. This is why the Bible, time and time again, pictures God as the divine Judge who beholds all our actions, every little word, and who alone can judge us with complete fairness. This is a comforting thought—and a frightening one as well! If we take seriously the Bible's images of the heavenly Judge, we ought to be always forthright and open in our words and deeds, knowing that nothing is concealed from him. We can also take solace in this: Wickedness and injustice may seem to triumph in this world, but their victory is not permanent.

A trivia tidbit: The Old English word doom *originally meant "judgment," and* doomsday *actually referred to Judgment Day, when God would reward or punish everyone.*

Regarding the Almighty, we cannot find him out; he is excellent in power, and in judgment, and in plenty of justice; he will not afflict.   JOB 37:23

Let the wickedness of the wicked come to an end; but establish the just, for the righteous God tests the hearts and minds.   PSALM 7:9

Truly there is a reward for the righteous: truly he is a God that judges the earth.   PSALM 58:11

To you, O LORD, belongs mercy, for you render to every man according to his work.   PSALM 62:12

Justice and judgment are the habitation of your throne: mercy and truth shall go before your face.   PSALM 89:14

All the ways of a man are clean in his own eyes; but the LORD weighs the spirits.   PROVERBS 16:2

Every way of a man is right in his own eyes, but the LORD ponders the hearts. To do justice and judgment is more acceptable to the LORD than sacrifice.   PROVERBS 21:2–3

God shall bring every work into judgment, with every secret thing, whether it be good, or whether it be evil.   ECCLESIASTES 12:14

There shall come forth a shoot from the stump of Jesse, and a branch shall grow out of his roots. And the Spirit of the LORD shall rest upon him, the Spirit of wisdom and understanding, the Spirit of counsel and might, the Spirit of knowledge and of the fear of the LORD. He shall not judge by what his eyes see, nor decide by what his ears hear; but with righteousness shall he judge the poor, and decide with equity for the meek of the earth.

ISAIAH 11:1–4

[NOTE: *The early Christians believed that this prophecy was fulfilled in the life of Jesus.*]

A good man out of the good treasure of the heart brings forth good things, and an evil man out of the evil treasure brings forth evil things. But I say to you, that every idle word that men shall speak, they shall give account of in the day of judgment. For by your words you shall be justified, and by your words you shall be condemned.   MATTHEW 12:35–37

What is a man profited, if he shall gain the whole world, and lose his own soul? Or what shall a man give in exchange for his soul? For the Son of man shall come in the glory of his Father with his angels, and then he shall reward every man according to his works.   MATTHEW 16:26–27

Whatever you have spoken in darkness shall be heard in the light, and what you have spoken in the ear in closets shall be proclaimed upon the housetops.   LUKE 12:3

You are inexcusable, O man, whoever you are that judges, for in passing judgment upon another, you condemn yourself; for you that judge do the same things. . . . And think you this, O man, that judges those who do such things, and do the same, that you shall escape the judgment of God? Or despise you the riches of his goodness and forbearance and longsuffering, not knowing that the goodness of God leads you to repentance?

ROMANS 2:1–4

Every one of us shall give account of himself to God.   ROMANS 14:12

With me it is a very small thing that I should be judged by you, or by any man; indeed, I judge not my own self. I know of nothing against myself, yet it is not this that justifies me, but he who judges me is the Lord. Therefore judge nothing before the appointed time, until the Lord comes, who will bring to light the hidden things of darkness and will reveal the purposes of hearts, and then shall every man have praise of God.

I CORINTHIANS 4:3–5

What have I to do with judging those who are outside? Do not you judge those who are within? But those who are outside, God judges. Therefore put away from among yourselves that wicked person.

I CORINTHIANS 5:12–13

If we would judge ourselves, we should not be judged. But when we are judged, we are chastened by the Lord, that we should not be condemned along with the world.   I CORINTHIANS 11:31–32

We must all appear before the judgment seat of Christ, so that everyone may receive recompense for the things done in his body, whether it be good or bad.   2 CORINTHIANS 5:10

God is not unrighteous to forget your work and labor of love, which you have showed toward his name, in that you have ministered to the saints, and do minister.   HEBREWS 6:10

It is appointed to men once to die, but after this the judgment.

HEBREWS 9:27

We know him that has said, "Vengeance belongs to me, I will recompense," says the Lord. And again, the Lord shall judge his people. It is a fearful thing to fall into the hands of the living God.   HEBREWS 10:30–31

Grumble not against one another, brethren, lest you are condemned.
Behold, the Judge stands before the door.   JAMES 5:9

Since you call on the Father, who without partiality judges according to
every man's work, live your lives here in reverent fear.   1 PETER 1:17

In the past you already spent enough time doing as the pagans do, walking
in debauchery, lusts, excess of wine, orgies, carousing, and abominable idolatries. They think it strange that you no longer join with them to the same
excess of dissipation, so they speak evil of you. They shall give account to
him that is ready to judge the living and the dead.   1 PETER 4:3–5

The Lord knows how to deliver the godly out of temptations, and to reserve
the unjust for the day of judgment to be punished.   2 PETER 2:9

The heavens and the earth which now exist have been reserved for fire until
the day of judgment and destruction of ungodly men. But, beloved, be not
ignorant of this one thing, that one day is with the Lord like a thousand
years, and a thousand years like one day. The Lord is not slow concerning
his promise, as some men believe; but he is longsuffering toward us, not
willing that any should perish, but that all should come to repentance. But
the day of the Lord will come as a thief in the night. Then the heavens shall
pass away with a great noise, and the elements shall melt with fervent heat,
the earth also and everything in it shall be burned up.   2 PETER 3:7–9

In this is our love made perfect, that we may have boldness in the day of
judgment: because as he is, so we are in this world. There is no fear in love,
but perfect love casts out fear: because fear has to do with punishment. He
that fears is not made perfect in love.   1 JOHN 4:17–18

I saw a great white throne, and him that sat on it. From his face the earth
and the heaven fled away, and there was found no place for them. And I saw
the dead, small and great, stand before God, and the books were opened,
and another book was opened, which is the Book of Life, and the dead were
judged out of those things which were written in the books, according to
their deeds. And the sea gave up the dead which were in it, and death and
hell delivered up the dead which were in them, and they were judged every
man according to their deeds. And death and hell were cast into the lake of

fire. This is the second death. And whoever was not found written in the Book of Life was cast into the lake of fire. REVELATION 20:11–15

See also God's Fairness, God's Mercy.

GOD'S COMPASSION FOR THE POOR

The great American songwriter Stephen Foster composed the song "Hard Times, Come Again No More." In it, he urged listeners, "Let us pause in life's pleasures and count its many tears, while we all sup sorrows with the poor." But it isn't easy to "pause in life's pleasures"—in fact, it is when we enjoy ourselves that we are least concerned about people who have less than we. But, according to the Bible, God is always counting the tears of the poor. Society's outcasts may feel neglected by their fellow human beings, but God has not forgotten them.

The LORD makes poor, and makes rich; he brings low, and lifts up. He raises up the poor out of the dust, and lifts up the beggar from the rubbish heap, to set them among princes, and to make them inherit the throne of glory, for the pillars of the earth are the LORD'S, and he has set the world upon them. I SAMUEL 2:7–8

This poor man cried, and the LORD heard him, and saved him out of all his troubles. PSALM 34:6

The LORD hears the poor, and despises not his prisoners. PSALM 69:35

He shall deliver the needy when he cries; the poor also, and him that has no helper. He shall spare the poor and needy, and shall save the souls of the needy. PSALM 72:12–13

He will regard the prayer of the destitute, and not despise their prayer. PSALM 102:17

He satisfies the longing soul, and fills the hungry soul with goodness.

PSALM 107:9

He shall stand at the right hand of the poor, to save him from those that condemn his soul. PSALM 109:31

He raises up the poor out of the dust, and lifts the needy out of the rubbish heap. PSALM 113:7

I know that the LORD will maintain the cause of the afflicted, and the right of the poor. PSALM 140:12

Whoever mocks the poor reproaches his Maker. PROVERBS 17:5

Rob not the poor because he is poor, neither oppress the needy in the courts, for the LORD will plead their cause, and will plunder those who have plundered them. PROVERBS 22:22–23

When the poor and needy seek water, and there is none, and their tongue fails for thirst, I the LORD will hear them, I the God of Israel will not forsake them. ISAIAH 41:17

Mary said, "My soul magnifies the Lord, and my spirit has rejoiced in God my Savior. For he has regarded the low estate of his handmaiden. Behold, from now on all generations shall call me blessed. For he who is mighty has done for me great things, and holy is his name. And his mercy is on those who fear him from generation to generation. He has showed strength with his arm; he has scattered the proud in the thoughts of their hearts. He has brought down the mighty from their seats, and exalted them of low estate. He has filled the hungry with good things, and the rich he has sent away empty." LUKE 1:46–53

Behold, some that are last shall be first, and some that are first shall be last.

LUKE 13:30

Hearken, my beloved brethren: has not God chosen the poor of this world to be rich in faith, heirs of the kingdom which he has promised to those who love him?   JAMES 2:5

See also Duty to the Poor.

GOD'S FAIRNESS

If any one human being was capable of total fairness, would we need nine justices on the Supreme Court or twelve people on a jury? Wouldn't one suffice? But humans, try as they might, are always biased in some way or another. We all have things in our backgrounds that skew our view of justice. God doesn't. He is the one Being who is capable of fairness without favoritism.

The LORD your God is God of gods, and LORD of lords, a great God, a mighty, and a terrible, who shows no partiality, nor takes bribes.

DEUTERONOMY 10:17

The LORD said to Samuel, "Look not on his appearance, or on the height of his stature, because I have refused him, for the LORD sees not as man sees. For man looks on the outward appearance, but the LORD looks on the heart."   I SAMUEL 16:7

Many that are first shall be last, and the last shall be first.

MATTHEW 19:30

There was a certain rich man, who was clothed in purple and fine linen, and feasted sumptuously every day. And there was a certain beggar named Lazarus, who lay at his gate, full of sores, and desiring to be fed with the crumbs which fell from the rich man's table; and the dogs came and licked his sores. And it came to pass, that the beggar died, and was carried by the angels to Abraham's side. The rich man also died, and was buried. And in hell he lifted up his eyes, being in torment, and he saw Abraham far off, with

Lazarus by his side. And he cried and said, "Father Abraham, have mercy on me, and send Lazarus, that he may dip the tip of his finger in water, and cool my tongue; for I am tormented in this flame." But Abraham said, "Son, remember that you in your lifetime received your good things, and likewise Lazarus evil things; but now he is comforted, and you are tormented."

LUKE 16:19–25

Peter opened his mouth, and said, "Truly I perceive that God shows no favoritism, but in every nation he accepts those who fear him and work righteousness."

ACTS 10:34–35

By your hardness and impenitent heart you store up for yourself wrath on the day of wrath, when God's righteous judgment will be revealed. He will repay every man according to his deeds: to those who by patient continuance in doing right seek for glory and honor and immortality, he will give eternal life; but to those who are contentious, and do not obey the truth, but obey unrighteousness, there will be indignation and wrath. There will be tribulation and anguish upon every soul of man that does evil, of the Jew first, and also of the Gentile; but there will be glory, honor, and peace for every man that works good, to the Jew first, and also to the Gentile, for there is no favoritism with God.

ROMANS 2:5–11

Whatever good thing any man does, the same shall he receive from the Lord, whether he is slave or free. And, you masters, do the same things to them. Do not threaten them, for you know that your Master also is in heaven, and there is no favoritism with him.

EPHESIANS 6:8–9

He that does wrong shall receive for the wrong which he has done, and there is no favoritism.

COLOSSIANS 3:25

Since you call on the Father, who without partiality judges according to every man's work, live your lives here in reverent fear.

I PETER 1:17

See also Equality/Fairness, Forgiveness, God As Judge, Revenge.

GOD'S GUIDANCE

The bookstores and television and radio have no shortage of advisers. This seems to suggest that many people are in need of advice. How else can so many psychologists, astrologers, diet experts, fitness pros, financial planners, and self-help gurus stay in business? How else can so many new (or recycled) religions flourish?

An obvious question arises: Can these so-called authorities be trusted? Or should we take all human advice with a grain of salt? The Bible says, yes, be a little skeptical of all human advice. Better yet, be a little skeptical of human goals. For the one goal the Bible offers us is distinctive: a rich, rewarding life now and forever in fellowship with God. All other goals pale next to this one, as do all human advisers. Human beings give advice; God gives guidance.

You are my lamp, O LORD, and the LORD will lighten my darkness.

2 SAMUEL 22:29

The LORD is my shepherd; I shall lack nothing. He makes me to lie down in green pastures: he leads me beside the still waters. He restores my soul: he leads me in the paths of righteousness for his name's sake. Yes, though I walk through the valley of the shadow of death, I will fear no evil, for you are with me; your rod and your staff they comfort me. You prepare a table before me in the presence of my enemies: you anoint my head with oil; my cup runs over. Surely goodness and mercy shall follow me all the days of my life, and I will dwell in the house of the LORD forever.   PSALM 23

The meek will he guide in judgment, and the meek will he teach his way.

PSALM 25:9

You are my rock and my fortress; therefore for your name's sake lead me, and guide me.   PSALM 31:3

I will instruct you and teach you in the way which you shall go; I will guide you with my eye.   PSALM 32:8

The steps of a good man are ordered by the LORD, and he delights in his way.

PSALM 37:23

This God is our God forever and ever; he will be our guide even to death.

PSALM 48:14

So foolish was I, and ignorant: I was like a beast before you. Nevertheless I am continually with you; you have held me by my right hand. You shall guide me with your counsel, and afterward receive me to glory. Whom have I in heaven but you? And there is none upon earth that I desire beside you. My flesh and my heart fail, but God is the strength of my heart, and my portion forever. PSALM 73:22–26

How shall a young man cleanse his way? By taking heed according to your word. PSALM 119:9

Your word is a lamp to my feet, and a light to my path.

PSALM 119:105

I have gone astray like a lost sheep; seek your servant; for I do not forget your commandments. PSALM 119:176

I will lift up my eyes to the hills, from whence comes my help. My help comes from the LORD, who made heaven and earth. He will not suffer your foot to be moved. The LORD shall preserve your going out and your coming in from this time forth, and even forevermore. PSALM 121:1–3, 8

Where shall I go from your Spirit? Or where shall I flee from your presence? If I ascend up into heaven, you are there; if I make my bed in the grave, behold, you are there. If I take the wings of the morning, and dwell in the uttermost parts of the sea, even there shall your hand lead me, and your right hand shall hold me. PSALM 139:7–10

In all your ways acknowledge him, and he shall direct your paths.

PROVERBS 3:6

The righteousness of the blameless shall direct his way, but the wicked shall fall by his own wickedness.   PROVERBS 11:5

A man's heart devises his way, but the LORD directs his steps.

PROVERBS 16:9

Where there is no vision, the people perish.   PROVERBS 29:18

The fear of man brings a snare, but whoever puts his trust in the LORD shall be safe.   PROVERBS 29:25

Your ears shall hear a voice behind you, saying, "This is the way, walk you in it," when you turn to the right hand, and when you turn to the left.

ISAIAH 30:21

I will bring the blind by a way that they knew not; I will lead them in paths that they have not known; I will make darkness light before them, and crooked things straight. These things will I do to them, and not forsake them.   ISAIAH 42:16

The LORD shall guide you continually, and satisfy your soul in drought, and make fat your bones. And you shall be like a watered garden, and like a spring of water, whose waters fail not.   ISAIAH 58:11

"I know the thoughts that I think about you," says the LORD, "thoughts of peace, and not of evil, to give you a future with hope. Then shall you call upon me, and you shall go and pray to me, and I will hearken to you. And you shall seek me, and find me, when you shall search for me with all your heart."   JEREMIAH 29:11–13

Whoever hears these sayings of mine, and does them, will be like a wise man who built his house upon a rock. And the rain descended, and the floods came, and the winds blew and beat upon that house, yet it fell not, for it was founded upon a rock. And everyone that hears these sayings of mine, and does them not, shall be like a foolish man who built his house upon the sand.

> "In all my perplexities and distresses the Bible has never failed to give me light and strength."
>
> —CONFEDERATE GENERAL ROBERT E. LEE

And the rain descended, and the floods came, and the winds blew and beat upon that house, and it fell, and great was the fall of it.

MATTHEW 7:24–27

If the blind lead the blind, both shall fall into the ditch.

MATTHEW 15:14

Jesus said to him, "I am the way, the truth, and the life; no man comes to the Father, but by me." JOHN 14:6

I will pray to the Father, and he shall give you another Comforter, that he may abide with you forever, the Spirit of truth. Him the world cannot receive, because it sees him not, neither knows him, but you know him; for he dwells with you, and shall be in you. JOHN 14:16–17, 26

When he, the Spirit of truth, is come, he will guide you into all truth.

JOHN 16:13

See also Faith, Hope, Obeying God, Trusting God.

GOD'S LOVE

It should give us more pleasure to think about God's love for us than about our love for God. After all, despite our best intentions, our feelings are always in flux. We may feel very loving toward God at some times but not at

others. Sometimes we may not even be conscious at all of our love for God.
But while our own feelings may come and go, God's love for us does not.
This is one of the beautiful themes of the Bible: His love for us is the most
steadfast thing in the universe. In other words, it is much more reliable than
human love.

Many sorrows shall be to the wicked, but he who trusts in the LORD, mercy shall encircle him. Be glad in the LORD, and rejoice, you righteous, and shout for joy, all you that are upright in heart.   PSALM 32:10–11

The eye of the LORD is upon those who fear him, upon those who hope in his mercy. Our soul waits for the LORD; he is our help and our shield.

PSALM 33:18, 20

Withhold not you your tender mercies from me, O LORD: let your loving-kindness and your truth continually preserve me.   PSALM 40:11

The LORD opens the eyes of the blind; the LORD raises those who are bowed down; the LORD loves the righteous.   PSALM 146:8

The one whom the LORD loves he corrects, just as a father corrects the son in whom he delights.   PROVERBS 3:12

The way of the wicked is an abomination to the LORD, but he loves him that follows after righteousness.   PROVERBS 15:9

"I know the thoughts that I think about you," says the LORD, "thoughts of peace, and not of evil, to give you a future with hope. Then shall you call upon me, and you shall go and pray to me, and I will hearken to you. And you shall seek me, and find me, when you shall search for me with all your heart."   JEREMIAH 29:11–13

The LORD has appeared to me long ago, saying, "Yes, I have loved you with an everlasting love; therefore with lovingkindness have I drawn you."

JEREMIAH 31:3

It is of the LORD 's mercies that we are not consumed, because his compassions fail not. They are new every morning: great is your faithfulness.

LAMENTATIONS 3:22–23

I will heal their backsliding, I will love them freely, for my anger is turned away from him. HOSEA 14:4

The Son of man has come to seek and to save that which was lost.

LUKE 19:10

The Word was made flesh, and dwelt among us, and we beheld his glory, the glory as of the only begotten of the Father, full of grace and truth.

JOHN 1:14

God so loved the world that he gave his only begotten Son, that whoever believes in him should not perish, but have everlasting life. For God sent not his Son into the world to condemn the world; but that the world through him might be saved. JOHN 3:16–17

He that has my commandments, and keeps them, he it is that loves me, and he who loves me shall be loved of my Father, and I will love him, and will manifest myself to him. . . . If a man love me, he will keep my words, and my Father will love him, and we will come to him, and make our abode with him. JOHN 14:21, 23

The love of God is shed abroad in our hearts by the Holy Spirit which is given to us. . . . God commends his love toward us, in this; while we were still sinners, Christ died for us. Much more then, being now justified by his blood, we shall be saved from wrath through him. For if, when we were enemies, we were reconciled to God by the death of his Son, much more, being reconciled, we shall be saved by his life. And not only this, but we also joy in God through our Lord Jesus Christ, by whom we have now received the atonement. ROMANS 5:5, 8–11

We know that all things work together for good to those who love God, to them who are the called according to his purpose.   ROMANS 8:28

Who shall separate us from the love of Christ? Shall tribulation, or distress, or persecution, or famine, or nakedness, or peril, or sword? As it is written, "For your sake we are killed all the day long; we are accounted as sheep for the slaughter." No, in all these things we are more than conquerors through him that loved us. For I am persuaded, that neither death, nor life, nor angels, nor principalities, nor powers, nor things present, nor things to come, nor height, nor depth, nor any other creature shall be able to separate us from the love of God, which is in Christ Jesus our Lord.

                                                        ROMANS 8:35–39

The grace of the Lord Jesus Christ, and the love of God, and the fellowship of the Holy Spirit be with you all.   2 CORINTHIANS 13:14

God, who is rich in mercy, out of his great love with which he loved us even when we were dead in sins, has made us alive—by grace you are saved—and has raised us up together and seated us with him in the heavenly places in Christ Jesus, so that in the ages to come he might show the immeasurable riches of his grace in his kindness toward us through Christ Jesus.

                                                        EPHESIANS 2:4–7

To know the love of Christ, which surpasses knowledge, that you might be filled with all the fullness of God.   EPHESIANS 3:19

Draw near to God, and he will draw near to you.   JAMES 4:8

Behold, what manner of love the Father has bestowed upon us, that we should be called the sons of God; and so the world knows us not, because it knew him not.   1 JOHN 3:1

He that loves not knows not God, for God is love. In this was revealed the love of God toward us, because God sent his only begotten Son into the world that we might live through him. In this is love, not that we loved God, but that he loved us, and sent his Son to be the sacrifice for our sins. Beloved, if God so loved us, we ought also to love one another. No man has seen God at any time. If we love one another, God dwells in us, and his love is perfected in us. In this we know that we dwell in him, and he in us, because he has given us of his Spirit.   I JOHN 4:8–13

As many as I love, I rebuke and chasten; be zealous therefore, and repent.

REVELATION 3:19

See also Comfort in Times of Trouble, Discipline and Correction, God's Guidance.

GOD'S MERCY

The poet Robert Frost observed that "all you really want in the end is mercy." He had a point. If most of us thought seriously enough about our good and bad deeds, we would realize that a fair reward—justice—from God would be the one thing we do not want. But the "good news" of the Bible is that God is kinder to us than we deserve. Being a loving Father, he is willing to give us what we did not really earn or deserve. Does this mean that we can live just as we please, knowing that God will accept us no matter what? Hardly. That would be the supreme ingratitude, wouldn't it? In the Bible's view of things, God's mercy becomes our motivation for living well.

The LORD, the LORD God, merciful and gracious, longsuffering, and abundant in goodness and truth, keeping mercy for thousands, forgiving iniquity and transgression and sin.   EXODUS 34:6–7

With the merciful you will show yourself merciful, and with the upright man you will show yourself upright.   2 SAMUEL 22:26

I am in a dire straits; let us fall now into the hand of the LORD; for his mercies are great, and let me not fall into the hand of man.

2 SAMUEL 24:14

O give thanks to the LORD, for he is good; for his mercy endures forever.

I CHRONICLES 16:34

You are a God ready to pardon, gracious and merciful, slow to anger, and of great kindness.　　　　　　　　　　　　　　　　　NEHEMIAH 9:17

Remember not the sins of my youth, nor my transgressions; according to your mercy remember me for your goodness' sake, O LORD.

　　　　　　　　　　　　　　　　　　　　　　　　　PSALM 25:7

All the paths of the LORD are mercy and truth to such as keep his covenant and his testimonies.　　　　　　　　　　　　　　　　PSALM 25:10

Behold, the eye of the LORD is upon them that fear him, upon them that hope in his mercy.　　　　　　　　　　　　　　　　　PSALM 33:18

The LORD is good; his mercy is everlasting; and his truth endures to all generations.　　　　　　　　　　　　　　　　　　PSALM 100:5

He forgives all your iniquities; he heals all your diseases; he redeems your life from destruction; he crowns you with lovingkindness and tender mercies; he satisfies your mouth with good things, so that your youth is renewed like the eagle's.

The LORD executes righteousness and judgment for all that are oppressed. He made known his ways to Moses, his deeds to the children of Israel. The LORD is merciful and gracious, slow to anger, and plenteous in mercy. He will not always punish, neither will he keep his anger forever. He has not dealt with us according to sins, nor rewarded us according to our offenses. For as the heaven is high above the earth, so great is his mercy toward those who fear him. As far as the east is from the west, so far has he removed our sins from us.

Like a father pities his children, so the LORD pities those who fear him. For he knows what we are made of; he remembers that we are dust. As for man, his days are like grass; as a flower of the field, so he flourishes. For the wind passes over it, and it is gone, and then its place shall be known no more. But the mercy of the LORD is from everlasting to everlasting upon those who fear him, and his righteousness to children's children.　　　PSALM 103:3–17

Sing, O heavens; and be joyful, O earth; and break forth into singing, O mountains. For the LORD has comforted his people, and will have mercy upon his afflicted.　　　　　　　　　　　　　　　　ISAIAH 49:13

"For a small moment have I forsaken you, but with great mercies will I gather you. In a little wrath I hid my face from you for a moment; but with everlasting kindness will I have mercy on thee," says the LORD your Redeemer. "For the mountains shall depart, and the hills be removed, but my kindness shall not depart from you, neither shall the covenant of my peace be removed," says the LORD that has mercy on thee.

ISAIAH 54:7–8, 10

Let the wicked forsake his way, and the unrighteous man his thoughts, and let him return to the LORD, and he will have mercy upon him.

ISAIAH 55:7

"Return, backsliding Israel," says the LORD, "and I will not cause my anger to fall upon you; for I am merciful, and I will not keep anger forever."

JEREMIAH 3:12

The LORD will not cast off forever. Though he causes grief, yet will he have compassion according to the multitude of his mercies. For he does not willingly afflict nor grieve the children of men.   LAMENTATIONS 3:31–33

As I live, says the LORD God, I have no pleasure in the death of the wicked; but desire that the wicked turn from his way and live. Turn, turn you from your evil ways; for why will you die, O house of Israel?

EZEKIEL 33:11

Who is a God like you, that pardons iniquity, and overlooks the transgression of the remnant of his heritage? He retains not his anger forever, because he delights in mercy. He will turn again, he will have compassion upon us; he will subdue our iniquities, and will cast all their sins into the depths of the sea.   MICAH 7:18–19

If you forgive men their trespasses, your heavenly Father will also forgive you. But if you forgive not men their trespasses, neither will your Father forgive your trespasses.   MATTHEW 6:14–15

The Son of man has come to save what was lost. What do you think? If a man has a hundred sheep, and one of them has gone astray, does he not leave the ninety-nine others, and goes into the mountains, and seeks what is gone astray? And if it happens that he finds it, truly I say to you, he rejoices more over that sheep than over the ninety-nine which went not astray. Even so, it is not the will of your Father who is in heaven that one of these little ones should perish. MATTHEW 18:11–14

His mercy is on those who fear him from generation to generation.

LUKE 1:50

Repent you therefore, and be converted, that your sins may be blotted out, when the times of refreshing shall come from the presence of the Lord. And he shall send Jesus Christ, who before was preached to you.

ACTS 3:19–20

The times of this ignorance God overlooked, but now he commands all men everywhere to repent. ACTS 17:30

God, who is rich in mercy, out of his great love with which he loved us even when we were dead in sins, has made us alive—by grace you are saved—and has raised us up together and seated us with him in the heavenly places in Christ Jesus, so that in the ages to come he might show the immeasurable riches of his grace in his kindness toward us through Christ Jesus.

EPHESIANS 2:4–7

Not by works of righteousness which we have done, but according to his mercy he saved us, by the washing of regeneration, and renewing of the Holy Spirit. TITUS 3:5

Let us therefore come boldly to the throne of grace, that we may obtain mercy and find grace to help in time of need. HEBREW 4:16

The Lord is not slow concerning his promise, as some men believe; but he is longsuffering toward us, not willing that any should perish, but that all should come to repentance. But the day of the Lord will come as a thief in the night. Then the heavens shall pass away with a great noise, and the elements shall melt with fervent heat, the earth also and everything in it shall be burned up. 2 PETER 3:9

See also Confession, Guilt, Repentance.

GUILT

An old proverb tells us, "A guilty conscience is one that works." But we are living in an anti-guilt age, constantly tempted to shift the blame for everything onto someone else. Blame one's parents, blame society, blame anything, but don't blame oneself. Nonetheless, guilty consciences cry out, and the only thing that will silence them is admitting one's sin and guilt and turning to a merciful God. The Bible presents God as one who can also overcome our vague feelings of guilt. Once past those, we can enjoy life as he intended.

Blessed is he whose offenses are forgiven, whose sin is covered. Blessed is the man to whom the LORD imputes no guilt, and in whose spirit there is no deceit. When I kept silent, my body wasted away through my groaning all the day long. For day and night your hand was heavy upon me; my strength was turned into the drought of summer. I acknowledged my sin to you, and my wrongdoings have I not hid. I said, "I will confess my offenses to the LORD," and you forgave the guilt of my sin. For this shall everyone that is godly pray to you in a time when you may be found; surely in the floods of great waters they shall not come near to him. You are my hiding place; you shall preserve me from trouble; you shall surround me with songs of deliverance.

PSALM 32:1–7

My iniquities have overwhelmed me; like a heavy burden they are too weighty for me. PSALM 38:4

Deliver me from bloodguiltiness, O God, God of my salvation, and my tongue shall sing aloud of your righteousness. PSALM 51:14

O God, you know my foolishness, and my sins are not hid from you.

PSALM 69:5

As far as the east is from the west, so far has he removed our sins from us. Like a father pities his children, so the LORD pities those who fear him. For he knows what we are made of; he remembers that we are dust.

PSALM 103:12–14

The way of man is perverse and strange, but as for the pure, his work is right.

PROVERBS 21:8

He that said to the wicked, "You are righteous," him shall the people curse; nations shall abhor him. But to those who rebuke him shall be delight, and a good blessing shall come upon them.

PROVERBS 24:24–25

In the year that King Uzziah died I saw the LORD sitting upon a throne, high and lifted up, and his robe's train filled the temple. Above it stood the seraphim; each one had six wings; with two he covered his face, and with two he covered his feet, and with two he flew. And one called to another and said, "Holy, holy, holy, is the LORD Almighty; the whole earth is full of his glory." And the posts of the door shook at the voice of him that called, and the temple was filled with smoke. Then said I, "Woe is me! for I am ruined! I am a man of unclean lips, and I dwell in the midst of a people of unclean lips, for my eyes have seen the King, the LORD Almighty."

ISAIAH 6:1–5

Ah sinful nation, a people laden with iniquity, a brood of evildoers, children given to corruption; they have forsaken the LORD, they have provoked the Holy One of Israel to anger and turned their backs upon him.

ISAIAH 1:4

The earth shall reel to and fro like a drunkard, and shall sway like a hut in a storm; and its offenses are so heavy upon it that it shall fall and not rise again.

ISAIAH 24:20

Let the wicked forsake his way, and the unrighteous man forsake his thoughts, and let him return to the LORD, and he will have mercy upon him, and to our God, for he will abundantly pardon.   ISAIAH 55:7

We acknowledge, O LORD, our wickedness, and the guilt of our fathers, for we have sinned against you.   JEREMIAH 14:20

The soul that sins is the one that shall die. The son shall not bear the guilt of the father, neither shall the father bear the guilt of the son; the righteousness of the righteous man shall be credited to him, and the wickedness of the wicked shall be charged to him.   EZEKIEL 18:20

If the wicked will turn from all his sins that he has committed, and keep all my statutes, and do what is lawful and right, he shall surely live, he shall not die. All his offenses that he has committed, they shall not be charged to him; in his righteousness that he has done he shall live.   EZEKIEL 18:21–22

All have sinned, and come short of the glory of God, and are justified freely by his grace through the redemption that is in Christ Jesus.

ROMANS 3:23–24

If any man be in Christ, he is a new creature; old things have passed away— behold, all things have become new. And all things are from God, who has reconciled us to himself through Jesus Christ, and has given to us the ministry of reconciliation, which is this: God was in Christ, reconciling the world to himself, not counting men's sins against them. And he has committed to us the word of reconciliation.   2 CORINTHIANS 5:17–19

Let us draw near with a true heart in full assurance of faith, having our hearts sprinkled from an evil conscience, and our bodies washed with pure water.   HEBREWS 10:22

If we walk in the light, as he is in the light, we have fellowship one with another, and the blood of Jesus Christ his Son cleanses us from all sin.

I JOHN 1:7

This is how we know that we are of the truth, and shall assure our hearts before him. For if our heart condemn us, God is greater than our heart, and he knows all things. Beloved, if our heart condemn us not, then we have confidence toward God.   I JOHN 3:19–21

See also Confession, God's Mercy, Repentance, Sin and Redemption.

HAPPINESS

An old gospel song says that "Happiness is to know the Savior." That pretty much sums up the Bible's view of happiness: People find true happiness in this world and the next by being in a proper relationship with God. Naturally this view doesn't square with the world's view of happiness. You might say that the most satisfying religion, the one that brings the most happiness in the short run, is the religion of worshiping oneself. But for the long haul, the old song holds true: Know and love and serve God, for this is the only way to ultimate happiness.

Happy is the man whom God corrects: therefore despise not the chastening of the Almighty; for he makes sore, and binds up; he wounds, and his hands make whole. JOB 5:17–28

The triumphing of the wicked is short, and the joy of the hypocrite but for a moment. JOB 20:5

His anger endures but a moment; in his favor is life. Weeping may endure for a night, but joy comes in the morning. You have turned my mourning into dancing; you have put off my sackcloth and circled me with gladness. PSALM 30:5, 11

They shall be abundantly satisfied with the prosperity of your house, and you shall make them drink from the river of your pleasures. For with you is the fountain of life; in your light shall we see light. PSALM 36:8

Delight yourself in the LORD, and he shall give you the desires of your heart. PSALM 37:4

I delight to do your will, O my God; indeed, your law is within my heart. PSALM 40:8

There is a river whose streams shall make glad the city of God, the holy place, the dwelling place of the most High.　　PSALM 46:4

Light is sown for the righteous, and gladness for the upright in heart.

　　　　　　　　　　　　　　　　　　　　PSALM 97:11

This is the day which the LORD has made; we will rejoice and be glad in it.

　　　　　　　　　　　　　　　　　　　　PSALM 118:24

They that sow in tears shall reap in joy.　　PSALM 126:5

Blessed is everyone that fears the LORD, that walks in his ways. For you shall eat the labor of your hands; happy shall you be, and it shall be well with you.　　PSALM 128:1–2

Happy is that people whose God is the LORD.　　PSALM 144:15

Happy is the man that finds wisdom, and the man that gets understanding. For it is more profitable than silver, and it gives greater return than fine gold. Wisdom is more precious than rubies, and all the things you can desire are not to be compared to it. Length of days is in its right hand, and in its left hand are riches and honor. Its ways are ways of pleasantness, and all its paths are peace. Wisdom is a tree of life and a blessing to those who lay hold upon it.　　PROVERBS 3:13–18

He that despises his neighbor sins, but he who has mercy on the poor, happy is he.　　PROVERBS 14:21

Whoever trusts in the LORD, happy is he.　　PROVERBS 16:20

I will greatly rejoice in the LORD, my soul shall be joyful in my God; for he has clothed me with the garments of salvation, he has covered me with the robe of righteousness, as a bridegroom decks himself with ornaments, and as a bride adorns herself with her jewels. For as the earth brings forth her buds, and as the garden causes the things that are sown in it to spring forth, so the LORD God will cause righteousness and praise to spring forth before all the nations. ISAIAH 61:10–11

I have come that they might have life, and that they might have it more abundantly. JOHN 10:10

The peace of God, which surpasses all understanding, shall keep your hearts and minds through Christ Jesus. PHILIPPIANS 4:7

If you suffer for righteousness' sake, happy are you, and be not afraid of their terror, neither be troubled. I PETER 3:14

Beloved, think it not strange concerning the fiery trial which is to try you, as though some strange thing happened to you. But rejoice in that you are sharing in Christ's sufferings, so that you may be glad and shout for joy when his glory is revealed. I PETER 4:12

Be not drunk with wine, which leads to immorality, but be filled with the Spirit, speaking to yourselves in psalms and hymns and spiritual songs, singing and making melody in your hearts to the Lord.

EPHESIANS 5:18–19

See also Contentment, Joy, Peace.

HATE

Comedian Buddy Hackett had this so say about grudges: "While you're holding a grudge, they're out dancing." Put another way, hatred does more harm to our own souls than it does to the person we hate. And, of course, hatred is just plain wrong. It's an old cliché, but a true one, that we ought to hate the sin but love the sinner. Why? Because God does. (One overlooked fact in our pro-tolerance age is that we are supposed to hate sin because we love the sinner.)

The flip side of hate is this: Innocent people are often hated. It is easy, and natural, to return hate for hate. But the Bible offers us a higher standard. Where there is hatred, sow love, and where there is harm, sow forgiveness.

You shall not hate your brother in your heart.   LEVITICUS 19:17

Consider my enemies, for they are many, and they hate me with cruel hatred.
                                                        PSALM 25:19

Evil shall slay the wicked, and they that hate the righteous shall be desolate.
                                                        PSALM 34:21

You have saved us from our enemies, and have put to shame them that hated us.   PSALM 44:7

They that hate me without a cause are more than the hairs of mine head; they that would destroy me, being my enemies wrongfully, are mighty. . . . Deliver me out of the mire, and let me not sink, let me be delivered from them that hate me, out of the deep waters.   PSALM 69:4, 14

Hatred stirs up quarrels, but love covers all sins.   PROVERBS 10:12

He that despises his neighbor sins.   PROVERBS 14:21

The bloodthirsty hate the upright.   PROVERBS 29:10

Let none of you imagine evil in your hearts against his neighbor, and love no false oath, for all these are things that I hate, says the LORD.
                                                        ZECHARIAH 8:17

You have heard that it has been said, "You shall love your neighbor, and hate your enemy." But I say to you, love your enemies, bless those who curse you, do good to those who hate you, and pray for those who spitefully use you and persecute you.   MATTHEW 5:43-44

If you forgive not men their offenses, neither will your Father forgive your offenses.   MATTHEW 6:15

You shall be hated by all men for my name's sake, but he who endures to the end shall be saved.   MATTHEW 10:22

Let all bitterness and wrath and anger and brawling and evil speaking be put away from you, along with all malice. And be kind one to another, tenderhearted, forgiving one another, just as God for Christ's sake has forgiven you.   EPHESIANS 4:31–32

Put off all these: anger, wrath, malice, blasphemy, filthy speaking out of your mouth.   COLOSSIANS 3:8

See that none repay evil for evil to any man, but always follow what is good, both among yourselves, and to all men.   I THESSALONIANS 5:15

Put them in mind to . . . speak evil of no man, not to be brawlers, but gentle, showing meekness to all men. For we ourselves also were sometimes foolish, disobedient, deceived, serving various lusts and pleasures, living in malice and envy, hateful, and hating one another.   TITUS 3:1–3

He that has shown no mercy shall have judgment without mercy.

JAMES 2:13

He that says he is in the light, and hates his brother, is in darkness even now. He that loves his brother dwells in the light, and there is no occasion of stumbling in him. But he who hates his brother is in darkness, and walks in darkness, and knows not where he goes, because that darkness has blinded his eyes.   I JOHN 2:9–11

In this is revealed which are the children of God and which are the children of the devil: whoever does not righteousness does not belong to God, nor is he who loves not his brother. For this is the message that you heard from the beginning, that we should love one another. Not as Cain, who was of that wicked one, and murdered his brother. And why did he slay him? Because his own works were evil, and his brother's were righteous.

Marvel not, my brethren, if the world hate you. We know that we have passed from death to life, because we love the brethren. He that loves not his brother abides in death. Whoever hates his brother is a murderer, and you know that no murderer has eternal life abiding in him.

1 JOHN 3:10–15

If a man say, "I love God," yet hates his brother, he is a liar, for if he loves not his brother whom he has seen, how can he love God whom he has not seen? And this commandment have we from him, that he who loves God loves his brother also.
1 JOHN 4:20–21

See also Anger, Enemies, Envy, Forgiveness, Mercy, Revenge.

HEALING

The Bible abounds with stories of miraculous healing, especially in the Gospels, which show Jesus as a great healer. As advanced as medical science is today, the medical experts know that there are still healings that are, medically speaking, impossible. So God still heals, though the mystery of why he sometimes heals and sometimes does not remains. The Bible promises that in eternity there will be no sickness or sorrow, so for people of faith there is an "ultimate healing" ahead.

Physical healing matters to God, for he made the human body and cares for it. Yet the worst sickness of all is the "soul sickness" that afflicts everyone, which is why Jesus the healer is also Jesus the Savior. No wonder some old hymns refer to him as "the Great Physician."

LORD, be merciful unto me; heal my soul; for I have sinned against you.

PSALM 41:4

Bless the LORD, O my soul, and all that is within me, bless his holy name. Bless the LORD, O my soul, and forget not all his benefits: he forgives all your iniquities, he heals all your diseases. PSALM 103:1–3

He heals the broken in heart and binds up their wounds.

PSALM 147:3

Heal me, O LORD, and I shall be healed. Save me, and I shall be saved.

JEREMIAH 17:14

Let us return to the LORD, for he has torn, and he will heal us; he has injured, but he will bind us up.   HOSEA 6:1

Jesus went about all Galilee, teaching in their synagogues, and preaching the gospel of the kingdom, and healing all manner of sickness and all manner of disease among the people.   MATTHEW 4:23

When he had called to him his twelve disciples, he gave them power against evil spirits, to drive them out, and to heal all manner of sickness and all manner of disease. "Heal the sick, cleanse the lepers, raise the dead, cast out devils; freely you have received, freely give."   MATTHEW 10:1, 8

The Spirit of the Lord is upon me, because he has anointed me to preach the gospel to the poor. He has sent me to heal the brokenhearted, to preach deliverance to the captives, and recovering of sight to the blind, to set at liberty those who are oppressed.   LUKE 4:18

Now when the sun was setting, all they that had any sick with diverse diseases brought them unto him; and he laid his hands on every one of them, and healed them.   LUKE 4:40

Peter and John went up together into the temple at the hour of prayer, being the ninth hour. And a certain man lame from his mother's womb was carried there and set down every day at the Beautiful Gate of the temple. He would ask alms from those who entered the temple, and seeing Peter and John about to go into the temple he asked for alms. And Peter, fixing his gaze upon him with John, said, "Look at us." And he gave heed to them, expecting to receive something from them. Then Peter said, "Silver and gold have I none, but such as I have give I you: In the name of Jesus Christ of Nazareth, rise up and walk." And Peter took him by the right hand and lifted him up, and immediately his feet and ankle bones received strength.

ACTS 3:1–7

God anointed Jesus of Nazareth with the Holy Spirit and with power. He went about doing good, and healing all that were oppressed by the devil, for God was with him.   ACTS 10:38

God has appointed some in the church—first apostles, then prophets, then teachers, and after that miracles, then gifts of healings.

1 CORINTHIANS 12:28

Confess your faults one to another, and pray one for another, that you may be healed. The fervent prayer of a righteous man works powerfully.

JAMES 5:16

In the midst of the street of it [heaven] and on either side of the river was the tree of life, which bore twelve sorts of fruits, and yielded her fruit every month, and the leaves of the tree were for the healing of the nations.

REVELATION 22:2

See also Sickness.

HEAVEN

Religious people have often been accused of being "otherworldly," neglecting life in this world by too much focus on the next. But one of the curiosities of history is that people who did the most to change the present world were those who had a powerful belief in the next world. Believing strongly in heaven is not really some form of escapism: It is simply giving attention to the world that will outlast this present one. The people in the Bible who looked forward to heaven loved and valued their lives in this world while all the time knowing that their permanent home was even finer.

The Bible assures us that heaven isn't just "later." Life lived in fellowship with God means that heaven already has begun. All the way to heaven is heaven.

The eternal God is your refuge, and underneath are the everlasting arms.

DEUTERONOMY 33:27

I know that my redeemer lives, and that he shall stand at the latter day upon the earth. JOB 19:25

You will show me the path of life. In your presence is fullness of joy. At your right hand there are pleasures forevermore. PSALM 16:11

Surely goodness and mercy shall follow me all the days of my life, and I will dwell in the house of the LORD forever. PSALM 23:6

Lay not up for yourselves treasures upon earth, where moth and rust corrupt, and where thieves break through and steal. But lay up for yourselves treasures in heaven, where neither moth nor rust do corrupt, and where thieves do not break through and steal; for where your treasure is, there will your heart be also. MATTHEW 6:19–21

Not every one that says to me, "Lord, Lord," shall enter into the kingdom of heaven; but he that does the will of my Father which is in heaven.

MATTHEW 7:21

Many shall come from the east and west, and shall sit down with Abraham, and Isaac, and Jacob, in the kingdom of heaven. MATTHEW 8:11

As you go, preach, saying, "The kingdom of heaven is at hand."

MATTHEW 10:7

Except you be converted, and become as little children, you shall not enter into the kingdom of heaven. MATTHEW 18:3

Rejoice, because your names are written in heaven. LUKE 10:20

God so loved the world that he gave his only begotten Son, that whoever believes in him should not perish, but have everlasting life. For God sent not his Son into the world to condemn the world, but that the world through him might be saved. JOHN 3:16–17

I give to them eternal life, and they shall never perish, neither shall any man snatch them out of my hand. My Father, who gave them to me, is greater than all, and no man is able to snatch them out of my Father's hand.

JOHN 10:28–29

Jesus said to her, "I am the resurrection and the life; he who believes in me, though he were dead, yet shall he live. And whoever lives and believes in me shall never die." JOHN 11:25–26

In my Father's house are many mansions; if it were not so, I would have told you. I go to prepare a place for you. And if I go and prepare a place for you, I will come again, and take you to myself, so that where I am, there you may be also. JOHN 14:2–3

He [Stephen], being full of the Holy Spirit, looked up steadfastly into heaven, and saw the glory of God, and Jesus standing at the right hand of God. ACTS 7:55

For now we see in a mirror, dimly, but then face to face.

I CORINTHIANS 13:12

If in this life only we have hope in Christ, we are of all men most miserable. But Christ has in fact risen from the dead, and has become the firstfruits of those who slept. I CORINTHIANS 15:19–20

We know that if this earthly tent we live in is destroyed, we have a building from God, a house not made with hands, eternal in the heavens. For in this tent we groan, earnestly desiring to be clothed with our dwelling from heaven. . . . For we who are in this tent do groan, being burdened, for we wish not to be unclothed but to be further clothed, so that mortality might be swallowed up by life. Now he who has made us for this very thing is God, who also has given to us the guarantee of the Spirit. Therefore we are always confident, knowing that, while we are at home in the body, we are absent from the Lord. (For we walk by faith, not by sight.)

2 CORINTHIANS 5:1–7

Our homeland is in heaven, and there we look for the Savior, the Lord Jesus Christ. He shall transform our wretched bodies so that it may be made like his glorious body. He will do this by the same power with which he can subdue all things.   PHILIPPIANS 3:20–21

If you then are risen with Christ, seek those things which are above, where Christ sits at the right hand of God. Set your affection on things above, not on things on the earth. For you are dead, and your life is hid with Christ in God. When Christ, who is our life, shall appear, then shall you also appear with him in glory.   COLOSSIANS 3:1–4

Walk worthy of God, who has called you to his kingdom and glory.
                                        I THESSALONIANS 2:12

You have in heaven a better and an enduring substance.
                                        HEBREWS 10:34

These all died in faith, not having received the promises, but having seen them far off, and were persuaded of them, and embraced them, and confessed that they were strangers and pilgrims on the earth. For they that say such things declare plainly that they seek a homeland. And truly, if they had been mindful of that country they had left behind, they might have had opportunity to return. But they desire a better country, that is, a heavenly one. Therefore God is not ashamed to be called their God, for he has prepared for them a city.   HEBREWS 11:13–16

You have come to Mount Zion, to the city of the living God, the heavenly Jerusalem, and to an innumerable company of angels, to the general assembly and church of the firstborn, which are inscribed in heaven, and to God the Judge of all, and to the spirits of just men made perfect.
                                        HEBREWS 12:22–23

Here have we no continuing city, but we seek one to come.
                                        HEBREWS 13:14

Blessed be the God and Father of our Lord Jesus Christ, who according to his abundant mercy has given us a new birth into a living hope by the resurrection of Jesus Christ from the dead, to an imperishable inheritance, one undefiled, which never fades away, reserved in heaven for you. You are protected by the power of God through faith for a salvation ready to be revealed in the last time. In this you greatly rejoice, though now for a time you are in heaviness through various trials.   I PETER 1:3–6

The heavens and the earth which now exist have been reserved for fire until the day of judgment and destruction of ungodly men. But, beloved, be not ignorant of this one thing, that one day is with the Lord like a thousand years, and a thousand years like one day. The Lord is not slow concerning his promise, as some men believe; but he is longsuffering toward us, not willing that any should perish, but that all should come to repentance. But the day of the Lord will come as a thief in the night. Then the heavens shall pass away with a great noise, and the elements shall melt with fervent heat, the earth also and everything in it shall be burned up.

2 PETER 3:7–10

To him that overcomes I will give fruit from the tree of life, which is in the midst of the paradise of God.   REVELATION 2:7

Him that overcomes I will make a pillar in the temple of my God, and he shall never leave there. I will write upon him the name of my God, and the name of the city of my God, which is the New Jerusalem, which comes down out of heaven from my God, and I will write upon him my new name.

REVELATION 3:12

I saw a new heaven and a new earth, for the first heaven and the first earth were passed away, and there was no more sea. And I John saw the holy city, New Jerusalem, coming down from God out of heaven, prepared as a bride adorned for her husband. And I heard a great voice out of heaven saying, "Behold, the dwelling place of God is with men, and he will dwell with them, and they shall be his people, and God himself shall be with them, and be their God. And God shall wipe away all tears from their eyes, and there shall be no more death, neither sorrow, nor crying, neither shall there be any more pain, for the former things have passed away."

Pearly Gates in Heaven?

How many cartoons have you seen of St. Peter standing at the gate of heaven? Is that in the Bible? No. But according to the New Testament, heaven does have gates. And yes, they are pearly gates: "The twelve gates were twelve pearls, each gate made of a single pearl" (Revelation 21:21).

And in case you were wondering, the same verse says that the street of heaven is paved thus: "The great street of the city was of pure gold, like transparent glass." (NIV)

And he who sat upon the throne said, "Behold, I make all things new." And he said to me, "Write, for these words are true and faithful." And he said to me, "It is done. I am Alpha and Omega, the beginning and the end. I will give to him that is thirsty the fountain of the water of life freely. He that overcomes shall inherit all things, and I will be his God, and he shall be my son. But the cowards, and unbelieving, and the abominable, and murderers, and whoremongers, and sorcerers, and idolaters, and all liars shall have their reward in the lake which burns with fire and brimstone. This is the second death."   REVELATION 21:1–8

I saw no temple there, for the Lord God Almighty and the Lamb are the temple of it. And the city had no need of the sun nor of the moon to shine on it, for the glory of God did lighten it, and the Lamb is its light. And the nations of those who are saved shall walk in the light of it, and the kings of the earth bring their glory and honor into it. And its gates shall not be shut at all by day, for there shall be no night there. And they shall bring the glory and honor of the nations into it. And there shall by no means enter into it anything that is impure, nor anything loathsome or deceitful, but only those whose names are written in the Lamb's book of life.

REVELATION 21:22–27

They shall see his face, and his name shall be on their foreheads. And there shall be no night there, and they need no lamp, nor the light of the sun. For the Lord God gives them light, and they shall reign forever and ever.

REVELATION 22:4–5

See also Eternal Life, Hell, Jesus' Second Coming.

HELL

Here is an unpopular topic, but one that still fascinates people. Most people today believe in some kind of afterlife, but the general view is that everyone will eventually get to heaven. Will they? Haven't we all known people so wrapped up in their own selfishness that they seemed to be already sealed up in their own private world? That, in essence, is what hell is all about: shutting oneself off from the goodness of God. Hell is saying "No" to the moral order that God established in the world. Saying that we don't believe in hell is like saying that people's evil and selfish acts do not really matter.

Jesus himself, the great teacher of love, the one who spoke so often of God's love for humanity, also taught that there is a hell. Difficult to accept? Perhaps—but also difficult to reject.

"As I live," says the LORD God, "I have no pleasure in the death of the wicked; but I desire that the wicked turn from his way and live. Turn, turn from your evil ways; for why will you die, O house of Israel?"

EZEKIEL 33:11

[Jesus:] Enter in at the narrow gate. For wide is the gate and broad is the way that leads to destruction, and many there are who go in that way.

MATTHEW 7:13

Fear not them which kill the body, but are not able to kill the soul; but rather fear him who is able to destroy both soul and body in hell.

MATTHEW 10:28

The Son of man shall send forth his angels, and they shall gather out of his kingdom all things that offend, and those who do evil, and shall cast them into a furnace of fire; there shall be wailing and gnashing of teeth. Then shall the righteous shine forth as the sun in the kingdom of their Father.

MATTHEW 13:41–43

The kingdom of heaven is like a net, that was cast into the sea, and gathered in every kind of fish. When it was full, they drew it to shore, and sat down, and gathered the good into baskets, but cast the bad away. So shall it be at the end of the world; the angels shall come forth, and separate the wicked from among the righteous, and shall cast them into the furnace of fire; there shall be wailing and gnashing of teeth.   MATTHEW 13:47–50

You serpents, you generation of vipers, how can you escape the damnation of hell?   MATTHEW 23:33

Cast the unprofitable servant into outer darkness; there shall be weeping and gnashing of teeth.   MATTHEW 25:30

He that shall blaspheme against the Holy Spirit never has forgiveness, but is in danger of eternal damnation.   MARK 3:29

He that believes and is baptized shall be saved; but he who believes not shall be damned.   MARK 16:16

If your hand causes you to sin, cut it off; it is better for you to go through life maimed than having two hands to go into hell, into the fire that never shall be quenched; where their worm dies not, and the fire is not quenched.

MARK 9:43–44

Depart from me, all you workers of evil. There shall be weeping and gnashing of teeth, when you shall see Abraham, Isaac, Jacob, and all the prophets in the kingdom of God, and you yourselves thrust out. And they shall come from the east and the west and the north and the south, and shall sit down in the kingdom of God. And, behold, some which are last shall be first, and there are first which shall be last.   LUKE 13:27–30

There was a certain rich man, who was clothed in purple and fine linen, and feasted sumptuously every day. And there was a certain beggar named Lazarus, who lay at his gate, full of sores, and desiring to be fed with the crumbs which fell from the rich man's table; and the dogs came and licked his sores.

And it came to pass, that the beggar died, and was carried by the angels to Abraham's side. The rich man also died, and was buried. And in hell he lifted up his eyes, being in torment, and he saw Abraham far off, with Lazarus by his side. And he cried and said, "Father Abraham, have mercy on me, and send Lazarus, that he may dip the tip of his finger in water, and cool my tongue; for I am tormented in this flame."

But Abraham said, "Son, remember that you in your lifetime received your good things, and likewise Lazarus evil things; but now he is comforted, and you are tormented. And beside all this, between us and you there is a great gulf fixed, so that they who would pass from here to you cannot."

LUKE 16:19–26

He that believes not is condemned already, because he has not believed in the name of the only begotten Son of God. And this is the condemnation: light has come into the world, and men loved darkness rather than light, because their deeds were evil.   JOHN 3:18–19

The wrath of God is revealed from heaven against all ungodliness and unrighteousness of men who hold the truth in unrighteousness. For what may be known about God is clearly revealed to, since God has shown it to them. For since the creation of the world, the invisible things of him, his eternal power and Godhead, are clearly seen, being understood by the things he has made. So they are without excuse; for when they knew God, they glorified him not as God, nor were thankful; but they became futile in their thoughts, and their foolish hearts were darkened. Professing themselves to be wise, they became fools. And they exchanged the glory of the eternal God for images made to look like mortal man and birds and animals and reptiles. ROMANS 1:18–22

They all will be condemned who believed not the truth, but took pleasure in unrighteousness. 2 THESSALONIANS 2:12

God spared not the angels that sinned, but cast them down to hell, and delivered them into chains of darkness, to be held for judgment.

2 PETER 2:4

The devil that deceived them was cast into the lake of fire and brimstone, where the beast and the false prophet are, and they shall be tormented day and night forever and ever. And death and hell were cast into the lake of fire. This is the second death. And whoever was not found written in the book of life was cast into the lake of fire. REVELATION 20:10, 14–15

The cowardly, and unbelieving, and the vile, and murderers, and whoremongers, and sorcerers, and idolaters, and all liars shall have their part in the lake which burns with fire and brimstone; which is the second death.

REVELATION 21:8

See also Eternal Life, Heaven, Jesus' Second Coming.

HOLINESS

How many people have you known who said that their main ambition was to be holy? It sounds laughable today, but in fact the Bible is clear that holiness is what God desires for mankind—not happiness, not health, but holiness. In other words, God's ultimate goal is to create saints. That strikes many people as self-righteous—and boring. But it isn't boring at all. It involves committing oneself to the highest form of life, striving to be (as the U.S. Army slogan has it) "all that you can be." Holiness doesn't require a long face and a somber heart; it just requires us to want to be like God.

When Abram was ninety-nine years old, the LORD appeared to him and said to him, "I am the Almighty God; walk before me, and be blameless."

GENESIS 17:1

Jacob said to his household, and to all that were with him, "Put away the strange gods that are among you, and be clean."   GENESIS 35:2

You shall be to me a kingdom of priests, and a holy nation.

EXODUS 19:6

You shall be holy, for I the LORD your God am holy.   LEVITICUS 19:2

You are a holy people to the LORD your God, and the LORD has chosen you to be a distinctive people to himself, above all the nations that are upon the earth.   DEUTERONOMY 14:2

Who shall ascend into the hill of the LORD? Or who shall stand in his holy place? He that has clean hands and a pure heart; he who has not lifted up his soul to an idol, nor swear by what is false. He shall receive the blessing from the LORD, and righteousness from the God of his salvation.

PSALM 24:3–5

There is a river whose streams make glad the city of God, the holy place where the Most High dwells.   PSALM 46:4

You that love the LORD, hate evil; he preserves the souls of his saints; he delivers them out of the hand of the wicked.   PSALM 97:10

Bless the LORD, O my soul, and all that is within me, bless his holy name.

PSALM 103:1

In the year that King Uzziah died I saw the LORD sitting upon a throne, high and lifted up, and his robe's train filled the temple. Above it stood the seraphim; each one had six wings; with two he covered his face, and with two he covered his feet, and with two he flew. And one called to another and said, "Holy, holy, holy, is the LORD Almighty; the whole earth is full of his glory." And the posts of the door shook at the voice of him that called, and the temple was filled with smoke. Then said I, "Woe is me! for I am ruined! I am a man of unclean lips, and I dwell in the midst of a people of unclean lips, for my eyes have seen the King, the LORD Almighty."

ISAIAH 6:1–5

A highway shall be there, and it shall be called The Way of Holiness. The unclean shall not travel over it; but it shall be for God's people.

ISAIAH 35:8

Behold, your salvation comes; behold, his reward is with him, and his recompense accompanies him. And they shall call them the Holy People, the Redeemed of the LORD. And you shall be called Sought Out, A City Not Forsaken.

ISAIAH 62:11–12

Blessed are they which do hunger and thirst after righteousness, for they shall be filled. Blessed are the merciful, for they shall obtain mercy. Blessed are the pure in heart, for they shall see God.

MATTHEW 5:6–8

A good man out of the good treasure of his heart brings forth what is good, and an evil man out of the evil treasure of his heart brings forth what is evil, for out of the abundance of the heart his mouth speaks.

LUKE 6:45

Being made free from sin, and become servants of God, you bear fruit leading to holiness, and the end is everlasting life.

ROMANS 6:22

I appeal to you, brethren, by the mercies of God, that you present your bodies a living sacrifice, holy and acceptable to God, which is your spiritual service. And be not conformed to this world, but be transformed by the renewing of your mind, that you may test what is the good and acceptable and perfect will of God.

ROMANS 12:1–2

Know you not that you are the temple of God, and that the Spirit of God dwells in you?

I CORINTHIANS 3:16

Whether you eat, or drink, or whatever you do, do all for the glory of God.

1 CORINTHIANS 10:31

Having these promises, dearly beloved, let us cleanse ourselves from all filthiness of the flesh and spirit, perfecting holiness in the fear of God.

2 CORINTHIANS 7:1

He has chosen us in him before the foundation of the world, that we should be holy and without blame before him in love.   EPHESIANS 1:4

Put on therefore, as the elect of God, holy and beloved, compassion, kindness, humbleness of mind, meekness, patience.   COLOSSIANS 3:12

Prepare your minds for action, be disciplined, and set your hope on the grace that will be brought to you at the revealing of Jesus Christ. As obedient children, do not be led by your lusts as when you lived in ignorance. But as he who has called you is holy, so be holy in everything you do, because it is written, "Be holy, for I am holy."   1 PETER 1:13

You are a chosen generation, a royal priesthood, a holy nation, a distinctive people, so you should show forth the praises of him who has called you out of darkness into his marvelous light.   1 PETER 2:9

If we say that we have fellowship with him, and walk in darkness, we lie, and do not do the truth. But if we walk in the light, as he is in the light, we have fellowship with one another, and the blood of Jesus Christ his Son cleanses us from all sin.   1 JOHN 1:6-7

Whatever is born of God overcomes the world.   1 JOHN 5:4

Holy, holy, holy, Lord God Almighty, who was, and is, and is to come.

REVELATION 4:8

I saw a new heaven and a new earth, for the first heaven and the first earth were passed away, and there was no more sea. And I John saw the holy city,

New Jerusalem, coming down from God out of heaven, prepared as a bride adorned for her husband. . . . There shall by no means enter into it anything impure, nor anything shameful or deceitful, but only they whose names are written in the Lamb's book of life.

Blessed are they that do his commandments, that they may have access to the tree of life, and may enter in through the gates into the city. For outside are dogs, and sorcerers, and whoremongers, and murderers, and idolaters, and whoever loves and practices falseness.

REVELATION 21:1-2, 27; 22:14-15

THE HOLY SPIRIT

The traditional view is that God is three "Persons"—Father, Son, and Holy Spirit. This view is based on the Bible. But over the centuries, belief in the Holy Spirit has been so neglected that most people had only the vaguest idea of what—or who—the Holy Spirit is. That has changed radically in recent years, and there is a healthy interest in the activity of the Spirit. Readers new to the Bible may be surprised to find that the Spirit is mentioned often—in fact, at the very beginning of the world itself.

In the beginning God created the heaven and the earth. And the earth was without form, and void, and darkness was upon the face of the deep. And the Spirit of God moved upon the face of the waters.   GENESIS 1:1-2

"As for me, this is my covenant with them," says the LORD; "my Spirit that is upon you, and my words which I have put in your mouth, shall not depart out of your mouth, nor out of the mouth of your offspring, nor out of the mouth of your children's children, from henceforth and forever."

ISAIAH 59:21

A new heart also will I give you, and a new spirit will I put within you. And I will take away the stony heart out of your flesh, and I will give you a heart of flesh. And I will put my Spirit within you, and cause you to walk in my statutes, and you shall keep my judgments, and do them. And you shall dwell in the land that I gave to your fathers, and you shall be my people, and I will be your God.   EZEKIEL 36:26–27

It shall come to pass afterward, that I will pour out my Spirit upon all flesh, and your sons and your daughters shall prophesy, your old men shall dream dreams, your young men shall see visions.   JOEL 2:28

[John the Baptist:] I indeed baptize you with water for repentance, but he who comes after me is mightier than I, whose shoes I am not worthy to carry; he shall baptize you with the Holy Spirit and with fire.

MATTHEW 3:11

It is not you that speak, but the Spirit of your Father who speaks in you.

MATTHEW 10:20

Go you therefore, and teach all nations, baptizing them in the name of the Father, and of the Son, and of the Holy Spirit.   MATTHEW 28:19

And it came to pass in those days, that Jesus came from Nazareth of Galilee, and was baptized by John in Jordan. And straightaway coming up out of the water, he saw the heavens opened, and the Spirit like a dove descending upon him. And there came a voice from heaven, saying, "You are my beloved Son, in whom I am well pleased."   MARK 1:9–11

Everyone that asks receives, and he who seeks finds, and to him that knocks it shall be opened. If a son shall ask bread of any of you that is a father, will he give him a stone? Or if he ask a fish, will he for a fish give him a serpent? Or if he shall ask an egg, will he offer him a scorpion? If you then, being evil, know how to give good gifts to your children, how much more shall your heavenly Father give the Holy Spirit to those who ask him?

LUKE 11:10–13

Whoever speaks a word against the Son of man, it shall be forgiven him, but to him that blasphemes against the Holy Spirit it shall not be forgiven.

LUKE 12:10

Jesus answered, "Truly, truly, I say to you, except a man be born of water and of the Spirit, he cannot enter into the kingdom of God. That which is born of the flesh is flesh, and what is born of the Spirit is spirit."

JOHN 3:5–6

It is the Spirit that gives life; the flesh profits nothing.   JOHN 6:63

I will pray to the Father, and he shall give you another Comforter, that he may abide with you forever; this is the Spirit of truth, whom the world cannot receive, because it sees him not, neither knows him. But you know him, for he dwells with you, and shall be in you. But the Comforter, which is the Holy Spirit, whom the Father will send in my name, he shall teach you all things, and bring all things to your remembrance, whatever I have said to you.   JOHN 14:16–17, 26

When he, the Spirit of truth, has come, he will guide you into all truth, for he shall not speak of himself; but whatever he shall hear, that shall he speak, and he will show you things to come. He shall glorify me, for he shall receive of mine, and shall show it to you.   JOHN 16:13–15

You shall receive power, after that the Holy Spirit has come upon you, and you shall be witnesses to me both in Jerusalem, and in all Judea, and in Samaria, and to the uttermost part of the earth.   ACTS 1:8

When the day of Pentecost had come, they [the apostles] were all together in one place. And suddenly there came a sound from heaven like the rushing of a mighty wind, and it filled all the house where they were sitting. And there appeared to them tongues of fire that separated and sat upon each of them. And they were all filled with the Holy Spirit, and began to speak with other tongues, as the Spirit gave them ability.   ACTS 2:1–4

Peter said to them, "Repent, and be baptized every one of you in the name of Jesus Christ for the forgiveness of sins, and you shall receive the gift of the Holy Spirit."   ACTS 2:38

When they had prayed, the place was shaken where they were assembled together; and they were all filled with the Holy Spirit, and they spoke the word of God with boldness.   ACTS 4:31

Stephen, being full of the Holy Spirit, looked up steadfastly into heaven, and saw the glory of God, and Jesus standing at the right hand of God.

ACTS 7:55

The law of the Spirit of life in Christ Jesus has made me free from the law of sin and death. Those who live according to the sinful nature set their minds on the things of the sinful nature; but those who live according to the Spirit set their minds on the things of the Spirit. For to be carnally minded is death; but to be spiritually minded is life and peace. If the Spirit of him that raised Jesus from the dead dwells in you, he who raised up Christ from the dead shall also give life to your mortal bodies through his Spirit that dwells in you. For those who are led by the Spirit of God are the sons of God. For you have not received the spirit of slavery to fall back again into fear; but you have received the Spirit of adoption. So when we cry, "Abba, Father," it is the Spirit itself that bears witness with our spirit that we are the children of God.   ROMANS 8:2, 5–6, 11, 14–16

We have received, not the spirit of the world, but the Spirit which is of God, so that we might know the things that are freely given to us of God. But the natural man receives not the things of the Spirit of God, for they are foolishness to him; neither can he know them, because they are spiritually discerned. But he who is spiritual judges all things, yet he himself is judged by no one else. For who has known the mind of the Lord, that he may instruct him? But we have the mind of Christ.

I CORINTHIANS 2:12, 14–16

Know you not that you are the temple of God, and that the Spirit of God dwells in you? If any man defile the temple of God, him shall God destroy; for the temple of God is holy, and his temple you are.

I CORINTHIANS 3:16–17

No man can say that Jesus is the Lord, except through the Holy Spirit.

I CORINTHIANS 12:3

You are plainly declared to be an epistle from Christ, prepared by us, written not with ink, but with the Spirit of the living God—not on tablets of stone, but on tablets of the human heart. God has also made us able ministers of the new covenant, not of the letter, but of the Spirit; for the letter kills, but the Spirit gives life. Now the Lord is that Spirit, and where the Spirit of the Lord is, there is liberty.   2 CORINTHIANS 3:3, 6, 17

We know that if this earthly tent we live in is destroyed, we have a building from God, a house not made with hands, eternal in the heavens. For in this tent we groan, earnestly desiring to be clothed with our dwelling from heaven. . . . For we who are in this tent do groan, being burdened, for we wish not to be unclothed but to be further clothed, so that mortality might be swallowed up by life. Now he who has made us for this very thing is God, who also has given to us the guarantee of the Spirit. Therefore we are always confident, knowing that, while we are at home in the body, we are absent from the Lord. (For we walk by faith, not by sight.)

2 CORINTHIANS 5:1–7

We through the Spirit wait for the hope of righteousness by faith.

GALATIANS 5:5

The sinful nature lusts against the Spirit, and the Spirit against the sinful nature, and these are contrary the one to the other; so that you cannot do the things that you would. But if you are led by the Spirit, you are not under the law. But the fruit of the Spirit is love, joy, peace, longsuffering, gentleness, goodness, faith, meekness, self-control; against such there is no law. And they that are Christ's have crucified the sinful nature with its passions and lusts. If we live in the Spirit, let us also walk in the Spirit.

GALATIANS 5:17–18, 22–25

Be not drunk with wine, which leads to immorality, but be filled with the Spirit.   EPHESIANS 5:18

Christ saved us not by works of righteousness which we have done, but according to his mercy, by the washing of regeneration, and renewing through the Holy Spirit.   TITUS 3:5

God and Mr. Huston

The 1966 movie The Bible, *directed by John Huston, actually covered only the first few chapters of Genesis, from the creation of the world to the life of Abraham. In the movie, director Huston played both Noah and the voice of God (which made it sound as if Noah were talking to himself).*

No prophecy of the scripture is of any private interpretation. For the prophecy came not in ages past by the will of man, but holy men of God spoke as they were moved by the Holy Spirit.　　2 PETER 1:20–21

He that keeps his commandments dwells in him, and he in him. And in this we know that he abides in us, by the Spirit which he has given us.

1 JOHN 3:24

See also Baptism of the Spirit/Gifts of the Spirit, God's Guidance.

HOPE

The great American songwriter Oscar Hammerstein II claimed that he just couldn't write a song without hope in it. He was an optimist, someone who focused more on the positive than on the negative. Most of us admire people with such an attitude. They seem to live sunnier lives and to be healthier in body and soul.

Well, the Bible is, strictly speaking, an optimistic book: It has a happy ending, with God and his people triumphing over evil and all pain and sorrow banished. True, it also contains a belief in hell, but it also makes clear that hell can be avoided. For those who cling to God, there is heaven. And the hope of heaven casts a glow over the present life, making the worst days endurable.

The needy shall not always be forgotten; the expectation of the poor shall not perish forever.   PSALM 9:18

O love the LORD, all you his saints, for the LORD preserves the faithful, and plentifully repays the arrogant. Be of good courage, and he shall strengthen your heart, all you that hope in the LORD.   PSALM 31:23–24

The eye of the LORD is upon those who fear him, upon those who hope in his mercy.   PSALM 33:18

Why are you cast down, O my soul? And why are you troubled within me? Hope in God, for I shall yet praise him, who is the help of my countenance, and my God.   PSALM 42:5

You are my hope, O LORD God; you are my trust since my youth. By you have I been sustained since my birth; you are he who took me out of my mother's womb. My praise shall be continually of you.   PSALM 71:5–6

Let Israel hope in the LORD, for with the LORD there is mercy, and with him is full redemption. And he shall redeem Israel from all his iniquities.
                                                    PSALM 130:7–8

The hope of the righteous shall be gladness, but the expectation of the wicked shall perish.   PROVERBS 10:28

Hope deferred makes the heart sick, but when the desire comes, it is a tree of life.   PROVERBS 13:12

The wolf shall dwell with the lamb, and the leopard shall lie down with the kid, and the calf and the young lion and the yearling together, and a little child shall lead them. And the cow and the bear shall feed; their young ones shall lie down together, and the lion shall eat straw like the ox. And the nursing child shall play on the hole of the cobra, and the weaned child shall put his hand on the viper's den. They shall not hurt nor destroy in all my holy mountain, for the earth shall be full of the knowledge of the LORD, as the waters cover the sea.   ISAIAH 11:6–9

You will keep him in perfect peace whose mind is stayed on you, because he trusts in you. ISAIAH 26:3

Blessed is the man that trusts in the LORD, and whose hope the LORD is.
JEREMIAH 17:7

"I know the thoughts that I think about you," says the LORD, "thoughts of peace, and not of evil, to give you a future with hope. Then shall you call upon me, and you shall go and pray to me, and I will hearken to you. And you shall seek me, and find me, when you shall search for me with all your heart." JEREMIAH 29:11–13

It is of the LORD's mercies that we are not consumed, because his compassions fail not. They are new every morning; great is your faithfulness. "The LORD is my portion," says my soul, "therefore will I hope in him." The LORD is good to those who wait for him, to the soul that seeks him. It is good that a man should both hope and quietly wait for the salvation of the LORD. LAMENTATIONS 3:22–26

Peace I leave with you, my peace I give to you; not as the world gives, give I to you. Let not your heart be troubled, neither let it be afraid.
JOHN 14:27

Hope makes not ashamed; because the love of God is shed abroad in our hearts by the Holy Spirit which is given to us. ROMANS 5:5

Whatever things were written in the past were written for our learning, that we through patience and comfort of the scriptures might have hope.
ROMANS 15:4

Now abide faith, hope, charity, these three. I CORINTHIANS 13:13

If in this life only we have hope in Christ, we are of all men most miserable.
I CORINTHIANS 15:19

We are troubled on every side, yet not distressed; we are perplexed, but not in despair; persecuted, but not forsaken; cast down, but not destroyed; always bearing about in the body the dying of the Lord Jesus, that the life also of Jesus might be made manifest in our body.

2 CORINTHIANS 4:8–10

We through the Spirit wait for the hope of righteousness by faith.

GALATIANS 5:5

At that time you were without Christ, being aliens from the commonwealth of Israel, and strangers from the covenants of promise, having no hope, and without God in the world. But now in Christ Jesus you who were once far off are brought near by the blood of Christ.   EPHESIANS 2:12–13

There is one body, and one Spirit, just as you are called in one hope of your calling.   EPHESIANS 4:4

We heard of your faith in Christ Jesus, and of the love which you have to all the saints, because of the hope laid up for you in heaven. You have heard of this hope before in the word of the truth, the gospel that has come to you. Just as brings forth fruit in all the world, so it bears fruit among you since the day you heard of it and knew the grace of God in truth.

COLOSSIANS 1:4–6

God made known among the Gentiles how great are the riches of the glory of this mystery, that is, Christ in you, the hope of glory.

COLOSSIANS 1:27

I would not have you ignorant, brethren, concerning those who have died, so that you may not sorrow as others who have no hope. For if we believe that Jesus died and rose again, even so, through Jesus, God will bring with him those who have died.   1 THESSALONIANS 4:13–14

Paul, a servant of God and an apostle of Jesus Christ, for the sake of the faith of God's elect and the knowledge of the truth that leads to godliness, in the hope of eternal life, which God, who cannot lie, promised before the world began.   TITUS 1:1–2

The grace of God has appeared, bringing salvation to all, teaching us to renounce ungodliness and worldly lusts, and in this present age to live soberly, righteously, and godly, looking for that blessed hope and the glorious appearing of the great God and our Savior Jesus Christ.   TITUS 2:12–13

Being justified by his grace, we should be made heirs according to the hope of eternal life.   TITUS 3:7

Now faith is the substance of things hoped for, the evidence of things not seen.   HEBREWS 11:1

Blessed be the God and Father of our Lord Jesus Christ, who according to his abundant mercy has given us a new birth into a living hope by the resurrection of Jesus Christ from the dead, to an imperishable inheritance, one undefiled, which never fades away, reserved in heaven for you. You are protected by the power of God through faith for a salvation ready to be revealed in the last time. In this you greatly rejoice, though now for a time you are in heaviness through various trials.   I PETER 1:3–6

Prepare your minds for action, be disciplined, and set your hope on the grace that will be brought to you at the revealing of Jesus Christ.

I PETER 1:13

See also Ambition, Eternal Life, Faith, Heaven, Trusting God.

HOSPITALITY

In a society that worships constant motion, maybe we neglect the art of hospitality. Being a warmhearted and generous host was highly valued in times past, and it was repaid by being a grateful and considerate guest. In a world of strangers passing one another on the streets, perhaps we need to return to an "open-door policy," entertaining not only friends and kin but also new neighbors, visitors in town, and even strangers. There is no restaurant or hotel that can quite compare with the genuine warmth of a home.

The New Testament shows that the first Christians placed high value on hospitality, even listing it as one of the gifts of the Holy Spirit. The warmth

of the Christian fellowship was one of the reasons that the new faith spread
so rapidly.

You shall not oppress a stranger, for you know the heart of a stranger, seeing
you were strangers in the land of Egypt.   EXODUS 23:9

If a stranger sojourns with you in your land, you shall not abuse him. But
the stranger that dwells among you shall be to you like one born among you,
and you shall love him as yourself; for you were strangers in the land of
Egypt.   LEVITICUS 19:33

Withdraw your foot from your neighbor's house, lest he grow weary of you,
and so hate you.   PROVERBS 25:17

When the Son of man shall come in his glory, and all the holy angels with
him, then shall he sit upon the throne of his glory. And before him shall be
gathered all nations, and he shall separate them one from another, as a
shepherd separates his sheep from the goats. And he shall set the sheep on
his right hand, and the goats on the left. Then shall the King say to them on
his right hand, "Come, you blessed of my Father, inherit the kingdom prepared for you from the foundation of the world. For I was hungry, and you
gave me food; I was thirsty, and you gave me drink; I was a stranger, and you
took me in; naked, and you clothed me; I was sick, and you visited me; I was
in prison, and you came to me."
    Then shall the righteous answer him, saying, "Lord, when did we see you
hungry, and fed you? Or thirsty, and gave you drink? When did we see you as
a stranger, and took you in? Or naked, and clothed you? Or saw you sick, or
in prison, and came to you?" And the King shall answer and say to them,
"Truly I say to you, when you have done it to one of the least of these my
brethren, you have done it to me."
    Then shall he say to them on his left hand, "Depart from me, you cursed,
into everlasting fire, prepared for the devil and his angels. For I was hungry,
and you gave me no food; I was thirsty, and you gave me no drink. I was a
stranger, and you took me not in; naked, and you clothed me not; sick, and
in prison, and you visited me not."
    Then shall they answer him, saying, "Lord, when did we see you hungry,
or thirsty, or a stranger, or naked, or sick, or in prison, and did not minister

---

Are You Being Served?

Some churches practice members washing one another's feet. This is based on John's Gospel, chapter 13, in which Jesus washes his disciples' feet and tells them that they should continue the practice. Foot washing was a gesture of hospitality in that era of sandals, mud, and dust. It was normally done by a servant, so Jesus used it as a symbol of his followers serving one another.

---

to you?" Then he will answer them, "Truly, I tell you, when you did not do it to one of the least of these, you did it not to me." These shall go away into everlasting punishment, but the righteous into life eternal.

MATTHEW 25:31–46

Whoever shall give you a cup of water to drink in my name, because you belong to Christ, truly I say to you, he shall not lose his reward.

MARK 9:41

When you make a dinner or a supper, summon not your friends, nor your brethren, neither your kinsmen, nor your rich neighbors; lest they also invite you again and return the favor. But when you make a feast, call the poor, the maimed, the lame, the blind. And you shall be blessed; for they cannot repay you, for you shall be repaid at the resurrection of the just.

LUKE 14:12–14

Let love be genuine. Abhor what is evil; hold fast to what is good. Be kindly affectioned one to another with brotherly love. Honor one another above yourselves. . . . Distributing to the needs of the saints; given to hospitality.

ROMANS 12:9–10, 13

Be not forgetful to entertain strangers, for in so doing some have entertained angels unawares.   HEBREWS 13:2

Show hospitality one to another without grudging.   1 PETER 4:9

See also Generosity, Kindness.

HUMILITY

The word humility *and the concept have gone out of fashion. We think of the humble person as someone with low self-esteem, but that is not accurate. The humble person is, according to the Bible, just a realist—one who measures him- or herself against the ultimate standard, God. By that lofty standard, we all come up short. Pride arises when we focus on other people's faults. Humility arises when we focus on our own.*

Humility can be a very liberating thing. It frees us from trying to "play God." It frees us to associate with people of any status or group. Best of all, it frees us to enter into a right relationship with God, who cannot fellowship with the selfish and the proud.

Now the man Moses was very meek, more than all the men who were on the face of the earth.   NUMBERS 12:3

The One who avenges blood remembers them; he forgets not the cry of the humble.   PSALM 9:12

LORD, you have heard the desire of the humble; you will prepare their heart, you will cause your ear to hear.   PSALM 10:17

The meek will he guide in judgment, and the meek will he teach his way.
                                                               PSALM 25:9

The meek shall inherit the earth, and shall delight themselves in the abundance of peace.   PSALM 37:11

Though the LORD be high, yet has he respect to the lowly, but the proud he perceives from far off.   PSALM 138:6

The LORD lifts up the meek; he casts the wicked down to the ground.

PSALM 147:6

The LORD takes pleasure in his people; he will beautify the meek with salvation.

PSALM 149:4

Better it is to be of a humble spirit with the lowly than to divide the spoil with the proud.

PROVERBS 16:19

Let another man praise you, and not your own mouth; a stranger, and not your own lips.

PROVERBS 27:2

Thus says the high and lofty One that inhabits eternity, whose name is Holy: "I dwell in the high and holy place, but also with him that is of a contrite and humble spirit, to revive the spirit of the humble, and to revive the heart of the contrite ones."

ISAIAH 57:15

He has showed you, O man, what is good, and what does the LORD require of you, but to do justly, and to love mercy, and to walk humbly with your God?

MICAH 6:8

Blessed are the poor in spirit, for theirs is the kingdom of heaven.

MATTHEW 5:3

Take my yoke upon you, and learn from me, for I am gentle and lowly in heart, and you shall find rest for your souls.

MATTHEW 11:29

Whoever will be chief among you, let him be your servant.

MATTHEW 20:27

Let him that thinks he stands take heed lest he fall.

I CORINTHIANS 10:12

God forbid that I should glory, except in the cross of our Lord Jesus Christ, by whom the world is crucified to me, and I to the world.

GALATIANS 6:14

Put on therefore, as the elect of God, holy and beloved, compassion, kind-ness, humbleness of mind, meekness, patience.   COLOSSIANS 3:12

God resists the proud, but gives grace to the humble. Humble yourselves in the sight of the Lord, and he shall lift you up.   JAMES 4:6, 10

Humble yourselves under the mighty hand of God, that he may exalt you in due time.   I PETER 5:6

See also Arrogance, Meekness/Gentleness, Pride.

HYPOCRISY

The state motto of North Carolina is "To be rather than to seem." The exact reverse of this is hypocrisy—to seem rather than to be. The Bible is consistently pro-honesty, so naturally it condemns hypocrisy, which is a form of lying. The Bible makes it clear that a hypocrite may be able to fool all the people all the time, but the all-knowing God sees past the facade. He does not care that people seem to be virtuous, only that they are. He is not pleased when people wear his uniform while they do the devil's work.

Some of the harshest words in the Bible are Jesus' speeches against reli-gious hypocrites. He was especially harsh against the group known as the Pharisees, people who often were genuinely religious but who placed too much emphasis on the visible side of faith while neglecting the unseen part—their own attitude toward God. Jesus condemned them because they were supposed to be the spiritual leaders, the "establishment," the authori-ties whom everyone respected.

The triumphing of the wicked is short, and the joy of the hypocrite is but for a moment.   JOB 20:4–5

He that works deceit shall not dwell within my house; he who tells lies shall not continue in my sight.   PSALM 101:7

To the wicked God says, "What right have you to recite my statutes, or to take my covenant in your mouth, seeing you hate my instruction, and cast my words behind you? When you saw a thief, then you joined in with him, and you have been partaker with adulterers. You give your mouth to evil, and your tongue frames deceit. You sit and speak against your brother; you slander your own mother's son." PSALM 50:16–20

Smooth lips with a wicked heart are like a glaze over a earthen pot. He that hates dissembles with his lips, and lays up deceit within him. When he speaks fair, believe him not, for there are seven abominations in his heart. Though hatred is covered by deceit, his wickedness shall be shown before the whole congregation. PROVERBS 26:23–26

This people draw near me with their mouth, and with their lips they honor me, but they have removed their heart far from me. Their worship of me is merely rules taught by men. ISAIAH 29:13

You are to them like a very lovely song by one that has a pleasant voice, and can play well on an instrument; for they hear your words, but they do not follow them. EZEKIEL 33:32

I hate, I despise your religious feasts, and I take no pleasure in your solemn assemblies. Though you offer me burnt offerings and food offerings, I will not accept them; neither will I accept the offerings of your fattened beasts. Take away from me the noise of your songs; I will not hear the melody of your harps. But let justice run down like waters, and righteousness like a mighty stream. AMOS 5:21–24

Hear this, O you that trample on the needy and bring ruin on the poor of the land, saying, "When will the new moon be over, so that we may sell corn? And the sabbath, so that we may offer wheat for sale. We will make the ephah small, and the shekel great, and falsify the weights. We will buy the poor for silver, and the needy for a pair of shoes, and sell the refuse of the wheat." The LORD has sworn by the excellency of Jacob, "Surely I will never forget any of their deeds. Shall not the land tremble for this, and everyone mourn that dwells there?" AMOS 8:4–8

Take heed that you do not your charity before men, to be seen by them: otherwise you have no reward from your Father who is in heaven. Therefore when you do your alms, do not sound a trumpet before you, as the hypocrites do in the synagogues and in the streets, that they may receive glory from men. Truly I say to you, they have their reward. But when you do alms, let not your left hand know what your right hand does, that your alms may be in secret, and your Father who sees in secret himself shall reward you openly.   MATTHEW 6:1-4

When you pray, do not do as the hypocrites do, for they love to pray standing in the synagogues and on the corners of the streets, so that they may be seen by men. Truly I say to you, they have their reward. Instead, when you pray, enter into your room and shut the door, and pray to thy Father who is in secret. And your Father who sees in secret shall reward you openly.

MATTHEW 6:5-6

When you fast, be not, like the hypocrites, with a sad face, for they disfigure their faces that men will know they are fasting. Truly I say to you, they have their reward. But when you fast, anoint your head and wash your face so that your fasting will not be known by men, but by your Father who is in secret; and your Father, who sees in secret, shall reward you openly.

MATTHEW 6:16-18

How can you say to your brother, "Let me pull out the speck out of your eye," and, behold, a plank is in your own eye? You hypocrite, first take out the plank from your own eye, and then shall you see clearly to take out the speck from your brother's eye.   MATTHEW 7:3-5

Jesus spoke to the multitude and to his disciples: "The scribes and the Pharisees sit in Moses' seat. You must observe and do whatever they tell you to observe. But do not do as they do, for they do not practice what they preach."   MATTHEW 23:1-3

Woe to you, scribes and Pharisees, hypocrites! For you tithe mint and anise and cummin, and have omitted the weightier matters of the law—judgment, mercy, and faith. These you ought to have done, without neglecting the other. You blind guides, who strain at a gnat and swallow a camel.

Woe to you, scribes and Pharisees, hypocrites! For you clean the outside of the cup and the platter, but within they are full of greed and self-indulgence. You blind Pharisee, first clean what is inside the cup and platter, so that the outside of them may be clean also.

Woe to you, scribes and Pharisees, hypocrites! For you are like white-washed tombs, which appear beautiful outwardly, but within are full of dead men's bones, and of all kinds of filth. Even so, you outwardly appear righteous to men, but within you are full of hypocrisy and dishonor.

Woe to you, scribes and Pharisees, hypocrites! You build the tombs of the prophets, and decorate the graves of the righteous, and say, "If we had lived in the days of our fathers, we would not have taken part in shedding the blood of the prophets."

You serpents, you generation of vipers, how can you escape the damnation of hell?   MATTHEW 23:23–30, 33

Why do you call me, "Lord, Lord," and not do the things which I say?

LUKE 6:46

Beware of the leaven of the Pharisees, which is hypocrisy. For there is nothing concealed that shall not be revealed, and nothing hid that shall not be known.   LUKE 12:1–2

Jesus spoke this parable to those who trusted in themselves that they were righteous, and despised others: "Two men went up into the temple to pray, one a Pharisee, and the other a tax collector. The Pharisee stood and prayed thus with himself: 'God, I thank you, that I am not like other men are, robbers, evildoers, adulterers, or like this tax collector. I fast twice a week, I give tithes of all that I possess.' And the tax collector, standing far off, would not lift up so much as his eyes to heaven, but beat his breast, saying, 'God, be merciful to me, a sinner.' I tell you, this man went to his house justified rather than the other, for every one that exalts himself shall be abased, and he who humbles himself shall be exalted."   LUKE 18:9–14

You who teach others, teach you not yourself? You that preach that a man should not steal, do you steal? You that say a man should not commit adultery, do you commit adultery? You that abhor idols, do you commit sacrilege? You that make your boast of the law, through breaking the law do you dishonor God? For the name of God is blasphemed among the Gentiles because of you.   ROMANS 2:21–24

Now the Spirit clearly says that in the last days some shall depart from the faith, giving heed to seducing spirits, and doctrines of devils, speaking lies in hypocrisy, having their conscience seared as with a hot iron.

1 TIMOTHY 4:1–2

They have a form of godliness, but deny its power; from such people turn away.   2 TIMOTHY 3:5

They profess that they know God, but in deeds they deny him, being detestable, and disobedient, and unfit to do anything good.

TITUS 1:16

A double-minded man is unstable in all his ways.   JAMES 1:8

Be doers of the word, and not hearers only, deceiving yourselves.

JAMES 1:22

If any man among you seems to be religious, and bridles not his tongue, but deceives his own heart, this man's religion is vain. Pure religion and undefiled before God and the Father is this: to visit the fatherless and widows in their affliction, and to keep himself unspotted from the world.

JAMES 1:26–27

The wisdom that is from above is first pure, then peaceable, gentle, submissive, full of mercy and good fruits, without partiality, and without hypocrisy.   JAMES 3:17

If we say that we have fellowship with him, and walk in darkness, we lie, and do not the truth. If we say that we have not sinned, we make him a liar, and his word is not in us.   I JOHN 1:6, 10

He that said, "I know him," and keeps not his commandments, is a liar, and the truth is not in him.   I JOHN 2:4

I know your works, that you have a reputation that you are alive, and you are dead.   REVELATION 3:1

See also Fellowship with Other Believers, Judging Others, Self-Righteousness.

IDOLATRY

We think of idols as things that primitive people worship in remote villages of the world. But, in fact, idolatry is universal, though idols take different shapes. Whatever any human being gives the heart to, that is his or her idol. No wonder the prophets of the Bible devoted so much energy trying to turn people away from idolatry and back to the one true God.

Which idols do we serve today? A shiny new car, a toned and muscular body, an unwrinkled and youthful face, a bigger house, or fame? The list is endless, maybe because the human heart is a sort of creative "idol finder," always finding some new object to serve. So the ancient words of the Bible still apply: God deserves our worship, but nothing else does.

You shall have no other gods besides me. You shall not make for yourselves any idol, or any likeness of anything that is in heaven above, or that is in the earth beneath, or that is in the water under the earth. You shall not bow down yourself to them, nor serve them, for I the LORD your God am a jealous God. EXODUS 20:3–5

Since you saw no form on the day that the LORD spoke to you at Horeb out of the midst of the fire, take good heed to yourselves, lest you corrupt yourselves and make an idol, in the form of any figure, the likeness of male or female, and lest you lift up your eyes to heaven, and when you see the sun, the moon, and the stars, even all the host of heaven, should be driven to worship them, and serve them. DEUTERONOMY 4:15

If we have forgotten the name of our God, or stretched out our hands to a strange god, shall not God find this out? For he knows the secrets of the heart. PSALM 44:20–21

Their idols are silver and gold, the work of men's hands. They that make them are like them; so is everyone that trusts in them.   PSALM 115:4, 8

Where are your gods that you have made for yourselves? Let them arise, if they can save you in the time of your trouble.   JEREMIAH 2:28

Where your treasure is, there will your heart be also.   LUKE 12:34

Now while Paul waited for them at Athens, his spirit was distressed, for he saw the city wholly given to idolatry.   ACTS 17:16

When they knew God, they glorified him not as God, nor were thankful; but they became futile in their thoughts, and their foolish hearts were darkened. Professing themselves to be wise, they became fools. And they exchanged the glory of the eternal God for images made to look like mortal man and birds and animals and reptiles. They changed the truth of God into a lie, and worshipped and served the creature more than the Creator.

ROMANS 1:22–25

We know that an idol is nothing in the world, and that there is none other God but one.   I CORINTHIANS 8:4

When you did not know God, you were slaves to those who by nature are not gods.   GALATIANS 4:8

A man is a slave to whatever masters him.   2 PETER 2:19

Love not the world, neither the things that are in the world. If any man love the world, the love of the Father is not in him. For all that is in the world, the cravings of the sinful nature, and the lust of the eyes, and the pride of life, is not of the Father, but is of the world. And the world passes away, and all its lusts, but he who does the will of God abides forever.   I JOHN 2:15–17

Little children, keep yourselves from idols.   I JOHN 5:21

JESUS AS SAVIOR

The Bible applies many titles to Jesus: Son of God, Christ, Lord, Master, and Suffering Servant. But one of the most frequently used titles for him is Savior. What exactly is he saving us from? Sin, of course. Or, put another way, he saves us from ourselves, from our worst instincts and impulses.

This notion that we need a Savior bothers many people. Can't we just pull ourselves up by our own bootstraps, do the best we can, and succeed? The multitude of books, videotapes, and television and radio shows offering personal advice suggests that most people do believe they need help. The beauty of the Bible is that it doesn't just offer advice—it offers a Person, someone so compassionate and giving that even unbelievers through the centuries have been deeply impressed by the words and deeds of Jesus. This is the gospel in its essence: Mankind needs a Savior, and that Savior is Jesus Christ.

Behold, the angel of the Lord appeared to him in a dream, saying, "Joseph, you son of David, fear not to take to you Mary your wife, for what is conceived in her is of the Holy Spirit. And she shall bring forth a son, and you shall call his name JESUS, for he shall save his people from their sins."

MATTHEW 1:20–21

The Son of man has power on earth to forgive sins.   MATTHEW 9:6

To you is born this day in the city of David a Savior, which is Christ the Lord.   LUKE 2:11

They brought to him a man sick with palsy, lying on a bed. And Jesus, seeing their faith, said to the man sick with palsy, "Son, be of good cheer; your sins are forgiven."   MATTHEW 9:2

As they were eating, Jesus took bread, and blessed it, and broke it, and gave it to the disciples, and said, "Take, eat; this is my body." And he took the cup, and gave thanks, and gave it to them, saying, "Drink all of it, for this is my blood of the new covenant, which is shed for many for the forgiveness of sins."   MATTHEW 26:26–28

I came not to call the righteous, but sinners to repentance.   LUKE 5:32

When they were come to the place which is called Calvary, there they cruci- fied him, and the criminals, one on the right hand, and the other on the left. Then said Jesus, "Father, forgive them, for they know not what they do."

LUKE 23:32–34

Repentance and forgiveness of sins should be preached in his name among all nations.   LUKE 24:47

John saw Jesus coming to him, and said, "Behold the Lamb of God, who takes away the sin of the world."   JOHN 1:29

Peter said to them, "Repent, and be baptized every one of you in the name of Jesus Christ for the forgiveness of sins, and you shall receive the gift of the Holy Spirit."   ACTS 2:38

Him has God exalted at his right hand to be a Prince and a Savior, to give re- pentance to Israel, and forgiveness of sins.   ACTS 5:31

God demonstrates his love toward us in this, while we were still sinners, Christ died for us.   ROMANS 5:8

Our old man is crucified with him, so that the body of sin might be de- stroyed, and that henceforth we should not serve sin.   ROMANS 6:6

The wages of sin is death, but the gift of God is eternal life through Jesus Christ our Lord.   ROMANS 6:23

God was in Christ, reconciling the world to himself, not counting men's sins against them; and he has committed to us the word of reconciliation.

2 CORINTHIANS 5:19

Handel-ing the Bible

If you want to hear the Bible's story of human sin, Jesus the Savior, and the final triumph of good over evil, just listen to George Frideric Handel's Messiah. *This great choral work is actually a collection of Bible verses set to beautiful music. The verses are on the theme of human sin and the salvation that Christ (the Messiah) offers.*

We have redemption through his blood, the forgiveness of sins, according to the riches of his grace. EPHESIANS 1:7

This is a faithful saying, and worthy of all acceptance: Christ Jesus came into the world to save sinners, of whom I am chief. 1 TIMOTHY 1:15

The appearing of our Savior Jesus Christ, who has abolished death, and has brought life and immortality to light through the gospel. 2 TIMOTHY 1:10

Christ also has once suffered for sins, the just for the unjust, so that he might bring us to God, being put to death in the flesh, but made alive by the Spirit. 1 PETER 3:18

Grow in grace, and in the knowledge of our Lord and Savior Jesus Christ. To him be glory both now and forever. 2 PETER 3:18

If we walk in the light, as he is in the light, we have fellowship one with another, and the blood of Jesus Christ his Son cleanses us from all sin. If we confess our sins, he is faithful and just to forgive us our sins, and to cleanse us from all unrighteousness. 1 JOHN 1:7, 9

We have seen and do testify that the Father sent the Son to be the Savior of the world.   1 JOHN 4:14

See also Justification, Sin and Redemption.

JESUS' SECOND COMING

When the twentieth century began, people were optimistic. They believed that human life was improving everyone, that mankind was progressing and evolving in the right way. So the Bible's words about a dramatic return of Jesus to judge the earth struck many people as crude and quaint. But after two world wars and dozens of other bloody conflicts, the century became less optimistic. The world seemed to be taking a step backward for every step forward. Contrary to the optimists, we aren't very close to creating heaven on earth. So maybe the belief in Jesus' return still has some appeal.

The earliest believers in Jesus had a firm hope that he would return—they just didn't know when, and Jesus and his apostles emphasized that no one could predict the time. This hasn't stopped clever (and sometimes misguided) people from trying. The message of the Bible is this: Since we cannot predict the time of his return, we must be ready at all moments. Clearly that is a life-affecting belief.

Who may abide the day of his coming? And who shall stand when he appears? For he is like a refiner's fire.   MALACHI 3:2

The Son of man shall come in the glory of his Father with his angels, and then he shall reward every man according to his works.

MATTHEW 16:27

Of that day and hour knows no man, no, not the angels of heaven, but my Father only. But as the days of Noah were, so shall also the coming of the Son of man be. For as in the days that were before the flood they were eating and drinking, marrying and giving in marriage, until the day that Noah entered into the ark, and knew not until the flood came, and took them all away, so shall also the coming of the Son of man be. Then shall two be in the field; the one shall be taken, and the other left. Two women shall be grinding at the mill; the one shall be taken, and the other left. Watch therefore, for you know not what hour your Lord comes.

MATTHEW 24:36–42

When the Son of man shall come in his glory, and all the holy angels with him, then shall he sit upon the throne of his glory. And before him shall be gathered all nations, and he shall separate them one from another, as a shepherd separates his sheep from the goats. And he shall set the sheep on his right hand, and the goats on the left. Then shall the King say to them on his right hand, "Come, you blessed of my Father, inherit the kingdom prepared for you from the foundation of the world. For I was hungry, and you gave me food; I was thirsty, and you gave me drink; I was a stranger, and you took me in; naked, and you clothed me; I was sick, and you visited me; I was in prison, and you came to me."

Then shall the righteous answer him, saying, "Lord, when did we see you hungry, and fed you? Or thirsty, and gave you drink? When did we see you as a stranger, and took you in? Or naked, and clothed you? Or saw you sick, or in prison, and came to you?" And the King shall answer and say to them, "Truly I say to you, when you have done it to one of the least of these my brethren, you have done it to me."

Then shall he say to them on his left hand, "Depart from me, you cursed, into everlasting fire, prepared for the devil and his angels. For I was hungry, and you gave me no food; I was thirsty, and you gave me no drink. I was a stranger, and you took me not in; naked, and you clothed me not; sick, and in prison, and you visited me not."

Then shall they answer him, saying, "Lord, when did we see you hungry, or thirsty, or a stranger, or naked, or sick, or in prison, and did not minister to you?" Then he will answer them, "Truly, I tell you, when you did not do it to one of the least of these, you did it not to me." These shall go away into everlasting punishment, but the righteous into life eternal.

MATTHEW 25:31–46

The Son of man is like a man taking a long journey, who left his house, and gave authority to his servants, and to every man his task, and commanded the doorkeeper to watch. Watch, therefore, for you know not when the master of the house returns, at evening, or at midnight, or at the cockcrowing, or in the morning. If he comes suddenly, let him not find you sleeping.

MARK 13:34–36

Whoever shall be ashamed of me and of my words, of him shall the Son of man be ashamed, when he shall come in his own glory, and in his Father's, and of the holy angels.

LUKE 9:26

Then shall they see the Son of man coming in a cloud with power and great glory. And when these things begin to come to pass, then look up, and lift up your heads; for your redemption draws near.

LUKE 21:27

Jesus spoke to them a parable: "Behold the fig tree, and all the trees; when they send forth shoots, you see and know that summer is near at hand. So likewise, when you see these things come to pass, know that the kingdom of God is near at hand. Truly I say to you, this generation shall not pass away till all be fulfilled. Heaven and earth shall pass away, but my words shall not pass away."

LUKE 21:28–33

Take heed to yourselves, lest at any time your hearts be overcharged with dissipation and drunkenness and the worries and cares of this life, and that day come upon you unawares, like a trap. It shall come upon all those who dwell on the face of the whole earth. Watch, therefore, and pray always, so that you may be accounted worthy to escape all these things that shall come to pass, and to stand before the Son of man.

LUKE 21:34–36

Behold, I show you a mystery: We shall not all sleep, but we shall all be changed, in a moment, in the twinkling of an eye, at the last trumpet; for the trumpet shall sound, and the dead shall be raised incorruptible, and we shall be changed.

I CORINTHIANS 15:51–52

Our citizenship is in heaven, and from there we expect the Savior, the Lord Jesus Christ. He will transform our lowly body, so that it may be made like his glorious body, by the power that makes him able to subdue all things to himself.

PHILIPPIANS 3:20–21

When Christ, who is our life, shall appear, then shall you also appear with him in glory. COLOSSIANS 3:4

The Lord himself shall descend from heaven with a shout, with the voice of the archangel, and with the trumpet of God, and the dead in Christ shall rise first. Then we who are alive and remain shall be caught up together with them in the clouds to meet the Lord in the air, and so shall we ever be with the Lord. I THESSALONIANS 4:15–17

You know that the day of the Lord comes like a thief in the night. For when they shall say, "Peace and safety," then sudden destruction comes upon them, like labor upon a woman with child, and they shall not escape. I THESSALONIANS 5:2–3

Rejoice in this, that you are sharers in Christ's sufferings. When his glory shall be revealed, you may be glad also with exceeding joy. I PETER 4:13

When the chief Shepherd shall appear, you shall receive a crown of glory that fades not away. I PETER 5:4

Beloved, now are we the sons of God, and it does not yet appear what we shall be. But we know that, when he shall appear, we shall be like him, for we shall see him as he is. I JOHN 3:2

Behold, he comes with clouds, and every eye shall see him, and they also which pierced him, and all peoples of the earth shall wail because of him. REVELATION 1:7

I will come on you as a thief, and you shall not know what hour I will come upon you. REVELATION 3:3

Behold, I come as a thief. Blessed is he who watches, and keeps his garments with him, lest he walk naked, and they see his shame. REVELATION 16:15

Behold, I come quickly, and my reward is with me, to give to every man according to what he has done. He who testifies these things said, "Surely I come quickly." Amen. Even so, come, Lord Jesus.

REVELATION 22:12, 20

See also Eternal Life, Heaven, Hell.

JOY

Religious people have a reputation—partly deserved, but partly not—for being gloomy. You would never guess this from the Bible. It is amazing how many times joy *is mentioned. Being in a right relationship with God and one's fellow man is a joyous thing. The person who knows where he or she stands with God can feel joy in any situation, for it is not dependent on externals.*

Joy, in the Bible's view, is not the same as pleasure or amusement. It is more enduring, for it is based not on the pleasant sensations of the moment but on the long view of things, enjoying the presence of God here and now but also looking forward to eternity.

The Bible could be called an anti-sin book. It is. But we need to remember that it is also pro-joy.

His anger endures but a moment; in his favor is life. Weeping may endure for a night, but joy comes in the morning. You have turned my mourning into dancing; you have put off my sackcloth and clothed me with gladness.

PSALM 30:5, 11

Our heart shall rejoice in him, because we have trusted in his holy name.

PSALM 33:21

There is a river whose streams make glad the city of God.   PSALM 46:4

My soul shall be satisfied as with delightful foods, and my mouth shall praise you with joyful lips.   PSALM 63:5

The righteous shall be glad in the LORD, and shall trust in him, and all the upright in heart shall glory.   PSALM 64:10

Let the righteous be glad; let them rejoice before God: indeed, let them exceedingly rejoice.   PSALM 68:3

The zeal for your house has consumed me.   PSALM 69:9

Blessed is the people that know the joyful sound; they shall walk, O LORD, in the light of your countenance. In your name shall they rejoice all the day, and in your righteousness shall they be exalted.   PSALM 89:15–16

Light is sown for the righteous, and gladness for the upright in heart.
                                    PSALM 97:11

This is the day which the LORD has made; we will rejoice and be glad in it.
                                    PSALM 118:24

They that sow in tears shall reap in joy.   PSALM 126:5

You shall go out with joy, and be led forth with peace: the mountains and the hills shall break forth before you into singing, and all the trees of the wood shall clap their hands.   ISAIAH 55:12

I will greatly rejoice in the LORD; my soul shall be joyful in my God; for he has clothed me with the garments of salvation, he has covered me with the robe of righteousness, as a bridegroom decks himself with ornaments, and as a bride adorns herself with her jewels. For as the earth brings forth her bud, and as the garden causes the things that are sown in it to spring forth, so the LORD God will cause righteousness and praise to spring forth before all the nations.   ISAIAH 61:10–11

Although the fig tree shall not blossom, nor fruit be on the vines, the produce of the olive fail, and the fields yield no food, the flock be cut off from the fold, and there be no herd in the stalls, yet I will rejoice in the LORD, I will joy in the God of my salvation.   HABAKKUK 3:17–18

Blessed are you when men hate you, and when they exclude you from their company, and insult you, and slander your name for the Son of man's sake. Rejoice in that day, and leap for joy, for, behold, your reward is great in heaven, for this is how their fathers treated the prophets.

LUKE 6:22–23

As the Father has loved me, so have I loved you: continue in my love. If you keep my commandments, you shall abide in my love, just as I have kept my Father's commandments and abide in his love. These things have I spoken to you, so that my joy might remain in you, and that your joy might be full.

JOHN 15:9–11

These things I have spoken to you, so that in me you might have peace. In the world you shall have tribulation, but be of good cheer; I have overcome the world. JOHN 16:33

The disciples were filled with joy, and with the Holy Spirit.

ACTS 13:52

We have access by faith into this grace in which we stand, and we rejoice in hope of the glory of God. And not only so, but we glory in tribulations also, knowing that tribulation produces patience; and patience, experience; and experience, hope. ROMANS 5:2–4

I am filled with comfort, I am exceeding joyful in all our tribulation.

2 CORINTHIANS 7:4

The fruit of the Spirit is love, joy, peace, longsuffering, gentleness, goodness, faith, meekness, self-control; against such there is no law.

GALATIANS 5:22–23

Be not drunk with wine, which leads to ruin, but be filled with the Spirit, speaking to yourselves in psalms and hymns and spiritual songs, singing and making melody in your heart to the Lord. EPHESIANS 5:18–19

Rejoice in the Lord always—again I say, rejoice. Let your gentleness be known to all men. The Lord is at hand. Be anxious for nothing; but in every-

Our word jubilee *comes from Leviticus 25, which describes the "jubilee year." The people of Israel were supposed to set aside every fiftieth year as "jubilee," during which any people who had been sold into slavery had to be freed.*

thing by prayer and supplication with thanksgiving let your requests be made known to God. And the peace of God, which surpasses all understanding, shall keep your hearts and minds through Christ Jesus.

PHILIPPIANS 4:4–7

You have come to Mount Zion, and to the city of the living God, the heavenly Jerusalem, and to an innumerable company of angels.

HEBREWS 12:22

My brethren, count it all joy when you fall into various temptations, knowing that the testing of your faith produces patience. But let patience have its full effect, so that you may be mature and complete, lacking nothing.

JAMES 1:2–4

Rejoice, since you are sharing in Christ's sufferings, so that when his glory shall be revealed, you may be glad also with exceeding joy.

I PETER 4:13

See also Eternal Life, Faith, Hope, Worldly Cares, Worry.

JUDGING OTHERS

If we could see inside the human heart as God can, then we would be in a position to judge others. But we can't, so we shouldn't. Again and again the Bible emphasizes this. None of us is ever completely fair and unbiased as

God is. None of us is completely unselfish as God is. Judging others is an attempt to "play God," to look down on the world from a pedestal, and this is strictly prohibited in the Bible.

Judging others is rooted in pride. We focus on the faults of others (which can always be found if we look hard enough) but forget our own imperfections. In a sense, judging others is an attempt to boost our own self-esteem. The Bible offers a better way to do this: Focus on our own failings, then commit to getting rid of them. This will leave little time and energy for judging others' shortcomings.

The LORD sees not as man sees, for man looks on the outward appearance, but the LORD looks on the heart.   I SAMUEL 16:7

Judge not, that you may not be judged. For with the judgment you make you shall be judged, and the measure you give shall be the measure you receive.
        MATTHEW 7:1–2

How can you say to your brother, "Let me pull out the speck out of your eye," and, behold, a plank is in your own eye? You hypocrite, first take out the plank from your own eye, and then shall you see clearly to take out the speck from your brother's eye.   MATTHEW 7:3–5

I say to you, so that every idle word that men shall speak, they shall give account of in the day of judgment.   MATTHEW 12:36

You are without excuse, O man, whoever you are, when you judge others; for in judging another, you condemn yourself, because you, the judge, are doing the same things. . . . And do you think, O man, that when you judge those who do such things, and do the same yourself, that you shall escape the judgment of God? Or do you despise the riches of his goodness and forbearance and longsuffering? Do you not know that the goodness of God leads you to repentance? But by your hardness and impenitent heart you store up for yourself wrath on the day of wrath, when the righteous judgment of God shall be revealed. And he will repay every man according to his deeds.   ROMANS 2:1,3–6

Who are you to judge another man's servant? To his own master he stands or falls. ROMANS 14:4

Why do you judge your brother? Or why do you look down on your brother? For we shall all stand before the judgment seat of Christ. So let us not judge one another any more, but rather resolve that no man put a stumblingblock or a hindrance in his brother's way. ROMANS 14:10, 13

With me it is a very small thing that I should be judged by you, or by any man; indeed, I judge not my own self. I know of nothing against myself, yet it is not this that justifies me, but he who judges me is the Lord. Therefore judge nothing before the appointed time, until the Lord comes, who will bring to light the hidden things of darkness and will reveal the purposes of hearts, and then shall every man have praise of God.
I CORINTHIANS 4:3–5

What have I to do to judge those who are outside [the church]? Do not you judge those who are within? But those who are outside God judges. Therefore put away from among yourselves that wicked person.
I CORINTHIANS 5:12–13

From now on we regard no man from the human point of view; indeed, though we have known Christ from the human point of view, we no longer know him in that way. 2 CORINTHIANS 5:16

Whoever has shown no mercy shall have judgment without mercy.
JAMES 2:12–13

Speak not evil one of another, brethren. . . . There is one lawgiver, who is able to save and to destroy. Who are you that judge another?
JAMES 4:11–12

Grumble not against one another, brethren, lest you are condemned. Behold, the Judge stands before the door. JAMES 5:9

See also Anger, Envy, God's Fairness, Hate, Hypocrisy, Self-Righteousness, The Tongue.

JUSTIFICATION

Remember the old highway signs that said "Get right with God"? That's what justification is all about: getting right with God. Put another way, we can be in a right relationship with God only when our backlog of selfish deeds has been canceled out. In contemporary terms, we have a lot of emotional and psychological baggage we need to unload. In the Bible's view, it is Christ who unloads the baggage for us. This is, the Bible tells us, the only way we can find acceptance with God.

Truly, truly, I say to you, he who hears my word and believes in him that sent me, has everlasting life, and shall not come into condemnation; but is passed from death to life.   JOHN 5:24

Through Christ all who believe are justified from all things, which could not be done by the law of Moses.   ACTS 13:39

All have sinned, and come short of the glory of God; being justified freely by his grace through the redemption that is in Christ Jesus.

ROMANS 3:23–24

Being justified by faith, we have peace with God through our Lord Jesus Christ. Much more then, since we are now justified through his blood, we shall be saved from wrath through him. And even more, we also joy in God through our Lord Jesus Christ, by whom we have now received the atonement.   ROMANS 5:1, 9, 11

As by one man's disobedience many were made sinners, so by the obedience of one shall many be made righteous.   ROMANS 5:19

Being made free from sin, and become servants of God, you bear fruit leading to holiness, and the end is everlasting life.   ROMANS 6:22

There is therefore now no condemnation for those who are in Christ Jesus.

ROMANS 8:1

With the heart man believes to righteousness, and with the mouth confession is made to salvation.   ROMANS 10:10

Know you not that the unrighteous shall not inherit the kingdom of God? Be not deceived: neither fornicators, nor idolaters, nor adulterers, nor homosexuals, nor abusers of themselves with mankind, nor thieves, nor covetous, nor drunkards, nor slanderers, nor swindlers shall inherit the kingdom of God. And such were some of you. But you are washed, you are sanctified, you are justified in the name of the Lord Jesus, and by the Spirit of our God.   1 CORINTHIANS 6:9–11

God was in Christ, reconciling the world to himself, not counting men's sins against them. And he has committed to us the word of reconciliation. For he has made him to be sin for us, who knew no sin, that we might be made the righteousness of God in him.   2 CORINTHIANS 5:19, 21

Being justified by his grace, we should be made heirs according to the hope of eternal life.   TITUS 3:7

See also Guilt, New Birth/New Life, Repentance, Salvation, Sin and Redemption.

KINDNESS

No one talks much about kindness anymore, for the word compassion *has become more trendy. Whatever word we use, we know instinctively that kindness is its own reward, that life has so many sorrows and burdens that kindness is an absolute necessity. All of this the Bible affirms, but with this added thought: We ought to show kindness because God does. As God extends to us more kindness than we probably deserve, so we ought to be kind not only to people we like but also to those we dislike. No, this isn't easy. There is probably no greater challenge in life than being kind to an enemy. But Jesus was, and in the area of kindness the world has no greater role model. The one who forgave the men who crucified him is a "tough act to follow," but we ought to at least make the attempt.*

Withhold not good from them who deserve it, when it is in your power to do it. Say not to your neighbor, "Go, and come again, and tomorrow I will give," when you have it with you now.   PROVERBS 3:27–28

The generous soul shall be made prosperous, and he that waters shall be watered himself.   PROVERBS 11:25

He that despises his neighbor sins, but he who has mercy on the poor, happy is he.   PROVERBS 14:21

Thus speaks the LORD Almighty, saying, "Execute true judgment, and show mercy and compassions every man to his brother."   ZECHARIAH 7:9

Blessed are the merciful, for they shall obtain mercy.   MATTHEW 5:7

Give to him that asks you, and turn not away from him that would borrow from you. MATTHEW 5:42

Then shall the King say to them on his right hand, "Come, you blessed of my Father, inherit the kingdom prepared for you from the foundation of the world; for I was hungry, and you gave me food; I was thirsty, and you gave me drink; I was a stranger, and you took me in; naked, and you clothed me; I was sick, and you visited me; I was in prison, and you came to me." MATTHEW 25:34–36

If you lend to them who will repay you, what reward have you? For sinners also lend to sinners, to receive as much again. Love your enemies, and do good; and lend, hoping for nothing in return. And your reward shall be great, and you shall be the children of the Highest, for he is kind to the ungrateful and to the evil. Be therefore merciful, as your Father also is merciful. LUKE 6:34–36

A certain man went down from Jerusalem to Jericho, and fell among thieves, who stripped him of his clothing and wounded him and departed, leaving him half dead. And by chance there came by a certain priest, and when he saw him, he passed by on the other side. And likewise a Levite, when he was at the place, came and looked at him, then passed by on the other side. But a certain Samaritan, as he journeyed, came where he was, and when he saw him, he had compassion on him, and went to him, and bound up his wounds, pouring in oil and wine, and set him on his own beast, and brought him to an inn, and took care of him. And on the next day when he departed, he took money, gave it to the innkeeper, and said to him, "Take care of him, and whatever else you spend, when I come again, I will repay you." LUKE 10:30–37

We, being many, are one body in Christ, and are all members of one another. Having then gifts differing according to the grace that is given to us. . . . Let love be genuine. Abhor what is evil; hold to what is good. Be kindly affectioned one to another with brotherly love, giving honor to one another instead of yourselves. ROMANS 12:5–10

The God of patience and consolation grant you to be likeminded toward one another according to Christ Jesus. ROMANS 15:5

Love endures long, and is kind; love envies not; love does not boast, is not arrogant, is not rude, is not self-seeking, is not easily provoked, thinks no evil; it rejoices not in wrongdoing, but rejoices in the truth; it bears all things, believes all things, hopes all things, endures all things.

I CORINTHIANS 13:4–7

Brethren, if a man is caught in a sin, you who are spiritual should restore him in the spirit of meekness. But take care, lest you also be tempted. Bear you one another's burdens, and so fulfill the law of Christ. For if a man think himself to be something, when he is nothing, he deceives himself.

GALATIANS 6:1–3

As we have any opportunity, let us do good to all men, especially to them who are of the household of faith. GALATIANS 6:10

Be kind to one another, tenderhearted, forgiving one another, just as God for Christ's sake has forgiven you. EPHESIANS 4:32

As the elect people of God, holy and beloved, put on compassion, kindness, humbleness of mind, meekness, patience; bear with one another, and forgive one another, if any man has a quarrel against any; just as Christ forgave you, so you also forgive. And above all these things put on love, which binds all things together in perfection. And let the peace of God rule in your hearts, to which you are called in one body. And be thankful.

COLOSSIANS 3:12–15

Be all of one mind, having compassion for one another; love as brethren, be tenderhearted, be courteous. I PETER 3:8

Above all things have constant love among yourselves, for love shall cover a multitude of sins. I PETER 4:8

Add to your faith virtue, and to virtue add knowledge; and to knowledge self-control, and to self-control patience, and to patience godliness; and to godliness brotherly kindness, and to brotherly kindness charity.

2 PETER 1:5−7

Whoever has this world's goods, and sees his brother in need, and has no pity on him, how dwells the love of God in him? My little children, let us not love merely in word, neither in speech, but in deed and in truth.

I JOHN 3:17−18

See also Generosity, Love for Others.

LAZINESS

We hear a lot about workaholics, but most employers probably agree that lazy workers far outnumber workaholics. In a society geared toward constant amusement, it is no wonder that the old ethic of hard work is dying out. "Keep your nose to the grindstone" has been replaced by "Why work when you can play?" While the Bible opposes idolatry—and that includes making an idol of one's job—it also has a lot to say about laziness and idleness. The Book of Proverbs is full of dire warnings for "the sluggard," the one who desires good things but is too lazy to work for them.

Go to the ant, you sluggard; consider her ways, and be wise. How long will you sleep, O sluggard? When will you arise out of your sleep? Yet a little sleep, a little slumber, a little folding of the hands to sleep—so shall your poverty come on you like a bandit, and scarcity like an armed man.

PROVERBS 6:6, 9–11

As vinegar to the teeth and as smoke to the eyes, so is the sluggard to those who send him. PROVERBS 10:26

He that tills his land shall be satisfied with bread, but he who chases worthless pursuits is void of understanding. PROVERBS 12:11

The slothful man does not roast his game, but the diligent man obtains good things. PROVERBS 12:27

The soul of the sluggard desires, and has nothing, but the soul of the diligent shall be made prosperous. PROVERBS 13:4

In all labor there is profit, but mere talk leads only to poverty.

PROVERBS 14:23

The way of the slothful man is overgrown with thorns, but the way of the righteous is made level. PROVERBS 15:19

He that is slothful in his work is brother to him that is a great waster.

PROVERBS 18:9

Slothfulness brings on deep sleep, and an idle soul shall suffer hunger.

PROVERBS 19:15

The craving of the slothful will be the death of him, for his hands refuse to labor. PROVERBS 21:25

The lazy man will not plow by reason of the cold; at harvest time he shall beg, and have nothing. PROVERBS 20:4

The thoughts of the diligent lead to abundance; but everyone who is hasty is led to poverty. PROVERBS 21:5

The drunkard and the glutton shall come to poverty, and drowsiness shall clothe a man with rags. PROVERBS 23:21

Behold what I have seen: it is good and fitting for one to eat and to drink, and to enjoy the good of all his labor that he does under the sun all the days of his life, which God gives him, for this is his lot; this is the gift of God.

ECCLESIASTES 5:18–19

By much slothfulness the building decays, and through idleness of the hands the house falls through. ECCLESIASTES 10:18

My beloved brethren, be steadfast, unmovable, always abounding in the work of the Lord, since you know that your labor is not in vain in the Lord.

I CORINTHIANS 15:58

When we were with you, this we commanded you, that if any would not work, neither should he eat. For we hear that there are some among you who are idle, not busy with work, but busybodies. Now to these we command by our Lord Jesus Christ, that with quietness they work and eat their own bread.

2 THESSALONIANS 3:10–12

See also Ambition, The Sabbath, Work.

LONELINESS

It is possible to be lonely even in the midst of a crowd. Thanks to home computers and at-home careers, people can live in their own cocoons, protected from the pain of human contact but also cut off from its pleasures. While electronic link-ups have brought us new forms of interaction and communication, loneliness still persists as a problem. It may be one of the worst problems of all because no one wants to talk about it. After all, who wants to admit to loneliness? Attempts to fill the void with pets, drugs, or endless amusements are only halfway measures. The real problem is not solved.

The Bible agrees with common sense in this area: Human beings are made to live in fellowship together. The Book of Genesis makes an interesting point: God created all things, declared that it was all "good," but then declared that the man by himself was "not good."

For the lonely person, the Bible offers this consolation: God is always there as a companion and defender.

The LORD God said, "It is not good that the man should be alone; I will make him a helper fit for him." And out of the ground the LORD God formed every beast of the field, and every bird of the air, and brought them to Adam to see what he would call them, and whatever Adam called every living creature, that was its name. And Adam gave names to all cattle, and to the fowl of the air, and to every beast of the field; but for Adam there was not found a helper fit for him.

GENESIS 2:18–20

Turn to me, and have mercy upon me, for I am desolate and afflicted.

PSALM 25:16

When my father and my mother forsake me, then the LORD will take me up.

PSALM 27:10

I am forgotten like a dead man; I am like a broken vessel.   PSALM 31:12

I am poor and needy, yet the LORD thinks upon me; you are my help and my deliverer.   PSALM 40:17

A father of the fatherless, and a judge of the widows, is God in his holy habitation. God sets the solitary in families; he brings out those which are bound with chains.   PSALM 68:4–6

Insults have broken my heart, and I am full of heaviness, and I looked for some to take pity, but there was none, and I looked for comforters, but I found none.   PSALM 69:20

Then all the disciples forsook him, and fled.   MATTHEW 26:56

I will be a Father to you, and you shall be my sons and daughters, says the Lord Almighty.   2 CORINTHIANS 6:18

See also Bad Company, Fellowship with God, Fellowship with Other Believers, Friends, Trendiness.

LOVE FOR GOD

A cathedral in Richmond, Virginia, has this inscription in stone over its doors: "If You Love Me, Keep My Commandments." Ouch. Wouldn't it be much easier to say that we love God without bothering with obeying him? Of course it would. But the Bible knows nothing about that kind of love. Our love for God is not measured by our words but by how well our lives conform to his will. The Bible presents him as a loving and merciful

Father—but a Father with morals and standards. Talking about our love for God while mistreating our fellow man and pursuing our own selfish interests is pure hypocrisy. According to the Bible, we are not spiritually healthy unless we love God fully.

You shall love the LORD your God with all your heart, and with all your soul, and with all your might.   DEUTERONOMY 6:5

Know that the LORD your God, he is God, the faithful God, who keeps covenant and mercy with those who love him and keep his commandments to a thousand generations.   DEUTERONOMY 7:9

Delight yourself also in the LORD, and he shall give you the desires of your heart.   PSALM 37:4

Whom have I in heaven but you? And there is none upon earth that I desire beside you.   PSALM 73:25

Because he has set his love upon me, therefore will I deliver him; I will set him on high, because he has known my name. He shall call upon me, and I will answer him; I will be with him in trouble; I will deliver him, and honor him. With long life will I satisfy him, and show him my salvation.

PSALM 91:14–16

I stretch forth my hands to you; my soul thirsts after you like a thirsty land.

PSALM 143:6

The LORD is near to all those who call upon him, to all that call upon him in truth. He will fulfill the desire of those who fear him; he also will hear their cry, and will save them. The LORD preserves all those who love him, but all the wicked will he destroy.   PSALM 145:18–20

Behold, a certain lawyer stood up, and tested him, saying, "Master, what shall I do to inherit eternal life?" Jesus said to him, "What is written in the law? What do you read there?" And he answering said, "You shall love the Lord your God with all your heart, and with all your soul, and with all your strength, and with all your mind, and your neighbor as yourself." And he said to him, "You have answered right; do this, and you shall live."

LUKE 10:25-28

Great multitudes followed after him, and he turned and said to them, "If any man come to me, and hate not his father, and mother, and wife, and children, and brethren, and sisters, indeed, and his own life also, he cannot be my disciple. And whoever does not carry his cross, and come after me, cannot be my disciple. Any of you who does not forsake all he has cannot be my disciple."

LUKE 14:25-27, 33

"If you love me, keep my commandments. And I will pray the Father, and he shall give you another Comforter, so that he may abide with you forever. He is the Spirit of truth, whom the world cannot receive, because it sees him not, neither knows him; but you know him, for he dwells with you, and shall be in you. I will not leave you comfortless; I will come to you. Yet a little while, and the world sees me no more; but you see me; because I live, you shall live also. At that day you shall know that I am in my Father, and you in me, and I in you. He that has my commandments, and keeps them, he it is that loves me, and he who loves me shall be loved of my Father, and I will love him, and will show myself to him."

Judas (not Iscariot) said to him, "Lord, how is it that you will reveal yourself to us, and not to the world?" Jesus answered and said to him, "If a man loves me, he will keep my words, and my Father will love him, and we will come to him, and make our abode with him. He that loves me not keeps not my sayings, and the word which you hear is not mine, but the Father's which sent me."

JOHN 14:15-24

Eye has not seen, nor has ear heard, neither have entered into the heart of man the things which God has prepared for those who love him.

I CORINTHIANS 2:9

God is not unrighteous; he will not forget your work and labor of love, which you have showed toward his name, in that you have ministered to the saints, and still do minister.

HEBREWS 6:10

If a man say, "I love God," and hates his brother, he is a liar, for if he loves not his brother whom he has seen, how can he love God whom he has not seen? And this commandment have we from him, so that he who loves God love his brother also.   I JOHN 4:20–21

This is love, that we walk after his commandments.   2 JOHN 1:6

Keep yourselves in the love of God, looking for the mercy of our Lord Jesus Christ to eternal life.   JUDE 21

See also Fellowship with God, Obeying God.

LOVE FOR OTHERS

It is a shame that we have only one word, love, *in English to cover all kinds of love. We are stuck with this one word to refer to family love, friendship, spiritual love, and (of course) sexual love. But the love spoken of in the Bible is a special kind—unselfish love—focused on giving, not getting. It isn't just a fleeting emotion, which can change in a moment, but something more durable, tougher—in fact,* eternal. *It involves vulnerability; after all, if we give unselfishly, there is a chance that whatever we love will not be grateful. But this is the kind of love that God shows humankind—unselfish giving, even when we respond by turning away. It is this same kind of love that the Bible commands us to show to one another, even if that means we risk being hurt. It is summarized most beautifully and memorably in the famous "love passage" in 1 Corinthians 13, given below.*

You shall love your neighbor as yourself. . . . The stranger that dwells with you shall be to you as one born among you, and you shall love him as yourself.   LEVITICUS 19:18, 34

Behold, how good and how pleasant it is for brethren to dwell together in unity!   PSALM 133:1

Hatred stirs up quarrels, but love covers all sins.   PROVERBS 10:12

He that covers over an offense fosters love; but he who repeats a matter separates true friends.   PROVERBS 17:9

A friend loves at all times, and a brother is born for adversity.
                                                                 PROVERBS 17:17

You have heard that it has been said, "You shall love your neighbor and hate your enemy." But I say to you, Love your enemies, bless them that curse you, do good to them that hate you, and pray for them which spitefully use you, and persecute you.   MATTHEW 5:43–44

Whoever welcomes a prophet in the name of a prophet shall receive a prophet's reward; and whoever receives a righteous man in the name of a righteous man shall receive a righteous man's reward. And whoever shall give one of these little ones a cup of cold water in the name of a disciple, truly I say to you, he shall by no means lose his reward.
                                                              MATTHEW 10:41–42

Whoever shall give you a cup of water to drink in my name, because you belong to Christ, truly I say to you, he shall not lose his reward.
                                                                      MARK 9:41

As you wish that men should do to you, do so to them. For if you love those who love you, what credit is that to you? For sinners also love those that love them. And if you do good to those who do good to you, what credit is that to you? For sinners also do the same. And if you lend to them of whom you hope to receive, what credit is that to you? For sinners also lend to sinners, to receive as much back again. But love you your enemies, and do good; and lend, hoping for nothing in return, and your reward shall be great, and you shall be the children of the Highest, for he is kind to the unthankful and to the evil. Be therefore merciful, as your Father also is merciful.
                                                                  LUKE 6:31–36

Behold, a certain lawyer stood up, and tested him, saying, "Master, what shall I do to inherit eternal life?" Jesus said to him, "What is written in the law? What do you read there?" And he answering said, "You shall love the

Lord your God with all your heart, and with all your soul, and with all your strength, and with all your mind, and your neighbor as yourself." And he said to him, "You have answered right; do this, and you shall live."

LUKE 10:25–28

A new commandment I give to you, that you love one another; as I have loved you.

JOHN 13:34

Greater love has no man than this, that a man lay down his life for his friends.

JOHN 15:13

The love of God is shed abroad in our hearts by the Holy Spirit which is given to us.

ROMANS 5:5

Let love be genuine. Abhor what is evil; hold fast to what is good. Be kindly affectioned one to another with brotherly love. Honor one another above yourselves. Rejoice with those who rejoice, and weep with those who weep. Be of the same mind one toward another. Do not be haughty, but be willing to associate with men of low estate. Be not wise in your own conceit.

ROMANS 12:9–10, 15–16

Owe no man anything, except to love one another; for he who loves another has fulfilled the law. The commandments—"You shall not commit adultery, you shall not murder, you shall not steal, you shall not bear false witness, you shall not covet," and any other commandment—are summed up in this saying, "You shall love your neighbor as yourself." Love does no harm to his neighbor; therefore love is the fulfilling of the law.

ROMANS 13:8–10

Though I speak in the tongues of men and of angels, but have not love, I am like a sounding gong or a tinkling cymbal. And though I have the gift of prophecy, and understand all mysteries, and all knowledge, and though I have such faith that I could move mountains, if I have not love, I am nothing. And though I bestow all my goods to feed the poor, and though I give my body to be burned, if I have not love, it gains me nothing.

Love is patient, love is kind; love envies not, boasts not, is not haughty, is not rude, is not self-seeking, is not easily provoked, thinks no evil; rejoices not in wrongdoing, but rejoices in the truth; love bears all things, believes all things, hopes all things, endures all things. Love never ends. But as for prophecies, they shall end; as for tongues, they shall cease; as for knowledge, it shall vanish away. For we know in part, and we prophesy in part. But when what is perfect is come, then what is partial will end. When I was a child, I spoke as a child, I understood as a child, I thought as a child. But when I became a man, I put away childish things. For now we see in a mirror, dimly; but then face to face. Now I know partially, but then shall I know just as also I am known.

And now abide faith, hope, love, these three; but the greatest of these is love. I CORINTHIANS 13

The fruit of the Spirit is love, joy, peace, longsuffering, gentleness, goodness, faith, meekness, self-control. GALATIANS 5:22–23

With all humility and gentleness and patience, bear with one another in love. Endeavor to keep the unity of the Spirit in the bond of peace. There is one body, and one Spirit, just as you are called in one hope of your calling. EPHESIANS 4:2–4

Walk in love, as Christ also has loved us, and has given himself for us an offering and a sacrifice to God. EPHESIANS 5:2

Let nothing be done through selfishness or vain conceit, but in humility let each esteem others better than himself. Look after not your own concerns, but let every man also look after the concerns of others. Let this mind be in you, the mind which was in Christ Jesus. PHILIPPIANS 2:3–5

God is not unrighteous; he will not forget your work and labor of love, which you have showed toward his name, in that you have ministered to the saints, and still do minister. And we desire that everyone of you show this same diligence to the very end. HEBREWS 6:10–11

Let brotherly love continue. Do not forget to entertain strangers, for in so doing some have entertained angels unawares. Remember those who are in prison as though you were fellow prisoners with them, and remember those who suffer adversity as though you were suffering along with them.

HEBREWS 13:1–3

If you fulfill the royal law according to the scripture, "You shall love your neighbor as yourself," you do well. JAMES 2:8

Now that you have purified your souls by obeying the truth so that you have genuine love for the brethren, see that you love one another deeply with a pure heart. I PETER 1:22

Be all of one mind, having compassion for one another; love as brethren, be tenderhearted, be courteous. I PETER 3:8

Above all things have devoted love among yourselves, for love covers multitude of sins. I PETER 4:8

He that loves his brother abides in the light, and there is nothing in him to cause him to stumble. I JOHN 2:10

In this is revealed which are the children of God and which are the children of the devil: whoever does not righteousness does not belong to God, nor is he who loves not his brother. For this is the message that you heard from the beginning, that we should love one another. Not as Cain, who was of that wicked one, and murdered his brother. And why did he slay him? Because his own works were evil, and his brother's were righteous.

Marvel not, my brethren, if the world hate you. We know that we have passed from death to life, because we love the brethren. He that loves not his brother abides in death. Whoever hates his brother is a murderer, and you know that no murderer has eternal life abiding in him.

This is how we know the love of God, because he laid down his life for us, and we ought to lay down our lives for the brethren. But whoever has this world's goods, and sees his brother has need, and withholds compassion from him, how can the love of God dwell in him? My little children, let us not love merely in word or in speech, but in deed and in truth.

I JOHN 3:10–19

By this we know that we love the children of God, when we love God, and keep his commandments.

I JOHN 5:2

See also Forgiving Others, Mercy.

LYING

Living in the video age, we wonder where truth ends and reality begins. Well, the Bible is heavily pro-reality, taking a harsh view of any kind of deception. Put in a more positive way, it is pro-truth. It takes for granted something we all know instinctively: The world functions best when people are honest and forthright about themselves and their intentions. Honesty is not only the best policy but also an obligation we owe to one another and to God.

True, some of the most successful people, including celebrities and leaders, are consummate liars. But if the public is fooled, God is not. If liars never receive their just deserts in this life, there is the afterlife to consider.

You shall not bear false witness against your neighbor.

EXODUS 20:16

The LORD will abhor the bloodthirsty and deceitful man.

PSALM 5:6

Everyone speaks falsely with his neighbor: with flattering lips they speak from a double heart. The LORD shall cut off all flattering lips, and the tongue that speaks proud things.

PSALM 12:2–3

Deliver my soul, O LORD, from lying lips, and from a deceitful tongue.

PSALM 120:2

Truthful lips shall be established forever, but a lying tongue lasts but for a moment.   PROVERBS 12:19

A faithful witness will not lie, but a false witness will utter lies.
                                                                        PROVERBS 14:5

A false witness shall not go unpunished, and he who speaks lies shall not escape.   PROVERBS 19:5

Differing weights are an abomination to the LORD, and a false scale is not good.   PROVERBS 20:23

A man that bears false witness against his neighbor is a club, and a sword, and a sharp arrow.   PROVERBS 25:18

Be not a witness against your neighbor without cause, and deceive not with your lips.   PROVERBS 24:28

Put away lying, speak every man truth with his neighbor, for we are members one of another.   EPHESIANS 4:25

Lie not one to another, seeing that you have put off the old man with his deeds.   COLOSSIANS 3:9

He that overcomes shall inherit all things, and I will be his God, and he shall be my son. But the fearful, and unbelieving, and the loathsome, and murderers, and whoremongers, and sorcerers, and idolaters, and all liars shall have their reward in the lake which burns with fire and brimstone, which is the second death.   REVELATION 21:7–8

See also Hypocrisy, The Tongue.

MARRIAGE

Ruth Bell Graham, Billy Graham's wife, advises people to "marry someone you don't mind adjusting to." That sounds simple enough, and it agrees with the section in the marriage ceremony about "for better and for worse." But considering the state of so many marriages, there must be a lot of spouses who aren't adjusting well to each other. What's wrong with marriage today? Everyone seems to think that marriage is tough in the modern world, but wasn't it always so? Hasn't it always been tempting to find fault with the person once the initial passion has cooled down? Hasn't the idea of adjusting and adapting been replaced with the idea of trading in a spouse the way one trades in an old car?

The Bible has a high view of marriage. It is a serious commitment, made for a lifetime. (The flip side is that it takes a dim view of adultery, which it does not treat at all lightly.) It involves caring for the other person as much as one cares for oneself, which can mean at times subordinating one's own desires to those of another. Yet, while marriage is a serious commitment and also, at its best, one of life's deepest pleasures, the Bible gives no hint that marriage is the best thing of all. Those who expect their marriages to be heaven are expecting too much. Only heaven is heaven.

Drink waters out of your own cistern, and running waters out of your own well. Should your springs be scattered abroad, and rivers of waters in the streets? Let them be for you alone, and not shared with strangers. Let your fountain be blessed, and rejoice in the wife of your youth. Let her be as the loving deer, the pleasant doe; let her breasts satisfy you at all times, and be you intoxicated always with her love.   PROVERBS 5:15–19

Whoever finds a wife finds a good thing, and obtains favor from the LORD.
                                                         PROVERBS 18:22

Live joyfully with the wife whom you love all the days of this meaningless
life under the sun.   ECCLESIASTES 9:9

It has been said, "Whoever shall put away his wife, let him give her a certifi-
cate of divorce"; but I say to you that whoever divorces his wife, except for
unfaithfulness, causes her to commit adultery, and whoever shall marry her
that is divorced commits adultery.   MATTHEW 5:31–32

To avoid sexual immorality, let every man have his own wife, and let every
woman have her own husband. Let the husband fulfill his marital duty to his
wife, and likewise the wife to her husband. I wish that all men were just as I
myself. But every man has his particular gift from God, one having one
kind, and one having another. I say to the unmarried and widows, it is good
for them if they remain just as I. But if they cannot control themselves, let
them marry, for it is better to marry than to burn.

                                      1 CORINTHIANS 7:2–3, 7–9

If any brother has an unbelieving wife, and she is pleased to dwell with him,
let him not divorce her. And the woman who has an unbelieving husband, if
he is pleased to dwell with her, let her not leave him. For the unbelieving
husband is sanctified by the wife, and the unbelieving wife is sanctified by
the husband. Otherwise your children would be unclean; but as it is, they
are holy. But if the unbelieving spouse departs, let him go; a brother or a sister is not under bondage in such cases. God has called us to peace.

                                      1 CORINTHIANS 7:12–15

Submit to one another out of reverence for Christ.

Wives, submit yourselves to your own husbands, as to the Lord. For the
husband is the head of the wife, just as Christ is the head of the church, and
he is the Savior of the body. Just as the church is subject to Christ, so let the
wives be to their own husbands in everything.

Husbands, love your wives, just as Christ loved the church and gave himself for it, that he might sanctify and cleanse it with the washing of water by
the word, so that he might present it to himself a glorious church, not having blemish or wrinkle or any such thing, but that it should be holy and
without fault. So ought men to love their wives as their own bodies. He that
loves his wife loves himself. For no man ever yet hated his own body, but

rather he nourishes and cherishes it, just as the Lord loves the church; for we are members of his body, of his flesh, and of his bones. For this cause shall a man leave his father and mother, and shall be joined to his wife, and the two shall be one flesh. This is a great mystery, but I speak concerning Christ and the church. Nevertheless let everyone of you in particular so love his wife just as himself, and the wife see that she reverence her husband.

EPHESIANS 5:21–33

Wives, submit yourselves to your own husbands, as it is fitting in the Lord. Husbands, love your wives, and be not harsh with them.

COLOSSIANS 3:18–19

This is the will of God, your sanctification, so that you should abstain from sexual immorality; that each one of you should know how to control his own body in holiness and honor, not in the lusts of immorality, like the pagans who do not know God; that no man go beyond and exploit his brother in any way; because the Lord is the avenger in all these things, just as we also have forewarned you and testified. For God has not called us to uncleanness, but to holiness.   I THESSALONIANS 4:3–7

The Spirit speaks clearly that in the last times some shall depart from the faith, giving heed to deceitful spirits and doctrines of demons, through the hypocrisy of liars whose consciences are seared with a hot iron. They will forbid people to marry, and command them to abstain from certain foods, which God has created to be received with thanksgiving by them who believe and know the truth.   I TIMOTHY 4:1–4

If any does not provide for his own, and especially for those of his own house, he has denied the faith, and is worse than an unbeliever.

I TIMOTHY 5:8

Marriage is honorable in all, and the bed undefiled, but whoremongers and adulterers God will judge.   HEBREWS 13:4

You wives, be subject to your own husbands, so that if they obey not the word, they also may without the word be won by the behavior of the wives, when they behold the purity and reverence of your conduct. Do not adorn

---

Honeymoon Law

Many of the rules in the Old Testament were quite sensible—and humane. There were laws, for example, to ensure the happiness of newlyweds and engaged couples:

"Has anyone become pledged to a woman and not married her? Let him go home, or he may die in battle and someone else marry her" (Deuteronomy 20:7).

"If a man has recently married, he must not be sent to war or have any other duty laid on him. For one year he is to be free to stay at home and bring happiness to the wife he has married" (Deuteronomy 24:5, NIV).

---

yourselves outwardly by braiding your hair, and by wearing gold, or by putting on clothing. Rather, let your adornment be the inner self of the heart, which never decays, the ornament of a meek and quiet spirit, which is of much value in the sight of God. Be like the holy women of ages past, who trusted in God and adorned themselves by being subject to their own husbands.

Likewise, you husbands, show consideration to your wives, giving them honor as the weaker sex, since you are both heirs together of the grace of life. I PETER 3:1–5, 7

See also Adultery, Children, Parents.

MEEKNESS/GENTLENESS

Meekness is not weakness, though we often assume that it is. The word suggests to us wimpiness, a doormat, or someone with pitifully low self-

esteem. This isn't the Bible's meaning, however. Perhaps the clearest summary of the Bible's teaching on meekness is found in an anonymous medieval book, The Cloud of Unknowing, *which tells us that "meekness is nothing else but a true knowing and feeling of man's self as he is." In other words, when we compare ourselves, however great we may be, we are still not very great when compared with God. So meekness is seeing ourselves realistically—not hating ourselves or putting ourselves down but realizing that we are not God.*

Gentleness is as neglected a quality as meekness. But it is praised mightily in the Bible, which predicts that someday the arrogant and proud will finally receive their reward, while the meek and gentle will inherit what is truly desirable.

The man Moses was very meek, above all the men which were on the face of the earth. NUMBERS 12:3

The meek shall eat and be satisfied; they shall praise the LORD that seek him; your heart shall live forever. PSALM 22:26

The meek will he guide in judgment, and the meek will he teach his way. PSALM 25:9

The meek shall inherit the earth, and shall delight themselves in the abundance of peace. PSALM 37:11

The LORD takes pleasure in his people; he will beautify the meek with salvation. PSALM 149:4

He that is slow to wrath is of great understanding, but he who is hasty of spirit exalts folly. PROVERBS 14:29

A soft answer turns away wrath, but grievous words stir up anger. PROVERBS 15:1

Scornful men bring a city into a trap, but wise men turn away wrath. PROVERBS 29:8

The patient in spirit is better than the proud in spirit.

ECCLESIASTES 7:8

The meek shall increase their joy in the LORD, and the poor among men shall rejoice in the Holy One of Israel.   ISAIAH 29:19

Seek you the LORD, all you meek of the earth, you who do as he commands; seek righteousness, seek meekness; it may be you shall be sheltered on the day of the LORD's anger.   ZEPHANIAH 2:3

Blessed are the meek, for they shall inherit the earth.   MATTHEW 5:5

Come to me, all you that labor and are heavy laden, and I will give you rest. Take my yoke upon you, and learn from me; for I am meek and lowly in heart, and you shall find rest for your souls.   MATTHEW 11:28–29

You call me Master and Lord, and you say rightly, for so I am. If I then, your Lord and Master, have washed your feet; you also ought to wash one another's feet. For I have given you an example, so that you should do as I have done to you. Truly, truly, I say to you, the servant is not greater than his Lord, nor is the one sent greater than he who sent him.   JOHN 13:3–17

Be of good comfort, be of one mind, live in peace, and the God of love and peace shall be with you.   2 CORINTHIANS 13:11

Brethren, if a man is caught in a sin, you who are spiritual should restore him in the spirit of meekness. But take care, lest you also be tempted. Bear one another's burdens, and so fulfill the law of Christ. For if a man think himself to be something, when he is nothing, he deceives himself.

GALATIANS 6:1–3

With all humility and meekness, with patience, bear with one another in love.   EPHESIANS 4:2

As the elect people of God, holy and beloved, put on compassion, kindness, humbleness of mind, meekness, patience; bear with one another, and forgive one another, if any man has a quarrel against any; just as Christ forgave you, so you also forgive. And above all these things put on love, which binds all things together in perfection. And let the peace of God rule in your hearts, to which you are called in one body. And be thankful.

COLOSSIANS 3:12–15

Follow peace with all men, and holiness, without which no man shall see the Lord. HEBREWS 12:14

Do not adorn yourselves outwardly by arranging your hair, or by wearing gold, or by putting on clothing. Rather, let your adornment be the inner man of the heart, which never decays, the ornament of a meek and quiet spirit, which is of much value in the sight of God. I PETER 3:3–4

Add to your faith virtue, and to virtue add knowledge; and to knowledge self-control; and to self-control patience; and to patience godliness; and to godliness brotherly kindness; and to brotherly kindness charity.

2 PETER 1:5–7

See also Arrogance, Pride, Self-Esteem, Selfishness.

MERCY

According to the Bible, mercy is an attribute of God. Though he is often depicted as the righteous Judge who punishes evil, he is also the Merciful One, always preferring that people depart from evil and do the good. Because he shows mercy to people who have done wrong, we too are to be merciful in our dealings with one another. This doesn't mean that we completely scrap our society's system of justice, of course, but it does mean that justice must be tempered with mercy.

Mercy is bound up with the whole idea of compassion. This is nowhere clearer than in Jesus' parable of the good Samaritan, found below in the quote from Luke 10.

With the merciful you will show yourself merciful, and with the upright man you will show yourself upright. 2 SAMUEL 22:26

Mercy and truth are met together; righteousness and peace have kissed each other. PSALM 85:10

The merciful man does good to his own soul, but he who is cruel troubles his own flesh. PROVERBS 11:17

A righteous man is considerate even for the life of his beast, but even the kindnesses of the wicked are cruel. PROVERBS 12:10

Hear the word of the LORD, you children of Israel, for the LORD has a controversy with the inhabitants of the land, because there is no truth, nor mercy, nor knowledge of God in the land. HOSEA 4:1

Blessed are the merciful, for they shall obtain mercy. MATTHEW 5:7

Love your enemies, and do good; and lend, hoping for nothing in return. And your reward shall be great, and you shall be the children of the Highest, for he is kind to the ungrateful and to the evil. Be therefore merciful, as your Father also is merciful. Give, and it shall be given to you. A good measure, pressed down, shaken together, and running over, shall men put into your lap. For the same measure you give will be the measure you get back. LUKE 6:35–38

A man willing to justify himself said to Jesus, "Who is my neighbor?" And Jesus answering said, "A certain man went down from Jerusalem to Jericho, and fell among thieves, who stripped him of his clothing and wounded him and departed, leaving him half dead. And by chance there came by a certain priest, and when he saw him, he passed by on the other side. And likewise a Levite, when he was at the place, came and looked at him, then passed by on the other side. But a certain Samaritan, as he journeyed, came where he was, and when he saw him, he had compassion on him, and went to him, and bound up his wounds, pouring in oil and wine, and set him on his own beast, and brought him to an inn, and took care of him. And on the next day when he departed, he took money, gave it to the innkeeper, and said to him, 'Take care of him, and whatever else you spend, when I come again, I will repay you.' Which now of these three, think you, was neighbor to him that fell among the thieves?" And he said, "He who showed mercy on him." Then said Jesus to him, "Go and do likewise." LUKE 10:29–37

As the elect people of God, holy and beloved, put on compassion, kindness, humbleness of mind, meekness, patience; bear with one another, and forgive one another, if any man has a quarrel against any; just as Christ forgave you, so you also forgive. And above all these things put on love, which binds all things together in perfection. And let the peace of God rule in your hearts, to which you are called in one body. And be thankful.

COLOSSIANS 3:12–15

Whoever has shown no mercy, he shall have judgment without mercy.

JAMES 2:13

If you have bitter envying and strife in your hearts, do not boast of it, and do not deny the truth. This so-called wisdom descends not from heaven, but is earthly, sensual, devilish. For where envying and strife are, there is disorder and every evil work. But the wisdom that is from above is first pure, then peaceable, gentle, and easy to be entreated, full of mercy and good fruits, without partiality, and without hypocrisy. JAMES 3:14–17

Do not repay evil for evil, or abuse for abuse, but, on the contrary, repay with blessing; knowing that you are called so that you should inherit a blessing. 1 PETER 3:9

See also Enemies, Forgiveness, God's Mercy.

MONEY

Benjamin Franklin, the great statesman and philosopher, had a lot of advice to give about making money, including such proverbs as "A penny saved is a penny earned." Despite such advice, Franklin wasn't foolish enough to believe that money could buy happiness. The practical-minded Franklin wrote, "The more a man has, the more he wants," then went on to quote Proverbs 15:16, which is quoted below. Like most sensible people, Franklin was aware that we need money to survive but also that it is not our ultimate source of happiness, for no matter how much money we have, it never brings satisfaction. Money can buy everything—except, of course, the things that truly matter, such as love, personality, freedom, and immortality.

The old saying "Money is the root of all evil" is in the Bible, or is it? The actual quote, found below, is "The love of money is the root of all evil." Money isn't evil in itself—in fact, it can do a great deal of good in the world—but our idolatry of it is evil.

A little that a righteous man has is better than the riches of many wicked.

PSALM 37:16

Surely they are in a turmoil for nothing; he heaps up riches, not knowing who will get them.

PSALM 39:6

Blessed is he who considers the poor; the LORD will deliver him in time of trouble.

PSALM 41:1

God sees that wise men die, likewise the fool and the brutish person perish, and leave their wealth to others. Their inward thought is that their houses shall continue forever, and their dwelling places to all generations. They call their lands after their own names. Nevertheless man, despite his wealth, does not endure; he is like the beasts that perish.

PSALM 49:10–12

Honor the LORD with your wealth.

PROVERBS 3:9

Riches are of no value on the day of wrath, but righteousness delivers from death.

PROVERBS 11:4

He that trusts in his riches shall fall, but the righteous shall flourish as a branch.

PROVERBS 11:28

The thoughts of the righteous are right, but the advice of the wicked is deceitful.

PROVERBS 12:5

Wealth hastily gotten shall be diminished, but he who gathers by labor shall increase.

PROVERBS 13:11

Better is little with the fear of the LORD than great treasure and trouble with it.

PROVERBS 15:16

How much better is it to get wisdom than gold! And to get understanding rather than silver! PROVERBS 16:16

Whoever mocks the poor insults his Maker, and he who is glad at calamities shall not go unpunished. PROVERBS 17:5

The rich and poor meet together; the LORD is the maker of them all. PROVERBS 22:2

He that oppresses the poor to increase his riches, and he who gives to the rich, shall surely come to want. PROVERBS 22:16

Rob not the poor, because he is poor; neither oppress the needy in the courts; for the LORD will plead their cause, and will ruin the soul of those that ruined them. PROVERBS 22:22–23

Labor not to be rich; be wise enough to desist. Will you set your eyes upon what is not there? For riches certainly make themselves wings; they fly away as an eagle toward heaven. PROVERBS 23:4–5

Riches are not forever, nor does the crown endure to every generation. PROVERBS 27:24

A faithful man shall abound with blessings, but he who makes haste to be rich shall not be innocent. PROVERBS 28:20

He that hastes to be rich has an evil eye, and considers not that poverty shall come upon him. PROVERBS 28:22

Give me neither poverty nor riches; feed me with food that I need; lest I be full, and deny you, and say, "Who is the LORD?" Or lest I be poor, and steal, and take the name of my God in vain. PROVERBS 30:8–9

He that loves silver shall not be satisfied with silver, nor shall he who loves abundance be satisfied with increase; this is also futile. When goods increase, those who consume them are increased, and what good is there to their owners, except seeing them with their eyes?

The sleep of a laboring man is sweet, whether he eat little or much, but the abundance of the rich will not let him sleep. There is a sore evil which I have seen under the sun, namely, riches kept by their owners to their harm. But those riches perish through misfortune, and he begets a son, but is nothing in his hand. As he came forth from his mother's womb, naked shall he return just as he came, and shall take nothing of his labor, which he may carry away in his hand.   ECCLESIASTES 5:10–15

There is an evil which I have seen under the sun, and it is common among men: a man to whom God has given riches, wealth, and honor, so that he lacks nothing at all that his soul desires, yet God does not enable him to enjoy these things, but a stranger enjoys them; this is futility, a grievous ill.

ECCLESIASTES 6:1–2

They shall cast their silver in the streets, and their gold shall be removed; their silver and their gold shall not be able to deliver them on the day of the wrath of the LORD; they shall not satisfy their souls, neither fill their bellies with it, because it is the stumblingblock of their wrongdoing.

EZEKIEL 7:19

Woe to him that gets evil gain for his house, so that he may set his nest on high, so that he may be delivered from the power of evil! You have devised shame for your house by cutting off many people, and you have sinned against your soul. For the stone shall cry out from the wall, and the beam out from the timber shall answer it. Woe to him that builds a town by bloodshed, and establishes a city by crime! Behold, has not the LORD Almighty determined that the people's labor is merely fuel for the fire, and that the nations shall weary themselves for nothing? For the earth shall be filled with the knowledge of the glory of the LORD, as the waters cover the sea.

HABAKKUK 2:9–14

Man shall not live by bread alone, but by every word that proceeds out of the mouth of God.   MATTHEW 4:4

Lay not up for yourselves treasures upon earth, where moth and rust corrupt, and where thieves break through and steal. But lay up for yourselves treasures in heaven, where neither moth nor rust do corrupt, and where thieves do not break through and steal; for where your treasure is, there will your heart be also. MATTHEW 6:19–21

No man can serve two masters, for either he will hate the one and love the other, or he will hold to the one, and despise the other. You cannot serve God and money. MATTHEW 6:24

Jesus said to them, "Children, how hard is it for those who trust in riches to enter into the kingdom of God! It is easier for a camel to go through the eye of a needle than for a rich man to enter into the kingdom of God." And they were astonished, saying among themselves, "Who then can be saved?" And Jesus looking upon them said, "With men it is impossible, but not with God, for with God all things are possible." MARK 10:24–27

Woe to you who are rich, for you have already received your consolation. Woe to you who are full, for you shall hunger. Woe to you that laugh now, for you shall mourn and weep. LUKE 6:24–25

Take heed, and beware of greed, for a man's life consists not in the abundance of the things he possesses. LUKE 12:15

Jesus spoke a parable to them, saying, "The ground of a certain rich man brought forth plentifully. And he thought to himself, 'What shall I do, because I have no room to store my yield?' And he said, 'This will I do: I will pull down my barns and build larger, and there will I store all my fruits and my goods. And I will say to my soul, Soul, you have much goods laid up for many years; take your ease, eat, drink, and be merry.' But God said to him, 'You fool, this night your soul shall be required of you. Then whose shall those things be, which you have provided?' So is he who lays up treasure for himself, and is not rich toward God." LUKE 12:16–21

You shall be enriched in every way for your generosity, which will produce thanksgiving to God. 2 CORINTHIANS 9:11

My God shall supply all your need according to his riches in glory by Christ Jesus. PHILIPPIANS 4:19

Having food and clothing, let us be content. But they that will be rich fall into temptation and a trap, and into many foolish and hurtful cravings, which drown men in destruction and ruin. The love of money is the root of all evil. Some who have coveted after it have wandered from the faith, and pierced themselves through with many sorrows.   I TIMOTHY 6:8–10

Command those who are rich in this world that they be not arrogant, nor trust in uncertain riches, but in the living God, who gives us richly all things to enjoy. Command that they do good, so that they be rich in good works, ready to distribute, willing to share, laying up in store for themselves a good foundation against the time to come, so that they may lay hold of eternal life.   I TIMOTHY 6:17–19

Let your lives be free from covetousness, and be content with such things as you have, for he has said, "I will never leave you, nor forsake you."

HEBREWS 13:5

The sun is no sooner risen with a burning heat, but it withers the grass, and the flower falls, and the beauty of it perishes. Likewise, the rich man shall fade away in the midst of his busy life.   JAMES 1:11

Listen, my beloved brethren: has not God chosen the poor of this world to be rich in faith, and heirs of the kingdom which he has promised to those who love him? But you have despised the poor. Do not rich men oppress you, and drag you into the courts? Do not they blaspheme that worthy name by which you are called? You do well if you fulfill the royal law according to the scripture, "You shall love your neighbor as yourself"; but if you show favoritism, you commit sin, and are convicted of the law as transgressors.

JAMES 2:5–9

Listen now, you rich men: weep and wail for the miseries that shall come upon you. Your riches have corrupted, and your garments are moth-eaten. Your gold and silver have cankered, and the rust of them shall be a witness against you, and shall eat your flesh as it were fire. You have heaped treasure together for the last days. Behold, the wages of the laborers who have harvested your fields, which you kept back by fraud, cry out, and the cries of the harvesters have entered into the ears of the Lord Almighty. You have lived in pleasure and luxury on the earth; you have fattened your hearts, as for a day of slaughter. You have condemned and killed the righteous, one who does not resist you.   JAMES 5:1-6

You say, "I am rich, and increased with goods, and have need of nothing," and you do not know that you are wretched, miserable, poor, blind, and naked; I counsel you to buy from me gold tested in the fire, so that you may be rich, and buy white clothing, so that you may be clothed, and so that the shame of your nakedness does not appear, and anoint your eyes with eye salve, so that you may see. As many as I love, I rebuke and chasten; be zealous therefore, and repent.   REVELATION 3:17-19

See also Ambition, Duty to the Poor, Generosity, Self-Esteem, Worry.

NATURE AND THE EARTH

Nature is beautiful. The Bible makes it clear that God takes pleasure in his own creation, and so does man. Polluting and deliberately spoiling natural beauty is wrong. But the Bible also makes it clear that nature, wonderful as it is, is not to be worshiped. A generation ago, people would have laughed at the idea that nature worship would become a popular religion, but that is exactly what has happened. The popular "Love Your Mother" bumper stickers suggest that people feel more of an affection for Mother Earth than for God the Father. But the invisible Creator, God, is the one thing people should worship. Everything else—the most awe-inspiring mountains, waterfalls, and canyons, even the vast cosmos itself—is something God created, so we may enjoy it or admire it but not worship it.

One other matter: Yes, mankind is part of nature, part of what God has created. But man is also a special part of it, given the role of tending and overseeing the natural world, a role that separates us from all other created things.

God said, "Let us make man in our image, after our likeness, and let them have dominion over the fish of the sea, and over the birds of the air, and over the cattle, and over all the earth, and over every creeping thing that creeps upon the earth."

And God blessed them, and God said to them, "Be fruitful, and multiply, and replenish the earth, and subdue it, and have dominion over the fish of the sea, and over the birds of the air, and over every living thing that moves upon the earth.   GENESIS 1:26, 28

God saw every thing that he had made, and, behold, it was very good.
                                                                    GENESIS 1:31

God blessed Noah and his sons, and said to them, "Be fruitful, and multiply, and replenish the earth. And the fear and dread of you shall be upon every beast of the earth, and upon every bird of the air, upon all that moves upon the earth, and upon all the fishes of the sea; into your hand are they delivered. Every moving thing that lives shall be food for you; just as I have given you the green plants, I give you all things."   GENESIS 9:1–3

You shall not make for yourself any graven image, or any likeness of anything that is in heaven above, or that is in the earth beneath, or that is in the water under the earth: you shall not bow down yourself to them, nor serve them, for I the LORD your God am a jealous God.   EXODUS 20:4–5

Take heed, lest you corrupt yourselves and make yourselves an idol, an image of some shape, formed like a man or woman, or like any beast that is on the earth, or any bird in the air, or like any creature in the waters below. And when you lift up your eyes to heaven, and when you see the sun, and the moon, and the stars, all the host of heaven, do not be driven to worship them, and serve them.   DEUTERONOMY 4:15–19

Stand still, and consider the wondrous works of God.   JOB 37:14

When I consider your heavens, the work of your fingers, the moon and the stars, which you have ordained—what is man, that you are mindful of him? And the son of man, that you visit him? For you have made him a little lower than the angels, and have crowned him with glory and honor. You made him to have dominion over the works of your hands; you have put all things under his feet: all sheep and oxen, yes, and the beasts of the field; the birds of the air, and the fish of the sea, and whatever passes through the paths of the seas. O LORD our LORD, how excellent is your name in all the earth!   PSALM 8:3–9

The heavens declare the glory of God, and the firmament shows his handiwork. Day to day utters speech, and night to night shows knowledge. There is no speech nor language, where their voice is not heard. Their voice is gone out through all the earth, and their words to the end of the world.   PSALM 19:1–4

O LORD God Almighty, who is a strong LORD like you? Or to your faithfulness round about you? You rule the raging of the sea: when its waves rise up, you still them. . . . The heavens are yours, the earth also is yours; as for the world and the fullness thereof, you have founded them.

PSALM 89:8–11

Long ago you laid the foundation of the earth, and the heavens are the work of your hands. They shall perish, but you shall endure: yes, all of them shall wear out like a garment; like clothing shall you change them, and they shall be changed. But you are the same, and your years shall have no end.

PSALM 102:25–27

The heaven, even the heavens, are the LORD'S, but the earth has he given to the children of men.
PSALM 115:16

The LORD by wisdom has founded the earth; by understanding has he established the heavens. By his knowledge the depths were divided, and the clouds drop down the dew.
PROVERBS 3:19–20

A righteous man is concerned for the life of his beast.
PROVERBS 12:10

Lift up your eyes to the heavens, and look upon the earth beneath, for the heavens shall vanish away like smoke, and the earth shall grow old like a garment, and they that dwell in it shall die in like manner, but my salvation shall be forever, and my righteousness shall not be abolished.
ISAIAH 51:6

Consider the lilies, how they grow; they toil not, they spin not, and yet I say to you that Solomon in all his glory was not arrayed like one of these.
LUKE 12:27

They changed the truth of God into a lie, and worshipped and served the creature more than the Creator.
ROMANS 1:25

The heavens and the earth which now exist have been reserved for fire until the day of judgment and destruction of ungodly men. But, beloved, be not ignorant of this one thing, that one day is with the Lord like a thousand

Nature Boys
The world's first "back to the land" movement was the Rechabites, a group in Israel. They lived in tents instead of houses and lived as nomads instead of settling down. They urged fellow Israelites to give up luxury and live simply as a way of getting close to God (see Jeremiah 35).

years, and a thousand years like one day. The Lord is not slow concerning his promise, as some men believe; but he is longsuffering toward us, not willing that any should perish, but that all should come to repentance. But the day of the Lord will come as a thief in the night. Then the heavens shall pass away with a great noise, and the elements shall melt with fervent heat, the earth also and everything in it shall be burned up.

2 PETER 3:7–10

Love not the world, neither the things that are in the world. If any man love the world, the love of the Father is not in him. For all that is in the world, the cravings of the sinful nature, and the lust of the eyes, and the pride of life, is not of the Father, but is of the world. And the world passes away, and all its lusts, but he who does the will of God abides forever.

1 JOHN 2:15–17

I saw a new heaven and a new earth, for the first heaven and the first earth were passed away, and there was no more sea. And I John saw the holy city, New Jerusalem, coming down from God out of heaven, prepared as a bride adorned for her husband. And I heard a great voice out of heaven saying, "Behold, the dwelling place of God is with men, and he will dwell with them, and they shall be his people, and God himself shall be with them, and be their God."

REVELATION 21:1–3

See also God As Creator, Heaven, Idolatry.

NEW BIRTH/NEW LIFE

The phrase "new and improved" is now part of the language. It is part of the Bible's language also, where the idea of moral and spiritual renewal is present everywhere. In fact, the Bible presents us two sides of moral renewal: We should always strive to improve ourselves, yet ultimately our being "born again" is through God's action. The explanation for this paradox is that the job is simply too big for us. We need a kind of spiritual "jump start" or, to use the familiar phrase from the Bible, to be "born again." While that phrase has been used so often that it seems worn and quaint, it fits in perfectly with our belief that we ought to always be improving, creating a "new me."

Our offenses are stronger than we are, but you shall blot them out.

PSALM 65:3

"Wash yourselves, make yourselves clean; put away the evil of your doings out of my sight. Cease to do evil; learn to do good; seek justice, relieve the oppressed, defend the fatherless, plead for the widow. Come now, and let us reason together," says the LORD; "though your sins be like scarlet, they shall be as white as snow; though they be red like crimson, they shall be like wool."

ISAIAH 1:16—18

Ho, everyone that thirsts, come to the waters; and he who has no money; come, buy, and eat; indeed, come, buy wine and milk without money and without cost. Why do you spend money for what is not bread, and why labor for what does not satisfy? Listen diligently to me, and eat what is good, and let your soul delight itself in richness. Incline your ear and come to me; hear, and your soul shall live, and I will make an everlasting covenant with you.

ISAIAH 55:1—3

Let the wicked forsake his way, and the unrighteous man his thoughts, and let him return to the LORD, and he will have mercy upon him.

ISAIAH 55:7

O LORD, the hope of Israel, all that forsake you shall be ashamed, and they that depart from me shall be written in the earth, because they have forsaken the LORD, the fountain of living waters. Heal me, O LORD, and I shall be healed; save me, and I shall be saved, for you are my praise.

JEREMIAH 17:13–14

"This shall be the covenant that I will make with the house of Israel after those days," says the LORD. "I will put my law in their minds and write it on their hearts, and will be their God, and they shall be my people. And no longer shall every man teach his neighbor, and every man his brother, saying, 'Know the LORD,' for they shall all know me, from the least of them to the greatest; for I will forgive their disobedience, and I will remember their sin no more."

JEREMIAH 31:33–34

I will give them one heart, and I will put a new spirit within you, and I will take the stony heart out of their flesh, and will give them a heart of flesh, that they may walk in my statutes, and keep mine commandments and do them, and they shall be my people, and I will be their God.

EZEKIEL 11:19–20

Rid yourselves of all your offenses you have done, and make you a new heart and a new spirit; for why will you die, O house of Israel?

EZEKIEL 18:31

I will sprinkle clean water upon you, and you shall be clean. From all your filthiness, and from all your idols will I cleanse you. A new heart also will I give you, and a new spirit will I put within you. And I will take away the stony heart out of your flesh, and I will give you a heart of flesh. And I will put my Spirit within you, and cause you to walk in my statutes, and you shall keep my judgments, and do them. And you shall dwell in the land that I gave to your fathers, and you shall be my people, and I will be your God.

EZEKIEL 36:25–28

Bring forth fruit in keeping with repentance.

MATTHEW 3:8

Every good tree brings forth good fruit; but a corrupt tree brings forth evil fruit. A good tree cannot bring forth evil fruit, neither can a corrupt tree bring forth good fruit. Every tree that brings not forth good fruit is cut down and cast into the fire. So by their fruits you shall know them. Not everyone that says to me, "Lord, Lord," shall enter into the kingdom of heaven, but only he who does the will of my Father who is in heaven.

MATTHEW 7:17–21

Truly I say to you, except you be converted, and become like little children, you shall not enter the kingdom of heaven. Whoever shall humble himself as this little child, the same is greatest in the kingdom of heaven. And whoever shall receive one such little child in my name receives me.

MATTHEW 18:3–5

There was a man of the Pharisees named Nicodemus, a leader of the Jews. He came to Jesus by night, and said to him, "Master, we know that you are a teacher come from God, for no man can do these miracles that you do, except God be with him." Jesus answered and said to him, "Truly, truly, I say to you, except a man be born again, he cannot see the kingdom of God." Nicodemus said to him, "How can a man be born when he is old? Can he enter the second time into his mother's womb, and be born?" Jesus answered, "Truly, truly, I say to you, except a man be born of water and of the Spirit, he cannot enter into the kingdom of God. That which is born of the flesh is flesh, and what is born of the Spirit is spirit. Marvel not that I said to you, 'You must be born again.' The wind blows where it chooses, and you hear the sound of it, but cannot tell where it comes from or where it goes; so is everyone that is born of the Spirit."   JOHN 3:1–8

Truly, truly, I say to you, he who hears my word, and believes in him that sent me, has everlasting life, and shall not come into condemnation; but is passed from death to life.   JOHN 5:24

Truly, truly, I say to you, he who believes in me has everlasting life.

JOHN 6:47

I am the light of the world; he who follows me shall not walk in darkness, but shall have the light of life.   JOHN 8:12

If the Son therefore shall make you free, you shall be free indeed.

JOHN 8:36

I am the door; if any man enter in by me, he shall be saved.

JOHN 10:9

Peter said to them, "Repent, and be baptized every one of you in the name of Jesus Christ for the forgiveness of sins, and you shall receive the gift of the Holy Spirit." ACTS 2:38

Repent you therefore, and be converted, that your sins may be blotted out, when the times of refreshing shall come from the presence of the Lord.

ACTS 3:19

We are buried with him by baptism into death, so that just as Christ was raised from the dead by the glory of the Father, so we too should walk in newness of life. For if we have been united with him in a death like his, we shall also be united with him in a resurrection like his. We know that our old man is crucified with him, so that the body of sin might be destroyed, and afterward we should not serve sin. For he who is dead is freed from sin. Now if we be dead with Christ, we believe that we shall also live with him.

ROMANS 6:4–8

Be not conformed to this world, but be transformed by the renewing of your mind, that you may prove what is the good and acceptable and perfect will of God. ROMANS 12:2

You are washed, you are sanctified, you are justified in the name of the Lord Jesus, and by the Spirit of our God. I CORINTHIANS 6:11

As in Adam all die, even so in Christ shall all be made alive.

I CORINTHIANS 15:22

If any man be in Christ, he is a new creature; old things are passed away; behold, all things are become new. 2 CORINTHIANS 5:17

I am crucified with Christ; nevertheless I live; yet not I, but Christ lives in me. And the life which I now live in the flesh I live by the faith of the Son of God, who loved me, and gave himself for me.   GALATIANS 2:20

By grace are you saved through faith, and that not of yourselves; it is the gift of God; not of works, lest any man should boast. For we are his workmanship, created in Christ Jesus for good works, which God has before ordained that we should walk in.   EPHESIANS 2:8–10

Be renewed in the spirit of your mind, and put on the new man, which after God is created in righteousness and true holiness.

EPHESIANS 4:23–24

Awake you that sleep, and arise from the dead, and Christ shall give you light.   EPHESIANS 5:14

Lie not one to another, seeing that you have put off the old man with his deeds and have put on the new man, which is renewed in knowledge after the image of him that created him.   COLOSSIANS 3:9–10

Not by works of righteousness which we have done, but according to his mercy he saved us, by the washing of regeneration, and renewing of the Holy Spirit; which he shed on us abundantly through Jesus Christ our Savior.   TITUS 3:5–6

You are a chosen generation, a royal priesthood, a holy nation, a distinctive people, so you should show forth the praises of him who has called you out of darkness into his marvelous light.   I PETER 2:9

We know that we have passed from death to life, because we love the brethren. He that loves not his brother abides in death.   I JOHN 3:14

Whoever believes that Jesus is the Christ is born of God, and everyone that loves the Father loves the Son as well.   I JOHN 5:1

Whoever is born of God overcomes the world, and this is the victory that overcomes the world, our faith. Who is it who overcomes the world? He who believes that Jesus is the Son of God.   I JOHN 5:4–5

God has given to us eternal life, and this life is in his Son. He that has the Son has life, and he who has not the Son of God has not life.

I JOHN 5:11–12

I saw a new heaven and a new earth, for the first heaven and the first earth were passed away. . . . And he that sat upon the throne said, "Behold, I make all things new." REVELATION 21:1, 5

See also Baptism of the Spirit/Gifts of the Spirit, Justification, Repentance, Salvation.

OBEYING GOD

The Bible offers us the Ten Commandments, not the Ten Suggestions. God did not base his moral laws on a poll of the human race or on the input from focus groups. Public opinion does not determine whether things are good or bad. In fact, like it or not, the Bible tells us to do certain things—period, end of discussion. While it is human nature to want to argue with every rule—especially those that get in the way of our selfish impulses— most of us feel, deep down, that rules are for our own good. This is precisely the position of the Bible: The rules are there not to deprive us of pleasure but to keep us from making a mess of our lives.

An old hymn sums up the life of faith in its title, "Trust and Obey." That's pretty much the essence of the Bible: Trust God, the One in charge of the universe, and obey him. The one who obeys God trusts God, and the one who trusts God obeys him.

If you will obey my voice and keep my covenant, then you shall be a distinctive treasure to me above all people, for all the earth is mine. And you shall be to me a kingdom of priests, a holy nation. EXODUS 19:5–6

Be strong, show yourself a man, and keep the charge of the LORD your God, to walk in his ways. I KINGS 2:2–3

If you will walk in my ways, to keep my statutes and my commandments, as your father David did walk, then I will lengthen your days.

I KINGS 3:14

Blessed is the man that walks not in the counsel of the ungodly, nor stands in the way of sinners, nor sits in the seat of the scornful. But his delight is in the law of the LORD, and on his law does he meditate day and night.

PSALM 1:1–2

All the paths of the LORD are mercy and truth to such as keep his covenant and his testimonies. PSALM 25:10

The mercy of the LORD is from everlasting to everlasting upon those who fear him, and his righteousness to children's children, to those that keep his covenant, and to those that remember his commandments to do them. The LORD has prepared his throne in the heavens, and his kingdom rules over all. Bless the LORD, you his angels, who excel in strength, that do his commandments, hearkening to the voice of his word. Bless you the LORD, all you his hosts; you ministers of his, that do his pleasure. PSALM 103:17–21

Praise the LORD. Blessed is the man that fears the LORD, who delights greatly in his commandments. PSALM 112:1

Blessed are they that keep his testimonies, and that seek him with their whole heart. PSALM 119:2

He that keeps the commandment keeps his own soul; but he who despises his ways shall die. PROVERBS 19:16

If you are willing and obedient, you shall eat the good of the land. ISAIAH 1:19

No man can serve two masters, for either he will hate one and love the other; or else he will hold to the one, and despise the other. You cannot serve God and money. MATTHEW 6:24

Not everyone that says to me, "Lord, Lord," shall enter into the kingdom of heaven, but only he who does the will of my Father who is in heaven. MATTHEW 7:21

Whoever hears these sayings of mine, and does them, will be like a wise man who built his house upon a rock. And the rain descended, and the floods came, and the winds blew and beat upon that house, yet it fell not, for it was founded upon a rock. And everyone that hears these sayings of mine, and does them not, shall be like a foolish man who built his house upon the sand. And the rain descended, and the floods came, and the winds blew and beat upon that house, and it fell, and great was the fall of it.

MATTHEW 7:24–27

Then said Jesus to those Jews which believed in him, "If you continue in my word, then you are my disciples indeed; and you shall know the truth, and the truth shall make you free."

JOHN 8:31–32

If you love me, keep my commandments.

JOHN 14:15

If you keep my commandments, you shall abide in my love; just as I have kept my Father's commandments, and abide in his love. These things have I spoken to you, so that my joy might remain in you, and that your joy might be complete. This is my commandment, that you love one another, as I have loved you. Greater love has no man than this, so that a man lay down his life for his friends. You are my friends, if you do whatever I command you.

JOHN 15:10–14

Know you not, that to whomever you yield yourselves as servants to obey, you are his slaves, whether slaves of sin to death, or slaves of obedience to righteousness? But, God be thanked, you were the servants of sin, but you have obeyed from the heart that form of doctrine which was delivered to you. Being then made free from sin, you became the servants of righteousness.

ROMANS 6:16–18

The carnal mind is hostile to God, for it is not subject to the law of God— indeed it cannot, and they that are in the flesh cannot please God. But you are not in the flesh, but in the Spirit, since the Spirit of God dwells in you. Now if any man have not the Spirit of Christ, he does not belong to him.

ROMANS 8:7–9

Whatever good thing any man does, the same shall he receive from the Lord.

EPHESIANS 6:8

Do those things which you have learned and received and heard and seen in me, and the God of peace shall be with you.   PHILIPPIANS 4:9

American author Mark Twain claimed, "Most people are bothered by those Scripture passages which they cannot understand. But for me, the passages in Scripture which trouble me most are those which I do understand."

Christ became the author of eternal salvation unto all them that obey him.

HEBREWS 5:9

By this we know that we love the children of God, when we love God, and keep his commandments. For this is the love of God, that we keep his commandments, and his commandments are not burdensome.

1 JOHN 5:2–3

Whoever transgresses and continues not in the doctrine of Christ does not have God. He that abides in the doctrine of Christ, he has both the Father and the Son.

2 JOHN 9

See also Faith, Fellowship with God, Trusting God.

OPPORTUNITIES

We are all familiar with the old proverb "The road to hell is paved with good intentions." There is another proverb like it: "Hell is roofed with lost opportunities." The Bible is a serious book, and throughout it is a sense of deep urgency: Turn away from doing wrong, turn to God, teach others to turn to God—and don't procrastinate. This sense of urgency has motivated preachers throughout the centuries, and from a psychological perspective it is highly effective. (Think of all the sales pitches you've ever heard—"If you act today," "You must act now," "For a limited time only," "Offer ends soon," and so on.) In a sense, all of life is urgent. None of us knows when it may end. If we plan to do the right thing, we ought to do it soon—or, even better, do it now.

Seek you the LORD while he may be found, call upon him while he is near.

ISAIAH 55:6

Into whatever city or town you enter, seek out someone in it who is worthy, and there abide till you leave. And when you come into a house, give it your greeting. And if the house be worthy, let your peace come upon it, but if it be not worthy, let your peace return to you. And whoever shall not receive you, nor hear your words, when you depart out of that house or city, shake the dust off your feet.   MATTHEW 10:7, 11-14

A certain man made a great banquet and invited many. And he sent his servant at supper time to say to those who were invited, "Come, for everything is ready now." But all of them began to make excuses. The first said to him, "I have bought a plot of land, and I must go and see it; I pray you to excuse me." And another said, "I have bought five teams of oxen, and I go to try them out; I pray you to excuse me." And another said, "I have married a wife, and therefore I cannot come." So that servant came, and told his lord these things. Then the master of the house, being angry, said to his servant, "Go out quickly into the streets and lanes of the city, and bring in here the poor, and the maimed, and the lame, and the blind." And the servant said, "Lord, it is done as you have commanded, and yet there is room." And the lord said to the servant, "Go out into the highways and byways and compel them to come in, so that my house may be filled. For I say to you, none of those men who were invited shall taste of my supper."

LUKE 14:16-24

Do you not say, "There are still four months, and then comes harvest"? Behold, I say to you, look around you, and look at the fields, for they are already ripe for harvesting.   JOHN 4:35

Only a little while is the light with you. Walk while you have the light, lest darkness come upon you, for he who walks in darkness knows not where he goes.   JOHN 12:35

Behold, now is the accepted time; behold, now is the day of salvation.

2 CORINTHIANS 6:2

Let us not be weary in doing right, for in due time we shall reap, if we do not give up. As we have opportunity, let us do good to all men, especially to them who are of the household of faith.   GALATIANS 6:9–10

See then that you walk carefully, not as fools but as wise men, making the most of the time, because the days are evil.   EPHESIANS 5:15–16

Walk in wisdom toward outsiders, making the most of opportunities. Let your speech be always with grace, seasoned with salt, so that you may know how you ought to answer every man.   COLOSSIANS 4:5–6

Behold, I stand at the door, and knock; if any man hear my voice, and open the door, I will come in to him, and will dine with him, and he with me.

REVELATION 3:20

The Spirit and the bride say, "Come." And let him that hears come. And let him that is thirsty come. And whoever will, let him take the water of life freely.   REVELATION 22:17

See also Witnessing/Evangelism.

OPPRESSION

The words victim *and* oppression *have been used so often that we begin to wonder just who the* really *oppressed people are. If everyone is oppressed (and sometimes it seems that way), then which ones are the* seriously *oppressed? The Bible takes oppression seriously, and it offers dire warnings to oppressors. The oppressed person isn't necessarily of any particular gender, race, ethnic background, or class—an oppressed person is anyone whose life is believed not to matter. Human history is full of examples of people treated as less than human, meaning that the oppressor is "playing God," holding himself up as higher, more important than the ones he oppresses.*

Our courts—including the court of public opinion—have some success in bringing justice to the oppressed, but they are not perfect. Ultimately, the Bible tells us, the One who can bring justice to the oppressed is God. From beginning to end, the Bible presents him as the friend and defender of the oppressed.

You shall neither mistreat a stranger nor oppress him, for you were strangers in the land of Egypt. You shall not afflict any widow, or fatherless child. If you afflict them in any way, and they cry at all to me, I will surely hear their cry; and my wrath shall grow hot, and I will kill you with the sword, and your wives shall be widows, and your children fatherless.

EXODUS 22:21–24

You shall not oppress a hired servant who is poor and needy, whether he is of your brethren or of your strangers that are in your land. At day's end you shall pay him his wages, neither shall the sun go down upon it; for he is poor, and is counting on it; lest he cry against you to the LORD, and it be sin to you.   DEUTERONOMY 24:14–15

The LORD will be a refuge for the oppressed, a refuge in times of trouble.

PSALM 9:9

LORD, you have heard the desire of the humble; you will prepare their heart, you will cause your ear to hear; to judge the fatherless and the oppressed, so that the man of the earth may no more oppress.   PSALM 10:17–18

Because of the oppression of the poor and the sighing of the needy, now will I arise, says the LORD; I will place them in the safety they long for.

PSALM 12:5

He shall judge the poor of the people, he shall save the children of the needy, and shall break in pieces the oppressor.   PSALM 72:4

He administers justice for the oppressed; he gives food to the hungry. The LORD looses the prisoners.   PSALM 146:7

> *"It is impossible to mentally or socially enslave a Bible-reading people."*
>
> —HORACE GREELEY, AMERICAN PUBLISHER AND POLITICIAN

Open your mouth on behalf of the mute, for all who are appointed to destruction. Open your mouth, judge righteously, and plead the cause of the poor and needy. PROVERBS 31:8–9

Learn to do well; seek judgment, relieve the oppressed, defend the fatherless, plead for the widow. ISAIAH 1:17

Woe to them that make unjust laws. ISAIAH 10:1

He that walks righteously, and speaks uprightly; he who despises the gain of oppressions, who withholds his hands from taking bribes, who stops his ears from hearing of bloodshed, and shuts his eyes from seeing evil—he shall dwell on high; his place of defense shall be the fortresses of rock; bread shall be given him; his waters shall not dry up. ISAIAH 33:15–16

Administer justice in the morning, and deliver him that is ruined out of the hand of the oppressor, lest my fury blaze out like fire, and burn that none can quench it, because of the evil of your doings. JEREMIAH 21:12

Woe to those who devise wrongdoing and work evil upon their beds! When the morning is light, they do it, because it is in the power of their hand. And they covet fields and take them by violence, and covet houses and take them away; they oppress a man and his house, even his heritage. Therefore, says the LORD, behold, against this family do I devise an evil, from which you shall not remove your necks; neither shall you go haughtily, for this time is evil. MICAH 2:1–3

The Spirit of the Lord is upon me, because he has anointed me to preach the gospel to the poor; he has sent me to heal the brokenhearted, to preach deliverance to the captives, and recovering of sight to the blind, to set at liberty those who are oppressed, to proclaim the year of the Lord's favor.

LUKE 4:18–21

God anointed Jesus of Nazareth with the Holy Spirit and with power; he went about doing good, and healing all that were oppressed by the devil; for God was with him.   ACTS 10:38

See also Kindness, Money.

PARENTS

Putting it mildly, the Bible's view of parenting differs from our contemporary view. The ancient world (and the modern world, at least until the last fifty years) believed in strictness and physical punishment for children, and, yes, "spare the rod and spoil the child" is found in the Bible. Yet some things have not changed: Parents in biblical days, as now, were expected to love their children, to keep them from harm, and to pass on to them whatever values they cherished. Then there is the flip side: Children should love and honor their parents, respecting them as authority figures just as the parents should respect the ultimate Authority Figure, God. We need to remember that God in the Bible is a complex figure—strict and highly moral but also loving and tender, merciful toward those who make mistakes. Parents are expected to be the same way toward their own children.

Honor your father and your mother, so that your days may be long upon the land which the LORD your God gives you.   EXODUS 20:12

Take to heart all the words which I declared to you today, all the words of this law, which you shall command your children to observe.

DEUTERONOMY 32:46

We will tell the generations to come the praises of the LORD, and his strength, and his wonderful works he has done. For he gave his testimony to Jacob, and established a law in Israel, which he commanded our fathers to make known to their children; that the generations to come might know them, even the children yet unborn, that they would in turn declare them to their children; so that they might put their hope in God, and not forget the works of God, but keep his commandments; and not be like their forefathers, a stubborn and rebellious generation, a generation whose heart was not steadfast and whose spirit was not faithful to God.   PSALM 78:4–8

As a father pities his children, so the LORD pities those who fear him. For he knows what we are made of; he remembers that we are dust.

PSALM 103:13–14

Whoever the LORD loves he corrects, just as a father corrects the son in whom he delights. PROVERBS 3:12

A good man leaves an inheritance to his children's children, and the wealth of the sinner is laid up for the righteous. PROVERBS 13:22

He that spares his rod hates his son, but he who loves him disciplines him diligently. PROVERBS 13:24

Chasten your son while there is hope, and let not your soul hold back because of his crying. PROVERBS 19:18

Train up a child in the way he should go, and when he is old he will not depart from it. PROVERBS 22:6

Foolishness is bound in the heart of a child; but the rod of correction shall drive it far from him. PROVERBS 22:15

Withhold not correction from the child, for if you beat him with the rod, he shall not die. You shall beat him with the rod, and shall deliver his soul from hell. PROVERBS 23:13–14

The rod and reproof give wisdom, but a child left to himself brings his mother to shame. Correct your son, and he shall give you rest; indeed, he shall give delight to your soul. PROVERBS 29:15, 17

You fathers, provoke not your children to wrath, but bring them up in the nurture and admonition of the Lord. EPHESIANS 6:4

Fathers, provoke not your children to anger, lest they be discouraged.

COLOSSIANS 3:21

If you endure chastening, God deals with you as with sons; for what son is he whom the father chastens not?   HEBREWS 12:7

See also Children, Marriage.

PATIENCE

William Penn, founder of the Pennsylvania colony (which bears his name), once wrote, "Patience and diligence, like faith, move mountains." But real patience, like real faith, is a rare quality. In an instant-gratification society like our own, patience seems even rarer. Yet most people know, deep down, what a desirable quality it is. While the patient person is quietly enduring the trial of the moment, others are groaning in frustration, cursing, and wasting valuable mental energy, and for what purpose? The Bible has high praise for the patient person—more praise, in fact, than for wisdom or bravery. The Bible calls people to be "God's diehards," enduring anything (with God's help) and coming out stronger for having endured.

Rest in the LORD, and wait patiently for him; do not fret yourself because of him who prospers, the one who succeeds in his wicked schemes. Cease from anger, and forsake wrath; do not fret yourself in any way to do evil. For evil-doers shall be cut off, but those that wait upon the LORD shall inherit the earth.   PSALM 37:7–9

A wrathful man stirs up strife, but he who is slow to anger appeases strife.
                                    PROVERBS 15:18

He that is slow to anger is better than the mighty, and he who rules his spirit better than he who takes a city.   PROVERBS 16:32

By patience is a prince persuaded, and a gentle tongue can break a bone.
                                    PROVERBS 25:15

The patient in spirit is better than the proud in spirit. Be not hasty in your spirit to be angry, for anger rests in the bosom of fools.

ECCLESIASTES 7:8–9

You shall be hated of all men for my name's sake, but he who endures to the end shall be saved. MATTHEW 10:22

Come to me, all you that labor and are heavy laden, and I will give you rest. Take my yoke upon you, and learn from me; for I am meek and lowly in heart, and you shall find rest for your souls. For my yoke is easy, and my burden is light. MATTHEW 11:28–30

In your patience possess you your souls. LUKE 21:19

We glory in tribulations, knowing that tribulation produces patience, and patience experience, and experience hope. ROMANS 5:3–4

If we hope for what we do not see, then we do with patience wait for it.

ROMANS 8:25

Whatever things were written in the past were written for our learning, so that through patience and comfort of the scriptures we might have hope. Now the God of patience and consolation grant you to be likeminded one toward another according to Christ Jesus. ROMANS 15:4–5

Love is patient, love is kind; love envies not; love boasts not, is not haughty, is not disrespectful, is not self-seeking, is not easily provoked, thinks no evil.

I CORINTHIANS 13:4–5

In all things we commend ourselves as ministers of God: in much patience, in hardships, calamities, distresses, beatings, imprisonments, riots, labors, sleepless nights, hunger; by purity, knowledge, patience, kindness, the Holy Spirit, by genuine love, the word of truth, the power of God, the armor of righteousness on the right hand and on the left.

2 CORINTHIANS 6:4–7

The fruit of the Spirit is love, joy, peace, patience, gentleness, goodness, faith, meekness, self-control. GALATIANS 5:22–23

Let us not be weary in doing good, for in due season we shall reap a harvest if we do not give up. GALATIANS 6:9

May you be strengthened with all might that comes from his glorious power, and may you patiently endure all things while joyfully giving thanks to the Father, who has made us fit to share in the inheritance of the saints in light. COLOSSIANS 1:11–12

Warn them that are idle, comfort the timid, support the weak, be patient toward all men. 1 THESSALONIANS 5:14

The servant of the Lord must not quarrel, but be gentle to all men, able to teach, patient. 2 TIMOTHY 2:24

Do not abandon your confidence, which brings a great reward. For you have need of patience, so that when you have done the will of God, you might receive what was promised. For in a little while, he who shall come will come, and will not delay. Now the just shall live by faith, but if any man shrinks back, my soul shall have no pleasure in him. HEBREWS 10:35–38

Seeing we are surrounded by so great a cloud of witnesses, let us lay aside every weight and the sin which does so easily beset us, and let us run with patience the race that is set before us, looking to Jesus, the author and finisher of our faith, who for the sake of the joy that was set before him endured the cross, disregarding the shame, and is seated at the right hand of the throne of God. Consider him who endured such hostility of sinners against himself, so that you may not grow weary and lose heart. HEBREWS 12:1–3

Know this, that the testing of your faith produces patience. But let patience finish its work, so that you may be mature and complete, lacking nothing. JAMES 1:3–4

Be patient, brethren, for the coming of the Lord. Behold, the farmer waits for the precious crop from the earth, and has long patience for it, until he receives the early and latter rains. Be you also patient; strengthen your hearts, for the coming of the Lord draws near. Do not grumble against each other, brethren, lest you are condemned; behold, the Judge stands outside the door.   JAMES 5:7–9

We count them happy which endure. You have heard of the patience of Job.
                                                                                   JAMES 5:11

If you endure when you are punished for doing wrong, what credit is that to you? But if you endure when you do right and suffer for it, this is pleasing to God. For to this were you called, because Christ also suffered for us, leaving us an example, so that you should follow his steps.
                                                                                   1 PETER 2:20–21

The Lord is not slow concerning his promise, as some men believe; but he is patient toward us, not willing that any should perish, but that all should come to repentance.   2 PETER 3:9

See also Frustration, Persecution, Perseverance, Worry.

PEACE

The Bible presents us with a story of Jesus and his disciples in a boat. A sudden storm blew up, the wind howled, and the waves washed over the boat—yet Jesus was asleep while his disciples were in a state of panic. When the Bible talks about peace, it is referring to this kind of inner peace. We can't control the storms around us, but we (with God's help) can control our reactions to them. Storms may rage, but our hearts can be at peace. This kind of peace can be (like panic) contagious—in the midst of tribulations, the one

who can remain at peace may "pass the peace" to those around him.
Of course, the key reason to be at peace, the Bible tells us, is this: God is in
control.

I will lay me down in peace and sleep, for you alone, LORD, make me dwell
in safety.   PSALM 4:8

The LORD will give strength to his people; the LORD will bless his people
with peace.   PSALM 29:11

Mark the blameless man, and behold the upright, for the reward of that
man is peace.   PSALM 37:37

Whom have I in heaven but you? And there is none upon earth that I desire
beside you. My flesh and my heart fail, but God is the strength of my heart,
and my portion forever.   PSALM 73:25–26

I will hear what God the LORD will speak, for he will speak peace to his
people, and to his saints, but let them not turn again to folly.
                                                                   PSALM 85:8

They that trust in the LORD shall be like Mount Zion, which cannot be
moved, but abides forever. As the mountains are round about Jerusalem, so
the LORD is round about his people from now and forevermore.
                                                                   PSALM 125:1–2

Deceit is in the heart of those who imagine evil, but to the counselors of
peace is joy.   PROVERBS 12:20

Better is a dinner of vegetables than a fattened calf and hatred with it.
                                                                   PROVERBS 15:17

When a man's ways please the LORD, he makes even his enemies to be at
peace with him.   PROVERBS 16:7

Better is a dry morsel, and quietness with it, than a house full of feasting, with strife.   PROVERBS 17:1

They shall beat their swords into plowshares, and their spears into pruning-hooks. Nation shall not lift up sword against nation, neither shall they learn war any more.   ISAIAH 2:4

To us a child is born, to us a son is given; and the government shall be upon his shoulder, and his name shall be called Wonderful Counselor, the Mighty God, the Everlasting Father, the Prince of Peace. Of the increase of his government and peace there shall be no end. He shall reign upon the throne of David and over his kingdom to establish it with justice and righteousness from that time on and forevermore.   ISAIAH 9:6–7
[NOTE: *Most people interpret this as a prophecy of Christ.*]

The wolf shall dwell with the lamb, and the leopard shall lie down with the kid, and the calf and the young lion and the yearling together, and a little child shall lead them. And the cow and the bear shall feed; their young ones shall lie down together, and the lion shall eat straw like the ox. And the nursing child shall play over the hole of the asp, and the weaned child shall put his hand on the adder's den. They shall not hurt nor destroy in all my holy mountain, for the earth shall be full of the knowledge of the LORD, as the waters cover the sea.   ISAIAH 11:6–9

You will keep him in perfect peace whose mind is stayed on you, because he trusts in you.   ISAIAH 26:3

There is no peace, says the LORD, for the wicked.   ISAIAH 48:22

All your children shall be taught by the LORD, and great shall be the peace of your children.   ISAIAH 54:13

Blessed are the peacemakers, for they shall be called the children of God.
                                                                    MATTHEW 5:9

When the evening had come, Jesus said to them, "Let us cross over to the other side." And when they had sent away the multitude, they took him even as he was in the boat. And there arose a great windstorm, and the waves beat into the boat, so that it was now full. And he was in the hind part of the ship, asleep on a pillow. And they awoke him, and said to him, "Master, do you not care that we perish?" And he arose, and rebuked the wind, and said to the sea, "Peace, be still!" And the wind ceased, and there was a great calm. And he said to them, "Why are you so fearful? How is it that ye have no faith?" And they feared exceedingly, and said to one another, "What manner of man is this, that even the wind and the sea obey him?"

MARK 4:35–41

Peace I leave with you, my peace I give to you, not as the world gives, give I to you. Let not your heart be troubled, neither let it be afraid.

JOHN 14:27

These things I have spoken to you, so that in me you might have peace. In the world you shall have tribulation, but be of good cheer; I have overcome the world. JOHN 16:33

Glory, honor, and peace to every man that does good. ROMANS 2:10

Being justified by faith, we have peace with God through our Lord Jesus Christ. ROMANS 5:1

To set the mind on the sinful nature is death, but to set the mind on the Spirit is life and peace. ROMANS 8:6

The kingdom of God is not food and drink, but righteousness and peace and joy in the Holy Spirit. ROMANS 14:17

The God of peace shall bruise Satan under your feet shortly.

ROMANS 15:13

God is not the author of confusion, but of peace.

I CORINTHIANS 14:33

> *Ever heard of the "Placemakers" Bible? A 1562 edition of the Bible contained this error in Matthew 5:9: "Blessed are the placemakers." It should read "Blessed are the peacemakers." Copies of this Bible are highly valued by rare book collectors.*

Be of good comfort, be of one mind, live in peace, and the God of love and peace shall be with you. 2 CORINTHIANS 13:11

The fruit of the Spirit is love, joy, peace, longsuffering, gentleness, goodness, faith, meekness, self-control; against such there is no law.

GALATIANS 5:22–23

Endeavor to keep the unity of the Spirit in the bond of peace. There is one body, and one Spirit, just as you are called in one hope of your calling.

EPHESIANS 4:3–4

The peace of God, which surpasses all understanding, shall keep your hearts and minds through Christ Jesus. PHILIPPIANS 4:7

Let the peace of God rule in your hearts, since you are called in one body, and be thankful. COLOSSIANS 3:15

Follow peace with all men, and holiness, without which no man shall see the Lord. HEBREWS 12:14

He that will love life, and see good days, let him refrain his tongue from evil and his lips from speaking deceit. 1 PETER 3:10

See also Freedom, Trusting God, Worldly Cares, Worry.

PERSECUTION

Human nature is curious: We praise dead saints and persecute the living ones. Jesus Christ was crucified, and many of his followers were persecuted and even executed. He predicted that it would be so, and history is full of tragic stories of good people being treated like the worst criminals. Why so? Maybe it's because bad people so often have the power and abuse the power they have. And, no doubt, immoral people cannot abide moral people for the obvious reason: "You're making us look bad."

William Penn, the great Quaker leader in England and America, knew about persecution firsthand, for the early Quakers were persecuted harshly. Penn wrote, "Whoever is right, the persecutor must be wrong."

O LORD my God, in you do I put my trust; save me from all them that persecute me, and deliver me: PSALM 7:1

The LORD is with me as a mighty awesome one; therefore my persecutors shall stumble, and they shall not prevail. They shall be greatly ashamed, for they shall not prosper. Their everlasting confusion shall never be forgotten.

JEREMIAH 20:11

The bloodthirsty hate the upright, and they seek the life of the righteous. An unjust man is an abomination to the just, and he who is upright is an abomination to the wicked.   PROVERBS 29:10, 27

Blessed are they which are persecuted for righteousness' sake, for theirs is the kingdom of heaven. Blessed are you, when men shall insult you and persecute you and say all manner of evil against you falsely, for my sake. Rejoice, and be exceedingly glad, for great is your reward in heaven, for so persecuted they the prophets who came before you.

MATTHEW 5:10—12

I send you forth as sheep in the midst of wolves; so be wise as serpents, and harmless as doves. Beware of men, for they will deliver you up to the councils, and they will flog you in their synagogues; and you shall be dragged before governors and kings for my sake, as a testimony to them and the Gentiles. But when they deliver you up, take no thought how or what you shall say, for it shall be given you in that same hour what you shall speak. For it is not you that speak, but the Spirit of your Father who speaks in you.

Brother shall betray brother to death, and the father the child, and the children shall rise up against their parents and cause them to be put to death. And you shall be hated by all men for my name's sake; but he who endures to the end shall be saved. When they persecute you in one city, flee to another, for truly I say to you, you shall not have gone over the cities of Israel till the Son of man has come.

The disciple is not above his master, nor the servant above his lord. It is enough for the disciple that he is like his master, and the servant like his lord. If they have called the master of the house Beelzebub, how much more shall they slander those of his household?

Fear not those who kill the body, but are not able to kill the soul, but rather fear him who is able to destroy both soul and body in hell.

Are not two sparrows sold for a penny? And one of them shall not fall on the ground without your Father. But the very hairs of your head are all numbered.

Whoever therefore shall acknowledge me before men, him will I acknowledge before my Father in heaven. But whoever shall deny me before men, him will I also deny before my Father which is in heaven.

MATTHEW 10:16–26, 28–33

Woe unto you, scribes and Pharisees, hypocrites! Because you build the tombs of the prophets, and decorate the sepulchres of the righteous, and say, "If we had been in the days of our fathers, we would not have been partakers with them in the blood of the prophets."   MATTHEW 23:29–30

Whoever will save his life shall lose it; but whoever shall lose his life for my sake and the gospel's shall save it.   MARK 8:35

They shall lay their hands on you, and persecute you, delivering you up to the synagogues, and into prisons, dragging you before kings and rulers for my name's sake. This shall be an opportunity to testify. Make up your mind not to worry beforehand as to how you will answer. For I will give you words and wisdom, which all your adversaries shall not be able to contradict nor resist.   LUKE 21:12–15

If the world hates you, you know that it hated me before it hated you. If you were of the world, the world would love its own, but because you are not of the world, but I have chosen you out of the world, therefore the world hates you. Remember what I told you: the servant is not greater than his master. If they have persecuted me, they will also persecute you; if they have kept my saying, they will keep yours also. But all these things will they do to you for my name's sake, because they know not him that sent me.

JOHN 15:18–21

We are children of God, and if children, then heirs—heirs of God, and joint heirs with Christ, if we suffer with him, so that we may be also glorified together.

Who shall separate us from the love of Christ? Shall tribulation, or distress, or persecution, or famine, or nakedness, or peril, or sword? As it is written, "For your sake we are killed all the day long; we are counted as sheep for the slaughter." No, in all these things we are more than conquerors through him that loved us.   ROMANS 8:16–17, 35–37

Even to this present hour we hunger, and thirst, and are naked, and are beaten, and have no certain dwelling place; we labor, working with our own hands; when insulted, we bless; when persecuted, we endure it; when slandered, we speak kindly. We are made to be the filth of the world, the dregs of all things.   I CORINTHIANS 4:10–13

We are troubled in every way, yet not distressed; we are perplexed, but not in despair; persecuted, but not abandoned; struck down, but not destroyed. We always bear in the body the dying of the Lord Jesus, so that the life of Jesus might be made visible in our body.   2 CORINTHIANS 4:8–10

In all things we commend ourselves as ministers of God, in much patience, in afflictions, hardships, calamities, beatings, imprisonments, riots, labors, sleepless nights, hunger. . . . We are treated as impostors, and yet we are true; as unknown, and yet are well known; as dying, and, see, we live; as punished, and yet not killed; as sorrowful, yet always rejoicing; as poor, yet making many rich; as having nothing, and yet possessing all things.

2 CORINTHIANS 6:4–5, 8–10

Share in suffering like a good soldier of Jesus Christ.   2 TIMOTHY 2:4

If we suffer, we shall also reign with him; if we deny him, he also will deny us.   2 TIMOTHY 2:12

All that will live godly in Christ Jesus shall suffer persecution.

2 TIMOTHY 3:12

Others had trial of cruel mockings and floggings, even slavery and imprisonment. They were stoned, they were sawn asunder, were tempted, were destitute, afflicted, tormented—of them the world was not worthy. They wandered in deserts, and in mountains, and in dens and caves of the earth.

HEBREWS 11:35–38

Consider him who endured such hostility of sinners against himself, so that you may not grow weary and lose heart.   HEBREWS 12:3

My brethren, take the prophets, who have spoken in the name of the Lord, for an example of suffering affliction, and of patience.   JAMES 5:10

If you endure when you are punished for doing wrong, what credit is that to you? But if you endure when you do right and suffer for it, this is pleasing to God. For to this were you called, because Christ also suffered for us, leaving us an example, so that you should follow his steps.   I PETER 2:20–21

If you suffer for righteousness' sake, happy are you. And be not afraid of their terror, neither be troubled; but in your hearts set apart Christ as Lord. Always be ready to give an answer to every man that asks you a reason for the hope that is in you, and do this with gentleness and respect. Keep a good conscience, so that when they speak evil of you, they that falsely accuse your good conduct in Christ may be ashamed. For it is better, if the will of God be so, that you suffer for doing right than for doing evil.

I PETER 3:14–17

Beloved, think it not strange concerning the fiery trial which is to test you, as though some strange thing happened to you. But rejoice, since you are sharing in Christ's sufferings, so that when his glory is revealed, you may be glad also with exceeding joy. If you are slandered for the name of Christ, happy are you, for the Spirit of glory and of God rests upon you.

I PETER 4:12–14

Behold, what manner of love the Father has bestowed upon us, so that we should be called the sons of God; therefore the world knows us not, because it knew him not. Marvel not, my brethren, if the world hate you.

I JOHN 3:1, 13

When he opened the fifth seal, I saw under the altar the souls of those who were slain for the word of God, and for the testimony they had given. They cried with a loud voice, saying, "How long, O Lord, holy and true, before you judge and avenge our blood on those who dwell on the earth?" And white robes were given to every one of them, and it was said to them, that they should rest yet a little longer, until their fellow servants and their brethren, that should be killed as they were, should be fulfilled.

REVELATION 6:9–11

Blessed are the dead which die in the Lord from henceforth. Yes, said the Spirit, that they may rest from their labors, and their deeds will follow them.

REVELATION 14:13

PERSEVERANCE

"Hang in there" is good advice, especially when the trend is to give up easily and move on. Faced with challenges in one's marriage, job, or plans, we find it tough to persevere, for we wonder whether our efforts will finally pay off. The Bible offers us no guarantees that all our earthly plans will bear the fruit we want, but it does guarantee that those who commit their lives to God will be rewarded. Even more, we receive the promise that God's people can endure anything this world has to offer. It may be tough for us to "hang in there," but the eternal God has outlasted every affliction that has ever plagued a human life. We can endure because he endures.

The LORD loves justice, and forsakes not his saints; they are preserved forever, but the seed of the wicked shall be cut off.   PSALM 37:28

The LORD will perfect that which concerns me. Your mercy, O LORD, endures forever; forsake not the works of your own hands.   PSALM 138:8

He who endures to the end shall be saved.   MATTHEW 10:22

Jesus said to him, "No man, having put his hand to the plow, and looking back, is fit for the kingdom of God."   LUKE 9:62

I give to them eternal life, and they shall never perish, neither shall any man pluck them out of my hand. My Father, which gave them me, is greater than all, and no man is able to pluck them out of my Father's hand.

JOHN 10:28–29

Abide in me, and I in you. As the branch cannot bear fruit by itself, except it abide in the vine; no more can you, except you abide in me. I am the vine, you are the branches: he who abides in me, and I in him, the same brings forth much fruit, for without me you can do nothing. If a man abides not in me, he is cast away as a branch, and withers up, and men gather them, and cast them into the fire, and they are burned. If you abide in me, and my words abide in you, you shall ask what you will, and it shall be done to you.

JOHN 15:4–7

[God] will render to every man according to his deeds: to them who by patient continuance in well doing seek for glory and honor and immortality, eternal life.   ROMANS 2:6–7

Who shall separate us from the love of Christ? Shall tribulation, or distress, or persecution, or famine, or nakedness, or peril, or sword? . . . No, in all these things we are more than conquerors through him who loved us. For I am persuaded, that neither death, nor life, nor angels, nor principalities, nor powers, nor things present, nor things to come, nor height, nor depth, nor any other creature, shall be able to separate us from the love of God, which is in Christ Jesus our Lord.   ROMANS 8:35–39

Let us not be weary in well doing, for in due season we shall reap, if we do not give up.   GALATIANS 6:9

You were in the past alienated and enemies in your mind by wicked works, yet now he has reconciled in the body of his flesh through death, to present you holy and unblameable and unreproveable in his sight. If you continue in the faith, grounded and settled, and be not moved away from the hope of the gospel, which you have heard, and which was preached to every creature which is under heaven.   COLOSSIANS 1:21–23

I am not ashamed, for I know whom I have believed, and am persuaded that he is able to keep that which I have entrusted to him for that day.
                                                            2 TIMOTHY 1:12

If we suffer, we shall also reign with him: if we deny him, he also will deny us.   2 TIMOTHY 2:12–13

The Lord shall deliver me from every evil work, and will preserve me to his heavenly kingdom: to whom be glory forever and ever. Amen.
                                                            2 TIMOTHY 4:18

We are made partakers in Christ, if we hold firmly to the end of the confidence we had at first.   HEBREWS 3:14

Blessed is the man that endures temptation, for when he is tested, he shall receive the crown of life, which the Lord has promised to those who love him.   JAMES 1:12

He that has an ear, let him hear what the Spirit said to the churches: To him that overcomes will I give to eat of the tree of life, which is in the midst of the paradise of God.   REVELATION 2:7

He that overcomes, the same shall be clothed in white clothing, and I will not blot out his name out of the Book of Life, but I will confess his name before my Father, and before his angels.   REVELATION 3:5

He that overcomes shall inherit all things, and I will be his God, and he shall be my son. REVELATION 21:7

See also God's Love, Patience, Temptation.

PERSONAL GROWTH

We could call our age the "Age of Improvement." Everyone is eagerly grasping for a diet, fitness regimen, career strategy, or "new attitude" to make life better, to lead to that elusive thing called "success." Well, the Bible is definitely pro-improvement and pro-growth. But it offers something that the world doesn't: a personal, loving God who sincerely desires each person to mature, to become more loving, more patient, and more zealous for everyone's good—in other words, becoming more like God. That doesn't rule out things like physical attractiveness, health, or success in one's career. But the Bible has its priorities: Concern yourself first with being a genuinely good person.

Better is a handful with quietness than both the hands full with toil and a chasing after the wind. ECCLESIASTES 4:6

Whoever hears these sayings of mine, and does them, will be like a wise man who built his house upon a rock. The rain descended, and the floods came, and the winds blew and beat upon that house, yet it fell not, for it was founded upon a rock. And everyone that hears these sayings of mine, and does them not, shall be like a foolish man who built his house upon the sand. The rain descended, and the floods came, and the winds blew and beat upon that house, and it fell, and great was the fall of it.

MATTHEW 7:24–27

What is a man profited, if he gain the whole world, and lose his soul? Or what shall a man give in exchange for his soul? MATTHEW 16:26

Whoever exalts himself shall be humbled, and he who humbles himself shall be exalted. MATTHEW 23:12

I am the vine, you are the branches. He who abides in me, and I in him, brings forth much fruit, for without me you can do nothing. If a man abide not in me, he is cast forth as a branch, and withers away; and men gather them, and cast them into the fire, and they are burned. If you abide in me, and my words abide in you, you shall ask what you desire, and it shall be done to you. In this is my Father glorified. If you bear much fruit, you are my disciples. As the Father has loved me, so have I loved you; continue in my love.   JOHN 15:5–9

I appeal to you, brethren, by the mercies of God, that you present your bodies a living sacrifice, holy, acceptable to God, which is your spiritual worship. And be not conformed to this world, but be transformed by the renewing of your mind, so that you may prove what is the good and acceptable and perfect will of God. Through the grace given to me I say to every man that is among you, not to think of himself more highly than he ought, but to think soberly, in accordance with the measure of faith God has given each man.   ROMANS 12:1–3

We all, with unveiled faces beholding as in a mirror the glory of the Lord, are transformed into the same image with ever-increasing glory, just as by the Spirit of the Lord.   2 CORINTHIANS 3:18

He that glories, let him glory in the Lord. For it is not he who commends himself who is approved, but whom the Lord commends.
                                                      2 CORINTHIANS 10:17–18

We must no longer be children, tossed to and fro and blown about by every wind of doctrine, by the trickery of men and by cunning craftiness in scheming deceitfully. But speaking the truth in love, we may grow into him in all things, who is the head, Christ.   EPHESIANS 4:14–15

Put aside the previous behavior of the old self, which is corrupt according to its deceitful lusts, and be renewed in the spirit of your mind, and clothe yourselves with the new man, created according to the likeness of God in righteousness and true holiness.   EPHESIANS 4:22–24

Be confident of this very thing, that he who has begun a good work among you will bring it to completion by the day of Jesus Christ. And I pray that your love may abound more and more in knowledge and in all judgment, that you may approve things that are excellent, that you may be sincere and without offense till the day of Christ, being filled with the fruits of righteousness, which are from Jesus Christ, to the glory and praise of God.

PHILIPPIANS 1:6, 9–11

This one thing I do: forgetting what lies behind and reaching forth to those things which are before, I press toward the mark for the prize of the high calling of God in Christ Jesus.   PHILIPPIANS 3:13–14

Set your affection on things above, not on things on the earth.

COLOSSIANS 3:2

This is the will of God, your sanctification, so that you should abstain from sexual immorality; that each one of you should know how to control his own body in holiness and honor, not in the lusts of immorality, like the pagans who do not know God; that no man go beyond and exploit his brother in any way; because the Lord is the avenger in all these things, just as we also have forewarned you and testified. For God has not called us to uncleanness, but to holiness.   1 THESSALONIANS 4:1–8

We are bound to thank God always for you, brethren, as it is appropriate, because that your faith grows exceedingly, and the love of everyone of you toward each other abounds.   2 THESSALONIANS 1:3

If you have bitter envying and strife in your hearts, do not boast of it, and do not deny the truth. This so-called wisdom descends not from heaven, but is earthly, sensual, devilish. For where envying and strife are, there is disorder and every evil work. But the wisdom that is from above is first pure, then peaceable, gentle, submissive, full of mercy and good fruits, without partiality, and without hypocrisy.   JAMES 3:14–17

Like newborn babes, desire the sincere milk of the word, so that you may grow steadily, now that you have tasted that the Lord is gracious.

1 PETER 2:2–3

> "No one ever did himself harm from reading the Book."
>
> —BENJAMIN FRANKLIN

His divine power has given us all things that pertain to life and godliness, through the knowledge of him that has called us to glory and virtue. Thus he has given us exceedingly great and precious promises, that by these you might be sharers in the divine nature, having escaped the corruption that is in the world through lust.

Add to your faith virtue, and to virtue add knowledge; and to knowledge add self-control; and to self-control add patience; and to patience add godliness; and to godliness add brotherly kindness; and to brotherly kindness add love. 2 PETER 1:3–7

See also **Ambition, Repentance, Self-Esteem, Success.**

POLITICS AND GOVERNMENT

Is politics a dirty business? Often, yes. One of the benefits of reading history is learning that things haven't changed much. When the New Testament was written, its authors were under the rule of the Roman Empire, which was notoriously tax hungry and corrupt. (The Roman emperors would qualify as some of the most immoral men ever to hold power.) The obvious reason that corruption is rampant in government is that it is the most unscrupulous people who seek and get political power. This never changes because human nature never changes. Good and moral leaders are the exception, not the rule.

The Bible takes an extremely realistic view of government power, "warts and all," and though it encourages people to be good citizens and to pray for their leaders, it also encourages people not to rely on government to solve all life's problems. Some of the Bible's most stinging words are directed at leaders who abuse the power and trust they have.

If my people, which are called by my name, shall humble themselves, and pray, and seek my face, and turn from their wicked ways; then will I hear from heaven, and will forgive their sin, and will heal their land.

2 CHRONICLES 7:14

With God is strength and wisdom; the deceived and the deceiver are his. He leads counselors away stripped, and makes the judges fools. He leads princes away stripped and overthrows the mighty. He silences the speech of trusted advisors and takes away the understanding of the elders. He pours contempt upon nobles and weakens the strength of the mighty. He makes nations great, and he destroys them. He enlarges the nations and scatters them again.

JOB 12:14, 16–21, 23

Why do the nations conspire, and the people plot in vain? The kings of the earth set themselves, and the rulers take counsel together against the LORD and against his anointed, saying, "Let us break their bonds asunder, and cast away their cords from us." He that sits in the heavens shall laugh; the LORD shall hold them in derision.

PSALM 2:1–4

You have rebuked the nations, you have destroyed the wicked, you have blotted out their name forever and ever. The nations have sunk down in the pit that they made; in the net which they hid is their own foot caught. Arise, O LORD; let not man prevail; let the nations be judged in your sight. Put them in fear, O LORD, that the nations may know themselves to be mere men.

PSALM 9:15, 19–20

The LORD brings the counsel of the nations to nothing; he frustrates the plans of the peoples. The counsel of the LORD stands forever, the thoughts of his heart to all generations. Blessed is the nation whose God is the LORD, and the people he has chosen for his inheritance. The LORD looks from heaven; he beholds all the sons of men. From the place of his habitation he looks upon all the inhabitants of the earth. He fashions their hearts alike; he observes all their deeds. There is no king saved by the multitude of an army; a mighty man is not delivered by great strength.

PSALM 33:10–16

Blessed is that man that makes the LORD his trust, and respects not the proud, nor those who turn aside to false gods.

PSALM 40:4

Be still, and know that I am God; I will be exalted among the nations, I will be exalted in the earth. The LORD Almighty is with us; the God of Jacob is our refuge. PSALM 46:10–11

God reigns over the nations; God sits upon the throne of his holiness.

PSALM 47:8

Do you decree righteousness, you rulers? Do you judge the people rightly? No, in your hearts you devise wickedness; your hands deal out violence on the land. PSALM 58:1–2

You, O LORD God Almighty, the God of Israel, awake to punish all the nations; show no mercy to any wicked transgressors. You, O LORD, shall laugh at them; you shall hold all the nations in derision. PSALM 59:5, 8

God be merciful to us, and bless us, and cause his face to shine upon us, that your way may be known upon earth, your saving health among all nations. Let the people praise you, O God; let all the people praise you. O let the nations be glad and sing for joy; for you shall judge the people righteously, and govern the nations upon earth. Let the people praise you, O God; let all the people praise you. PSALM 67:1–5

Give the king your judgments, O God, and your righteousness to the king's son. He shall judge your people with righteousness, and your poor with justice. The mountains shall bring peace to the people, and the little hills, by righteousness. He shall judge the poor of the people, he shall save the children of the needy, and shall break in pieces the oppressor.

PSALM 72:1–4

Arise, O God, judge the earth; for all the nations belong to you.

PSALM 82:8

All the gods of the nations are idols, but the LORD made the heavens. Honor and majesty are before him; strength and beauty are in his sanctuary. Give to the LORD, O you families of the peoples, give to the LORD glory and strength. PSALM 96:5–7

It is better to trust in the LORD than to put confidence in man. It is better to trust in the LORD than to put confidence in princes.   PSALM 118:8–9

Unless the LORD watches over the city, the watchman keeps his vigil in vain.
                                                                         PSALM 127:1

Happy is that people whose God is the LORD.   PSALM 144:15

Put not your trust in rulers, nor in mortal man, in whom there is no help. His breath goes forth, he returns to the earth; in that very day his thoughts perish.

   Happy is he who has the God of Jacob for his help, whose hope is in the LORD his God, who made heaven and earth, the sea and all that is in it; who keeps truth forever; who administers justice for the oppressed; who gives food to the hungry. The LORD looses the prisoners; the LORD opens the eyes of the blind; the LORD raises up those who are bowed down; the LORD loves the righteous.   PSALM 146:3–8

Righteousness exalts a nation, but sin is a reproach to any people.
                                                                    PROVERBS 14:34

He that says to the wicked, "You are righteous," him shall the people curse; nations shall abhor him.   PROVERBS 24:24

Where there is no vision, the people perish.   PROVERBS 29:18

The fear of man brings a trap, but whoever puts his trust in the LORD shall be safe.   PROVERBS 29:25

He shall judge among the nations, and shall reprove many people. And they shall beat their swords into plowshares, and their spears into pruninghooks; nation shall not lift up sword against nation, neither shall they learn war any more.   ISAIAH 2:4

Woe to them . . . which justify the wicked for reward, and take away the righteousness of the righteous from him!   ISAIAH 5:22–23

Behold, the nations are as a drop in the bucket, and are regarded as small dust on the scales. Behold, he takes up the isles as a very little thing. . . . All nations before him are as nothing, and they are counted to him less than nothing, mere emptiness.   ISAIAH 40:15–17

It is he who sits upon the circle of the earth, and the inhabitants of it are like grasshoppers; he stretches out the heavens like a curtain and spreads them out as a tent to dwell in; he brings the princes to nothing; he makes the judges of the earth to be emptiness.   ISAIAH 40:22–23

Thus says the LORD: "Cursed be the man that trusts in man, and relies on flesh for his strength, and whose heart departs from the LORD. For he shall be like a bush in the desert, and shall not see when good comes; but he shall inhabit parched places in the wilderness, in a salt land where no one dwells. Blessed is the man that trusts in the LORD, and whose hope the LORD is."
                                                         JEREMIAH 17:5–7

Jesus called them [his disciples] to him, and said, "You know that the rulers of the Gentiles lord it over them, and they that are great are tyrants over them. But it shall not be so with you; but whoever will be great among you, let him be your servant; and whoever will be chief among you, let him be your servant; just as the Son of man came not to be served, but to serve, and to give his life a ransom for many."   MATTHEW 20:25–28

Then the Pharisees went and plotted how they might entrap him in his talk. And they sent to him their disciples, along with the Herodians, saying, "Teacher, we know that you are sincere, and teach the way of God in truth, showing no deference to anyone, for you do not regard men with partiality. Tell us therefore what you think of this: Is it lawful to give taxes to Caesar or not?" But Jesus perceived their wickedness, and said, "Why do you test me, you hypocrites? Show me the tribute money." And they brought to him a coin. And he said to them, "Whose image and title are on this?" They said to him, "Caesar's." Then said he to them, "Render to Caesar the things that are Caesar's, and to God the things that are God's."
                                                       MATTHEW 22:15–21

Jesus, being full of the Holy Spirit, returned from the Jordan, and was led by the Spirit into the wilderness. And the devil took him to a high mountain and showed him all the kingdoms of the world in a moment of time. And the devil said to him, "All this power will I give you, and the glory of them, for that is delivered to me, and I give it to whomever I wish. If you will worship me, all shall be yours." And Jesus answered and said to him, "Get behind me, Satan, for it is written, 'You shall worship the Lord your God, and him only shall you serve.'"   LUKE 4:1, 5–8

Honor all men. Love the brotherhood. Fear God. Honor the king.

                                                    I PETER 2:17

He [the angel] cried mightily with a loud voice, "Babylon the great is fallen, is fallen, and has become the dwelling place of demons, and the haunt of every foul spirit, and a home for every unclean and loathsome thing. For all nations have drunk the wine of the wrath of her fornication, and the kings of the earth have committed fornication with her, and the merchants of the earth have grown rich through the abundance of her luxury." And I heard another voice from heaven, saying, "Come out of her, my people, so that you do not take part in sins, and that you do not share in her plagues. For her sins have reached unto heaven, and God has remembered her evils. . . . Alas, alas that great city Babylon, that mighty city! In one hour has your judgment come." . . . Rejoice over her, O heaven, and you holy apostles and prophets, for God has avenged you on her. And a mighty angel took up a stone like a great millstone and cast it into the sea, saying, "Thus with violence shall that great city Babylon be overthrown, and shall be found no more."   REVELATION 18:2–5, 10, 20–21

See also Citizenship, Power.

POWER

Throw the word power *in the title of a book, and it is almost guaranteed to sell. Why? Because it is human to want to have power and control. In his classic* Democracy in America, *Alexis de Tocqueville wrote, "The affections of men generally turn towards power." Strictly speaking, there is nothing wrong with this. It is normal and healthy to want to move from*

Abraham Lincoln's speech at the 1858 Republican Convention in Springfield, Illinois, included one of his most quoted lines: "A house divided against itself cannot stand." (Lincoln was referring to the North-South division that was occurring in the country.) Lincoln borrowed his line from Matthew 12:25: "Every kingdom divided against itself is brought to desolation; and every city or house divided against itself shall not stand."

childhood dependence on others to some degree of independence, having power over one's own destiny. This is maturity, a natural and good thing that God approves of. But the Bible, with its "no rose-colored glasses" attitude, takes a harsh and realistic look at the human craving for power. For many people it goes beyond personal independence, for most people who want power want to control others. It's an old cliché but a true one: Power corrupts. As far as the Bible is concerned, the only powerful being who cannot be corrupted is God.

You may say in your heart, "My power and the might of my hand have gotten me this wealth." But remember the LORD your God, for it is he that gives you power to get wealth.   DEUTERONOMY 8:17–18

How are the mighty fallen, and the weapons of war perished!

2 SAMUEL 1:27

God drags away the mighty by his power: though they rise up, they cannot be sure of life. Though they may feel they are resting securely, yet his eyes are upon their ways. They are exalted for a little while, but are gone and brought low; they are taken out of the way as all others.

JOB 24:22–24

I have seen the wicked in great power, and spreading himself like a green bay tree. Yet he passed away, and, lo, he was no more.   PSALM 37:35–36

Thus says the LORD: "Let not the wise man glory in his wisdom, neither let the mighty man glory in his might, let not the rich man glory in his riches. Let him that glories glory in this, that he understands and knows me, that I am the LORD who exercise lovingkindness, judgment, and righteousness in the earth; for in these things I delight."   JEREMIAH 9:24

You have plowed wickedness, you have reaped iniquity; you have eaten the fruit of lies, because you did trust in your way, in the multitude of your mighty men.   HOSEA 10:13

Not by might, nor by power, but by my spirit, says the LORD Almighty.
   ZECHARIAH 4:6

Jesus called them [his disciples] to him, and said, "You know that the rulers of the Gentiles lord it over them, and they that are great are tyrants over them. But it shall not be so with you; but whoever will be great among you, let him be your servant; and whoever will be chief among you, let him be your servant; just as the Son of man came not to be served, but to serve, and to give his life a ransom for many."   MATTHEW 20:25–28

Then Jesus spoke to the multitude and to his disciples: "The scribes and the Pharisees sit in Moses' seat. They love the places of honor at feasts and the chief seats in the synagogues, and to be greeted in the marketplace and called by men, 'Rabbi, Rabbi.' But be not called 'Rabbi,' for one alone is your Master, and that is Christ, and you are all brethren. And call no man 'father' upon the earth, for one alone is your Father, who is in heaven. Neither be called 'master,' for one alone is your Master, and that is Christ. But he who is greatest among you shall be your servant. And whoever exalts himself shall be humbled, and he who humbles himself shall be exalted."
   MATTHEW 23:1–2, 6–12

The devil took him to a high mountain and showed him all the kingdoms of the world in a moment of time. And the devil said to him, "All this power will I give you, and the glory of them; for that is delivered to me; and I give it to whomever I wish. If you will worship me, all shall be yours." And Jesus answered and said to him, "Get behind me, Satan; for it is written, 'You shall worship the Lord your God, and him only shall you serve.'"

LUKE 4:5–8

Seek not you what you shall eat or what you drink, neither be worrisome. For all these things does the pagan world run after, and your Father knows that you need these things. Rather, seek the kingdom of God; and all these things shall be added to you. Fear not, little flock; for it is your Father's good pleasure to give you the kingdom.   LUKE 12:29–32

That which is highly esteemed by men is abomination in the sight of God.

LUKE 16:15

How can you believe, you who receive praise from one another, and seek not the praise that comes from God only?   JOHN 5:44

Jesus answered, "My kingdom is not of this world. If my kingdom were of this world, then my servants would fight, so that I should not be delivered to the Jews; but now is my kingdom not from here."   JOHN 18:36

Set your affection on things above, not on things on the earth.

COLOSSIANS 3:2

He that overcomes, and keeps my works unto the end, to him will I give power over the nations.   REVELATION 2:26

You are worthy, O Lord, to receive glory and honor and power, for you have created all things, and for your pleasure they are and were created.

REVELATION 4:11

See also Ambition, Humility, Meekness/Gentleness, Politics and Government, Spiritual Power, Success.

> *"Throughout the history of the Western world, the Scriptures have been the greatest instigators of revolt against the worst forms of tyranny."*
>
> —THOMAS HUXLEY, ENGLISH AGNOSTIC AND SCIENTIST

PRAYER

Prayer is making a sort of comeback, as even skeptics and unbelievers admit that prayer leads to mental and even physical benefits. For those less skeptical, prayer has always been important, the means of communication between the heart and the God who made all things. Mother Teresa of Calcutta claimed that prayer "enlarges the heart." Judging from her own saintly life, this must be true.

One thing that runs counter to our nature is this matter of praying for our enemies. The Bible demands this, hard as it is to do. Yet those who have done so affirm that nothing makes us love a person as much as praying for that person.

Why are some prayers answered while some are not? No one knows. The Bible gives no explanation except this: "Keep praying, and trust." Perhaps God's timetable is different from our own. And perhaps some of the things we pray for are things we never needed anyway.

The famous Lord's Prayer, by the way, is quoted below in Matthew 6:9–13.

You, Solomon my son, know the God of your father, and serve him with a perfect heart and with a willing mind, for the LORD searches all hearts and understands all the imaginations of the thoughts. If you seek him, he will be found by you; but if you forsake him, he will cast you off forever.

I CHRONICLES 28:9

The eyes of the LORD are upon the righteous, and his ears are open to their cry. The righteous cry, and the LORD hears, and delivers them out of all their troubles.

PSALM 34:15, 17

Call upon me in the day of trouble; I will deliver you.   PSALM 50:15

As for me, I will call upon God, and the LORD shall save me. Evening, and morning, and at noon will I pray, and cry aloud, and he shall hear my voice.

PSALM 55:16–17

Because he has set his love upon me, I will deliver him; I will set him on high, because he has known my name. He shall call upon me, and I will answer him; I will be with him in trouble; I will deliver him, and honor him. With long life will I satisfy him, and show him my salvation.

PSALM 91:14–16

He will regard the prayer of the destitute, and not despise their prayer. This shall be written for the generations to come, and the people yet to be created shall praise the LORD. For he has looked down from the height of his sanctuary; from heaven does the LORD behold the earth, to hear the groaning of the prisoner, to loose those that are appointed to death.

PSALM 102:17–20

Out of the depths have I cried to you, O LORD. LORD, hear my voice; let your ears be attentive to the voice of my pleading.   PSALM 130:1–2

The LORD is near to all those who call upon him, to all that call upon him in truth. He will fulfill the desire of those who fear him; he will hear their cry, and will save them.   PSALM 145:18–19

The LORD is far from the wicked, but he hears the prayer of the righteous.

PROVERBS 15:29

Before they call, I will answer, and while they are still speaking, I will hear.

ISAIAH 65:24

"I know the thoughts that I think about you," says the LORD, "thoughts of peace, and not of evil, to give you a future with hope. Then shall you call upon me, and you shall go and pray to me, and I will hearken to you. And you shall seek me, and find me, when you shall search for me with all your heart."   JEREMIAH 29:11–13

When you pray, enter into your room, and when you have shut your door, pray to your Father who is in secret, and your Father who sees in secret shall reward you openly. But when you pray, do not heap up empty phrases as the pagans do, for they think that they shall be heard by speaking so much. Be not like them, for your Father knows what things you have need of before you even ask him.   MATTHEW 6:6–8

Our Father which art in heaven, hallowed be thy name. Thy kingdom come. Thy will be done in earth, as it is in heaven. Give us this day our daily bread. And forgive us our debts, as we forgive our debtors. And lead us not into temptation, but deliver us from evil: For thine is the kingdom, and the power, and the glory, for ever. Amen.   MATTHEW 6:9–13

Ask, and it shall be given you; seek, and you shall find; knock, and it shall be opened to you. For everyone that asks receives, and he who seeks finds, and to him that knocks it shall be opened. What man is there among you who, if his son ask for bread, will give him a stone? Or if he ask for a fish, will he give him a serpent? If you then, being evil, know how to give good gifts to your children, how much more shall your Father who is in heaven give good things to those who ask him?   MATTHEW 7:7–11

If you shall say to this mountain, "Be moved and be cast into the sea," it shall be done. And if you believe, whatever you ask in prayer, you shall receive.   MATTHEW 21:21–22

Whatever things you desire when you pray, believe that you receive them, and you shall have them. And when you stand praying, forgive, if you have anything against anyone, so that your Father who is in heaven may forgive you your sins.   MARK 11:24–25

Bless those who curse you, and pray for those who spitefully use you.

                                              LUKE 6:28

Jesus said to them, "Suppose you have a friend, and you go to him at midnight, and say to him, 'Friend, lend me three loaves; for a friend of mine on his journey has come to me, and I have nothing to set before him'? And he from within shall answer, 'Trouble me not; the door is shut, and my children and I are asleep. I cannot rise and give you anything.' I say to you, though he will not rise and give him anything, because he is his friend, yet because of his persistence, he will rise and give him as much as he needs."

LUKE 11:5–8

Jesus spoke a parable to make this point, that men ought always to pray and not give up: "There was in a city a judge, who feared not God nor respected man. And there was a widow in that city, and she came to him, saying, 'Give me justice against my adversary.' And for awhile he would not, but finally he said to himself, 'Though I fear not God nor respect man, yet because this widow troubles me, I will give her justice, lest she wear me out with her continual coming.'" And the Lord said, "Hear what the unjust judge said. And shall not God avenge his elect, who cry to him day and night, though he bear long with them? I tell you that he will avenge them speedily."

LUKE 18:1–8

If you abide in me, and my words abide in you, you shall ask what you desire, and it shall be done to you.   JOHN 15:7

The Spirit also helps us in our weakness, for we know not how to pray as we ought. But the Spirit himself intercedes for us with groanings which are too deep for words.   ROMANS 8:26

Through him [Christ] we have access by one Spirit to the Father.

EPHESIANS 2:18

Be anxious for nothing, but in everything by prayer and supplication with thanksgiving let your requests be made known to God. And the peace of God, which passes all understanding, will keep your hearts and minds in Christ Jesus.   PHILIPPIANS 4:6

Let us therefore come boldly to the throne of grace, so that we may obtain mercy and find grace to help in time of need.   HEBREWS 4:16

If any of you lack wisdom, let him ask God, who gives to all men generously without finding fault, and it shall be given him. But let him ask in faith, without doubting. For he who doubts is like a wave of the sea driven and tossed by the wind. For let not that man think that he shall receive anything from the Lord. JAMES 1:5–7

Is any among you afflicted? Let him pray. Is any merry? Let him sing psalms. Is any sick among you? Let him call for the elders of the church, and let them pray over him, anointing him with oil in the name of the Lord. And the prayer of faith shall save the sick, and the Lord shall raise him up, and if he has committed sins, they shall be forgiven him. Confess your faults one to another, and pray one for another, so that you may be healed. The fervent prayer of a righteous man is powerful and effective. Elijah was a man, subject to the same passions as we are, and he prayed earnestly that it might not rain, and it rained not on the earth for the space of three years and six months. And he prayed again, and the heaven gave rain, and the earth brought forth its fruit. JAMES 5:13–18

The eyes of the Lord are on the righteous, and his ears are open to their prayers; but the face of the Lord is against those who do evil.

I PETER 3:12

Whatever we ask, we receive of him, because we keep his commandments and do those things that are pleasing in his sight. I JOHN 3:22

This is the confidence that we have in him, that, if we ask anything according to his will, he hears us. I JOHN 5:14

See also Confession, Fellowship with God, God's Guidance, Thankfulness.

PRIDE

If only people could be beautiful, intelligent, successful, and powerful without looking down on others. But how often does that happen? Part of the pleasure in worldly success is the joy of conceit, the delight in feeling superior to others. Most of us dislike this quality in others (though not necessarily in ourselves). No wonder tradition makes pride the worst of the "seven deadly sins." Needless to say, the Bible opposes the "pedestal people," those who take the attitude of "I am my own god." In the Bible's view of things,

---

The Strangest Place to Pray

"They took Jonah and threw him overboard. . . . But the LORD *provided a great fish to swallow Jonah, and Jonah was inside the fish three days and three nights. From inside the fish Jonah prayed to the* LORD *his God."*

JONAH 1:15, 17; 2:1 (NIV)

---

one who is always looking down is not able to see what is above him. The famous evangelist D. L. Moody preached that "God sends no one away empty except those who are full of themselves."

You may say in your heart, "My power and the might of my hand have gotten me this wealth." But remember the LORD your God, for it is he that gives you power to get wealth.   DEUTERONOMY 8:17–18

Talk no more so exceedingly proud; let not arrogance come out of your mouth, for the LORD is a God who knows, and by him actions are weighed.   1 SAMUEL 2:3

The afflicted people you will save, but your eyes are upon the haughty, so that you may bring them down.   2 SAMUEL 22:28

For the wicked boasts of his heart's desire, and blesses the covetous, whom the LORD abhors. The wicked, through the pride of his countenance, will not seek after God; God is not in his thoughts at all.   PSALM 10:3

The LORD shall cut off all flattering lips, and the tongue that speaks proud things.   PSALM 12:3

You will save the afflicted people; but will bring down haughty looks.   PSALM 18:27

O love the LORD, all you his saints, for the LORD preserves the faithful, and plentifully pays back the proud.   PSALM 31:23

There is no fear of God before his eyes, for he flatters himself in his own eyes.   PSALM 36:1–2

You have rebuked the proud that are cursed, those who err from your commandments.   PSALM 119:21

Though the LORD be high, yet has he respect to the lowly, but the proud he knows from far off.   PSALM 138:6

Be not wise in your own eyes; fear the LORD, and depart from evil.
                                   PROVERBS 3:7

Surely he scorns the scornful, but he gives grace to the lowly.
                                   PROVERBS 3:34

When pride comes, then comes shame, but with the lowly is wisdom.
                                   PROVERBS 11:2

Only by pride comes strife, but with the well-advised is wisdom.
                                   PROVERBS 13:10

The LORD will destroy the house of the proud, but he will establish the boundaries of the widow.   PROVERBS 15:25

Everyone that is proud in heart is an abomination to the LORD; he shall not be unpunished. Pride goes before destruction, and a haughty spirit before a fall. Better it is to be of a humble spirit with the lowly than to divide the spoil with the proud.   PROVERBS 16:5, 18–19

See you a man wise in his own conceit? There is more hope for a fool than for him.   PROVERBS 26:12

Let another man praise you, and not your own mouth; a stranger, and not your own lips.   PROVERBS 27:2

He that is of a proud heart stirs up strife, but he who puts his trust in the LORD shall be made prosperous.   PROVERBS 28:25

A man's pride shall bring him low, but honor shall uphold the humble in spirit.   PROVERBS 29:23

The lofty looks of man shall be humbled, and the haughtiness of men shall be bowed down, and the LORD alone shall be exalted in that day.

ISAIAH 2:11

Woe to those who are wise in their own eyes, and prudent in their own sight!

ISAIAH 5:21

I will punish the world for their evil, and the wicked for their wrongdoing, and I will cause the arrogance of the proud to cease, and will lay low the haughtiness of the ruthless.   ISAIAH 13:11

How you are fallen from heaven, O Lucifer, son of the morning! How you are cut down to the ground, you who did weaken the nations! For you have said in your heart, "I will ascend into heaven, I will raise my throne above the stars of God. I will sit upon the mount of the assembly, in the utmost heights. I will ascend above the clouds. I will be like the Most High." Yet you shall be brought down to hell, to the depths of the pit.

ISAIAH 14:12–15

[NOTE: *Tradition says that this Lucifer was an angel who became proud, rebelled against God, and became Satan, the devil.*]

Behold, his soul which is lifted up is not upright in him, but the just shall live by faith.   HABAKKUK 2:4

Behold, the day comes and burns like an oven, and all the proud, indeed, all that do wickedly, shall be stubble, and the day that comes shall burn them up, says the LORD Almighty, and not a root nor branch will be left of them. But to you that fear my name shall the Sun of righteousness arise with healing in his wings. MALACHI 4:1–2

Blessed are the poor in spirit, for theirs is the kingdom of heaven. Blessed are the meek, for they shall inherit the earth. MATTHEW 5:3, 5

Jesus answered and said, "I thank you, O Father, Lord of heaven and earth, that you have hid these things from the wise and prudent, and have revealed them to babes." MATTHEW 11:25

Jesus sat down and called the twelve, and said to them, "If any man desire to be first, the same shall be last of all, and servant of all." MARK 9:35

Many that are first shall be last, and the last first. MARK 10:31

He has shown strength with his arm; he has scattered the proud in the imagination of their hearts. He has put down the mighty from their seats, and lifted up those of low estate. He has filled the hungry with good things, and the rich he has sent away empty. LUKE 1:51–53

When you are invited by any man to a wedding, do not sit in the places of honor, lest a more distinguished guest than you be present, and he who invited you come and say to you, "Give this man your place," and you go in disgrace to the lowest place. LUKE 14:8–9

Jesus said to them, "You are they that justify yourselves before men; but God knows your hearts, for what is highly esteemed among men is abomination in the sight of God." LUKE 16:15

Jesus spoke this parable to those who trusted in themselves that they were righteous, and despised others: "Two men went up into the temple to pray, one a Pharisee, and the other a tax collector. The Pharisee stood and prayed thus with himself, 'God, I thank you, so that I am not like other men are, robbers, evildoers, adulterers, or like this tax collector. I fast twice a week, I give tithes of all that I possess.' And the tax collector, standing far off, would not lift up so much as his eyes to heaven, but beat his breast, saying, 'God, be merciful to me, a sinner.' I tell you, this man went to his house justified rather than the other, for everyone that exalts himself shall be abased, and he who humbles himself shall be exalted."   LUKE 18:9–14

Love is patient, and is kind; love envies not; love boasts not, is not proud, is not rude, is not easily provoked, thinks no evil.

1 CORINTHIANS 13:4–5

He that glories, let him glory in the Lord. For it is not he who commends himself who is approved, but he whom the Lord commends.

2 CORINTHIANS 10:17–18

Let nothing be done through selfishness or vain conceit, but in humility let each esteem others better than himself. Look after not your own concerns, but let every man also look after the concerns of others. Let this mind be in you, the mind which was in Christ Jesus.   PHILIPPIANS 2:3–5

If a man think himself to be something, when he is nothing, he deceives himself.   GALATIANS 6:3

God resists the proud, but gives grace to the humble.   JAMES 4:6

Listen, now, you who say, "Today or tomorrow we will go into such a city, and continue there a year, and buy and sell, and make money." And yet you do not know what will happen tomorrow. For what is your life? It is like a vapor that appears for a little time, and then vanishes away. Rather, you ought to say, "If the Lord wills, we shall live, and do this or that."

JAMES 4:13–15

Love not the world, neither the things that are in the world. If any man love the world, the love of the Father is not in him. For all that is in the world, the cravings of the sinful nature, and the lust of the eyes, and the pride of life, is not of the Father, but is of the world. And the world passes away, and all its lusts, but he who does the will of God abides forever.

1 JOHN 2:15–17

See also Hypocrisy, Meekness/Gentleness, Money, Self-Esteem, Self-Righteousness.

REPENTANCE

"I'm sorry" are two of the finest words in the language—assuming they are sincere, that is. While some people believe that a tearful apology is enough, this isn't the Bible's view at all. In the words of Martin Luther, "To do so no more is the truest repentance." We aren't sorry until we are ashamed enough not to repeat our wrongdoings.

The Bible could easily be called "The Book of Repentance." It presents a God who judges mankind's failures but who is willing to accept us if only we repent. This is sound not only spiritually but also psychologically. We mature inwardly when we can look objectively at our failures (the Bible uses the classic word sins, *naturally), realize the harm we have done to ourselves and others, and feel such shame that we resolve to lead a new life.*

The Bible's finest quotation on repentance is Jesus' parable of the prodigal son, found below in Luke 15:11–23.

You, Solomon my son, know the God of your father, and serve him with a perfect heart and with a willing mind, for the LORD searches all hearts and understands all the imaginations of the thoughts. If you seek him, he will be found by you; but if you forsake him, he will cast you off forever.

I CHRONICLES 28:9

If my people, which are called by my name, shall humble themselves, and pray, and seek my face, and turn from their wicked ways; then will I hear from heaven, and will forgive their sin, and will heal their land.

2 CHRONICLES 7:14

I acknowledged my sin to you, and my offenses have I not hid. I said, "I will confess my wrongdoing to the LORD," and you forgave the guilt of my sin.

PSALM 32:5

The LORD is near to those who are of a broken heart, and saves such as are of a contrite spirit.   PSALM 34:18

Purge me with hyssop, and I shall be clean. Wash me, and I shall be whiter than snow. Make me to hear joy and gladness; let the bones which you have broken rejoice. Hide your face from my sins, and blot out all my iniquities. Create in me a clean heart, O God, and renew a right spirit within me.

   Cast me not away from your presence, and take not your Holy Spirit from me. Restore to me the joy of your salvation, and uphold me with your free spirit. Then will I teach transgressors your ways, and sinners shall be converted to you.   PSALM 51:7–13

The sacrifices of God are a broken spirit. A broken and a contrite heart, O God, you will not despise.   PSALM 51:16–17

He is our God, and we are the people of his pasture, and the sheep of his hand. Today if you will hear his voice, harden not your heart.
                                                           PSALM 95:7–8

He heals the broken in heart, and binds up their wounds.
                                                           PSALM 147:3

He that covers his sins shall not prosper, but whoever confesses and forsakes them shall have mercy.   PROVERBS 28:13

I have blotted out, like a thick cloud, your offenses and your sins. Return to me; for I have redeemed you.   ISAIAH 44:22

Seek the LORD while he may be found, call you upon him while he is near. Let the wicked forsake his way, and the unrighteous man his thoughts, and let him return to the LORD, and he will have mercy upon him, and to our God, for he will abundantly pardon.   ISAIAH 55:6–7

Thus says the high and lofty One who inhabits eternity, whose name is Holy: "I dwell in the high and holy place, but also with him that is of a contrite and humble spirit, to revive the spirit of the humble, and to revive the heart of the contrite ones."   ISAIAH 57:15

To this man will I look, him that is poor and of a contrite spirit, who trembles at my word.   ISAIAH 66:2

If the wicked will turn from all his sins that he has committed, and keep all my statutes, and do what is lawful and right, he shall surely live, he shall not die. All his offenses that he has committed, they shall not be charged to him; in his righteousness that he has done he shall live.

EZEKIEL 18:21–22

Rend your heart, and not your garments, and turn unto the LORD your God: for he is gracious and merciful, slow to anger, and of great kindness.

JOEL 2:13

[John the Baptist:] I baptize you with water for repentance, but he who comes after me is mightier than I, whose shoes I am not worthy to bear; he shall baptize you with the Holy Spirit, and with fire.

MATTHEW 3:11

Go and learn what that means, "I will have mercy, and not sacrifice," for I have not come to call the righteous, but sinners to repentance.

MATTHEW 9:13

The time is fulfilled, and the kingdom of God is at hand; repent, and believe the gospel.   MARK 1:15

Jesus said to them, "They that are well need not a physician, but they that are sick. I came not to call the righteous, but sinners to repentance."

LUKE 5:31–32

There were present at that season some who told him of the Galileans whose blood Pilate had mingled with their sacrifices. And Jesus said to them, "Do you suppose that these Galileans were sinners above all the Galileans, because they suffered such things? I tell you, no; but, unless you repent, you shall all likewise perish."   LUKE 13:1–3

What man of you, having a hundred sheep, if he loses one of them, does not leave the ninety-nine in the wilderness and go after what is lost, until he finds it? And when he has found it, he lays it on his shoulders, rejoicing. And when he comes home, he calls together his friends and neighbors, saying to them, "Rejoice with me; for I have found my lost sheep." I say to you, that likewise there shall be joy in heaven over one sinner that repents, more than over ninety-nine righteous persons, who need no repentance.

What woman, having ten pieces of silver, if she lose one piece, does not light a candle, and sweep the house, and seek diligently till she finds it? And when she has found it, she calls her friends and her neighbors together, saying, "Rejoice with me, for I have found the piece which I had lost." Likewise, I say to you, there is joy in the presence of the angels of God over one sinner that repents.   LUKE 15:4–10

A certain man had two sons. And the younger of them said to his father, "Father, give me my share of the inheritance." And he divided up his property. And not many days after the younger son gathered his belongings and took a journey to a far country, and there squandered his property in riotous living. And when he had spent everything, there came a severe famine in that land, and he was in dire need. And he went and hired himself to a citizen of that country, who sent him into his fields to feed swine. And he would gladly have filled his belly with the husks that the swine ate, and no man gave him anything. And when he came to himself, he said, "How many hired servants of my father's have bread enough and to spare, and I perish with hunger! I will arise and go to my father, and will say to him, 'Father, I have sinned against heaven and before you, and am no longer worthy to be called your son. Make me as one of your hired servants.'" And he arose, and went to his father. But when he was still a long way off, his father saw him, and had compassion. And he ran, and fell on his neck, and kissed him. And the son said to him, "Father, I have sinned against heaven, and in your sight, and am no longer worthy to be called your son." But the father said to his servants, "Bring forth the best robe, and put it on him, and put a ring on his hand, and shoes on his feet. And bring here the fatted calf, and kill it, and let us eat, and be merry."   LUKE 15:11–23

Peter said to them, "Repent, and be baptized everyone of you in the name of Jesus Christ for the forgiveness of sins, and you shall receive the gift of the Holy Spirit."   ACTS 2:38

Repent and be converted, so that your sins may be blotted out, so that times of refreshing may come from the presence of the Lord.   ACTS 3:19–20

The times of this ignorance God overlooked; but now he commands all men everywhere to repent, because he has appointed a day in the which he will judge the world in righteousness by that man whom he has ordained.

ACTS 17:30–31

If you shall confess with your mouth the Lord Jesus, and shall believe in your heart that God has raised him from the dead, you shall be saved. For with the heart man believes to righteousness, and with the mouth confession is made to salvation. For the scripture says, "Whoever believes in him shall not be ashamed."   ROMANS 10:9–11, 13

Awake, you that sleep, and arise from the dead, and Christ shall give you light.   EPHESIANS 5:14

Draw near to God, and he will draw near to you. Cleanse your hands, you sinners, and purify your hearts, you double-minded. Be afflicted, and mourn, and weep; let your laughter be turned to mourning, and your joy to heaviness. Humble yourselves in the sight of the Lord, and he shall lift you up.   JAMES 4:8–10

The Lord is not slow concerning his promise, as some men believe; but he is longsuffering toward us, not willing that any should perish, but that all should come to repentance.   2 PETER 3:9

If we confess our sins, he is faithful and just to forgive us our sins, and to cleanse us from all unrighteousness.   I JOHN 1:9

As many as I love, I rebuke and chasten; be zealous therefore, and repent.

REVELATION 3:19

See also Confession, Justification, New Birth/New Life.

REVENGE

The phrase "turn the other cheek" comes from Jesus' Sermon on the Mount. On the subject of revenge, he turned the world's standards upside down: Instead of hitting back when someone strikes you on one cheek, let him strike the other. Did Jesus mean this literally? That question misses the point: Jesus was saying that our "natural" response to an injury is all wrong. Instead of getting mad, then getting even, Jesus—and the whole Bible, in fact—holds up a much higher standard. The higher wisdom says to the angry person, "Yes, you could retaliate, but you will only be setting in motion a pointless sequence of one insult or injury after another. Do the nobler thing: Break the chain."

No one said this was easy. It sounds good to say, "I'll let God take revenge, not me." But it requires a bending over backwards of the soul to do this. Most people, in their saner moments, would say that it is worth the effort.

You shall not avenge nor bear any grudge against the children of your people, but you shall love your neighbor as yourself; I am the LORD.

LEVITICUS 19:18

O God, to whom vengeance belongs, show yourself. Lift up yourself, you judge of the earth; render a reward to the proud. LORD, how long shall the wicked, how long shall the wicked triumph? PSALM 94:1–3

Say not, "I will recompense evil"; but wait on the LORD, and he shall save you. PROVERBS 20:22

Whoever digs a pit shall fall in it, and he who rolls a stone, it will roll back upon him. PROVERBS 26:27

You have heard it said, "an eye for an eye, and a tooth for a tooth"; but I say to you, resist not evil, but whoever strikes you on your right cheek, turn to him the other also. And if any man sue you at the law, and take away your coat, let him have your cloak also. And whoever shall compel you to go a mile, go with him two. Give to him that asks you, and turn not away from him that would borrow from you.

You have heard that it has been said, "You shall love your neighbor, and hate your enemy." But I say to you, love your enemies, bless those who curse you, do good to those who hate you, and pray for those who spitefully use you and persecute you; that you may be the children of your Father who is in heaven.   MATTHEW 5:38-44

Shall not God avenge his own elect, who cry day and night to him, though he bear long with them? I tell you that he will avenge them speedily.

LUKE 18:7-8

Pay back no man evil for evil. Take thought for what is noble in the sight of all men. If it be possible, as much as lies in you, live peaceably with all men. Dearly beloved, avenge not yourselves, but rather give place to wrath, for it is written, "Vengeance is mine; I will repay, says the Lord."

ROMANS 12:17-19

If your enemy hungers, feed him; if he thirsts, give him drink; for in so doing you shall heap coals of fire on his head.   ROMANS 12:20

It is a righteous thing with God to repay with affliction those who afflict you, and to relieve the afflicted as well as us, when the Lord Jesus shall be revealed from heaven with his mighty angels, in flaming fire taking vengeance on those who know not God and obey not the gospel of our Lord Jesus Christ.   2 THESSALONIANS 1:5-8

I saw under the altar the souls of those who had been slain for the word of God, and for the testimony they had given. And they cried with a loud voice, "How long, O Lord, holy and true, before you avenge our blood on those who dwell on the earth?" And white robes were given to every one of them.

REVELATION 6:9-11

See also Anger, Enemies, Envy, Forgiveness, Hate.

"Eye for an Eye" . . . Progressive Morals?
Yes, the idea of "eye for an eye, tooth for a tooth"
really is in the Bible:
"If anyone injures his neighbor, whatever he has
done must be done to him: fracture for fracture, eye
for eye, tooth for tooth. As he has injured the other,
so he is to be injured" (Leviticus 24:19–20, NIV).

This law from the Old Testament strikes us as
spiteful and vindictive (or "mean spirited," to use
the now-popular phrase). In the New Testament,
Jesus taught a higher ethic: "You have heard that it
was said, 'Eye for eye, and tooth for tooth.' But I tell
you, Do not resist an evil person. If someone strikes
you on the right cheek, turn to him the other also"
(Matthew 5:38–39, NIV). Doesn't that sound bet-
ter—more "Christian"?

For the record, the Old Testament law was pretty
compassionate and progressive. "Eye for eye, tooth
for tooth" was a limit. It meant "tit for tat"—but no
more. The common custom (human nature never
changes!) was (and is) to get more than even. But the
enlightened law in Leviticus said, No, if you're in-
jured you can't take two teeth because you lost one
tooth. It was actually a progressive law. Jesus took it
a step further.

We wonder: How would the Bible authors view
personal-injury lawsuits today?

RIGHTEOUSNESS

The problem with the word righteous *is that we always want to tack* self *onto it. Self-righteousness is bad; righteousness is good, even if the word itself has gone out of fashion. Certainly the* idea *of righteousness is still with us. Consider how we talk about people: "She's got a lot of compassion," "He's a caring person," "She's deeply committed to what she believes," or "He's involved in his community." Isn't this righteousness we're talking about?*

Putting it mildly, righteousness is one of the main themes of the Bible. The main assumption is that God is righteous and that we should imitate him. The New Testament gives us Jesus, not only the teacher and the miracle worker but also one whom people believed to be totally righteous. The fact that he was executed illustrates another theme of the Bible: Being right with God often means being in trouble with mankind.

It shall be our righteousness, if we observe to do all these commandments before the LORD our God, as he has commanded us.

DEUTERONOMY 6:25

Blessed is the man that walks not in the counsel of the ungodly, nor stands in the way of sinners, nor sits in the seat of the scornful. But his delight is in the law of the LORD, and in his law does he meditate day and night. And he shall be like a tree planted by rivers of water, who brings forth his fruit in his season; his leaf shall not wither, and whatever he does shall prosper. The ungodly are not so, but are like the chaff which the wind drives away. Therefore the ungodly shall not stand in the judgment, nor sinners in the congregation of the righteous. The LORD knows the way of the righteous, but the way of the ungodly shall perish.　　　　　PSALM 1

You, LORD, will bless the righteous; with favor will you protect him as with a shield.　　　　　PSALM 5:12

The LORD examines the righteous, but the wicked and him that loves violence his soul hates.　　　　　PSALM 11:5

Many are the afflictions of the righteous, but the LORD delivers him out of them all. Evil shall slay the wicked, and they that hate the righteous shall be desolate. PSALM 34:19, 21

A little that a righteous man has is better than the riches of many wicked. The righteous shall inherit the land, and dwell therein forever.

PSALM 37:16, 29

Cast your burden upon the LORD, and he shall sustain you; he shall never allow the righteous to be moved. PSALM 55:22

Truly there is a reward for the righteous; truly he is a God who judges in the earth. PSALM 58:11

The LORD God is a sun and shield; the LORD will give grace and glory; no good thing will he withhold from those who walk uprightly.

PSALM 84:11

The righteous shall flourish like the palm tree; he shall grow like a cedar in Lebanon. PSALM 92:12

Light is sown for the righteous, and gladness for the upright in heart.

PSALM 97:11

The LORD opens the eyes of the blind; the LORD raises up those who are bowed down; the LORD loves the righteous. PSALM 146:8

The curse of the LORD is on the house of the wicked, but he blesses the dwelling of the just. PROVERBS 3:33

The path of the just is like a shining light, which shines more and more to the perfect day. PROVERBS 4:18

Evil pursues sinners, but good shall be repaid to the righteous.

PROVERBS 13:21

Better is a little with righteousness than great revenues without right.

PROVERBS 16:8

The righteous considers the cause of the poor, but the wicked have no concern for them.

PROVERBS 29:7

For as the earth brings forth her bud, and as the garden causes the things that are sown in it to spring forth, so the LORD God will cause righteousness and praise to spring forth before all the nations.

ISAIAH 61:11

The soul that sins is the one that shall die. The son shall not bear the guilt of the father, neither shall the father bear the guilt of the son; the righteousness of the righteous man shall be credited to him and the wickedness of the wicked shall be credited to him. But if the wicked will turn from all his sins that he has committed, and keep all my statutes, and do what is lawful and right, he shall surely live, he shall not die.

EZEKIEL 18:20–23

Let judgment run down as waters, and righteousness as a mighty stream.

AMOS 5:24

Blessed are they that hunger and thirst after righteousness, for they shall be filled. Blessed are they that are persecuted for righteousness' sake, for theirs is the kingdom of heaven.

MATTHEW 5:6, 10

Take heed that you do not your alms before men, to be seen by them; otherwise you have no reward from your Father who is in heaven.

MATTHEW 6:1

Jesus said to them, "They that are well have no need of a physician, but they that are sick; I came not to call the righteous, but sinners to repentance."

MARK 2:17

Being made free from sin, you became the servants of righteousness.

ROMANS 6:18

If any man be in Christ, he is a new creature; old things have passed away; behold, all things have become new. For he has made him to be sin for us, who knew no sin, that through him we might be made the righteousness of God. 2 CORINTHIANS 5:17, 21

The fruit of the Spirit is love, joy, peace, longsuffering, gentleness, goodness, faith, meekness, self-control; against such there is no law. And they that are Christ's have crucified the sinful nature with its passions and lusts. If we live in the Spirit, let us also walk in the Spirit. GALATIANS 5:22–25

There is laid up for me a crown of righteousness, which the Lord, the righteous judge, shall give me at that day, and not to me only, but to all that love his appearing. 2 TIMOTHY 4:8

The fruit of righteousness is sown in peace by those who make peace.

JAMES 3:18

You also, like living stones, are built into a spiritual house, a holy priesthood, to offer up spiritual sacrifices, acceptable to God by Jesus Christ. But you are a chosen generation, a royal priesthood, a holy nation, a distinctive people; that you should show forth the praises of him who has called you out of darkness into his marvelous light. In time past you were not a people, but are now the people of God. I PETER 2:5, 9–10

If we confess our sins, he is faithful and just to forgive us our sins, and to cleanse us from all unrighteousness. I JOHN 1:9

See also Justification, Obeying God, Self-Righteousness.

THE SABBATH

We have the Bible to thank for the concept of the weekend. In biblical times, the notion of taking one day out of seven as a no-work day was quite radical. As more and more people work from their homes, with hours that they set for themselves, and as more businesses open earlier and earlier on Sundays, the old concept of the Sabbath is being forgotten. But it will be a long, long time before the idea of Sunday as a special day completely disappears.

Remember the sabbath day, to keep it holy. Six days shall you labor, and do all your work; but the seventh day is the sabbath of the LORD your God. In it you shall not do any work, you, nor your son, nor your daughter, your manservant, nor your maidservant, nor your cattle, nor the stranger that is within your gates. For in six days the LORD made heaven and earth, the sea, and all that in them is, and rested the seventh day; therefore the LORD blessed the sabbath day and made it holy. EXODUS 20:8–11

Speak to the children of Israel, saying, "Truly my sabbaths you shall keep, for it is a sign between me and you throughout your generations; that you may know that I am the LORD that sanctifies you. You shall keep the sabbath, for it is holy to you; everyone that defiles it shall surely be put to death, for whoever does any work then, that soul shall be cut off from among his people. Six days may work be done; but in the seventh is the sabbath of rest, holy to the LORD. Whoever does any work in the sabbath day, he shall surely be put to death. Therefore the children of Israel shall keep the sabbath, to observe the sabbath throughout their generations, for a perpetual covenant. It is a sign between me and the children of Israel forever, for in six days the LORD made heaven and earth, and on the seventh day he rested, and was refreshed. EXODUS 31:13–17

Reverence my sabbaths, and they shall be a sign between me and you, so that you may know that I am the LORD your God.　　　EZEKIEL 20:20

There was a man who had a withered hand. And they asked him [Jesus], "Is it lawful to heal on the sabbath day?" (They wished to trap him.) And he said to them, "What man is there among you, who, having one sheep, and if it fall into a pit on the sabbath day, will he not lay hold of it, and lift it out? How much better then is a man than a sheep? Therefore it is lawful to do well on the sabbath." Then said he to the man, "Stretch forth your hand." And he stretched it forth, and it was restored whole, like the other.

MATTHEW 12:10–13

Jesus said to them, "The sabbath was made for man, and not man for the sabbath; therefore the Son of man is Lord also of the sabbath."

MARK 2:27–28

See also **Work.**

SALVATION

Salvation means, in the most literal sense, being saved—as in saved from a fire, a flood, or an illness. Sometimes this is the meaning of the word in the Bible. But most of the time salvation refers to "saving one's soul." The word has gone out of style, but all the self-help books, seminars, conventions, therapists, support groups, and so on suggest that many (maybe most) people feel the need to be saved from something. In the Bible, that something is sin, that tendency toward selfishness that wrecks our relations with others and with God. Like most ancient peoples, the people of the Bible believed in sacrifice—giving up something you value as a sign to God that you are sorry for your wrongs. (Things haven't changed much. Think of people today who try to "save themselves" by strict diets or grueling exercise routines.) In the New Testament, the idea of sacrifice shifts to Jesus, the perfect and sinless man who takes the place of the animals and other items that were sacrificed.

A note about the idea of salvation in the Bible: It is not really about human improvement but about transformation.

The LORD is near to those who are of a broken heart, and saves such as are of a contrite spirit. PSALM 34:18

The salvation of the righteous is from the LORD; he is their strength in the time of trouble. PSALM 37:39

Restore to me the joy of your salvation, and uphold me with your free Spirit. PSALM 51:12

Truly my soul waits upon God; from him comes my salvation. PSALM 62:1

O come, let us sing to the LORD; let us make a joyful noise to the Rock of our salvation. PSALM 95:1

The LORD preserves the simple; I was brought low, and he helped me. PSALM 116:6

The LORD himself shall give you a sign: behold, a virgin shall conceive and bear a son, and shall call his name "Immanuel." ISAIAH 7:14

The people that walked in darkness have seen a great light; they that dwell in the land of the shadow of death, upon them has the light shined. For to us a child is born, to us a son is given, and the government shall be upon his shoulder, and his name shall be called Wonderful, Counselor, the Mighty God, the Everlasting Father, the Prince of Peace. ISAIAH 9:2, 6

Then the eyes of the blind shall be opened, and the ears of the deaf shall be unstopped. Then shall the lame man leap like a deer, and the tongue of the mute shall sing, for in the wilderness shall waters break out, and streams in the desert. ISAIAH 35:5–6

He shall feed his flock like a shepherd: he shall gather the lambs with his arm, and carry them in his bosom, and shall gently lead those that are with young. ISAIAH 40:11

Politically Corrected?

Noah Webster, of dictionary fame, produced a "corrected" version of the King James Bible, making it more American by changing the British spelling of certain words.

Surely he has borne our griefs, and carried our sorrows; yet we accounted him stricken, struck down by God, and afflicted. But he was wounded for our offenses, he was bruised for our iniquities. The punishment that made us whole was upon him, and with his wounds we are healed.

ISAIAH 53:4–5

"I know the thoughts that I think about you," says the LORD, "thoughts of peace, and not of evil, to give you a future with hope. Then shall you call upon me, and you shall go and pray to me, and I will hearken to you. And you shall seek me, and find me, when you shall search for me with all your heart."

JEREMIAH 29:11–13

Rejoice greatly, O daughter of Zion; shout, O daughter of Jerusalem; behold, your King comes to you; he is just, and having salvation; lowly, and riding on a donkey.

ZECHARIAH 9:9

[NOTE: *This Old Testament prophecy was fulfilled centuries later when Jesus rode into Jerusalem on a donkey.*]

Enter in by the narrow gate. For wide is the gate and broad is the way that leads to destruction, and many there are who go in that way. But narrow is the gate, and narrow is the way, which leads to life, and few there are that find it.

MATTHEW 7:13–14

Come to me, all you that labor and are heavy laden, and I will give you rest. Take my yoke upon you, and learn from me; for I am meek and lowly in heart, and you shall find rest for your souls. For my yoke is easy, and my burden is light.   MATTHEW 11:28–30

Whoever will save his life shall lose it, and whoever will lose his life for my sake shall find it.   MATTHEW 16:25

The time is fulfilled, and the kingdom of God is at hand; repent, and believe the gospel.   MARK 1:15

The Son of man came not to be served, but to serve, and to give his life a ransom for many.   MARK 10:45

Jesus said to them, "Go into all the world and preach the gospel to every creature. He that believes and is baptized shall be saved; but he who believes not shall be damned."   MARK 16:15–16

The Son of man is come to seek and to save what was lost.   LUKE 19:10

Jesus answered and said to him, "Truly, truly, I say to you, except a man be born again, he cannot see the kingdom of God." Nicodemus said to him, "How can a man be born when he is old? Can he enter the second time into his mother's womb, and be born?" Jesus answered, "Truly, truly, I say to you, except a man be born of water and of the Spirit, he cannot enter into the kingdom of God. That which is born of the flesh is flesh, and what is born of the Spirit is spirit. Marvel not that I said to you, 'You must be born again.'"   JOHN 3:3–7

God so loved the world that he gave his only begotten Son, that whoever believes in him should not perish, but have everlasting life. For God sent not his Son into the world to condemn the world; but that the world through him might be saved.   JOHN 3:16–17

I am the door; if any man enter in by me, he shall be saved, and shall go in and out, and find pasture.   JOHN 10:9

I am not ashamed of the gospel of Christ, for it is the power of God to salvation to everyone that believes.　ROMANS 1:16

What the law could not do, because of the weakness of human nature, God did by sending his own Son in the likeness of sinful flesh.　ROMANS 8:3

If you confess with your mouth the Lord Jesus, and shall believe in your heart that God has raised him from the dead, you shall be saved.

ROMANS 10:9

The preaching of the cross is foolishness to those who perish; but to us who are saved it is the power of God. For it is written, "I will destroy the wisdom of the wise, and will bring to nothing the understanding of the prudent."

1 CORINTHIANS 1:18–19

If any man be in Christ, he is a new creature; old things have passed away—behold, all things have become new. And all things are from God, who has reconciled us to himself through Jesus Christ, and has given to us the ministry of reconciliation, which is this: God was in Christ, reconciling the world to himself, not counting men's sins against them. And he has committed to us the word of reconciliation. Now then we are ambassadors for Christ, as if God did appeal to you through us; we pray you on behalf of Christ, be reconciled to God. For our sake he made him to be sin who knew no sins, so that we might become the righteousness of God.

2 CORINTHIANS 5:17–21

Behold, now is the accepted time; behold, now is the day of salvation.

2 CORINTHIANS 6:2

You he has made alive, you who were dead in trespasses and sins. In time past you walked according to the course of this world, following the prince of the power of the air, the spirit that now works in the children of disobedience. All of us once lived among them in the lusts of our sinful nature, fulfilling the desires of the sinful nature and of the mind, and we were by nature the children of wrath, like everyone else.

But God, who is rich in mercy, out of the great love with which he loved us even when we were dead in sins, has made alive us together with Christ—by grace you are saved—and has raised us up and made us sit together in heavenly places in Christ Jesus, so that in the ages to come he might show the immeasurable riches of his grace in his kindness toward us through Christ Jesus. For by grace are you saved through faith, and that not of yourselves; it is the gift of God—not of works, lest any man should boast.

EPHESIANS 2:1–9

Buried with him in baptism, you also are risen with him through the faith of the operation of God, who has raised him from the dead. And you, being dead in your sins and the uncircumcision of your flesh, he has made alive together with him, having forgiven you all sins.   COLOSSIANS 2:12–13

This is a faithful saying, and worthy of full acceptance, that Christ Jesus came into the world to save sinners.   I TIMOTHY 1:15

This is good and acceptable in the sight of God our Savior, who wishes all men to be saved, and to come to the knowledge of the truth. For there is one God, and one mediator between God and men, the man Christ Jesus; who gave himself a ransom for all.   I TIMOTHY 2:3–6

The grace of God that brings salvation has appeared to all men.

TITUS 2:11

Not by works of righteousness which we have done, but according to his mercy he saved us, by the washing of regeneration, and renewing of the Holy Spirit.   TITUS 3:5

How shall we escape, if we neglect so great salvation?   HEBREWS 2:3

Since the children are partakers of flesh and blood, Jesus also himself likewise took part in the same; that through death he might destroy him that had the power of death, that is, the devil; . . . For we have not a high priest who cannot be touched with the feeling of our infirmities; but was in all points tempted as we are, yet without sin.   HEBREWS 2:14, 4:15

See also Justification, New Birth/New Life, Repentance, Sin and Redemption.

SELF-CONTROL/SELF-DENIAL

In this area, the Bible pretty much agrees with modern thought and with common sense: The greatest burden we have to carry in life is the self. It is certainly one of the hardest things to control, probably because most people don't try. This is surprising, considering that the concept of "No pain, no gain" is widely accepted. We take it for granted that the perfect body can't be had by wishful thinking—it takes hard work and (horrors!) self-denial. No athlete becomes a superstar by luck and hope—it takes hours upon hours of self-denial. Self-control and self-denial are all about having goals that make short-term pleasures seem trivial by comparison. The idea is that a person's desire to be a better self—the best possible self—means forgoing certain pleasures, including such dubious pleasures as vengeance, immorality, following the crowd, and losing one's temper. Simply put, the capacity to say "No" determines one's capacity to say "Yes" to greater things.

Set a watch, O LORD, before my mouth; keep the door of my lips.
PSALM 141:3

His own iniquities ensnare the wicked, and he is held with the cords of his sins. He shall die for lack of discipline, and in the greatness of his folly he shall be lost.   PROVERBS 5:22–23

He that has no rule over his own spirit is like a city that is broken down and without walls.   PROVERBS 25:28

I say to you, resist not evil, but whoever shall strike you on your right cheek, turn to him the other also. MATTHEW 5:39

Then said Jesus to his disciples, "If any man will come after me, let him deny himself, and take up his cross, and follow me. For whoever will save his life shall lose it, and whoever will lose his life for my sake shall find it. For what is a man profited, if he shall gain the whole world, and lose his own soul? Or what shall a man give in exchange for his soul? For the Son of man shall come in the glory of his Father with his angels, and then he shall reward every man according to his works." MATTHEW 16:24–27

Whoever among you that forsakes not all that he has, he cannot be my disciple. LUKE 14:33

For those who are self-seeking, who do not obey the truth but obey unrighteousness, there will be indignation and wrath. ROMANS 2:8

If you live according to the sinful nature, you shall die; but if through the Spirit you put to death the deeds of the body, you shall live. ROMANS 8:12–13

Put you on the Lord Jesus Christ, and make no provision for the sinful nature, to fulfill its lusts. ROMANS 13:14

I am crucified with Christ; nevertheless I live; yet not I, but Christ lives in me; and the life which I now live in the flesh I live by the faith of the Son of God, who loved me, and gave himself for me. GALATIANS 2:20

Walk in the Spirit, and you shall not fulfill the lust of the sinful nature. For the sinful nature lusts against the Spirit, and the Spirit against the sinful nature, and these are contrary to one another, so that you cannot do the things that you wish. GALATIANS 5:16–17

The fruit of the Spirit is love, joy, peace, longsuffering, gentleness, goodness, faith, meekness, self-control: against such there is no law. And they that are Christ's have crucified the sinful nature with its passions and lusts. If we live in the Spirit, let us also walk in the Spirit. GALATIANS 5:22–25

Since you are dead with Christ to the principles of the world, why, as though living in the world, are you subject to regulations—"Touch not, taste not, handle not"? All such regulations will perish with use and are merely human commandments and teachings. These things have indeed an appearance of wisdom in promoting self-imposed worship, false humility, and severe treatment of the body, but are of no value in controlling self-indulgence.

COLOSSIANS 2:20-23

God has not given us the spirit of fear; but of power, and of love, and of a self-discipline.

2 TIMOTHY 1:7

Denying ungodliness and worldly lusts, we should live soberly, righteously, and godly in this present world.

TITUS 2:12

Dearly beloved, I urge you as strangers and pilgrims, abstain from fleshly lusts, which war against the soul. Live such honorable lives among the pagans that, though they speak of you as evildoers, they may see your good works and glorify God when he comes.

I PETER 2:11-12

Be self-controlled, be vigilant; because your adversary the devil walks about like a roaring lion, seeking whom he may devour.

I PETER 5:8

Add to your faith virtue, and to virtue add knowledge; and to knowledge self-control; and to self-control patience; and to patience godliness; and to godliness brotherly kindness; and to brotherly kindness charity.

2 PETER 1:5-7

See also Anger, Hate, Obeying God, Revenge, Selfishness, Temptation.

SELF-DECEPTION

Of all the forms of dishonesty human beings practice, this may be the most destructive. People deceive themselves because (obviously) they are uncomfortable with who they really are. They prefer the illusion to reality. The "unreal" self, the illusionary self, is probably prettier, smarter, more moral, and more successful and no doubt has a brighter future than the real self.

Well, comforting and comfortable as illusions are, the Bible is strongly anti-illusion and is especially harsh toward people who turn a blind eye to their own sins. No form of moral blindness is condemned more than the person who justifies his or her own wrongdoings, calling good evil and evil good.

Be sure your sin will find you out. NUMBERS 32:23

God drags away the mighty by his power: though they rise up, they cannot be sure of life. Though they may feel they are resting securely, yet his eyes are upon their ways. They are exalted for a little while, but are gone and brought low; they are taken out of the way as all others. JOB 24:22–24

The fool has said in his heart, "There is no God." They are corrupt, they have done abominable deeds, there is none that does good. PSALM 14:1

In my prosperity I said, "I shall never be moved." PSALM 30:6

There is no fear of God before his eyes, for he flatters himself in his own eyes. PSALM 36:1–2

All the ways of a man are clean in his own eyes; but the LORD weighs the spirits. PROVERBS 16:2

There is a way that seems right to a man, but the end thereof are the ways of death. PROVERBS 16:25

He that trusts in his own heart is a fool, but whoever walks wisely shall be delivered. PROVERBS 28:26

Woe to those who are wise in their own eyes and shrewd in their own sight! ISAIAH 5:21

We have made lies our refuge, and under falsehood have we hid ourselves. ISAIAH 28:15

Woe to those who go to great depths to hide their plans from the LORD. Their works are done in the dark, and they say, "Who sees us? And who knows us?" ISAIAH 29:15

You have trusted in your wickedness; you have said, "No one sees me." Your wisdom and your knowledge have perverted you, and you have said in your heart, "I am, and no on else beside me." But disaster shall come upon you; you shall not know from whence it came, and calamity shall fall upon you.

ISAIAH 47:10–11

"My thoughts are not your thoughts, neither are your ways my ways," says the LORD. "For as the heavens are higher than the earth, so are my ways higher than your ways, and my thoughts than your thoughts."

ISAIAH 55:8–9

Thus says the LORD, "Cursed be the man that trusts in man, and makes flesh his strength, and whose heart departs from the LORD."

JEREMIAH 17:5

Thus says the LORD: deceive not yourselves.   JEREMIAH 37:9

The terror you cause, and the pride of your heart, have deceived you.

JEREMIAH 49:16

They have seduced my people, saying, "Peace," and there was no peace.

EZEKIEL 13:10

Woe to those who are at ease in Zion.   AMOS 6:1

Take heed that the light which is in you is not darkness.   LUKE 11:35

He spoke a parable to them, saying, "The ground of a certain rich man brought forth plentifully. And he thought within himself, saying, What shall I do, because I have no room to store my fruits? And he said, This will I do; I will pull down my barns, and build larger, and there will I store all my fruits and my goods. And I will say to my soul, Soul, you have much goods laid up for many years; take your ease, eat, drink, and be merry. But God said to him, 'You fool, this night your soul shall be required of you. Then whose shall those things be, which you have provided?' So is he who lays up treasure for himself, and is not rich toward God."   LUKE 12:16–21

When they knew God, they glorified him not as God, nor were thankful; but they became futile in their thoughts, and their foolish hearts were darkened. Professing themselves to be wise, they became fools.

ROMANS 1:21–22

Be not deceived; God is not mocked, for whatever a man sows, that shall he reap.

GALATIANS 6:7

When they shall say, "Peace and safety," sudden destruction comes upon them, like labor upon a woman with child, and they shall not escape.

I THESSALONIANS 5:3

Listen, now, you who say, "Today or tomorrow we will go into such a city, and continue there a year, and buy and sell, and make money." And yet you do not know what will happen tomorrow. For what is your life? It is like a vapor, that appears for a little time, and then vanishes away. Rather, you ought to say, "If the Lord wills, we shall live, and do this or that."

JAMES 4:13–15

See also Arrogance, Pride.

SELF-ESTEEM

You get the impression that many people today have fragile egos that need constant stroking. Maintaining that "I'm special" feeling has become some people's key goal in life. In theory, anything could nourish the "I'm special" feeling: losing weight, gaining weight, a new job, higher pay, a promotion, a more attractive spouse, running a marathon—whatever. The Bible takes a more sensible view of self-esteem: We aren't right with ourselves unless we are in a right relationship with one another and with God, and we can't be in a right relationship with others while our attention is focused on feeding our own hungry egos. Put another way, we have to combat the "I'm special" feeling with the feeling that "Everyone else is special, too." In other words, the Bible asks us to be adults, not infants, whose attention is focused only on themselves. That sort of fixation is appropriate for a ten-month-old but not for an adult. The Bible's message is this: Grow up; you will find your self-esteem most healthy when you can forget about it and love and enjoy others.

The LORD sees not as man sees; for man looks on the outward appearance, but the LORD looks on the heart.   I SAMUEL 16:7

Who can understand his own errors? Cleanse me from secret faults.

PSALM 19:12

Blessed is that man that makes the LORD his trust, and respects not the proud, nor those who turn aside to false gods.   PSALM 40:4

God sees that wise men die, likewise the fool and the brutish person perish, and leave their wealth to others. Their inward thought is that their houses shall continue forever, and their dwelling places to all generations. They call their lands after their own names. Nevertheless man, despite his wealth, does not endure; he is like the beasts that perish.   PSALM 49:9–12

In God I have put my trust; I will not fear what man can do to me.

PSALM 56:4

O LORD, you have searched me and known me. You know my sitting down and my rising up; you understand my thoughts from afar. You encompass my path and my lying down, and you know all my ways. There is not a word on my tongue, but, lo, O LORD, you know it altogether. You press upon me behind and before, and lay your hand on me. Such knowledge is too wonderful for me; it is so high I cannot attain it.

Where can I go from your Spirit? Where can I flee from your presence? If I ascend up to heaven, you are there; if I make my bed in the grave, behold, you are there. If I take the wings of the morning, and dwell in the uttermost parts of the sea, even there shall your hand lead me, and your right hand shall hold me. If I say, "Surely the darkness shall cover me, and the light around me turn to night." The darkness and light to you are both alike.

You created my inmost parts; you knit me together in my mother's womb. I will praise you, for I am fearfully and wonderfully made; marvelous are your works, and my soul knows this well. My body was not hid from you when I was made in secret, and made in the depths of the earth. Your eyes beheld my substance while I was still incomplete, and in your book all my members were written.

How precious are your thoughts to me, O God! How great is the sum of them! If I should count them, they are more in number than the sand. When I awake, I am still with you. Search me, O God, and know my heart; try me, and know my thoughts. See if there is any wicked way in me, and lead me in the way everlasting. PSALM 139

For men to seek their own glory is not glory. PROVERBS 25:27

Boast not of tomorrow, for you know not what a day may bring forth. PROVERBS 27:1

I said in my heart, "Come now, I will test you with mirth, therefore enjoy pleasure." But behold, this also is meaningless. ECCLESIASTES 2:1

I considered that all labor and every skill come from man's envy of his neighbor. This is also meaningless, a chasing after the wind. ECCLESIASTES 4:4

Better what the eyes see than the wandering of desire; this is also meaningless, a chasing after the wind. ECCLESIASTES 6:9

You will keep him in perfect peace, whose mind is stayed on you; because he trusts in you. ISAIAH 26:3

He gives power to the weary, and to those who have no might he increases strength. ISAIAH 40:29

Let him that glories glory in this, that he understands and knows me, that I am the LORD who practice lovingkindness, justice, and righteousness in the earth; for in these things I delight, says the LORD. JEREMIAH 9:24

You are the salt of the earth, but if the salt has lost its savor, how can it be salty again? It is no longer good for anything, but to be cast out, and to be trampled underfoot.

You are the light of the world. A city that is set on a hill cannot be hid. Neither do men light a candle and put it under a bushel, but on a candle-stick, and it gives light to all that are in the house. Let your light so shine before men that they may see your good works and glorify your Father who is in heaven. MATTHEW 5:13–16

Seek first the kingdom of God, and his righteousness, and all these other things shall be given to you. Take no thought for the morrow, for tomorrow shall bring worries of its own. Sufficient for each day is its own trouble. MATTHEW 6:33–34

Are not two sparrows sold for a penny? And one of them shall not fall to the ground without your Father. But the very hairs of your head are all num-bered. So fear not: you are of more value than many sparrows. MATTHEW 10:29–31

He that finds his life shall lose it, and he who loses his life for my sake shall find it. MATTHEW 10:39

Come to me, all you that labor and are heavy laden, and I will give you rest. Take my yoke upon you, and learn from me, for I am meek and lowly in heart, and you shall find rest for your souls. For my yoke is easy, and my burden is light. MATTHEW 11:28–30

What is a man profited, if he gain the whole world and lose his own soul? Or what shall a man give in exchange for his soul? MATTHEW 16:26

I have come that they might have life, and that they might have it more abundantly. JOHN 10:10

By the grace given to me I say to every man that is among you not to think more highly of himself than he ought to think, but to think soberly, in accordance with the measure of faith God has given to each man. For as we have many members in one body, and all members have not the same function, so we, being many, are one body in Christ, and everyone members one of another. ROMANS 12:3–6

With me it is a very small thing that I should be judged by you, or by any man; indeed, I judge not my own self. I know of nothing against myself, yet it is not this that justifies me, but he who judges me is the Lord. Therefore judge nothing before the appointed time, until the Lord comes, who will bring to light the hidden things of darkness and will reveal the purposes of hearts, and then shall every man have praise of God.

I CORINTHIANS 4:3–4

He that glories, let him glory in the Lord. For it is not he who commends himself who is approved, but the one whom the Lord commends.

2 CORINTHIANS 10:17–18

To keep me from being too exalted through the abundance of the revelations, there was given to me a thorn in the flesh, the messenger of Satan to torment me, lest I should be exalted above measure. For this thing I appealed to the Lord three times, that it might depart from me. And he said to me, "My grace is sufficient for you, for my strength is made perfect in weakness." Most gladly therefore will I glory in my infirmities, that the power of Christ may rest upon me. Therefore I take pleasure in infirmities, in insults, in hardships, in persecutions, in calamities for Christ's sake, for when I am weak, then am I strong.

2 CORINTHIANS 12:7–10

If a man think himself to be something, when he is nothing, he deceives himself. But let every man test his own work, and then shall he have rejoicing in himself alone, and not in another. For every man shall bear his own burden.

GALATIANS 6:3–5

God forbid that I should glory, except in the cross of our Lord Jesus Christ, by whom the world is crucified to me, and I to the world.

GALATIANS 6:14

The things that were gain to me, these I counted as loss for Christ. More than that, I count all things as loss because of the excellency of the knowledge of Christ Jesus my Lord, for whom I have suffered the loss of all things, and do count them as rubbish, so that I may win Christ.

PHILIPPIANS 3:7–8

In the last days perilous times shall come. For men shall be lovers of their own selves, covetous, boastful, proud, blasphemers, disobedient to parents, ungrateful, unholy, without natural affection, merciless, slanderers, without self-control, cruel, despisers of those who are good, treacherous, rash, conceited, lovers of pleasure more than lovers of God.

2 TIMOTHY 3:1-4

You are a chosen generation, a royal priesthood, a holy nation, a distinctive people, so you should show forth the praises of him who has called you out of darkness into his marvelous light. In time past you were not a people, but now are the people of God.

1 PETER 2:9-10

Do not adorn yourselves outwardly by arranging your hair, or by wearing gold, or by putting on clothing. Rather, let your adornment be the inner man of the heart, which never decays, the ornament of a meek and quiet spirit, which is of much value in the sight of God.

1 PETER 3:3-4

See also Ambition, The Body, Contentment, Worldly Cares, Worry.

SELFISHNESS

An old proverb says, "Men are not against you, they are merely for themselves." That isn't much consolation. In practice the "every man for himself" philosophy does lead to people being against one another. We could probably attribute war and most other afflictions that people bring on one another to this root problem: selfishness. Most people accept this, yet we generally hate the selfishness of other people, not our own. Funny, but in all the schemes for improving humanity, everyone thinks of ways to diminish someone else's selfishness—but not their own.

From the Bible's point of view, selfishness is a form of idolatry, worshiping something (one's own ego) instead of God. This is not only psychologically unhealthy but, according to the Bible, just plain sin. What is the alternative? Hating oneself? Of course not. The alternative to selfishness is opening one's eyes to the needs and wants of others, learning to say "we" and "all of us" more often and to say "I" less often.

A man who separates himself from others seeks his own desire, and he rejects all wise advice.

PROVERBS 18:1

He that is first to present his case seems just, until another comes and examines him.

PROVERBS 18:17

For men to seek their own glory is not glory.

PROVERBS 25:27

As you wish that men should do to you, do so to them. For if you love those who love you, what credit is that to you? For sinners also love those that love them. And if you do good to those who do good to you, what credit is that to you? For sinners also do the same. And if you lend to them of whom you hope to receive, what credit is that to you? For sinners also lend to sinners, to receive as much back again. But love you your enemies, and do good; and lend, hoping for nothing in return, and your reward shall be great, and you shall be the children of the Highest, for he is kind to the unthankful and to the evil. Be therefore merciful, as your Father also is merciful.

LUKE 6:31–36

For those who are self-seeking, who do not obey the truth but obey unrighteousness, there will be indignation and wrath.

ROMANS 2:8

Let no man seek his own good, but the good of every other man.

I CORINTHIANS 10:24

Now the works of the sinful nature are obvious, which are these; adultery, fornication, impurity, debauchery, idolatry, witchcraft, hatred, discord, jealousy, wrath, strife, seditions, heresies, envyings, murders, drunkenness, carousing, and the like. I warn you, as I have also told you in the past, so that those who do such things shall not inherit the kingdom of God.

GALATIANS 5:19–21

Bear one another's burdens, and so fulfill the law of Christ.

GALATIANS 6:2

Since you are dead with Christ to the principles of the world, why, as though living in the world, are you subject to regulations—"Touch not, taste not, handle not"? All such regulations will perish with use and are merely human commandments and teachings. These things have an appearance of wisdom in promoting self-imposed worship, false humility, and severe treatment of the body, but are of no value in controlling self-indulgence.

COLOSSIANS 2:20–23

In the last days perilous times shall come. For men shall be lovers of their own selves, covetous, boastful, proud, blasphemers, disobedient to parents, ungrateful, unholy, without natural affection, merciless, slanderers, without self-control, cruel, despisers of those who are good, treacherous, rash, conceited, lovers of pleasure more than lovers of God.

2 TIMOTHY 3:1–4

Denying ungodliness and worldly lusts, we should live soberly, righteously, and godly in this present world. TITUS 2:12

Where envying and strife are, there is confusion and every evil work.

JAMES 3:16

Where do these conflicts and disputes among you arise from? Do they not come from your cravings that war within you? You crave, and have not, so you kill. You desire to have, and cannot obtain, so you fight and war. You have not because you ask not. You ask, and receive not, because you ask wrongly, so that you may spend it upon your pleasures. You adulterers and adulteresses, know you not that the friendship of the world is enmity with God? Whoever therefore will be a friend of the world is the enemy of God. Do you think it is for nothing that the scripture says, "He yearns jealously for the spirit that he has made to dwell in us"? But he gives more grace, therefore as the scripture says, "God resists the proud, but gives grace to the humble." JAMES 4:1–6

Whoever has this world's goods, and sees his brother in need, and has no pity on him, how dwells the love of God in him? My little children, let us not love merely in word, neither in speech, but in deed and in truth.

I JOHN 3:17–18

See also Ambition, Self-Control/Self-Denial, Self-Esteem.

SELF-RIGHTEOUSNESS

Most people talk today as if self-righteousness was worse than no righteousness at all. It isn't, according to the Bible, but it is condemned heartily. Why? The Bible is pro-reality and anti-deception, and self-righteousness is a way of deceiving oneself and others (but not God, who sees the heart). It also gives real righteousness a bad name, just as anything counterfeit brings down the value of the real thing. God, the Bible tells us, doesn't want people who strike a moral pose, who seem righteous and admirable. He wants the real thing—in fact, he prefers people who do good things without drawing attention to themselves. In other words, God wants people to be good because they want to be.

The attitude of self-righteousness is neatly summed up in the Bible's phrase "holier than thou." This is found below in the quotation from Isaiah 65.

The way of a fool is right in his own eyes, but he who listens to advice is wise.

PROVERBS 12:15

There is a way that seems right to man, but in the end it leads to death.

PROVERBS 14:12

All the ways of a man are clean in his own eyes; but the LORD weighs the spirits.　　　PROVERBS 16:2

Whoever boasts himself of a gift he does not give is like clouds and wind without rain.　　　PROVERBS 25:14

For men to seek their own glory is not glory.　　　PROVERBS 25:27

Do you see a man wise in his own conceit? There is more hope for a fool than for him.　　　PROVERBS 26:12

He that covers his sins shall not prosper, but whoever confesses and forsakes them shall have mercy.　　　PROVERBS 28:13

He that is of a proud heart stirs up strife, but he who puts his trust in the LORD shall be made prosperous.　　　PROVERBS 28:25

He that trusts in his own heart is a fool, but whoever walks wisely shall be delivered.   PROVERBS 28:26

There is a generation that is pure in their own eyes, and yet is not washed from their filthiness. There is generation—O how lofty are their eyes! and their eyelids are lifted up.   PROVERBS 30:12–13

Woe to those who call evil good, and good evil, who put darkness for light, and light for darkness, who put bitter for sweet, and sweet for bitter! Woe to those who are wise in their own eyes, and shrewd in their own sight!

ISAIAH 5:20–21

We are all like an unclean thing, and all our righteousnesses are as filthy rags, and we all fade as a leaf; and our wrongdoings, like the wind, have taken us away.   ISAIAH 64:6

These are a people that provoke me to anger continually to my face . . . who say, "Stand by yourself, come not near me; for I am holier than thou."

ISAIAH 65:3–5

Judge not, so that you may not be judged. For with the judgment you make you shall be judged, and the measure you give shall be the measure you receive.   MATTHEW 7:1–2

How can you say to your brother, "Let me pull out the speck out of your eye," and, behold, a plank is in your own eye? You hypocrite, first take out the plank from your own eye, and then shall you see clearly to take out the speck from your brother's eye.   MATTHEW 7:3–5

Many will say to me in that day, "Lord, Lord, have we not prophesied in your name? And in your name have we not cast demons? And in your name done many wonderful works?" And then will I profess to them, "I never knew you; depart from me, you evildoers."   MATTHEW 7:22–23

It came to pass, as Jesus sat at food in the house, behold, many tax collectors and sinners came and sat down with him and his disciples. And when the Pharisees saw it, they said to his disciples, "Why does your Master eat

with tax collectors and sinners?" But when Jesus heard that, he said to
them, "They that are whole need not a physician, but they that are sick. But
go and learn what that means, 'I will have mercy, and not sacrifice,' for I am
not come to call the righteous, but sinners to repentance."

MATTHEW 9:10–13

Woe to you, scribes and Pharisees, hypocrites! For you are like whitewashed
tombs, which indeed appear beautiful outwardly, but inside are full of dead
men's bones, and of all uncleanness. MATTHEW 23:27

Woe to you, scribes and Pharisees, hypocrites! Because you build the tombs
of the prophets and decorate the sepulchres of the righteous, and you say, 'If
we had been in the days of our fathers, we would not have been partakers
with them in the blood of the prophets.' MATTHEW 23:29–30

Jesus said to them, "You are the ones who justify yourselves before men; but
God knows your hearts, for what is highly esteemed among men is abomination in the sight of God." LUKE 16:15

Jesus spoke this parable to those who trusted in themselves that they were
righteous, and despised others: "Two men went up into the temple to pray,
one a Pharisee, and the other a tax collector. The Pharisee stood and prayed
thus with himself, 'God, I thank you, so that I am not like other men are,
robbers, evildoers, adulterers, or like this tax collector. I fast twice a week, I
give tithes of all that I possess.' And the tax collector, standing far off,
would not lift up so much as his eyes to heaven, but beat his breast, saying,
'God, be merciful to me, a sinner.' I tell you, this man went to his house justified rather than the other, for everyone that exalts himself shall be abased,
and he who humbles himself shall be exalted." LUKE 18:9–14

He that glories, let him glory in the Lord. For it is not he who commends
himself is approved, but him whom the Lord commends.

2 CORINTHIANS 10:17–18

If a man think himself to be something, when he is nothing, he deceives
himself. GALATIANS 6:3

By grace are you saved through faith, and that not of yourselves; it is the gift of God—not of works, lest any man boast.   EPHESIANS 2:8–9

See also Hypocrisy, Judging Others, Righteousness, Self-Esteem.

SEXUALITY

If sex were nothing more than bodily friction, it would probably not be debated endlessly as it is. But, try as we might to exclude it, emotion somehow gets into the picture, and we are faced with that awkward and age-old problem: What good is sex without love? True, some people can enjoy mechanical, impersonal, meaningless sex. But aside from the physical risks (which are considerable!), this type of sex is far from ideal—in fact, so far from the ideal that multitudes of people through the centuries were willing to postpone sexual intimacy until they found it in the emotional intimacy of marriage. Does this sound quaint? Granted, it is rarer than it was, and so is total fidelity to one's spouse. No matter: The Bible makes no apologies for having a higher sexual morality than the human race at large.

By the way, the Bible is not anti-sex. The fact that an erotically charged book like the Song of Solomon is part of the Bible proves that. But the Bible views sex as too noble and beautiful a thing, too rich an experience, to be reduced to merely a physical technique or recreation. Far from being anti-sex, the Bible is pro-sexuality-in-all-its-emotionally-intimate-splendor.

By means of a whorish woman a man is reduced to a piece of bread, and the adulteress will prey on your precious life.   PROVERBS 6:26

A whore is a deep ditch, and a wayward woman is a narrow well.

          PROVERBS 23:27

Whoever loves wisdom rejoices his father, but he who keeps company with prostitutes wastes his substance.   PROVERBS 29:3

Those things which come from the mouth come forth from the heart, and they defile the man. For out of the heart proceed evil thoughts, murders, adulteries, fornications, thefts, false witness, blasphemies.

MATTHEW 15:17–19

The wrath of God is revealed from heaven against all ungodliness and unrighteousness of men who hold the truth in unrighteousness. For what may be known about God is clearly revealed, since God has shown it to them. For since the creation of the world, the invisible things of him, his eternal power and Godhead, are clearly seen, being understood by the things he has made. So they are without excuse; for when they knew God, they glorified him not as God, nor were thankful; but they became futile in their thoughts, and their foolish hearts were darkened. Professing themselves to be wise, they became fools. . . .

Therefore God gave them up to uncleanness through the lusts of their own hearts, to dishonor their own bodies between themselves. . . . God gave them up to vile affections, for even their women exchanged the natural use into what is against nature. And likewise also the men, leaving the natural use of the woman, burned in their lust toward one another; men with men doing what is shameful, and receiving in themselves the appropriate recompense for their error. And just as they did not like to retain God in their knowledge, God gave them over to a depraved mind, to do those things which should never be done.

ROMANS 1:18–22, 24, 26–28

They that live according to the sinful nature set their minds on the things of the sinful nature; but they that live according to the Spirit set their minds on the things of the Spirit. For to be carnally minded is death; but to be spiritually minded is life and peace. The carnal mind is hostile toward God, for it is not subject to the law of God, neither can be. So then they that are in the sinful nature cannot please God. But you are not in the sinful nature, but in the Spirit, if the Spirit of God dwells in you. Now if any man have not the Spirit of Christ, he is none of his. For if you live after the sinful nature, you shall die; but if you through the Spirit put to death the deeds of the body, you shall live.

ROMANS 8:5–9, 13

I wrote to you in a letter not to keep company with the sexually immoral— not referring to the immoral of this world, or the covetous, or swindlers, or idolaters, since you would then have to leave the world. But now I write to you not to keep company with any man that is called a brother, if he be sexually immoral, or covetous, or an idolater, or a drunkard, or a swindler; with such a one have no fellowship. I CORINTHIANS 5:9–11

Know you not that the unrighteous shall not inherit the kingdom of God? Be not deceived—neither fornicators, nor idolaters, nor adulterers, nor homosexuals, nor abusers of themselves with mankind, nor thieves, nor covetous, nor drunkards, nor slanderers, nor swindlers shall inherit the kingdom of God. And such were some of you. But you are washed, you are sanctified, you are justified in the name of the Lord Jesus and by the Spirit of our God.

Know you not that your bodies are the members of Christ? Shall I then take the members of Christ, and make them the members of a prostitute? God forbid. . . . Flee fornication. Every sin that a man does is outside his, but he who commits fornication sins against his own body.

I CORINTHIANS 6:9–11, 15–18

To avoid fornication, let every man have his own wife, and let every woman have her own husband. I CORINTHIANS 7:2

This I say then: walk in the Spirit, and you shall not fulfill the lust of the sinful nature. GALATIANS 5:16

Now the works of the sinful nature are plain, which are these; adultery, fornication, uncleanness, debauchery . . . those who do such things shall not inherit the kingdom of God. GALATIANS 5:19–21

He that sows to please his sinful nature shall reap corruption; but he who sows to please the Spirit shall reap life everlasting. GALATIANS 6:8

Fornication, and all uncleanness, or covetousness, let it not even be mentioned among you, as becomes saints. EPHESIANS 5:3

This you know, that no whoremonger, nor unclean person, nor covetous man, nor an idolater has any inheritance in the kingdom of Christ and of God. EPHESIANS 5:5

Try to discern what is acceptable to the Lord. And have no fellowship with the unfruitful works of darkness, but rather expose them. For it is a shame even to speak of those things which are done by them in secret. But all things that are reproved are exposed by the light.　　EPHESIANS 5:10–13

Put to death whatever in you is earthy—fornication, uncleanness, inordinate affection, evil immorality, and covetousness, which is idolatry. Because of these things the wrath of God comes on the children of disobedience. These are the ways you followed when you were living among them. But now you also put off all these—anger, wrath, malice, blasphemy, filthy communication out of your mouth. Lie not one to another, seeing that you have put off the old man with his deeds and have put on the new man, which is renewed in knowledge after the image of him that created him.

COLOSSIANS 3:5–10

This is the will of God, your sanctification, that you should abstain from fornication.　　I THESSALONIANS 4:3

In that he himself [Christ] was tempted, he is able to comfort those who are tempted.　　HEBREWS 2:18

We have not a high priest [Christ] who cannot be touched with the feeling of our frailties; but he was in all points tempted like we are, yet without sin.

HEBREWS 4:15

Marriage is honorable in all, and the bed undefiled, but whoremongers and adulterers God will judge.　　HEBREWS 13:4

There shall by no means enter into it [heaven] anything that is impure, nor anything loathsome or deceitful, but only those whose names are written in the Lamb's book of life.　　REVELATION 21:27

Blessed are they that do his commandments, that they may have access to the tree of life and may enter through the gates into the city. For outside are the dogs, and sorcerers, and whoremongers, and murderers, and idolaters, and whoever loves and makes a lie.　　REVELATION 22:14–15

See also Adultery, The Body, Self-Control/Self-Denial, Temptation.

SICKNESS

Medical science has made amazing strides in curing and preventing a multitude of sicknesses. Some illnesses that were certain death a hundred years ago are now practically unheard of. Even so, some things are still beyond cure, and we have no guarantee that every sickness has a solution. (Even if this ever occurred, we would face the problem of the gradual decline of an aging population.) Medical science was hardly a science at all in biblical times, so the best way of treating a sick person was to make him or her comfortable and pray to God. We can do much more than that now, of course, but no doctor worth his or her salt ever rules out the role of faith or the role of miracles in healing. Even unbelieving doctors admit that people of faith have an advantage in any healing process, just as they admit that some people who seemed certain to die made an amazing recovery—"cause of cure unknown," except, perhaps, to the eye of faith.

This is my comfort in my affliction, for your word has made me alive.

PSALM 119:50

Heal me, O LORD, and I shall be healed; save me, and I shall be saved, for you are my praise. JEREMIAH 17:14

I will restore health to you, and I will heal your wounds, says the LORD.

JEREMIAH 30:17

When Jesus had called to him his twelve disciples, he gave them power against evil spirits, to cast them out, and to heal all manner of sickness and all manner of disease. MATTHEW 10:1

Heal the sick, cleanse the lepers, raise the dead, cast out demons; freely you have received, freely give. MATTHEW 10:8

The Spirit of the Lord is upon me, because he has anointed me to preach the gospel to the poor; he has sent me to heal the brokenhearted, to preach deliverance to the captives, and recovering of sight to the blind, to set at liberty those who are oppressed. LUKE 4:18

As Jesus passed by, he saw a man who had been blind from birth. And his disciples asked him, "Master, who sinned, this man, or his parents, so that he was born blind?" Jesus answered, "Neither this man sinned, nor his parents; but this happened so that the works of God should be revealed in him."

JOHN 9:1–3

Peter and John went together to the temple at the hour of prayer, being the ninth hour. And a certain man lame from birth was carried, whom they laid daily at the Beautiful Gate of the temple, to ask alms of those who entered into the temple. Seeing Peter and John about to go into the temple, he asked them for alms. And Peter, fixing his gaze upon him, along with John, said, "Look at us." And he gave heed to them, expecting to receive something of them. Then Peter said, "Silver and gold have I none, but such as I have give I you: In the name of Jesus Christ of Nazareth, rise up and walk." And he took him by the right hand, and lifted him up, and immediately his feet and ankle bones received strength.

ACTS 3:1–7

There are diversities of gifts, but the same Spirit. And there are differences of services, but the same Lord. And there are diversities of activities, but it is the same God who works all in all. But the manifestation of the Spirit is given to every man to profit all.

For to one is given by the Spirit the word of wisdom; to another the word of knowledge by the same Spirit; to another faith by the same Spirit; to another the gifts of healing by the same Spirit; to another the working of miracles; to another prophecy; to another discerning of spirits; to another various kinds of tongues; to another the interpretation of tongues. But in all these work that one and the selfsame Spirit, allotting to every man individually as he chooses.

1 CORINTHIANS 12:4–11

Though our outward man perish, yet the inward man is renewed day by day.

2 CORINTHIANS 4:16

We know that if this earthly tent we live in is destroyed, we have a building from God, a house not made with hands, eternal in the heavens. For in this tent we groan, earnestly desiring to be clothed with our dwelling from heaven. . . . For we who are in this tent do groan, being burdened, for we wish not to be unclothed but to be further clothed, so that mortality might be swallowed up by life. Now he who has made us for this very thing is God, who also has given to us the guarantee of the Spirit. Therefore we are always confident, knowing that, while we are at home in the body, we are absent from the Lord. (For we walk by faith, not by sight.)

2 CORINTHIANS 5:1–7

To keep me from being too exalted through the abundance of the revelations, there was given to me a thorn in the flesh, the messenger of Satan to torment me, lest I should be exalted above measure. For this thing I appealed to the Lord three times, that it might depart from me. And he said to me, "My grace is sufficient for you, for my strength is made perfect in weakness." Most gladly therefore will I glory in my infirmities, that the power of Christ may rest upon me. Therefore I take pleasure in infirmities, in insults, in hardships, in persecutions, in calamities for Christ's sake, for when I am weak, then am I strong.

2 CORINTHIANS 12:7–10

Is any among you afflicted? Let him pray. Is any merry? Let him sing psalms. Is any sick among you? Let him call for the elders of the church, and let them pray over him, anointing him with oil in the name of the Lord. And the prayer of faith shall save the sick, and the Lord shall raise him up, and if he has committed sins, they shall be forgiven him.

JAMES 5:13–15

Confess your faults one to another, and pray one for another, so that you may be healed. The fervent prayer of a righteous man is powerful and effective.

JAMES 5:16

See also The Body, Comfort in Times of Trouble, Eternal Life, God's Love, Healing, Patience.

SIN AND REDEMPTION

Talk shows on television and radio bring up a thousand different grievances that human beings have against one another, and no matter what horrible thing has been done, no one refers to it as a "sin." But if the word sin has gone out of style, the idea hasn't. Amid all the yelling and name-calling, a theme comes through: One person, through selfishness, neglected or abused another. In other words, an "I" cared more for its own desires than for the welfare of others.

This is, basically, the Bible's view of sin: selfishness. It is a kind of idolatry, worshiping and serving one's own ego at the expense of others (and of God, who is the only thing worth truly worshiping). This is sin (singular), the root problem, which results in all kinds of selfish and immoral acts, the sins (plural). The Bible is concerned about both. A key theme is that all human beings need to be set free from sin—redeemed, to use the Bible's word. It is as if people are so mired in their own selfishness that they can't just "improve themselves out of it" but need divine aid. According to the New Testament, Jesus is God's answer to the sin problem.

Psalm 51, below, is attributed to Israel's King David, caught in his adultery. The psalm is one of the most touching, heartfelt confessions of sin in the world—the Bible's great "sin song," which not only confesses sin but also asks for and expects redemption from God.

Be sure your sin will find you out.   NUMBERS 32:23

They have all gone astray, they have all together become filthy; there is none that does good, no, not one.   PSALM 14:3

Have mercy upon me, O God, according to your lovingkindness; according to the multitude of your tender mercies, blot out my offenses. Wash me thoroughly from my iniquity, and cleanse me from my sin. For I acknowledge my offenses, and my sin is ever before me. Against you, you only, have I sinned, and done this evil in your sight; that you might be justified when you speak, and be blameless when you pass judgment. Behold, I was formed in iniquity, and in sin did my mother conceive me. Behold, you desire truth in the inward being, and in the hidden part you shall make me to know wisdom.

Purge me with hyssop, and I shall be clean. Wash me, and I shall be whiter than snow. Make me to hear joy and gladness; let the bones which you have broken rejoice. Hide your face from my sins, and blot out all my iniquities. Create in me a clean heart, O God, and renew a right spirit within me. Cast me not away from your presence, and take not your Holy Spirit from me. Restore to me the joy of your salvation, and uphold me with your free spirit. Then will I teach transgressors your ways, and sinners shall be converted to you.   PSALM 51:1–13

There is not a just man upon earth, who does good, and sins not.

ECCLESIASTES 7:20

"Wash yourselves, make yourselves clean; put away the evil of your doings out of my sight; cease to do evil; learn to do good; seek justice, relieve the oppressed, defend the fatherless, plead for the widow. Come now, and let us reason together," says the LORD; "though your sins be like scarlet, they shall be as white as snow; though they be red like crimson, they shall be like wool."

ISAIAH 1:16–18

All we like sheep have gone astray; we have turned everyone to his own way, and the LORD has laid on him the iniquity of us all.

ISAIAH 53:6

Your iniquities have separated you and your God, and your sins have hid his face from you, so that he will not hear.

ISAIAH 59:2

We are all like an unclean thing, and all our righteousnesses are as filthy rags, and we all fade as a leaf, and our wrongdoings, like the wind, have taken us away.

ISAIAH 64:6

Can the Ethiopian change his skin, or the leopard his spots? Neither can you do good, you that are accustomed to do evil.

JEREMIAH 13:23

The heart is deceitful above all things, and desperately wicked; who can understand it?

JEREMIAH 17:9

The soul that sins, it shall die.

EZEKIEL 18:4

When Jesus heard it, he said to them, "They that are well have no need of a physician, but they that are sick; I came not to call the righteous, but sinners to repentance."

MARK 2:17

Jesus spoke this parable to those who trusted in themselves that they were righteous, and despised others: "Two men went up into the temple to pray, one a Pharisee, and the other a tax collector. The Pharisee stood and prayed thus with himself, 'God, I thank you, so that I am not like other men are, robbers, evildoers, adulterers, or like this tax collector. I fast twice a week, I give tithes of all that I possess.' And the tax collector, standing far off, would not lift up so much as his eyes to heaven, but beat his breast, saying, 'God, be merciful to me, a sinner.' I tell you, this man went to his house justified rather than the other, for everyone that exalts himself shall be abased, and he who humbles himself shall be exalted."   LUKE 18:9–14

John saw Jesus coming to him, and said, "Behold the Lamb of God, who takes away the sin of the world."   JOHN 1:29

The wrath of God is revealed from heaven against all ungodliness and unrighteousness of men who hold the truth in unrighteousness. For what may be known about God is clearly revealed, since God has shown it to them. For since the creation of the world, the invisible things of him, his eternal power and Godhead, are clearly seen, being understood by the things he has made. So they are without excuse; for when they knew God, they glorified him not as God, nor were thankful; but they became futile in their thoughts, and their foolish hearts were darkened. Professing themselves to be wise, they became fools. And they exchanged the glory of the eternal God for images made to look like mortal man and birds and animals and reptiles. Therefore God gave them up to uncleanness through the lusts of their own hearts, to dishonor their own bodies between themselves. They changed the truth of God into a lie, and worshipped and served the creature more than the Creator.   ROMANS 1:18–25

All have sinned, and come short of the glory of God, being justified freely by his grace through the redemption that is in Christ Jesus, whom God put forward as a sacrifice of atonement by faith in his blood.

ROMANS 3:23–24

Jesus was delivered for our offenses, and was raised again for our justification.   ROMANS 4:25

God demonstrates his love toward us, in that while we were still sinners, Christ died for us.   ROMANS 5:8

Our old self is crucified with him, so that the body of sin might be destroyed, and that from now on should not serve sin. For sin shall not have

Calvin Coolidge, America's thirtieth president, was notoriously tightlipped. Leaving church one Sunday, he was asked what the preacher had preached on. He replied, "Sin." Asked what the preacher had said about it, Coolidge stated, "He was against it."

dominion over you, for you are not under the law, but under grace. Being made free from sin, you became the servants of righteousness. For the wages of sin is death; but the gift of God is eternal life through Jesus Christ our Lord.   ROMANS 6:6, 14, 18, 23

God was in Christ, reconciling the world to himself, not counting men's sins against them. For he has made him to be sin for us, who knew no sin; that we might be made the righteousness of God in him.
                                                     2 CORINTHIANS 5:19, 21

This is a faithful saying, and worthy of full acceptance, that Christ Jesus came into the world to save sinners.   I TIMOTHY 1:15

The prayer of faith shall save the sick, and the Lord shall raise him up, and if he has committed sins, they shall be forgiven him.   JAMES 5:15

If we walk in the light, as he is in the light, we have fellowship one with another, and the blood of Jesus Christ his Son cleanses us from all sin. If we say that we have no sin, we deceive ourselves, and the truth is not in us. If we confess our sins, he is faithful and just to forgive us our sins, and to cleanse us from all unrighteousness. If we say that we have not sinned, we make him a liar, and his word is not in us.   I JOHN 1:7–10

See also Confession, Justification, Repentance, Righteousness, Salvation, Self-Righteousness.

SPIRITUAL POWER

When Jesus told the Roman governor Pontius Pilate, "My kingdom is not of this world," he was summing up the Bible's view of power. Pilate represented an empire based on military might, on power rooted in the desire to dominate others. Jesus represented something greater and more enduring: spiritual power rooted in compassion. Rome had the power to crucify Jesus, and it did so. Jesus had a greater power: He forgave those who crucified him. He also performed miracles of healing and exorcism, miracles performed not for show but for the genuine love of those who benefited from those miracles.

Jesus' followers were, as he predicted, also able to draw upon spiritual power to benefit humankind. The power "not of this world" is still being manifested, not only in miracles of healing but in countless acts of compassion as well.

He gives power to the weary, and to those who have no might he increases strength. Even the youths shall faint and be weary, and the young men shall utterly fall; but they that wait upon the LORD shall renew their strength; they shall mount up with wings as eagles; they shall run, and not be weary, and they shall walk, and not faint. ISAIAH 40:29–31

"Not by might, nor by power, but by my Spirit," says the LORD Almighty. ZECHARIAH 4:6

When Jesus had called to him his twelve disciples, he gave them power against evil spirits, to cast them out, and to heal all manner of sickness and all manner of disease. MATTHEW 10:1

The blind receive their sight, and the lame walk, the lepers are cleansed, and the deaf hear, the dead are raised up, and the poor have the gospel preached to them. MATTHEW 11:5

If you have faith the size of a mustard seed, you shall say to this mountain, "Move from here to yonder place," and it shall move, and nothing shall be impossible to you. MATTHEW 17:20

Evil spirits, when they saw him, fell down before him, and cried, saying, "You are the Son of God." MARK 3:11

Jesus said to them, "Go into all the world, and preach the gospel to every creature. He that believes and is baptized shall be saved; he who believes not shall be damned. And these signs shall follow those who believe; in my name shall they cast out demons; they shall speak with new tongues; they shall handle serpents, and if they drink any deadly poison, it shall not hurt them; they shall lay hands on the sick, and they shall recover." After the Lord had spoken to them, he was taken up into heaven, and sat on the right hand of God. And they went forth, and preached everywhere, the Lord working with them, and confirming the word with signs following.

MARK 16:15–20

The Spirit of the Lord is upon me, because he has anointed me to preach the gospel to the poor; he has sent me to heal the brokenhearted, to preach deliverance to the captives, and recovering of sight to the blind, to set at liberty those who are oppressed. LUKE 4:18

They were all amazed, and spoke among themselves, saying, "What is this teaching! With authority and power he commands the evil spirits, and they come out." LUKE 4:36

The man out of whom the demons had departed begged Jesus that he might stay with him, but Jesus sent him away, saying, "Return to your house, and show the great things God has done for you." And he went his way and published throughout the whole city the great things Jesus had done for him.

LUKE 8:38–39

The Lord appointed seventy others also, and sent them two by two ahead of him into every city and place that he himself would go. . . . The Seventy returned again with joy, saying, "Lord, even the demons are subject to us through your name." And he said to them, "I beheld Satan fall like lightning from heaven. Behold, I give to you power to tread on serpents and scorpions, and over all the power of the enemy, and nothing shall by any means hurt you. Nevertheless, do not rejoice that the spirits are subject to you, but rather rejoice because your names are written in heaven."

LUKE 10:1, 17–20

If I with the finger of God cast out demons, no doubt the kingdom of God is come upon you.   LUKE 11:20

You shall receive power after the Holy Spirit is come upon you, and you shall be witnesses to me both in Jerusalem, and in all Judea, and in Samaria, and to the uttermost parts of the earth.   ACTS 1:8

Fear came upon every soul, and many wonders and signs were done by the apostles.   ACTS 2:43

There came a multitude from the cities near Jerusalem, bringing sick folks and those who were vexed with evil spirits, and they were healed every one.
                                                                          ACTS 5:16

God anointed Jesus of Nazareth with the Holy Spirit and with power. He went about doing good, and healing all that were oppressed by the devil; for God was with him.   ACTS 10:38

The preaching of the cross is foolishness to those who perish; but to us who are saved it is the power of God. For it is written, "I will destroy the wisdom of the wise, and will bring to nothing the understanding of the prudent."
                                                            I CORINTHIANS 1:18-19

My speech and my preaching was not with persuasive words of man's wisdom, but with demonstration of the Spirit and of power, so that your faith should not rest on man's wisdom but on the power of God.
                                                              I CORINTHIANS 2:4-5

The kingdom of God is not in word, but in power.
                                                               I CORINTHIANS 4:20

Now there are diversities of gifts, but the same Spirit. And there are differences of services, but the same Lord. And there are diversities of activities, but it is the same God who works all in all. But the manifestation of the Spirit is given to every man to profit all.

  For to one is given by the Spirit the word of wisdom; to another the word of knowledge by the same Spirit; to another faith by the same Spirit; to another the gifts of healing by the same Spirit; to another the working of miracles; to another prophecy; to another discerning of spirits; to another various kinds of tongues; to another the interpretation of tongues. But in all these work that one and the selfsame Spirit, allotting to every man individually as he chooses.   1 CORINTHIANS 12:4–11

We have this treasure in earthen vessels, so that the excellency of the power may be of God and not of us.   2 CORINTHIANS 4:7

The weapons of our warfare are not earthly, but are mighty through God to the pulling down of strongholds.   2 CORINTHIANS 10:4

The Lord said to me, "My grace is sufficient for you, for my strength is made perfect in weakness." Most gladly will I glory in my frailties, so that the power of Christ may rest upon me.   2 CORINTHIANS 12:9

Our gospel came not to you in word only, but also in power, and in the Holy Spirit, and in much assurance.   1 THESSALONIANS 1:5

God has not given us the spirit of fear; but of power, and of love, and of a sound mind.   2 TIMOTHY 1:7

Confess your faults one to another, and pray one for another, so that you may be healed. The fervent prayer of a righteous man is powerful and effective.   JAMES 5:16

His divine power has given us all things that pertain to life and godliness, through the knowledge of him that has called us to glory and virtue. Thus he has given us exceedingly great and precious promises, so that by these you might be sharers in the divine nature, having escaped the corruption that is in the world through lust.

Add to your faith virtue, and to virtue add knowledge; and to knowledge add self-control; and to self-control add patience; and to patience add godliness; and to godliness add brotherly kindness; and to brotherly kindness add love.   2 PETER 1:3–7

See also Angels, God's Guidance, Healing, The Holy Spirit, Power.

SUCCESS

Everyone wants to be a success—the question is, A successful what? A successful moneymaker? Spouse? Parent? Entrepreneur? Athlete? Envy of the neighborhood? While there is nothing wrong with setting such goals in life and pursuing those goals, the Bible has a different view of success. The only real success, ultimately, is being a good and moral person. While achieving this will never merit a cover story in Time, *it may bring the greatest satisfaction of all. There are plenty of true stories of people who sought and achieved worldly success but then found themselves unsatisfied and restless. What about the stories of people who sought to live in a loving relationship with their fellow man and with God? The stories of those anonymous people are never told, but perhaps they should be.*

Wise men die, likewise the fool and the senseless perish, and leave their wealth to others. Their inward thought is that their houses shall continue forever, and their dwelling places to all generations; they call their lands after their own names. Nevertheless man, despite his honors, abides not; he is like the beasts that perish. Such is the fate of the foolish, and of their followers who approve their sayings. Like sheep they are laid in the grave; death shall feed on them; and the upright shall have dominion over them in the morning; and their beauty shall decay in the grave, far from their dwelling. But God will redeem my soul from the power of the grave; for he shall receive me.

Be not afraid when one is made rich, when the glory of his house is increased, for when he dies he shall carry nothing with him; his glory shall not descend with him. Though while he lived he was counted as blessed—and men will praise you when you prosper—he shall go to the generation of his fathers; they shall never see light. Man that is held in honor and lacking in understanding is like the beasts that perish. PSALM 49:10–20

Incline my heart to your commandments, and not to covetousness. Turn away my eyes from beholding worthless things. PSALM 119:36–37

Grant not, O LORD, the desires of the wicked; further not his wicked plans, lest they become proud. PSALM 140:8

Without advice plans are thwarted, but with many advisors they are established.   PROVERBS 15:22

Commit your works to the LORD, and your plans shall succeed.

PROVERBS 16:3

There is no wisdom nor understanding nor plan that can succeed against the LORD.   PROVERBS 21:30

I communed with my own heart, saying, "I have come to great estate, and have gotten more wisdom than all they that were before me in Jerusalem." Indeed, my heart had great experience of wisdom and knowledge. And I gave my heart to know wisdom, and to understand madness and folly; I perceived that this also is a chasing after the wind. For in much wisdom is much grief, and he who increases knowledge increases sorrow.

ECCLESIASTES 1:16–18

I made great works; I built houses; I planted vineyards; I was great, and increased more than all that were before me in Jerusalem; and my wisdom remained with me. And whatever my eyes desired I kept not from them; I withheld not my heart from any joy; for my heart rejoiced in all my labor, and this was my portion of all my labor.

Then I looked on all the works that my hands had made, and on the labor that I had labored to do, and, behold, all was meaningless, a chasing after the wind, and there was no profit under the sun.

ECCLESIASTES 2:4, 9–11

The desire accomplished is sweet to the soul.   JOEL 13:19

Then was Jesus led by the Spirit into the wilderness to be tempted by the devil. . . . The devil took him to an exceedingly high mountain, and showed him all the kingdoms of the world, and their glory. And he said to him, "All these things will I give you, if you will fall down and worship me." Then said Jesus to him, "Get away, Satan, for it is written, 'You shall worship the Lord your God, and him only shall you serve.'"

MATTHEW 4:1, 8–10

What is a man profited, if he shall gain the whole world, and lose his own soul? Or what shall a man give in exchange for his soul?

MATTHEW 16:26

Jesus sat down, and called the twelve disciples, and said to them, "If any man desire to be first, the same shall be last of all, and servant of all."

MARK 9:35

Woe to you that are rich! For you have received your consolation. Woe to you that are full! For you shall hunger. Woe to you that laugh now! For you shall mourn and weep.

LUKE 6:24–25

Take heed, and beware of covetousness, for a man's life consists not in the abundance of the things he possesses.

LUKE 12:15

I am come that they might have life, and that they might have it more abundantly.

JOHN 10:10

He that loves his life shall lose it, and he who hates his life in this world shall keep it to life eternal.

JOHN 12:25

If you were of the world, the world would love its own, but because you are not of the world, but I have chosen you out of the world, the world hates you.

JOHN 15:19

Jesus answered, "My kingdom is not of this world. If my kingdom were of this world, then my servants would fight, so that I should not be delivered to the Jews; but now is my kingdom not from here."

JOHN 18:36

Be not conformed to this world, but be transformed by the renewing of your mind.

ROMANS 12:2

Where is the wise? Where is the scribe? Where is the debater of this age? Has not God made foolish the wisdom of this world?

I CORINTHIANS 1:20

Let no man deceive himself. If any man among you seem to be wise in this world, let him become a fool, that he may be wise. For the wisdom of this world is foolishness with God. For it is written, "He catches the wise in their own craftiness." And again, "The Lord knows the thoughts of the wise, that they are futile." Therefore let no man glory in men.

I CORINTHIANS 3:18–20

You are bought with a price; do not be the slaves of men.

I CORINTHIANS 7:23

We are those that use this world, yet are not caught up in it, for the world in its present form is passing away.   I CORINTHIANS 7:31

From now on we regard no man from a human point of view. Though we knew Christ from the human point of view, we no longer know him in this way. If any man be in Christ, he is a new creature; old things have passed away—behold, all things have become new. And all things are from God, who has reconciled us to himself through Jesus Christ, and has given to us the ministry of reconciliation.   2 CORINTHIANS 5:16–18

God forbid that I should glory, except in the cross of our Lord Jesus Christ, by whom the world is crucified to me, and I to the world.

GALATIANS 6:14

Command those who are rich in this world that they be not arrogant, nor trust in uncertain riches, but in the living God, who gives us richly all things to enjoy. Command that they do good, so that they be rich in good works, ready to distribute, willing to share, laying up in store for themselves a good foundation against the time to come, so that they may lay hold of eternal life.   I TIMOTHY 6:17–19

My beloved brethren, has not God chosen the poor of this world to be rich in faith, and heirs of the kingdom which he has promised to those who love him?   JAMES 2:5

Know you not that the friendship of the world is enmity with God? Whoever will be a friend of the world is the enemy of God.

JAMES 4:4

His divine power has given to us all things we need for life and godliness, through the knowledge of him that has called us to glory and virtue. Through these he has given us exceedingly great and precious promises, that by these you might share in the divine nature, having escaped the corruption that is in the world through lust.   2 PETER 1:3–4

Love not the world, neither the things that are in the world. If any man love the world, the love of the Father is not in him. For all that is in the world, the cravings of the sinful nature, and the lust of the eyes, and the pride of life, is not of the Father, but is of the world. And the world passes away, and all its lusts, but he who does the will of God abides forever.

1 JOHN 2:15–17

See also Ambition, Laziness, Self-Esteem, Work, Worry.

TEMPTATION

We might gather from the media that the worst temptation that faces contemporary man is the temptation to eat something fattening. Is a calorierich dessert really the worst thing Satan can tempt us with? The Bible takes a more sober view of this subject: Our baser impulses, or Satan, or perhaps both, frequently coax us to do what is selfish and then hang the consequences on ourselves or others. The result? Aside from gaining a few extra pounds (which the Bible doesn't treat with the same seriousness, as we moderns do), we fall into the pattern of taking the easy way out morally, of growing lazy on the inside, and of never saying "No" to ourselves, even when we know we should.

Jesus himself was tempted, but he resisted successfully. So can we, according to the Bible, but how many people seek out the promised divine help when faced with a temptation?

Beware that you forget not the LORD your God, in not keeping his commandments, and his judgments, and his statutes, which I command you this day; lest when you have eaten and are full, and have built goodly houses, and dwell in them, and when your herds and your flocks multiply, and your silver and your gold is multiplied, and all that you have is multiplied; then your heart be made proud, and you forget the LORD your God, who brought you out of the land of Egypt, from the house of slavery; and you say in your heart, "My power and the might of my hand have gotten me this wealth." But you shall remember the LORD your God, for it is he who gives you power to get wealth, so that he may establish his covenant which he swore to your fathers, as it is this day. DEUTERONOMY 8:11–14, 17–18

My son, if sinners entice you, do not give in. Walk not with them; keep your foot from their path, for their feet run to do evil and make haste to shed blood. PROVERBS 1:10, 15–16

Enter not into the path of the wicked, and go not in the way of evil men.

PROVERBS 4:14

The fear of the LORD is a fountain of life, to depart from the snares of death.

PROVERBS 14:27

Whoever causes the righteous to go astray in an evil way, he shall fall himself into his own pit; but the upright shall have good things to possess.

PROVERBS 28:10

He that walks righteously, and speaks uprightly, who despises the gain of oppressions, who keeps his hands from taking of bribes, who stops his ears against hearing of bloodshed, and shuts his eyes from seeing evil—he shall dwell on high; his place of defense shall be the rocky fortress. Bread shall be given him; his waters shall not fail.

ISAIAH 33:15–16

Enter in at the narrow gate. For wide is the gate and broad is the way that leads to destruction, and many there are who go in that way. But narrow is the gate, and narrow is the way, which leads to life, and few there are that find it.

MATTHEW 7:13–14

Whoever shall cause one of these little ones who believe in me to sin, it were better for him that a millstone were hung about his neck, and that he were drowned in the depth of the sea.

MATTHEW 18:6

Watch and pray, so that you enter not into temptation; the spirit is willing, but the flesh is weak.

MATTHEW 26:41

Sin shall not have dominion over you, for you are not under the law, but under grace.

ROMANS 6:14

The flesh lusts against the Spirit, and the Spirit against the flesh, and the two are contrary to one another; so that you cannot do the things that you wish.

GALATIANS 5:17

Let him that thinks he stands firm take heed lest he fall. There has no temptation overtaken you but such as is common to man. But God is faithful; he will not allow you to be tempted above what you can bear. But with the temptation he will also make a way to escape, so that you may be able to bear it. I CORINTHIANS 10:12–13

Brethren, if a man is caught in a sin, you who are spiritual should restore him in the spirit of meekness. But take care, lest you also be tempted. Bear you one another's burdens, and so fulfill the law of Christ. For if a man think himself to be something, when he is nothing, he deceives himself. GALATIANS 6:1–3

Put on the whole armor of God, so that you may be able to stand against the wiles of the devil. For we struggle not against flesh and blood, but against principalities, against powers, against the rulers of the darkness of this world, against spiritual wickedness in high places. Therefore take up the whole armor of God, so that you may be able to withstand on the evil day, and having done all, to stand firm. Stand therefore, having your waist belted with truth, and having on the breastplate of righteousness, and your feet shod with the preparation of the gospel of peace. Above all, take up the shield of faith, with which you shall be able to quench all the fiery arrows of the wicked. And take the helmet of salvation, and the sword of the Spirit, which is the word of God. EPHESIANS 6:11–17

Since Jesus himself has endured being tempted, he is able to help those who are tempted. HEBREWS 2:18

We have not a high priest who cannot be touched with the feeling of our frailties; but he was in all points tempted as we are, yet without sinning. HEBREWS 4:15

My brethren, count it all joy when you fall into various temptations, knowing that the testing of your faith produces patience. But let patience have its full effect, so that you may be mature and complete, lacking nothing. JAMES 1:2–4

Blessed is the man that endures temptation, for when he is tested, he shall receive the crown of life, which the Lord has promised to those who love him. JAMES 1:12

> *"The New Testament is the best book the world has ever known or ever will know."*
>
> —ENGLISH NOVELIST CHARLES DICKENS, AUTHOR OF *A Christmas Carol, David Copperfield, Great Expectations,* AND OTHER CLASSICS

Let no man say when he is tempted, "I am tempted by God," for God cannot be tempted with evil, neither tempts he any man. But every man is tempted when he is drawn away by his own cravings and enticed. Then when lust has conceived, it brings forth sin; and sin, when it is completed, brings forth death. JAMES 1:13–16

Submit yourselves to God. Resist the devil, and he will flee from you.

JAMES 4:7

The Lord knows how to deliver the godly out of temptations, and to reserve the unjust for punishment on the day of judgment. 2 PETER 2:9

See also Self-Control/Self-Denial, Sin.

THANKFULNESS

We may not mind being ingrates, but we are surely peeved when faced with someone else's ingratitude. According to the Bible, most of mankind falls into the category of ingrates—angry at God when things go wrong but forgetting him completely when things go well. God faces the same problem that we face: hearing more gripes than thank-you's. If being grateful for the good times comes hard for most of us, imagine the difficulty of thanking God for the bad times. Yet some amazing and saintly people have learned to do so, finding that the worst of times do teach us patience and humility.

Interestingly, the Bible presents thankfulness to God as the best motivation for living a good life. Fear of hell or other punishment motivates some people, but what pleases God most is people who live moral lives not because they fear him but because they love him. Of the three kinds of giving—grudge giving, duty giving, and thanksgiving—God prefers the last.

You have turned my mourning into dancing; you have put off my sackcloth and clothed me with gladness; to the end that my glory may sing praise to you, and not be silent. O LORD my God, I will give thanks to you forever.

PSALM 30:11–12

We your people and sheep of your pasture will give you thanks forever; we will show forth your praise to all generations.

PSALM 79:13

It is a good thing to give thanks unto the LORD, and to sing praises unto your name, O Most High; to show forth your lovingkindness in the morning, and your faithfulness every night; upon an instrument of ten strings, and upon the lyre, upon the harp with a solemn sound. For you, LORD, have made me glad through your work. I will triumph in the works of your hands.

PSALM 92:1–4

Make a joyful noise to the LORD, all you lands. Enter into his gates with thanksgiving, and into his courts with praise; be thankful to him, and bless his name.

PSALM 100:1, 4

Bless the LORD, O my soul, and all that is within me, bless his holy name. Bless the LORD, O my soul, and forget not all his benefits; he forgives all your iniquities; he heals all your diseases; he redeems your life from destruction; he crowns you with lovingkindness and tender mercies. He satisfies your mouth with good things, so that your youth is renewed like the eagle's.

PSALM 103:1–5

Praise you the LORD. O give thanks to the LORD; for he is good, for his mercy endures forever. PSALM 106:1

I have come that they might have life, and that they might have it more abundantly. JOHN 10:10

Thanks be to God, who gives us the victory through our Lord Jesus Christ. I CORINTHIANS 15:57

Thanks be to God, who always causes us to triumph in Christ, and through us in every place spreads the sweet savor of his knowledge. 2 CORINTHIANS 2:14

You shall be enriched in every way for your generosity, which will produce thanksgiving to God. 2 CORINTHIANS 9:11

Speak to yourselves in psalms and hymns and spiritual songs, singing and making melody in your heart to the Lord. Give thanks always for all things to God and the Father in the name of our Lord Jesus Christ. EPHESIANS 5:19–20

Be anxious for nothing, but in everything by prayer and supplication with thanksgiving let your requests be made known to God. And the peace of God, which passes all understanding, will keep your hearts and minds in Christ Jesus. PHILIPPIANS 4:6

Give thanks to the Father, who has made us fit to be partakers of the inheritance of the saints in light. COLOSSIANS 1:12

Let the peace of God rule in your hearts, to which you are called in one body. And be thankful. Let the word of Christ dwell in you richly in all wisdom, teaching and admonishing one another in psalms and hymns and spiritual songs, singing with grace in your hearts to the Lord. COLOSSIANS 3:15–16

Rejoice evermore. Pray without ceasing. In every thing give thanks, for this is the will of God in Christ Jesus concerning you. I THESSALONIANS 5:16–18

Every creature of God is good, and nothing is to be refused if it be received with thanksgiving; for it is made holy by the word of God and prayer.

I TIMOTHY 4:4–5

Every good gift and every perfect gift is from above, and comes down from the Father of lights, with whom is no changing, and no shadow of turning.

JAMES 1:17

See also Fellowship with God, Obeying God, Prayer.

THE TONGUE

Sticks and stones may break our bones, but words can do even worse. Concerning this issue of the harm that can be done by a wayward tongue, we and the Bible are in complete agreement. Unfortunately, our loathing for the harm that other people can do with their tongues doesn't always lead us to modify our own tongues, does it?

One of the Ten Commandments specifically forbids bearing false witness against another person. This shows the importance that God places on truthfulness, on not using words to harm another person. Regrettably, while people take seriously the commandments prohibiting murder, stealing, and adultery, they go on their merry way using criticism and slander to do immeasurable harm. While our society has laws against slander and libel, they go only so far, and no laws can truly prevent the wickedness of malicious words. Control of the tongue lies with the individual.

You shall not bear false witness against your neighbor.

EXODUS 20:16

You shall not go about as a talebearer among your people.

LEVITICUS 19:16

Keep your tongue from evil, and your lips from speaking deceit. Depart from evil, and do good; seek peace, and pursue it. The eyes of the LORD are upon the righteous, and his ears are open to their cry.

PSALM 34:12–15

The words of the wicked man's mouth are smoother than butter, but war is in his heart; his words are softer than oil, yet they are drawn swords.

PSALM 55:21

Swords are in their lips, for they say, "Who can hear us?"   PSALM 59:7

They delight in lies; they bless with their mouths, but inwardly they curse.

PSALM 62:4

Whoever secretly slanders his neighbor, him will I cut off; him that has a haughty look and a proud heart will not I endure.   PSALM 101:5

In the multitude of words there is no lack of sin, but he who controls his lips is wise.   PROVERBS 10:19

He that is void of wisdom despises his neighbor, but a man of understanding holds his peace. A talebearer reveals secrets, but he who is of a faithful spirit keeps a secret.   PROVERBS 11:12–13

There is one who speaks like the piercings of a sword, but the tongue of the wise is health.   PROVERBS 12:18

A soft answer turns away wrath, but harsh words stir up anger.

PROVERBS 15:1

A man finds joy in giving an apt answer, and how good is a word spoken in due season!   PROVERBS 15:23

Pleasant words like a honeycomb, sweet to the soul, and health to the body.

PROVERBS 16:24

A perverse man sows strife, and a whisperer separates close friends.

PROVERBS 16:28

He that has a perverse heart finds no good, and he who has a perverse tongue falls into mischief.   PROVERBS 17:20

A fool's mouth is his destruction, and his lips are the trap of his soul.

PROVERBS 18:7

The words of a talebearer are like wounds, and they go down into the innermost parts.

PROVERBS 18:8

He that goes about as a talebearer reveals secrets; therefore have no dealings with him that flatters with his lips.

PROVERBS 20:19

The north wind brings rain, so a backbiting tongue brings angry looks.

PROVERBS 25:23

Where there is no wood, the fire goes out; where there is no gossip, the strife ceases.

PROVERBS 26:20

Listen to me, you that know righteousness, the people in whose heart is my law: fear not the criticism of men, nor be afraid of their insults. For the moth shall eat them up like a garment, and the worm shall eat them like wool. But my righteousness shall be forever, and my salvation from generation to generation.

ISAIAH 51:7–8

Blessed are you when men shall slander you and persecute you, and shall say all manner of evil against you falsely, for my sake. Rejoice, and be exceedingly glad, for great is your reward in heaven, for so persecuted they the prophets who were before you.

MATTHEW 5:11–12

O generation of vipers, how can you, being evil, speak good things? For out of the abundance of the heart the mouth speaks. A good man out of the good treasure of the heart brings forth good things, and an evil man out of the evil treasure brings forth evil things. But I say to you, so that every idle word that men shall speak, they shall give account of in the day of judgment. For by your words you shall be justified, and by your words you shall be condemned.

MATTHEW 12:33–37

Those things that come out of the mouth come forth from the heart, and they defile the man. For out of the heart proceed evil thoughts, murders,

adulteries, fornications, thefts, false witness, blasphemies: these are the things that defile a man.
                                                    MATTHEW 15:18–20

Whatever you have spoken in darkness shall be heard in the light; and what you have spoken in private shall be proclaimed upon the housetops.
                                                    LUKE 12:3

Let all bitterness and wrath and anger and brawling and evil speaking be put away from you, along with all malice. And be kind one to another, tenderhearted, forgiving one another, just as God for Christ's sake has forgiven you.
                                                    EPHESIANS 4:31–32

Now put off all these; anger, wrath, malice, blasphemy, filthy language out of your mouth. Lie not one to another, seeing that you have put off the old man with his deeds; and have put on the new man, which is renewed in knowledge after the image of him that created him.
                                                    COLOSSIANS 3:8–10

Whatever you do in word or deed, do all in the name of the Lord Jesus.
                                                    COLOSSIANS 3:17

Shun profane and vain babblings, for they will lead to more ungodliness.
                                                    2 TIMOTHY 2:16

If any man among you seem to be religious, and does not control his tongue, but deceives his own heart, this man's religion is worthless.
                                                    JAMES 1:26

We put bits in horses' mouths so that they may obey us, and we direct their whole body. Behold also ships, which though they be so large, and are driven by fierce winds, yet are they guided by a small rudder, wherever the pilot chooses. Even so, the tongue is a little member, yet it boasts great things. Behold, a great forest is set aflame by a little fire! And the tongue is a fire, a world of iniquity; so is the tongue among our members, so that it defiles the whole body, and sets on fire the course of nature, and it is set on fire by hell. For every kind of beasts and birds and serpents and things in the sea is tamed, and has been tamed by mankind, but the tongue can no man tame. It is an unruly evil, full of deadly poison. With it we bless God, even the Father, and with it we curse men, who are made in the image of God. Out of the same mouth proceed blessing and cursing. My brethren, these things ought not to be. JAMES 3:3–10

Speak not evil one of another, brethren. . . . There is one lawgiver, he is able to save and to destroy. Who are you that judge another? JAMES 4:11–12

Lay aside all malice, and all deceit and hypocrisies and envies and all evil speakings. I PETER 2:1

He that will love life, and see good days, let him refrain his tongue from evil, and let his lips speak no deceit. I PETER 3:10

See also Anger, Envy, Hate, Judging Others, Self-Righteousness.

TRENDINESS

An old French proverb says "Vogue without, vague within." Put another way, if you are trendy on the outside, you may be empty on the inside. Not all trends are necessarily bad, of course. God isn't overly concerned about our hairstyles, the width of men's neckties, or the latest food trend. He is concerned, however, with following the crowd in regard to morality. This is the lazy way to maintain morality, certainly the easiest way, since it doesn't call for much decision making on our part. But it has to be the worst way—as Jesus put it, "Wide is the gate and broad is the way that leads to destruction, and many there are that go in that way." What would happen if people could forget about what others would say and ask themselves, "Is this right?" or even "Would this please God?" That, according to the Bible, is the "narrow way" that leads to life.

You shall not follow the crowd to do evil. EXODUS 23:2

You shall not be afraid of the face of man; for judgment is God's. DEUTERONOMY 1:17

Enter not into the path of the wicked, and go not in the way of evil men.

PROVERBS 4:14

Do not call a conspiracy all that this people calls conspiracy; do not fear what it fears, nor be in dread. But the LORD Almighty, him you shall regard as holy, him alone shall you fear and dread.   ISAIAH 8:12–13

Enter in at the narrow gate. For wide is the gate and broad is the way that leads to destruction, and many there are that go in that way. But narrow is the gate, and narrow is the way, which leads to life, and few there are that find it.   MATTHEW 7:13–14

Among the chief [Jewish] rulers many believed in him [Jesus], but because of the Pharisees they did not confess their faith in him, fearing they should be put out of the synagogue; for they loved the praise of men more than the praise of God.   JOHN 12:42–43

All the Athenians and strangers there spent their time in nothing else but to tell or to hear some new thing.   ACTS 17:21

Be not conformed to this world, but be transformed by the renewing of your mind, so that you may test what is the good and acceptable and perfect will of God.   ROMANS 12:2

It is written, "I will destroy the wisdom of the wise, and will bring to nothing the understanding of the prudent." Where is the wise? Where is the scribe? Where is the debater of this world? Has not God made foolish the wisdom of this world?   I CORINTHIANS 1:19–20

The wisdom of this world is foolishness with God. For it is written, "He catches the wise in their own craftiness."   I CORINTHIANS 3:19

Do not be deceived: bad company corrupts goods morals.

I CORINTHIANS 15:33

Set your affection on things above, not on things on the earth.

COLOSSIANS 3:2

Know you not that the friendship of the world is enmity with God? Whoever will be a friend of the world is the enemy of God.

JAMES 4:4

Love not the world, neither the things that are in the world. If any man love the world, the love of the Father is not in him. For all that is in the world, the cravings of the flesh, and the lust of the eyes, and the pride of life, is not of the Father, but is of the world. And the world passes away, and all its lusts, but he who does the will of God abides forever.   I JOHN 2:15–17

All that is in the world, the cravings of the flesh, and the lust of the eyes, and the pride of life, is not of the Father, but is of the world. And the world passes away, and all its lusts, but he who does the will of God lives forever.

I JOHN 2:16–17

Marvel not, my brethren, if the world hates you.   I JOHN 3:13

See also Bad Company, Friends, Temptation, Worldly Pleasures.

TRUSTING GOD

Any parent, or anyone who has ever been a child (which includes everyone), knows that every father or mother does things that the child cannot understand. What is the usual response of the child? Trust. True, the child can respond with tantrums, screaming, "It's not fair," and crying and sulking. But part of growing up is learning to accept situations, trusting that the parent is watching and protecting no matter what. What is true of human parents is true, the Bible says, of God as well, only more so. God is in charge regardless of how frustrated or perplexed we may be.

Jesus, who took pleasure in referring to God as Father, several times spoke of the childlike trust that was a trait of God's people. It is one of the sweet ironies of the Bible: To mature spiritually, we must become like children, trusting someone wiser and greater than ourselves.

God is not a man, that he should lie, nor a son of man, that he should change his mind.   NUMBERS 23:19

Some trust in chariots, and some in horses, but we will remember the name of the LORD our God. PSALM 20:7

Trust in the LORD, and do good; so shall you dwell in the land, and you shall be fed. Delight yourself in the LORD, and he shall give you the desires of your heart. Commit your way to the LORD; trust also in him, and he shall bring it to pass. PSALM 37:3–5

Blessed is that man that makes the LORD his trust, and respects not the proud, nor such as turn aside to false gods. PSALM 40:4

God is our refuge and strength, a very present help in trouble. Therefore will we not fear, though the earth be removed, and though the mountains be carried into the depths of the sea. PSALM 46:1–2

O LORD Almighty, blessed is the man that trusts in you. PSALM 84:12

God shall cover you with his feathers, and under his wings shall you trust; his truth shall be your shield and protection. PSALM 91:4

Trust in the LORD with all your heart, and lean not on your own understanding. PROVERBS 3:5

The fear of man brings a trap, but whoever puts his trust in the LORD shall be safe. PROVERBS 29:25

Behold, God is my salvation; I will trust, and not be afraid.
ISAIAH 12:2

You will keep him in perfect peace whose mind is stayed on you, because he trusts in you. ISAIAH 26:3

"My thoughts are not your thoughts, neither are your ways my ways," says the LORD. "For as the heavens are higher than the earth, so are my ways higher than your ways, and my thoughts than your thoughts."
ISAIAH 55:8–9

Blessed is the man that trusts in the LORD, and whose hope the LORD is.

JEREMIAH 17:7

The just shall live by faith.

HABAKKUK 2:4

Why take thought for clothing? Consider the lilies of the field, how they grow; they toil not, neither do they spin. And yet I say to you, even Solomon in all his glory was not arrayed like one of these. If God so clothes the grass of the field, which exists today and tomorrow is cast into the oven, shall he not much more clothe you, O you of little faith? Therefore take no thought, saying, "What shall we eat?" or "What shall we drink?" or "What shall we wear?" The pagans worry about all these things. Your heavenly Father knows that you have need of all these things. But seek first the kingdom of God and his righteousness, and all these other things shall be given to you.

MATTHEW 6:28–33

If you have faith the size of a mustard seed, you shall say to this mountain, "Move from here to another place," and it shall move, and nothing shall be impossible to you.

MATTHEW 17:20

Jesus called a little child unto him, and set him in the midst of them, and said, "Truly I say to you, except you be converted, and become as little children, you shall not enter into the kingdom of heaven. Whoever therefore shall humble himself as this little child, the same is greatest in the kingdom of heaven."

MATTHEW 18:2–4

They brought young children to him, that he should touch them; and his disciples rebuked those that brought them. But when Jesus saw it, he was much displeased, and said to them, "Let the little children to come unto me, and forbid them not; for of such is the kingdom of God. Truly I say unto you, whoever shall not receive the kingdom of God as a little child, he shall not enter therein."

MARK 10:13–15

Fear not, little flock; for it is your Father's good pleasure to give you the kingdom.

LUKE 12:32

Who shall separate us from the love of Christ? Shall tribulation, or distress, or persecution, or famine, or nakedness, or peril, or sword? No, nor height, nor depth, nor any other creature shall be able to separate us from the love of God, which is in Christ Jesus our Lord.   ROMANS 8:35, 39

We should not trust in ourselves, but in God who raises the dead.

2 CORINTHIANS 1:9

Every good gift and perfect gift is from above, and comes down from the Father of lights, with whom is no variation, nor shadow of turning.

JAMES 1:17

See also Faith, God's Guidance, Hope, Obeying God.

VIOLENCE

According to Genesis, violence is as old as humanity. When there were only four people on earth (Adam, his wife, and two sons), one of the sons murdered the other. Call it history or call it legend, but we know that violence is indeed an ancient pastime for man, one that God clearly detests. Since the Bible takes a realistic view of mankind, warts and all, it is full of violence, but always with the understanding that God intended man to be at peace with all creation, not murdering or warring. Jesus is presented as the Prince of Peace, one who bestows not only inward peace to his followers but also, at the end of time, eternal and unbroken peace on the entire world.

Abel was a keeper of sheep, but Cain was a tiller of the ground. And it came to pass that Cain brought to the LORD an offering of the fruit of the ground. And Abel also brought of the firstlings of his flock, their fat portions. And the LORD had looked favorably on Abel and his offering. But on Cain and to his offering he did not look favorably. And Cain was very angry, and his countenance fell. And the LORD said to Cain, "Why are you angry? And why is your countenance fallen? If you do well, shall you not be accepted? And if you do not do well, sin lurks at the door. Sin desires you, but you must master him."

And Cain talked with Abel his brother, and it came to pass, when they were in the field, that Cain rose up against Abel his brother and killed him. And the LORD said to Cain, "Where is Abel your brother?" And he said, "I know not; am I my brother's keeper?" And God said, "What have you done? The voice of your brother's blood cries to me from the ground. And now are you cursed from the earth, which has opened its mouth to receive your brother's blood from your hand." GENESIS 4:2–11

The earth was corrupt before God, and the earth was filled with violence. And God looked upon the earth, and, behold, it was corrupt; for all flesh

> *The commonly used word* Armageddon *is from the Bible—specifically, Revelation 16:16, which speaks of a great battle at the end of time, at a place called Armageddon.*

had corrupted his way upon the earth. And God said to Noah, "The end of all flesh is come before me; for the earth is filled with violence through them; and, behold, I will destroy them with the earth."

GENESIS 6:11–13

The God of my rock, in him will I trust: he is my shield, and the horn of my salvation, my high tower, and my refuge, my Savior; you save me from violence.

2 SAMUEL 22:3

He made a pit and dug it, and has fallen into it himself. His mischief shall return upon his own head, and his violent dealing shall come down upon his own pate.

PSALM 7:15–16

The LORD examines the righteous; but the wicked and him that loves violence his soul hates.

PSALM 11:5

Do you decree righteousness, you rulers? Do you judge the people rightly? No, in your hearts you devise wickedness; your hands deal out violence on the land.

PSALM 58:1–2

Pride surrounds them like a chain; violence covers them like a garment.

PSALM 73:6

Let not an evil speaker be established in the earth; evil shall hunt the violent man to overthrow him.

PSALM 140:11

Envy not the oppressor, and choose none of his ways.   PROVERBS 3:31

They eat the bread of wickedness, and drink the wine of violence. But the path of the just is as the shining light, that shines more and more to the perfect day.   PROVERBS 4:17–18

A violent man entices his neighbor, and leads him into the way that is not good.   PROVERBS 16:29

Violence shall no more be heard in your land, nor ruin nor destruction within your borders. But you shall call your walls Salvation, and your gates Praise.   ISAIAH 60:18

The rich men are full of violence, and the inhabitants have spoken lies, and their tongue is deceitful in their mouth.   MICAH 6:12

I say to you, resist not evil; but whoever shall strike you on your right cheek, turn to him the other also.   MATTHEW 5:39

Blessed are the peacemakers, for they shall be called the children of God.
                                                                         MATTHEW 5:9

One of those who were with Jesus stretched out his hand, and drew his sword, and struck a servant of the high priest's, and cut off his ear. Then said Jesus to him, "Put away your sword into its place, for all they that take the sword shall perish with the sword."   MATTHEW 26:51–52

Let your speech be always with grace, seasoned with salt, so that you may know how you ought to answer every man.   COLOSSIANS 4:6

Though I was once a blasphemer and a persecutor and a violent man, I was shown mercy because I acted in ignorance and unbelief.
                                                                1 TIMOTHY 1:13 (NIV)

On either side of the river [in heaven] was the tree of life, which bore twelve manner of fruits, and yielded her fruit every month; and the leaves of the tree were for the healing of the nations. And there shall be no more curse.
                                                              REVELATION 22:2–3

See also Anger, Enemies, Hate, Peace, Revenge.

WISDOM AND DISCERNMENT

The mad, evil scientist is a fixture in horror and science fiction movies. Is this because we suspect, deep down, that highly intelligent people are not necessarily good people? People can be as vain about their knowledge and intelligence as they can about physical beauty, and the Bible views the arrogant wise guy just as it does the arrogant beauty. The Bible is not anti-intelligence—far from it. But it takes a realistic view of man's inclination to worship knowledge for its own sake rather than for the good it can do. This is why the Bible has little praise for knowledge—what we might today call facts or data—and much praise for wisdom. Wisdom goes deeper than knowledge, penetrating to the soul, so the writers of the Bible believed that all true wisdom came from God. In the Bible, the only truly wise man is one who is morally upright, for in a world where God sees all our deeds, only a fool would behave badly.

[Solomon:] "Now, O LORD my God, you have made your servant king in place of David my father, and I am but a little child; I know not how to go out or come in. And your servant is in the midst of your people you have chosen, a great people that cannot be numbered nor counted. Give your servant an understanding heart to judge your people, so that I may discern between good and evil. For who is able to judge this, your great people?"

And the speech pleased the LORD, that Solomon had asked this thing. And God said to him, "Because you have asked this thing, and have not asked for yourself long life, nor riches for yourself, nor vengeance on your enemies, but have asked for yourself understanding to discern what is right, behold, I have done according to your word. Lo, I have given you a wise and understanding heart, so that there is none like you before you, nor after you shall any arise like you."   I KINGS 3:7–12

He catches the wise in their own craftiness, and the schemes of the cunning are swept away.   JOB 5:13

Inquire, I pray you, of the former ages, and prepare yourself to the search of their forefathers. For we were born but yesterday, and know nothing, because our days on earth are a shadow. Shall not they teach you and tell you and utter words out of their hearts?   JOB 8:8–10

With him is wisdom and strength; he has counsel and understanding.
                                                             JOB 12:13

Surely there is a mine for silver, and a place for gold which they refine. But where shall wisdom be found? And where is the place of understanding? Man knows not the price of it, neither is it found in the land of the living. The deep says, "It is not in me," and the sea says, "It is not with me." It cannot be gotten for gold, neither shall silver be weighed as its price. Whence then comes wisdom? And where is the place of understanding, seeing it is hid from the eyes of all living, and kept close from the fowls of the air?

God understands the way to it, and he knows its place. And to man he says, "Behold, the fear of the LORD, that is wisdom, and to depart from evil is understanding."   JOB 28:1, 12–15, 19–20, 23, 28

The price of wisdom is above rubies.   JOB 28:18

The law of the LORD is perfect, converting the soul. The testimony of the LORD is sure, making wise the simple.   PSALM 19:7

The fool says in his heart, "There is no God."   PSALM 53:1

Teach us to number our days, that we may apply our hearts to wisdom.
                                                           PSALM 90:12

The fear of the LORD is the beginning of wisdom. A good understanding have all they that do his commandments.   PSALM 111:10

You through your commandments have made me wiser than my enemies, for they are ever with me.   PSALM 119:98

The LORD gives wisdom; out of his mouth comes knowledge and understanding. He lays up sound wisdom for the righteous; he is a shield to those who walk uprightly.   PROVERBS 2:5-7

Be not wise in your own eyes; fear the LORD, and depart from evil. It shall be health to your body and nourishment to your bones.

PROVERBS 3:7-8

Happy is the man that finds wisdom, and the man that gets understanding. For it is more profitable than silver, and it gives greater return than fine gold. Wisdom is more precious than rubies, and all the things you can desire are not to be compared to it. Length of days is in its right hand, and in its left hand are riches and honor. Its ways are ways of pleasantness, and all its paths are peace. Wisdom is a tree of life and a blessing to those who lay hold upon it.   PROVERBS 3:13-18

Wisdom is the principal thing; therefore get wisdom, and with all your getting get understanding.   PROVERBS 4:7

Wisdom is better than rubies, and all the things that may be desired are not to be compared to it.   PROVERBS 8:11

The wise in heart will receive commandments, but a babbling fool comes to ruin.   PROVERBS 10:8

How much better is it to get wisdom than gold, and to get understanding rather than silver!   PROVERBS 16:16

He that gets wisdom loves his own soul. He that keeps understanding shall find good.   PROVERBS 19:8

Better is a poor and a wise child than an old and foolish king, who will no longer take advice.   ECCLESIASTES 4:13

The quiet words of wise men are heard more than the cry of a ruler of fools.

ECCLESIASTES 9:17

Woe unto them that are wise in their own eyes, and prudent in their own sight!   ISAIAH 5:21

You have trusted in your wickedness; you have said, "No one sees me." Your wisdom and knowledge have perverted you, and you have said in your heart, "I am, and no one else beside me."   ISAIAH 47:10

My people is foolish; they have not known me; they are senseless children, and they have no understanding. They are wise to do evil, but to do good they have no knowledge.   JEREMIAH 4:22

Thus says the LORD: "Let not the wise man glory in his wisdom, neither let the mighty man glory in his might, let not the rich man glory in his riches. But let him that glories glory in this, that he understands and knows me, that I am the LORD who exercise lovingkindness, judgment, and righteousness, in the earth; for in these things I delight," says the LORD.

JEREMIAH 9:23

Whoever hears these sayings of mine, and does them, will be like a wise man who built his house upon a rock. And the rain descended, and the floods came, and the winds blew and beat upon that house, yet it fell not, for it was founded upon a rock. And everyone that hears these sayings of mine, and does them not, shall be like a foolish man who built his house upon the sand. And the rain descended, and the floods came, and the winds blew and beat upon that house, and it fell, and great was the fall of it.

MATTHEW 7:24–27

O the depth of the riches of the wisdom and knowledge of God! How unsearchable are his judgments, and his ways past finding out!

ROMANS 11:33

Where is the wise? Where is the scribe? Where is the debater of this world? Has not God made foolish the wisdom of this world? For since, in the wisdom of God, the world did not know God through wisdom, it pleased God through the foolishness of preaching to save those who believe. The foolishness of God is wiser than men, and the weakness of God is stronger than men. But God has chosen the foolish things of the world to confound the wise, and God has chosen the weak things of the world to confound the mighty.   I CORINTHIANS 1:20–21, 25–27

We have received, not the spirit of the world, but the Spirit which is of God, so that we might know the things that are freely given to us of God. But the natural man receives not the things of the Spirit of God, for they are foolishness to him; neither can he know them, because they are spiritually discerned. But he who is spiritual judges all things, yet he himself is judged by no one else. For who has known the mind of the Lord, that he may instruct him? But we have the mind of Christ.   I CORINTHIANS 2:12, 14–16

The wisdom of this world is foolishness with God. For it is written, "He catches the wise in their own craftiness."   I CORINTHIANS 3:19

The manifestation of the Spirit is given to every man to profit all. For to one is given by the Spirit the word of wisdom; to another the word of knowledge by the same Spirit; to another faith by the same Spirit; to another the gifts of healing by the same Spirit; to another the working of miracles; to another prophecy; to another discerning of spirits; to another various kinds of tongues; to another the interpretation of tongues. But in all these work that one and the selfsame Spirit, allotting to every man individually as he chooses.   I CORINTHIANS 12:7–8, 11

He has abounded toward us in all wisdom and understanding.

EPHESIANS 1:8

Whatever things are true, whatever things are honest, whatever things are just, whatever things are pure, whatever things are lovely, whatever things are admirable—if anything is excellent or praiseworthy—think on these things.   PHILIPPIANS 4:8

Let the word of Christ dwell in you richly in all wisdom; teaching and admonishing one another in psalms and hymns and spiritual songs, singing with grace in your hearts to the Lord.   COLOSSIANS 3:16

> *"The Bible is not the only means to furnish a mind, but without a book of similar gravity, read with the gravity of the potential believer, it will remain unfurnished."*
>
> —ALLAN BLOOM, IN HIS AWARD-WINNING BESTSELLER
> *The Closing of the American Mind* (1987)

If any of you lack wisdom, let him ask of God, who gives to all men generously. JAMES 1:5

Who is a wise man and endowed with knowledge among you? Let him show it with good conduct, in deeds done in the meekness that comes from wisdom. If you have bitter envying and strife in your hearts, do not boast of it, and do not deny the truth. This so-called wisdom descends not from heaven, but is earthly, sensual, devilish. For where envying and strife are, there is disorder and every evil work. But the wisdom that is from above is first pure, then peaceable, gentle, and easy to be entreated, full of mercy and good fruits, without partiality, and without hypocrisy. JAMES 3:13–17

See also False Teachings/Heresy

WITNESSING/EVANGELISM

When people stumble onto something good, they cannot help talking about it. Go to any college campus and observe the intensity of committed environmentalists, young Republicans, young Democrats, animal rights activists, and so on. They don't convert everyone, of course, but inevitably their enthusiasm is passed on to some, and the movements grow. This is what happened in the Bible with people of faith: Believing that they had encountered the power of God, they couldn't help talking. More important, their changed lives showed that something truly dramatic had happened.

*They "talked the talk" and (usually) "walked the walk." Some who heard
the message were not impressed, but many were. And so the faith lives on,
not primarily through the theologians and the Bible scholars but through
everyday people who witness to God not only with their words but also
with lives reflecting the compassion and mercy of God.*

*Of the quotes below, probably the most famous is Matthew 28:19–20,
known as Jesus' "Great Commission" to his disciples.*

How beautiful on the mountains are the feet of him that brings good tidings, who proclaims peace, who brings tidings of good, who proclaims, who
says to Zion, "Your God reigns." ISAIAH 52:7

The Spirit of the LORD God is upon me; because the LORD has anointed me
to preach good tidings to the meek; he has sent me to bind up the brokenhearted, to proclaim liberty to the captives, and the opening of the prison to
those who are bound. ISAIAH 61:1

Walking by the Sea of Galilee, Jesus saw two brothers, Simon (called Peter)
and Andrew his brother, casting a net into the sea; for they were fishermen.
And he said to them, "Follow me, and I will make you fishers of men."
MATTHEW 4:18–19

You are the salt of the earth, but if the salt has lost its savor, how can it be
salty again? It is no longer good for anything, but to be cast out, and to be
trampled underfoot.

You are the light of the world. A city that is set on a hill cannot be hid.
Neither do men light a candle and put it under a bushel, but on a candle-
stick, and it gives light to all that are in the house. Let your light so shine before men that they may see your good works and glorify your Father who is
in heaven. MATTHEW 5:13–16

I send you forth as sheep in the midst of wolves; be wise as serpents, and
harmless as doves. MATTHEW 10:16

Whoever shall confess me before men, him will I confess before my Father
who is in heaven. But whoever shall deny me before men, him will I deny before my Father who is in heaven. MATTHEW 10:32–33

This gospel of the kingdom shall be preached in all the world for a witness to all nations, and then shall the end come.   MATTHEW 24:14

Go you therefore, and teach all nations, baptizing them in the name of the Father, and of the Son, and of the Holy Spirit; teaching them to observe all things I have commanded you, and, lo, I am with you always, even to the end of the world.   MATTHEW 28:19–20

Jesus said to them, "Go into all the world and preach the gospel to every creature. He that believes and is baptized shall be saved; but he who believes not shall be condemned. And these signs shall follow those who believe: In my name shall they cast out demons; they shall speak with new tongues; they shall handle serpents, and if they drink any deadly poison, it shall not hurt them; they shall lay hands on the sick, and they shall recover." After the Lord had spoken to them, he was received up into heaven, and sat on the right hand of God. And they went forth, and preached everywhere, the Lord working with them and confirming the word with signs following.
         MARK 16:15–20

Why do you call me "Lord, Lord," and not do the things I say?
         LUKE 6:46

Whoever shall be ashamed of me and of my words, of him shall the Son of man be ashamed when he shall come in his own glory, and in his Father's, and of the holy angels.   LUKE 9:26

The harvest is truly great, but the laborers are few. Ask the Lord of the harvest to send forth laborers into his harvest.   LUKE 10:2

They shall lay their hands on you, and persecute you, delivering you up to the synagogues, and into prisons, dragging you before kings and rulers for my name's sake. This shall be an opportunity to testify. Make up your mind not to worry beforehand as to how you will answer. For I will give you words and wisdom, which all your adversaries shall not be able to contradict nor resist.   LUKE 21:12–15

Among the chief [Jewish] leaders many believed in him, but because of the Pharisees they did not confess him, lest they be put out of the synagogue; for they loved the praise of men more than the praise of God.

JOHN 12:42–43

You shall receive power after the Holy Spirit has come upon you; and you shall be witnesses to me both in Jerusalem, and in all Judea, and in Samaria, and to the uttermost parts of the earth.

ACTS 1:8

The word of God grew and multiplied.

ACTS 12:24

Open their eyes, and turn them from darkness to light, and from the power of Satan to God, so that they may receive forgiveness of sins, and inheritance among those who are made holy by faith.

ACTS 26:18

Woe is me if I preach not the gospel!

I CORINTHIANS 9:16

Though I am free from all men, yet I have made myself servant of all, that I might win the more. And to the Jews I became as a Jew, so that I might win the Jews; to the weak became I as weak, so that I might win the weak. I am made all things to all men, so that I might by all means save some. And this I do for the gospel's sake, so that I might share in its blessings.

I CORINTHIANS 9:19–20, 22–23

God was in Christ, reconciling the world to himself, not counting men's sins against them. And he has committed to us the word of reconciliation.

2 CORINTHIANS 5:19

We are ambassadors for Christ, as though God did appeal to you through us. We pray you on behalf of Christ, be reconciled to God.

2 CORINTHIANS 5:20

Do everything without murmuring and arguing, that you may be blameless and innocent, the sons of God without fault in the midst of a crooked and perverse generation, among whom you shine as lights in the world, holding forth the word of life.

PHILIPPIANS 2:14–16

Whatever you do in word or deed, do all in the name of the Lord Jesus, giving thanks to God and the Father through him.　　　COLOSSIANS 3:17

Walk in wisdom toward outsiders, making the most of opportunities. Let your speech be always with grace, seasoned with salt, so that you may know how you ought to answer every man.　　　COLOSSIANS 4:5—6

Study to lead a quiet life, and to do your own business, and to work with your own hands, as we commanded you, so that you may walk honestly toward outsiders, and that you may have lack of nothing.

I THESSALONIANS 4:11—12

God has not given us the spirit of fear, but of power, and of love, and of self-discipline. Be not ashamed of the testimony of our Lord, nor of me as his prisoner. But share in suffering for the gospel according to the power of God.　　　2 TIMOTHY 1:7—8

Dearly beloved, I urge you as strangers and pilgrims, abstain from fleshly lusts, which war against the soul. Live such honorable lives among the pagans that, though they speak of you as evildoers, they may see your good works and glorify God when he comes.　　　I PETER 2:11—12

Sanctify the Lord God in your hearts, and be ready always to give an answer to every man that asks you a reason for the hope that is in you.

I PETER 3:15

See also Opportunities.

WORK

"Thank God it's Friday" suggests that people live for the weekend, as if their weekday jobs were a necessary evil. This isn't the Bible's view at all. As seen in the first quotation below, God gave Adam and Eve the job of tending the Garden of Eden. But as the second quote shows, after the two

disobeyed God, work was changed from a pleasant task to a sweaty burden. That is pretty much what it has been for most human beings through history, and only in our own time have so many people had sweat-free and (relatively) easy work to do. We should be thankful for this, but most people aren't, always feeling underpaid and overworked.

The Bible has many things to say about work, such as commanding employers to treat their workers with care and (the flip side) commanding employees to work diligently. The New Testament puts a very positive spin on work: We can work, as we can do everything else in life, to the glory of God. This is a good thing to remember at the end of a day that seems to have produced little of value.

God created man in his own image, in the image of God created he him; male and female created he them. And God blessed them, and God said to them, "Be fruitful, and multiply, and replenish the earth, and subdue it, and have dominion over the fish of the sea, and over the birds of the air, and over every living thing that moves upon the earth." And the LORD God took the man and put him into the garden of Eden to work it and to tend it.

GENESIS 1:27–28, 2:15

To Adam he said, "Because you have listened to the voice of your wife, and have eaten of the tree, of which I commanded you, saying, 'You shall not eat of it,' cursed is the ground because of you. In sorrow shall you eat of it all the days of your life; thorns and thistles shall it bring forth for you, and you shall eat the plants of the field. In the sweat of your face shall you eat bread, till you return to the ground; for out of it were you taken, for dust you are, and to dust shall you return." GENESIS 3:17–19

Remember the sabbath day, to keep it holy. Six days shall you labor, and do all your work; but the seventh day is the sabbath of the LORD your God. In it you shall not do any work, you, nor your son, nor your daughter, your manservant, nor your maidservant, nor your cattle, nor the stranger that is within your gates. For in six days the LORD made heaven and earth, the sea, and all that in them is, and rested the seventh day; therefore the LORD blessed the sabbath day and made it holy. EXODUS 20:8–11

You shall not defraud your neighbor, nor rob him; the wages of him that you hired shall not stay with you all night until the morning.

LEVITICUS 19:13

You shall not oppress a hired servant who is poor and needy, whether he is of your brethren or of your strangers that are in your land. At day's end you shall pay him his wages, neither shall the sun go down upon it; for he is poor, and is counting on it; lest he cry against you to the LORD, and it be sin to you.   DEUTERONOMY 24:14–15

He that tills his land shall be satisfied with bread, but he who chases worthless pursuits is void of understanding.   PROVERBS 12:11

The hand of the diligent shall rule, but the lazy will be forced into slave labor.   PROVERBS 12:24

The slothful man does not roast what he took in hunting, but the diligent man gains precious wealth.   PROVERBS 12:27

In all labor there is profit, but mere talk leads only to poverty.

PROVERBS 14:23

He that is slothful in his work is brother to him that is a great waster.

PROVERBS 18:9

The thoughts of the diligent lead only to prosperity, but those of the hasty lead only to want.   PROVERBS 21:5

Do you see a man diligent in his business? He shall stand before kings.

PROVERBS 22:29

He that tills his land shall have plenty to eat, but he who follows after foolish fantasies shall have poverty.   PROVERBS 28:19

I looked on all the works that my hands had made, and on the labor that I had labored to do, and, behold, all was meaningless, a chasing after the wind, and there was no profit under the sun.   ECCLESIASTES 2:11

The sleep of a laboring man is sweet, whether he eats little or much, but the abundance of the rich will not allow him to sleep.

ECCLESIASTES 5:12

Behold what I have seen: it is good and fitting for one to eat and to drink, and to enjoy the good of all his labor that he does under the sun all the days of his life, which God gives him, for this is his lot; this is the gift of God.

ECCLESIASTES 5:18–19

Whatever your hand finds to do, do it with your might.

ECCLESIASTES 9:10

Jesus entered into a certain village, and a certain woman named Martha received him into her house. And she had a sister called Mary, who also sat at Jesus' feet, and listened to his word. But Martha was occupied with many tasks, and she came to him and said, "Lord, do you not care that my sister has left me to serve alone? Tell her to help me." And Jesus answered and said to her, "Martha, Martha, you are anxious and troubled about many things. One thing is needed, and Mary has chosen the better, which shall not be taken away from her."   LUKE 10:38–42

Labor not for the food which perishes, but for that food which endures to everlasting life, which the Son of man shall give to you.   JOHN 6:27

[Paul:] I have coveted no man's silver, or gold, or apparel. Yes, you yourselves know, that my hands have supported myself and my companions. I have showed you all things, how that in laboring you ought to support the weak, and to remember the words of the Lord Jesus, how he said, "It is more blessed to give than to receive."   ACTS 20:33–35

Be not slothful in business; be fervent in spirit, serving the Lord.

ROMANS 12:11

We are laborers together with God; you are God's field, you are God's building.   I CORINTHIANS 3:9

Whether you eat, or drink, or whatever you do, do all for the glory of God.

                                    1 CORINTHIANS 10:31

My beloved brethren, be steadfast, unmovable, always abounding in the work of the Lord, since you know that your labor is not in vain in the Lord.

                                    1 CORINTHIANS 15:58

He who sows sparingly shall reap also sparingly, and he who sows bountifully shall reap also bountifully.   2 CORINTHIANS 9:6

Let him that stole steal no more, but rather let him labor, working with his hands the thing which is good, so that he may be able to give to those in need.

                                    EPHESIANS 4:28

Serve with good will, as doing it for the Lord, not for men.

                                    EPHESIANS 6:6–7

From the Lord you shall receive the reward of the inheritance, for you serve the Lord Christ.   COLOSSIANS 3:24

Study to lead a quiet life, and to do your own business, and to work with your own hands, as we commanded you, so that you may walk honestly toward outsiders, and that you may lack nothing.

                                    1 THESSALONIANS 4:11–12

Now we command you, brethren, in the name of our Lord Jesus Christ, that you withdraw yourselves from every brother who is idle and not living according to the tradition he received from us. For you know how you ought to follow us, for we were not idle while among you, nor did we eat any man's bread without paying; but we labored night and day so that we might not burden any of you. This was not because we have no right, but in order to make ourselves an example to you to follow. For even when we were with you, this we commanded you: If any will not work, neither should he eat. For we hear that there are some of you are living in idleness, not working at all, mere busybodies. Now such as these we command and exhort by our

Lord Jesus Christ, so that with quietness they work and earn their own living.   2 THESSALONIANS 3:6–12

If any provide not for his own, and specially for those of his own house, he has denied the faith, and is worse than an infidel.   I TIMOTHY 5:8

Listen now, you rich men; weep and wail for the miseries that shall come upon you. Behold, the wages of the laborers who have harvested your fields, which you kept back by fraud, cry out, and the cries of the harvesters have entered into the ears of the Lord Almighty. You have lived in pleasure and luxury on the earth; you have fattened your hearts, as for a day of slaughter.

JAMES 5:1, 4–5

See also Laziness, Money, The Sabbath, Success.

WORLDLY CARES

Some world religions teach detachment from the world, even living (so far as possible) without food or clothing. The Bible takes a more down-to-earth view of human capacities, recognizing that we are material beings with material needs and that we can take reasonable steps to meet those needs. But the Bible also recognizes that worldly cares can weigh us down, sapping the joy from life by making us anxious over the question "What will happen to me?" The Bible insists that God is more concerned with the question "Are you, at this present moment, living right?"

It is vain you rise up early and stay up late, to eat the bread of anxiety; for he gives his beloved sleep.   PSALM 127:2

Remove far from me vanity and lies; give me neither poverty nor riches; feed me with food that I need.   PROVERBS 30:8

Do not call a conspiracy all that this people calls conspiracy; do not fear what it fears, nor be in dread. But the LORD Almighty, him you shall regard as holy, him alone shall you fear and dread.   ISAIAH 8:12–13

I say to you, take no thought for your life, what you shall eat, or what you shall drink; nor yet for your body, what you shall wear. Is not life more than food, and the body than clothing? Behold the birds of the air, for they neither sow nor reap, nor gather into barns; yet your heavenly Father feeds them. Are you not much better than they? Which of you by worrying can add one day to his life span?

Why take thought for clothing? Consider the lilies of the field, how they grow; they toil not, neither do they spin. And yet I say to you, even Solomon in all his glory was not arrayed like one of these. If God so clothes the grass of the field, which exists today and tomorrow is cast into the oven, shall he not much more clothe you, O you of little faith? Therefore take no thought, saying, "What shall we eat?" or "What shall we drink?" or "What shall we wear?" The pagans worry about all these things. Your heavenly Father knows that you have need of all these things. But seek first the kingdom of God and his righteousness, and all these other things shall be given to you.

Take therefore no thought for tomorrow, for tomorrow has worries of its own. Sufficient to each day is its own trouble.   MATTHEW 6:25–34

Come to me, all you that labor and are heavy laden, and I will give you rest. Take my yoke upon you, and learn from me; for I am meek and lowly in heart, and you shall find rest for your souls. For my yoke is easy, and my burden is light.   MATTHEW 11:28–30

Are not five sparrows sold for two pennies, and not one of them is forgotten before God? But even the very hairs of your head are all numbered. So fear not; you are of more value than many sparrows.   LUKE 12:6–7

Seek not you what you shall eat or what you drink, neither be worrisome. For all these things does the pagan world run after, and your Father knows that you need these things. Rather, seek the kingdom of God; and all these things shall be added to you. Fear not, little flock; for it is your Father's good pleasure to give you the kingdom.   LUKE 12:29–32

Take heed to yourselves, lest at any time your hearts be weighed down with dissipation and drunkenness and worries of this life, and so that day come upon you unawares.   LUKE 21:34

Be anxious for nothing, but in everything by prayer and supplication with thanksgiving let your requests be made known to God. And the peace of God, which surpasses all understanding, will keep your hearts and minds in Christ Jesus.   PHILIPPIANS 4:6

My God shall supply all your need according to his riches in glory by Christ Jesus.   PHILIPPIANS 4:19

Godliness with contentment is great gain. For we brought nothing into this world, and it is certain we can carry nothing out. And having food and clothing, let us be content.   I TIMOTHY 6:6–8

Let your lives be free from covetousness, and be content with such things as you have, for he has said, "I will never leave you, nor forsake you."
                                                                HEBREWS 13:5

Every good gift and every perfect gift is from above, and comes down from the Father of lights, with whom is no variableness, nor shadow of turning.
                                                                JAMES 1:17

See also Anxiety, Contentment, Eternal Life, Hope, Trusting God, Worry.

WORLDLY PLEASURES

Since God made the world, what is wrong with being "worldly"? Doesn't God want us to enjoy the world and its pleasures? The Bible says yes, but.... The "but" is this: It is easy to get so caught up in pleasure seeking that we forget the One who made everything. It's the old idolatry problem that the Bible brings up again and again: We are more inclined to worship things instead of the Creator of all things. Chasing one amusement and pleasure after another may keep us busy, and some people spend their whole lives doing it, but there are serious doubts about whether this is our ultimate purpose.

Even in laughter the heart is sorrowful, and mirth may end in grief.
                                                                PROVERBS 14:13

Folly is joy to him that is lacking in wisdom, but a man of understanding walks uprightly. PROVERBS 15:21

Whoever is full loathes honey, but to the hungry even bitter food is sweet. PROVERB 27:7

Is there any thing of which it may be said, "See, this is new"? No, it has already been, from long ago, before our time. ECCLESIASTES 1:10

I sought in my heart to give myself to wine, yet acquainting my heart with wisdom, and to lay hold on folly, till I might see what was that good for the sons of men, what they should do under the heaven all the days of their life. I made great works; I built houses; I planted vineyards; I made gardens and orchards. . . . I amassed silver and gold, and the treasure of kings. . . . So I was great, and I surpassed all who were before me in Jerusalem; also my wisdom remained with me. And whatever my eyes desired I did not deny them. I did not deny my heart any joy; for my heart rejoiced in all my labor, and this was my reward for all my labor.

Then I looked on all the works that my hands had made, and on the labor that I had labored to do, and, behold, all was meaningless, a chasing after the wind, and there was no profit under the sun.

ECCLESIASTES 2:3–11

There is a grievous evil I have seen under the sun: riches kept by the owner to his own harm. His riches perish through misfortunes, and when he fathers a son, there is nothing in his hand to leave him. As he came forth from his mother's womb, naked shall he return, to go as he came, and there is nothing of his labor which he may carry away in his hand. And this also is a grievous evil, that just exactly as he came, so shall he go; and what profit has he who has labored for the wind? All his days he eats in darkness, and he has much sorrow and wrath with his sickness. ECCLESIASTES 5:13–17

Better what the eyes see than the wandering of the desire; this is futile, a chasing after the wind. ECCLESIASTES 6:9

Woe to those who rise up early in the morning, so that they may follow strong drink; who linger until night, inflamed by wine! Your feasts have the

Isaac Asimov, author of numerous books of science and science fiction, also published a Guide to the Bible.

harp and the lyre, the tambourine and pipes and wine, but they regard not the deeds of the LORD, nor consider the work of his hands.

ISAIAH 5:11–12

You that are given to pleasures, that dwell carelessly, that say in your heart, "I am, and there is no one else; I shall not be a widow, nor shall I know the loss of children"—but these two things shall come to you in a moment in one day: the loss of children, and widowhood. They shall come upon you in full measure for the multitude of your sorceries, and for the abundance of your enchantments. For you have trusted in your wickedness; you have said, "No one sees me." Your wisdom and your knowledge have perverted you, and you have said in your heart, "I am, and no one else beside me." But disaster shall come upon you; you shall not know from whence it came, and calamity shall fall upon you.

ISAIAH 47:8–11

Seek you first the kingdom of God, and his righteousness, and all these things shall be added to you.

MATTHEW 6:32–33

I have come that they might have life, and that they might have it more abundantly.

JOHN 10:10

He that loves his life shall lose it, and he who hates his life in this world shall keep it to life eternal.

JOHN 12:2

Peace I leave with you, my peace I give to you; not as the world gives, give I to you. Let not your heart be troubled, neither let it be afraid.

JOHN 14:27

Let us walk honestly, as in the daylight; not in orgies and drunkenness, not in sexual immorality and debauchery, not in quarreling and jealousy. But put you on the Lord Jesus Christ, and make no provision for the sinful nature, to fulfill its lusts.   ROMANS 13:13–14

You must no longer live as the pagans do, in the futility of their minds. Their understanding is darkened, alienated from the life of God through the ignorance that is in them, because of the blindness of their hearts. Being past feeling, they have given themselves over to immorality, to do greedily every kind of uncleanness. But you have not learned Christ in this way. Surely you heard of him and have been taught by him, in accordance with the truth that is in Jesus. You were taught to put away your former way of life, the old man, which is corrupt and deluded by its lusts, and to be renewed in the spirit of your minds.   EPHESIANS 4:18–22

In the past we ourselves were foolish, disobedient, deceived, serving various lusts and pleasures, living in malice and envy, hated and hating one another. But after that the kindness and love of God our Savior toward man appeared.   TITUS 3:3–4

In the past you already spent enough time doing as the pagans do, walking in debauchery, lusts, excess of wine, orgies, carousing, and abominable idolatries. They think it strange that you no longer join with them to the same excess of dissipation, so they speak evil of you. They shall give account to him that is ready to judge the living and the dead.   I PETER 4:3–5

These [false teachers], like brute beasts, made to be taken and destroyed, speak evil of the things they do not understand. They shall utterly perish in their own corruption, and shall receive the reward of unrighteousness, as they that count it pleasure to carouse in broad daylight. They are blots and blemishes, reveling in their immoral pleasures while they feast with you. They have eyes full of adultery, and they cannot cease from sin. They entice unstable souls. They have hearts trained in greed. Accursed children! They have forsaken the right way, and are gone astray. . . . They are wells without water, clouds blown along by a storm, for whom deepest darkness is reserved forever. When they speak empty and boastful words, they entice through the immoral lusts of the sinful nature those who have just escaped from those who live in error. While they promise them liberty, they themselves are the slaves of corruption. For a man is a slave to whatever has mastered him.   2 PETER 2:12–19

See also Joy, Success.

WORRY

"Don't worry, be happy" makes for a nice song, but the advice itself is hard to follow. It is human nature to think ahead, and many of our thoughts of the future are unpleasant. No wonder: We like to be in control of our lives, and our fears that we won't be in control are our worries. According to the Bible, God equips us to face each day as it comes, but he does not equip us to bear the burdens of both today and tomorrow. Worry never diminishes tomorrow's sorrows, but it does diminish today's pleasures. Better to leave the matter to the one who is in control.

The last quotation in this section, from the Book of Revelation, reminds us that though this world is not worry free, heaven is.

In my distress I called upon the LORD, and cried to my God; he heard my voice out of his temple, and my cry came before him, into his very ears.

PSALM 18:6

Cast your burden upon the LORD, and he shall sustain you; he shall never allow the righteous to be moved.   PSALM 55:22

When I said, "My foot slips," your mercy, O LORD, held me up.

PSALM 94:18

In the multitude of my thoughts within me, your comforts delight my soul.

PSALM 94:19

Praise the LORD. Blessed is the man that fears the LORD, who delights greatly in his commandments. His offspring shall be mighty upon earth; the generation of the upright shall be blessed. Wealth and riches shall be in his house, and his righteousness endures forever. Light shines in the darkness for the upright; he is gracious and full of compassion and righteous. A good man shows kindness, and lends; he will guide his affairs with discretion. Surely he shall never be moved; the righteous shall be kept in everlasting remembrance. He shall not be afraid of evil tidings; his heart is fixed, trusting in the LORD. His heart is established and shall not be afraid.

PSALM 112:1–8

Trouble and anguish have taken hold on me; yet your commandments are my delights.

PSALM 119:143

Search me, O God, and know my heart; examine me, and know my thoughts.

PSALM 139:23

I looked on my right hand, and there was no man that would know me; I had no refuge me; no man cared for my soul. I cried to you, O LORD; I said, "You are my refuge and my portion in the land of the living." Attend to my cry; for I am brought very low; deliver me from my persecutors; for they are stronger than I.

PSALM 142:4–6

The way of a fool is right in his own eyes, but he who listens to counsel is wise.

PROVERBS 12:15

Heaviness in the heart of man makes it stoop, but a good word makes it glad.

PROVERBS 12:25

Fret not yourself because of evil men, neither be you envious of the wicked.

PROVERBS 24:19

What does man gain from all his labor, from all his anxious striving and toiling under the sun? For all his days are sorrowful, and his work brings grief; yes, his heart takes not rest in the night. This is also futility.

ECCLESIASTES 2:22–23

Blessed is the man that trusts in the LORD, and whose hope the LORD is. For he shall be as a tree planted by the waters, that spreads out her roots by the river, and shall not wilt when heat comes, but her leaf shall be green, and shall not be anxious in the year of drought, nor shall cease from yielding fruit.   JEREMIAH 17:7–8

I say to you, take no thought for your life, what you shall eat, or what you shall drink; nor yet for your body, what you shall wear. Is not life more than food, and the body than clothing? Behold the birds of the air, for they neither sow nor reap, nor gather into barns; yet your heavenly Father feeds them. Are you not much better than they? Which of you by worrying can add one day to his life span?

Why take thought for clothing? Consider the lilies of the field, how they grow; they toil not, neither do they spin. And yet I say to you, even Solomon in all his glory was not arrayed like one of these. If God so clothes the grass of the field, which exists today and tomorrow is cast into the oven, shall he not much more clothe you, O you of little faith? Therefore take no thought, saying, "What shall we eat?" or "What shall we drink?" or "What shall we wear?" The pagans worry about all these things. Your heavenly Father knows that you have need of all these things. But seek first the kingdom of God and his righteousness, and all these other things shall be given to you.

Take therefore no thought for tomorrow, for tomorrow has worries of its own. Sufficient to each day is its own trouble.   MATTHEW 6:25–34

I send you forth as sheep in the midst of wolves; so be wise as serpents, and harmless as doves. Beware of men, for they will deliver you up to the councils, and they will flog you in their synagogues; and you shall be dragged before pilots and kings for my sake, as a testimony to them and the Gentiles. But when they deliver you up, take no thought how or what you shall say, for it shall be given you in that same hour what you shall speak. For it is not you that speak, but the Spirit of your Father who speaks in you.

MATTHEW 10:16–20

Take heed to yourselves, lest at any time your hearts be weighed down with dissipation and drunkenness and worries of this life.   LUKE 21:34

Peace I leave with you, my peace I give to you; not as the world gives, give I to you. Let not your heart be troubled, neither let it be afraid.

JOHN 14:27

If God be for us, who can be against us? He that spared not his own Son, but delivered him up for us all, how shall he not also freely give us all things?

ROMANS 8:31–32

Be anxious for nothing, but in everything by prayer and supplication with thanksgiving let your requests be made known to God. And the peace of God, which passes all understanding, will keep your hearts and minds in Christ Jesus. Finally, brethren, whatever things are true, whatever things are honest, whatever things are just, whatever things are pure, whatever things are lovely, whatever things are of good report; if there are any virtue, and if there are any praise, think on these things.   PHILIPPIANS 4:6–8

Listen, now, you who say, "Today or tomorrow we will go into such a city, and continue there a year, and buy and sell, and make money." And yet you do not know what will happen tomorrow. For what is your life? It is like a vapor, that appears for a little time, and then vanishes away. Rather, you ought to say, "If the Lord wills, we shall live, and do this or that."

JAMES 4:13–15

Humble yourselves under the mighty hand of God so that he may exalt you in due time; cast all your care upon him; for he cares for you.

I PETER 5:6–7

I John saw the holy city, new Jerusalem, coming down from God out of heaven. . . . And I heard a great voice out of heaven saying, "Behold, the dwelling place of God is with men, and he will dwell with them, and they shall be his people, and God himself shall be with them, and be their God.

"And God shall wipe away all tears from their eyes; and there shall be no more death, neither sorrow, nor crying, neither shall there be any more pain, for the former things are passed away."   REVELATION 21:2–4

See also Anxiety, Contentment, Joy, Peace, Trusting God, Worldly Cares.

Topical Index

A

B

C

Calling   See Opportunities, Witnessing/Evangelism, Work

Challenges   See Comfort in Times of Trouble, Patience, Trusting God

Change   See New Birth/New Life, Personal Growth, Repentance, Salvation, Self-Esteem

Character   See Righteousness

Charity   See Duty to the Poor, Generosity, God's Compassion for the Poor

Church   See Fellowship with Other Believers

Cleansing   See The Holy Spirit, Personal Growth

Commitment   See New Birth/New Life, Repentance

Companionship   See Fellowship with God, Fellowship with Other Believers, Friends, Loneliness, Marriage

Compassion   See Duty to the Poor, Generosity, Kindness, Love for Others

Conformity   See Bad Company, Trendiness

Conservation   See Nature and the Earth

Conversion   See New Birth/New Life, Repentance, Salvation, Sin and Redemption

Courage   See Enemies, Fear, Hope, Perseverance, Trusting God

Covetousness   See Envy

Creation   See Nature and the Earth

Criticism   See Envy, Judging Others, Self-Righteousness, The Tongue

Cursing   See The Tongue

D

Deceit   See Lying

Decisions   See God's Guidance, Obeying God, Trusting God

Demons   See The Devil

Despair   See Comfort in Times of Trouble, Hope, Trusting God

Dieting   See The Body, Food

Direction   See God's Guidance

Disagreements   See Conflict, Enemies, Forgiveness

Disappointment   See Comfort in Times of Trouble, Hope

Discernment   See Wisdom and Discernment

Discipleship   See Fellowship with Other Believers, Opportunities, Witnessing/Evangelism

Gratitude   See Thankfulness

Grief   See Comfort in Times of Trouble, Death, Patience, Perseverance, Sickness, Trusting God

Growth   See Obeying God, Personal Growth, Self-Esteem

H

Happiness   See Contentment, Hope, Joy, Peace

Healing   See The Body, Comfort in Times of Trouble, Eternal Life, Heaven, Patience, Sickness

Health   See The Body, Comfort in Times of Trouble, Eternal Life, Heaven, Sickness

Help   See Comfort in Times of Trouble, Faith, Hope, God's Guidance, God's Love

Home   See Children, Parents, Marriage

Homosexuality   See The Body, Righteousness, Selfishness, Sexuality

Honesty   See Lying

Humility   See Meekness/Gentleness, Pride

Husbands   See Marriage

I

Identity   See Personal Growth, Self-Esteem

Idleness   See Laziness

Idolatry   See The Body, Love for God, Obeying God, Selfishness, Worldly Pleasures

Illness   See Sickness

Immorality   See The Body, Righteousness, Selfishness, Sexuality

Immortality   See Eternal Life, Heaven, Hell, Hope

Individuality   See God's Fairness

Infidelity   See Adultery, Marriage

Inspiration   See The Bible, The Holy Spirit

Integrity   See Righteousness

Intelligence   See Wisdom and Discernment

J

Jealousy   See Envy

Jesus Christ   See Heaven, Jesus' Second Coming, Salvation

Justice   See God As Judge, God's Fairness, Heaven, Hell, Mercy

K

Knowledge   See Ambition, Success, Wisdom and Discernment

L

Labor   See Laziness, Work
Laughter   See Contentment, Joy
Law   See Citizenship, Politics and Government
Legalism   See False Beliefs, Freedom, Hypocrisy
Liberty   See Freedom

M

Materialism   See Ambition, Money, Selfishness, Success, Worldly
   Pleasures
Maturity   See Aging, Personal Growth
Meaning   See Hope, Personal Growth, Self-Esteem
Mission   See Opportunities, Witnessing/Evangelism
Morality   See Obeying God, Righteousness, Sin and Redemption
Mothers   See Children, Marriage, Parents
Mourning   See Death, Eternal Life, Hope

N

Nature   See Nature and the Earth
New Age   See False Beliefs
Nurture   See Children, Fellowship with God, Fellowship with Other
   Believers, Parents, Personal Growth
Nutrition   See The Body, Food

O

Occult   See False Beliefs
Old Age   See Aging
Opposition   See Enemies, Fear, Hope, Perseverance, Trusting God

P

Pain   See Comfort in Times of Trouble, Patience, Sickness, Trusting God
Peer Pressure   See Bad Company, Friends, Temptation, Trendiness
Perfection   See Personal Growth

Wives   See Marriage

World   See Nature and the Earth

Worship   See Baptism of the Spirit/Gifts of the Spirit, Fellowship with God, Fellowship with Other Believers, Love for God, Obeying God, Prayer, Thankfulness

Wrath   See Anger

Wrath of God   See God As Judge, Heaven, Hell, Jesus' Second Coming

Z

Zeal   See Opportunities, Witnessing\Evangelism